Corporate Social Strategy

WITHDRAWN

Firms are increasingly called upon to address social issues such as poverty and human rights violations. The demand for corporate social responsibility (CSR) is directed mainly at top management in multinational corporations who are reminded that, in addition to helping to make the world a better place, their commitment to social action will be rewarded by lasting customer loyalty and profits. But is it true that firms that engage in social action will be rewarded with a good name, competitive advantage, superior profits and corporate sustainability? What if it is true for some firms and not for others? This book addresses these and other questions by explaining the how and why of creating value and competitive advantage through corporate social action. It shows how and when firms can develop successful corporate social strategies that establish strong commitments to shareholders, employees, and other stakeholders.

BRYAN W. HUSTED holds the Erivan K. Haub Chair in Business and Sustainability at the Schulich School of Business, York University, Canada. He also holds a joint appointment at the EGADE Business School, Tecnológico de Monterrey, Mexico. For many years, he held the Alumni Association Chair in Business Ethics and Corporate Sustainability at the Instituto de Empresa in Spain. He is also a national researcher (level II) of the National Research System (SNI) of Mexico.

DAVID BRUCE ALLEN is Dean of the Faculty of Management and Law at the University of Surrey in Guildford, UK. His research has been published in leading journals. In addition to his academic work, Professor Allen has held top management positions in the movie, publishing, and consulting industries. He received his M.B.A from New York University, M.F.A. in Fiction from the Iowa Writers' Workshop, and Ph.D. from the University of Iowa. Professor Allen was Chair of the Strategy Department at IE Business School, a Resident Filmmaker at the Sundance Film Institute, and a Fulbright Lecturer in American Studies.

Corporate Social Strategy

Stakeholder Engagement and Competitive Advantage

BRYAN W. HUSTED

Schulich School of Business, York University, Canada
Tecnológico de Monterrey, Mexico

DAVID BRUCE ALLEN

University of Surrey, Guildford, UK

CAMBRIDGE
UNIVERSITY PRESS

CAMBRIDGE UNIVERSITY PRESS
Cambridge, New York, Melbourne, Madrid, Cape Town, Singapore,
São Paulo, Delhi, Dubai, Tokyo, Mexico City

Cambridge University Press
The Edinburgh Building, Cambridge CB2 8RU, UK

Published in the United States of America by Cambridge University Press, New York

www.cambridge.org
Information on this title: www.cambridge.org/9780521149631

First published 2011

Printed in the United Kingdom at the University Press, Cambridge

A catalogue record for this publication is available from the British Library

Library of Congress Cataloguing in Publication data
Husted, Bryan, 1957–
    Corporate social strategy : stakeholder engagement and competitive advantage /
    Bryan W. Husted, David Bruce Allen.
        p.   cm.
    Includes bibliographical references and index.
    ISBN 978-0-521-19764-9 (hardback) – ISBN 978-0-521-14963-1 (pbk.)
    1. Social responsibility of business.   2. Social entrepreneurship.
    3. Social action– Economic aspects.   4. Strategic planning–
    Social aspects.   I. Allen, David Bruce, 1951–
    II. Title.
    HD60.H875 2010
    658.4′08–dc22
    2010033025

ISBN 978-0-521-19764-9 Hardback
ISBN 978-0-521-14963-1 Paperback

Contents

Figures

Tables

Acknowledgments

We began our joint research in 1997, which has now culminated in this book. Our work started when Bryan served as the full-time director of the Alumni Association Chair in Business Ethics and Corporate Sustainability at the Instituto de Empresa. Since then we have received invaluable assistance and support from many people and organizations. We would like to express our debt of gratitude for their advice, guidance, and support.

A major debt is owed to José Salazar Cantú of the Tecnológico de Monterrey who played a major role in our thinking about the theory of the firm, game theory, and methods of evaluation. David Bach of the IE Business School also enriched our understanding of the non-market environment and stakeholders.

We would also like to acknowledge the very substantial research assistance that we received from Iuliana Dutkay, Gerardo Garza, Beatriz Mota, Erika Rodríguez, José Gazca, Manuel Valencia, Ana Laura Ambriz, Carlos López, Rodrigo García, Mario González, and César Villegas.

We received very important support from Sandra Camacho at the Tecnológico de Monterrey, Mary Amati at York University, and Carmen Diez and Maribel Trabanca at the Instituto de Empresa. A special word of thanks goes to Victoria Gimeno, director of the IE Alumni Association, and Mariano Oyarzabal, former president of the board of directors of the IE Alumni Association, for their constant support for this and other projects of the Ethics Chair.

Many people helped us by commenting on drafts of one or more chapters: Mike Russo, Claire Husted, Hector Viscencio, Jorge Ibarra, Irene Henriques, Steve Wartick, Alejandro Ibarra, Roberto Santillan, Thomas Donaldson, Donald Siegel, Alicia Coduras, Juan Santaló, and Alejandro Ruelas-Gossi. Special thanks must go to Yuliya Shymko who read the book chapter by chapter and whose perceptive and challenging commentaries, at the very least, obligated us to work a good deal harder.

We owe a debt of gratitude to colleagues at the Schulich School of Business at York University and at the IE Business School for setting high standards of scholarship during the writing of this book. In addition, during the research phase, colleagues at the Tecnológico de Monterrey provided magnificent collegial support. Special thanks go to Edwin M. Epstein, Bryan's dissertation supervisor, for his moral support at a particularly difficult time during the writing phase.

We acknowledge funding for this research from a number of sources. The Alumni Association Ethics Chair provided significant support for research assistance throughout the research phase of the project. The Erivan K. Haub Chair in Business and Sustainability at the Schulich School of Business provided similar financial support during the writing phase. In addition, Bryan received a research grant from the Consejo Nacional de Ciencia y Tecnología (Mexico), which funded a project entitled, "Estudio Exploratorio sobre la Estrategia Social de la Empresa," including the surveys in Mexico and Spain that formed the basis for much of this study. Bryan also benefited from collaboration on a grant from the Social Sciences and Humanities Research Council of Canada led by Sanjay Sharma (SSHRC Award 410–2005–0200) for a project entitled, "Organizational capabilities, institutional influences, and environmental management systems: A comparative study of the NAFTA countries." This grant helped to fund the case studies on Quali and Amanco discussed in Chapter 8.

We would also like to express our appreciation for permission to reproduce and adapt portions of several previously published papers. An earlier version of Chapter 2 appeared in the *Journal of Business Ethics*, volume 27 (Husted and Allen, 2000). In addition, an earlier version of Chapter 3 appeared in *Journal of Management Studies*, volume 43 (Husted and Salazar Cantú, 2006). We drew heavily from the Husted and Allen (2007b) article published in *Journal of Business Ethics* in preparing Chapter 4 and from the Husted and Allen (2007a) article published in *Long Range Planning* in preparing Chapter 5. An earlier version of Chapter 10 appeared in *Long Range Planning*, volume 36 (Husted, 2003). The Husted and Allen (2006) article published in the *Journal of International Business Studies*, volume 37, was adapted for Chapter 11. The Husted (2005) article published in *Journal of Business Ethics*, volume 60, provided the basis for the section on real options in Chapter 12. In addition, José Salazar Cantú has given us permission to use two co-authored papers published in the *Proceedings of the International Association for Business and Society*. An earlier version of the game-theory portion of Chapter 6 appeared in the *Proceedings of the Thirteenth Annual Meeting* (Husted and Salazar Cantú, 2002), while an earlier version of the methods for social project evaluation in Chapter 12 appeared in the *Proceedings of the Nineteenth Annual Meeting* (Salazar Cantú and Husted, 2008). Finally, Sage gave permission to reprint Figure 2 of Barney (1991) in Chapter 8 and the *MIT Sloan Management Review* granted permission to reprint the (ia)³ framework figure from Bach and Allen (2010) in Chapter 7.

1 | *Introduction*

Everywhere business creates wealth, there is a chorus imploring firms to respond to community needs, large and small. The most urgent, at times strident, calls are addressed to multinational enterprises (MNEs). CEOs of multinationals are told repeatedly that they have a special obligation to society to use their firms' assets, global reach, and unique skills to address the challenges of poverty, illness, and human rights violations in innovative ways. They are also reminded with equal fervor that if the satisfaction of helping to make the world a better place were not sufficient incentive, that their firms' commitment to social action will be rewarded by lasting customer loyalty and profits.

For the most part, CEOs agree. Moreover, given the magnitude of the world's ills and pandemic dissatisfaction with government, they understand, and may even feel honored that governments, NGOs, and other civil society groups turn to the business community for resources and solutions. Not surprisingly, social action and CSR[1] are embraced by all – investors, management, employees, governments, NGOs, the press, and academics like ourselves.

Dramatic events, such as the Hurricane Katrina disaster, provide strong evidence for this new role of business in society. As the perception that government could not provide relief grew, firms announced a battery of employee, philanthropic, and relief aid projects. Wal-Mart, frequently portrayed as a villain in the mass media, and whose expansion has been subject to numerous "stop Wal-Mart" campaigns in cities throughout the US, announced it was relocating thousands of its employees to jobs at other Wal-Marts and opened its warehouses

---

[1] The term CSR stands for corporate social responsibility and is sometimes employed to cover all actions by the firm that are deemed ethical and/or benefit society, and are pursued altruistically. Later on, we will have a good deal more to say about the institution of CSR.

for aid relief, leveraging its logistics expertise. Wal-Mart's actions were reported widely on television and in the press. Wal-Mart was not alone in pitching in. *The New York Times* picked up on the widespread corporate efforts in a Sept. 14, 2005 article entitled "Storm and Crisis: The Helping Hands; When Good Will Is Also Good Business," which began "Corporate good will in the aftermath of Hurricane Katrina has been anything but run-of-the-mill. Amgen, the biotechnology company, is donating $2.5 million to relief efforts, focusing on dialysis and cancer patients. On top of millions of dollars in cash and equipment, General Electric donated a mobile power plant" (Hafner *et al.* 2005).

Following Katrina, Americans expected firms to help. As firms responded, the media publicized their efforts, and firms earned goodwill that might later be translated into profits.

The logic, as such, is simple, direct, impeccable, and promulgated in every developed country in the world. Good deeds lead to a reputation advantage and, hence, profits. But this is not the whole of the argument in favor of corporate social action. Strategy gurus Kanter, Porter, and Prahalad have all written *Harvard Business Review* articles explaining how some of the best innovation and new market opportunities come out of social action projects and social entrepreneurship. As *The New York Times* reported recently, "Perhaps for less altruistic reasons, but often with positive results for the poor, corporations have made India a laboratory for extending modern technological conveniences to those long deprived. Nokia, for instance, develops many of its ultralow-cost cell phones here. Citibank first experimented here with a special ATM that recognizes thumbprints – to help slum dwellers who struggle with PINs" (Giriharadis, 2007).

Competitive advantage and fortune apparently await those who can provide products and services to "the bottom of the pyramid." As firms address environmental and social problems via social action projects, the message of business opportunity and reputation building appears to be unbeatable; who would not want to do well by doing good and reap praise for it?

But is it true that firms that engage in social action will be rewarded with a good name, competitive advantage, superior profits, and corporate sustainability? What if it is true for some firms and not for others? How do positive social activities get weighed against less positive actions by the same company? To what extent are home market and foreign market activities compatible? Are there situations in which corporate social action has a positive financial impact and others when it does not? Are there specific management processes involved with achieving financial reward through corporate social action? Are there significant risks in engaging in corporate social action? Ought firms to have a corporate social strategy? Do we need a new theory of the firm that moves beyond both the traditional economic efficiency model and the emergent stakeholder model? Does corporate social responsibility (CSR) require that firms engage in disinterested or altruistic actions divorced from thoughts of profit? And finally, are the rules for social strategy different in different countries?

In a decade of research into these questions, we have found that firms will do a far better job at creating economic value and social value if they include social action programs in the strategic decision-making process.

When we say "the decision-making process" we mean just that: firms must decide yes or no – a great deal, some, or even none – on social action programs. Social action, like all corporate activities, may be strategic or not, beneficial or harmful to the bottom line. However, as our research has also shown, to date few firms truly understand what this means. Too often, social action is an expense. Corporate communications informs stakeholders of the firm's good deeds; praise is expected in return. On occasion, a reputation advantage seems to be attached to the good works. Sometimes, in an unpleasant turn of events, the same company that benefited from engaging in social action is accused of not adequately sharing these benefits with its customers and the community; another firm is criticized as "unethical" or "uncaring" when it abandons a social action project or defends a policy a stakeholder considers wrong. Doing good, management finds out, is not quite as simple as it first appears.

At the very least, all firms subject to stakeholder demands for CSR need to consider their social action projects as part of their strategy. Those firms that believe social action can also be a vital part of their competitive advantage require a well-developed *corporate social strategy* that is fully integrated with business strategy. CEOs and top management need to know the full story on how business can positively engage stakeholders and satisfy their legitimate needs, while maintaining, and even improving, competitive advantage. Telling that story is largely what this book is about.

Surprisingly, management research has just begun to consider the issues carefully. Over the last two decades, research has mostly been stuck on developing a theory of the firm that incorporates stakeholder aspirations, and links corporate profitability to corporate social responsibility without saying very much about either how to decide what to do or how to actually get it done. One recent effort, the July 2007 *Academy of Management Review* Special Topic Forum on "Business As Social Change Agents" set out to explain the strategic benefits of social action, but was judged even by the editors themselves to fall far short of offering much in the way of examples of social action entrepreneurship and leadership, instead, "Most of the papers address factors that affect whether firms will undertake socially responsible action" (Bies *et al.*, 2007: 791). Whether is, of course, important, but without the how, and the who, the prospects for social change will be unaffected. Part of the problem is that researchers must finally come to acknowledge that demonstrating a causal relationship between positive CSR spending and firm financial performance is a dead end. Even Michael Barnett's "Stakeholder Influence Capacity and the Variability of Financial Returns to Corporate Social Responsibility" (2007) and Mackey *et al.*'s "Corporate Social Responsibility and Firm Performance: Investor Preferences and Corporate Strategies" (2007), both in the same Special Topic Forum, recognize the consistent failures of previous CSR and stakeholder research in which financial performance is the dependent variable, but nonetheless, despite efforts to dissect CSR and stakeholder influence, run smack into the same problem.

The reason for this was explained with exquisite preciseness and tact by James March and Robert Sutton (1997) in "Organizational Performance as a Dependent Variable" over a decade ago.

Most studies of organizational performance define performance as a dependent variable and seek to identify variables that produce variations in performance. Researchers who study organizational performance in this way typically devote little attention to the complications of using such a formulation to characterize the causal structure of performance phenomena. These complications include the ways in which performance advantage is competitively unstable, the causal complexity surrounding performance, and the limitations of using data based on retrospective recall of informants. Since these complications are well-known and routinely taught, a pattern of acknowledging the difficulties but continuing the practice cannot be attributed exclusively to poor training, lack of intelligence, or low standards. Most researchers understand the difficulties of inferring causal order from the correlations generated by organizational histories, particularly when those correlations may be implicit in the measurement procedures used. We suggest that the persistence of this pattern is due, in part, to the context of organizational research. Organizational researchers live in two worlds. The first demands and rewards speculations about how to improve performance. The second demands and rewards adherence to rigorous standards of scholarship. (March and Sutton, 1997)

Accordingly, one of our goals is to help shift the conversation away from performance outcomes and back on to the variables, the concrete behaviors, that go into creating competitive advantage itself and value creation. Over the last decade we have worked to come up with alternative approaches to understanding how corporate social action functions. When this work has sufficient weight and empirical evidence, then it makes sense to talk about economic and social value creation and, in turn, corporate performance.

The corporate performance dependent variable is not the only stumbling block we face in offering corporate social strategy as a possible alternative to current practice. Some researchers have concluded that the lack of a clear correlation (positive or negative) between corporate social performance and corporate financial performance supports the ethical argument that doing good is good in itself and that rewards for doing good are irrelevant. If this is correct, then the only thing firms must do is decide what is right and behave accordingly; unfortunately, as we will discuss later on, management may not always be in a position to be ethical arbiters.

Another group of researchers, among them C. K. Prahalad (2005) and Stuart Hart (2007), argue persuasively that doing good is the task of social entrepreneurs who will change the world and get rich providing goods and services for the base of the pyramid.

Though both these arguments have considerable merit, we believe that neither responds to the questions we raise nor provides established firms, particularly multinationals, with much needed strategic tools for deciding on and managing social action programs effectively. For their part, academic researchers face the challenge of investigating the strategic opportunities inherent in social action programs that may either supplement or displace traditional strategic options.

Several researchers have made promising advances, in particular linking social outcomes with stakeholder theory. The aim has been to identify which stakeholders matter and under what circumstances. For example, Hillman and Keim's (2001) work on primary and secondary stakeholders and social benefits found that different market and nonmarket participants have varying impacts on firm competitive advantage. Such targeted research has helped to introduce academic rigor and realistic expectations to the CSR domain.

Nonetheless, CSR research has lagged far behind the demands of businesses, NGOs, and other civil society and government organizations that seek a clearer understanding of the firm's contribution to social welfare. Accordingly, one of our key objectives is to develop a theory of firm strategic behavior that explains how firms can integrate business strategy and social strategy to increase overall economic and social value creation.

Hence, in seeking to explain firm financial and social performance, we respond to key strategy questions regarding investment in corporate social action. Not all social issues should claim the attention of managers and be invested in; and even worthy social action projects may be rejected by specific stakeholder groups, exposing the firm to new, perhaps debilitating demands. Addressing such strategy formulation questions is essential to understanding how firms may employ social activities to achieve competitive advantage and, hence, superior returns.

We believe that this book will provide new directions for studying the role of social action programs within the firm's corporate strategy. While there are energetic calls for a more strategic CSR and several efforts to explain how it might work, there has been neither sustained theory development nor a meaningful discussion of how to put corporate social strategy into practice. We intend to do both. The book examines both the why of corporate social strategy – that is, it analyzes why and under what conditions social action programs create value for the firm – as well as the how of social strategy. In addition, we provide several examples of firms that are on the road to doing so.

In summary, we believe this book is the first to set out a fully developed strategy for corporate social action. In this introductory chapter, we begin by examining current research in the area and then explore the potential role of corporate social action in the search for competitive advantage. This discussion leads us to propose and define the concept of corporate social strategy; we dedicate much of the chapter to locating social strategy within the field of strategic management. Additionally, we lay out the road map for the rest of this book.

The road to corporate social strategy

One of the most vexing research questions in management is the ambiguous relationship between corporate social responsibility and financial performance (Griffin and Mahon, 1997; Preston and O'Bannon, 1997; Russo and Fouts, 1997; Waddock and Graves, 1997; Hillman and Keim, 2001; Margolis and Walsh, 2001, 2003; Orlitzky *et al.*, 2003). Though initially of concern principally to researchers in social issues management, the emergence of stakeholder theory as an alternative to restrictive economic theories of the firm (Freeman, 1984) has pushed the question of CSR's impacts on corporate performance to the forefront of a reinvigorated debate over the theory of the firm.

As a result, two Academy of Management journals have dedicated special issues to stakeholder management and CSR. The 1995 *Academy of Management Review* "Shifting Paradigms: Societal Expectations and Corporate Performance," held the consensus view that firms must meet the demands of both shareholders and other stakeholders. A framework for stakeholder theory was proposed based on the distinction between normative, descriptive, and instrumental stakeholder approaches (Donaldson and Preston, 1995); among the key research questions that emerged was how to move beyond the normative belief that CSR is good for stakeholders and shareholders, and to demonstrate the instrumental value of CSR for firms.

Four years later, in the *Academy of Management Journal* (1999), the special research forum on "Stakeholders, Social Responsibility and Performance" reviewed the results of recent empirical research. The verdict was, at best, neutral. Particularly telling were the findings of Berman *et al.* (1999). Only two of five stakeholder groups (employees and customers), both directly related to the firm's value chain, were shown to have a positive influence on firm performance. None of the nonmarket stakeholders were found to have any effect. Disappointing results have long been the bane of CSR and stakeholder research. Continuing research has sought to disentangle the moderating and mediating variables muddying the relationship between social action and firm performance as we seek to explain how nonmarket factors impact corporate performance (Hillman and Keim, 2001; McWilliams and Siegel, 2001). These recent studies have been careful to take into account previous work and have rigorously employed statistical modeling (Orlitzky *et al.*, 2003), but they have not significantly changed the landscape (Margolis and Walsh, 2003).

During the last decade there has been little advance in research methodology, though slowly we have come to understand that the complexity of corporate behavior precludes demonstrating that corporate social action (or any other firm activity, for that matter) is positively correlated with financial performance. Nor have we advanced appreciably in the practical task of providing good working models for managers of how to create competitive advantage and economic and social value through social action.

Where we ought to go from here is a significant challenge, given the pressures on business firms to increase profits, increase corporate social action, and help fix the world's problems. We argue that social action is a strategic tool that managers need to learn how to employ. Academic researchers must investigate the strategic choices generated by treating social action as a set of business opportunities that may also interact with traditional strategic options. Our challenge is to develop a theory of the firm in which we contribute to solving the world's ills while maintaining or increasing firm profitability. Understood in terms of joint financial and social performance, we are asked to answer questions of strategy formulation including: (1) how much to invest in social action?; (2) what social activities should be invested in?; (3) will these investments satisfy stakeholders or, on the contrary, may the firm open itself up to new, perhaps debilitating, demands from stakeholders?; (4) should the firm invest in projects that management judges to be financially and socially beneficial, or should investment decisions be left to external NGO and civil society professionals? Answering such questions involves explaining how firms may employ social activities to achieve competitive advantage and, hence, superior returns.

As we have indicated briefly above, the relationship between CSR and financial performance has taken on special relevance as non-business organizations, including the United Nations (Global Compact), and ethical investment funds (Calvert Social Index Fund, Domini Social Equity Fund) insist that there is a positive relationship between CSR and economic performance – despite the mixed empirical evidence! In an environment in which social action is a requisite of doing business, figuring out how to do it and under what circumstances is fundamental. One of our key objectives in this book is to formulate a model of corporate social strategy that more clearly sets out the conditions under which engaging in social change programs can create competitive advantage and lead to superior financial as well as social performance.[2]

In developing our model, we draw on the most relevant recent efforts to link CSR activities to superior financial performance and incorporate CSR into the theory of the firm (Burke and Logsdon, 1996; Berman *et al.*, 1999; Reinhardt, 1999; Rowley and Berman, 2000; Aragón-Correa and Sharma, 2003). As discussed previously, there is no necessary link between CSR and profitability, nor could there be. Only after considering a specific firm activity or group of activities as part of a defined strategy will it make sense to analyze whether the firm has a competitive advantage and, hence, the possibility of creating wealth (Porter, 1996).

For example, in looking at the relationship of response to categories of stakeholders and firm performance, Berman *et al.* (1999) find that only market stakeholders are linked to improved financial performance. However, as we will argue more fully later on in Chapter 4, we believe that a social strategy formulation model based on the commitment of the firm to the strategic use of social action in seeking competitive advantage can incorporate both market and nonmarket stakeholders. With respect to the theory of the firm, Aragón-Correa and Sharma (2003) detail a model of proactive environmental strategy that parallels our work. While quite useful, especially in drawing a strong relationship between the general business environment and a proactive environmental strategy, the model focuses specifically on environmental strategy and improvements in product performance and reduction of environmental damage. Here, the link is between a specific set of easily identifiable firm activities that are part of core operations. Social action programs are a more difficult challenge precisely because they are much more difficult to link to

---

[2] The terms "social action" and "social change" are used synonymously throughout this chapter. We may assume that firms that engage in social action pretend to achieve some positive social change.

specific firm operations and the route to obtaining benefits much more complex. Social strategy embraces both environment and social action. In this book, we focus principally on social action because the strategic opportunities are as large and complex as the demands being placed on firms. In sum, despite having gotten bogged down in the often sterile debate over profitability, previous research has provided evidence that when linked to competitive advantage, CSR may entail either reduced costs (e.g., environmental savings), product or service improvement (e.g., social product attributes that add value) or improved reputation (e.g., buyers prefer products sold by socially responsible firms) (Fombrun and Shanley, 1990; Reinhardt, 1999). While reminding us that some firms have created competitive advantage in certain situations, research has yet to address two key questions: how can firms manage social action to create competitive advantage as well as achieve its social objectives? What do managers need to know about social action and competitive advantage if they are to integrate social change activities into core firm processes?

In answering these questions, we position CSR and social action within the mainstream of the management literature. CSR traditionally refers to activities that "further some social good, beyond the interests of the firm and that which is required by law" (McWilliams and Siegel, 2001). We juxtapose CSR with social action as a way to emphasize the broad range of social activities in which a firm may become involved. In principle, we agree with Marquis *et al.* (2007: 926) who define corporate social action as "behaviors and practices that extend beyond immediate profit maximization goals and are intended to increase social benefits or mitigate social problems for constituencies external to the firm." This approach is similar to prior attempts to define CSR in terms of welfare economics in which corporate social responsibility is defined as the firm's obligation to respond to the externalities created by market action (Sethi, 1978). Externalities are positive or negative impacts of a firm's production on the utility or production of a third party. For example, a negative externality is created when the firm emits noxious gases that affect the health of its neighbors (Sethi, 1978). A positive externality occurs when a company opens operations in the inner city and its presence drives down crime in the area (Keim, 1978).

To this argument, we add the proviso that social action is more likely to lead to both positive financial and positive social performance where it is designed and implemented *as part of* the strategic process (Liedtka, 2000; Grant, 2003). The pursuit of competitive advantage and, hence, superior financial performance may be achieved through social action just as it may be achieved via the advantageous application of other firm resources, depending on the competitive situation of the firm. When firms create competitive advantage via social action in the pursuit of economic and social value creation, we call this *corporate social strategy*.

Defining corporate social strategy

At this point, as we move to introduce our model of corporate social strategy, we would like to insert a brief note on stakeholder management theory. On several occasions, we have already mentioned stakeholder theory in conjunction with CSR. Researchers in stakeholder management have worked on most of the same issues with similar results. Not surprisingly, in the twenty years since Freeman (1984) proposed strategic stakeholder management, research specifying the nature of the link between stakeholder management and financial performance (Murray and Montanari, 1986; Burke and Logsdon, 1996; Mahon and McGowan, 1998; Maignan *et al.*, 1999) has had as little success as CSR, and as little impact within the field of strategic management. Another goal of this book is to reintegrate firm social behavior into strategy, recuperating the tradition of Barnard (1938) and Andrews (1971).

Despite methodological failings, research has consistently sought to demonstrate the potential for achieving strategic benefits from social action. Both CSR and stakeholder management research suggest that doing good works for society or engaging in ethical behavior: (1) builds support from stakeholders that is necessary to firm survival (Clarkson, 1995); (2) creates competitive advantage by reducing agency and transaction costs (Jones, 1995); and (3) improves reputation (Orlitzky *et al.* 2003). In both CSR and stakeholder management research, the relationship between social responsibility and financial performance was thus postulated to occur in a manner similar to that depicted in Figure 1.1.

In contrast, in our work we argue that these links are unlikely to occur by simply including a social action program, but require integrating social change activities within firm competitive strategy – as

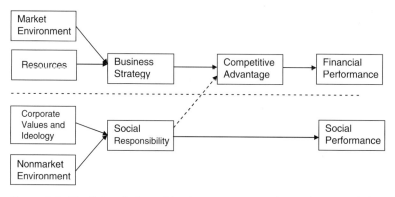

Figure 1.1: Traditional view of business strategy and social responsibility

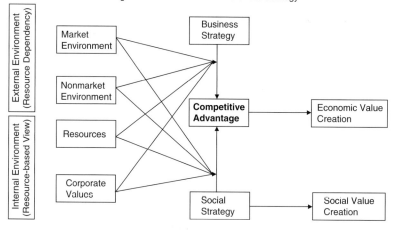

Figure 1.2: Integrated view of business and social strategy

seen in Figure 1.2 – in the same way that firms organize other potential sources of competitive advantage. Figures 1.1 and 1.2 translate
the relationship between social action, business strategy, and corporate performance into a model for formulating corporate social
strategy based on four elements: (1) market environment; (2) nonmarket environment; (3) firm resources; and (4) corporate identity
and values. (In Chapter 4, we provide a thorough review of the
model as well as carefully considering how firms may implement
social strategy).

By no means, however, do we wish to argue that social strategy has been invented by us. Since the Medici – to whom we will return later on – firms have engaged in stakeholder management, philanthropy, government relations, sponsorship and nearly all the activities that may comprise an effective social strategy program.

However, as we have progressed, and professional CSR has become the norm rather than the exception, the same pressures that made firms responsible also led them to eschew practical strategic arguments for social action. As a result, though social strategy is always an option, it is rarely taken up seriously. This, we believe, is a loss for the firm and for society. As a socioeconomic actor, the firm inevitably participates in a broad range of activities that influence economic and social life. Social strategy focuses on activities where the social dimension of corporate activity may be joined with the economic dimension in such a way as to enhance both economic and social value creation. Though, as we will repeat several times, social strategy is not for all firms, the only way management can be sure is to include social strategy in the normal set of strategic options when it comes to time to do strategic planning. Our aim is to facilitate the process.

For those firms that choose a social strategy, there is a great deal to be gained by replacing the hit-and-miss approaches to CSR developed to date with a strategic approach that gives the socially responsible firm the same fair chance of success as those firms that consider their social responsibility to be the generation of profit.

Frankly, beyond encouragement (Kanter, 1999) and Porter and Kramer's (2006) seminal article, strategic management has done little to model how firms prosper via social change activities. In fact, customarily, the social dimension of corporate activity has been described as "nonmarket," while the economic activities have been termed "market" activities (Baron, 1995), demonstrating the clear division between the two types of activities. As indicated in Figures 1.1 and 1.2, the interaction of market environment and non-market environment provides the firm with new opportunities to seek competitive advantage and enhance both financial and social performance.

Our approach tracks traditional strategic management by arguing quite simply that those who are able to innovate in social strategy are more likely to achieve competitive advantage and superior returns

(Porter, 1980; Porter and Kramer, 2002). Innovation is, in effect, the ability to recognize and fulfill customer needs and expectations. In some cases, these needs and expectations may have an important social dimension. Finding ways to serve customer groups with social needs may be a stimulus to innovation (Hart and Sharma, 2004). Consequently, identifying those opportunities and creating competitive strategies to take advantage of them is part of the firm's strategy agenda.

Our model also builds on different strands within the CSR literature, especially the outcomes approach to corporate social performance, which focuses on the measurement and evaluation of corporate impacts on society (Preston, 1990; Clarkson, 1995). The firm's social projects allow it to achieve measurable social objectives as well as improve corporate financial performance in those cases where the social action is linked to product and service innovation, process innovation, or corporate reputation (Fombrun and Shanley, 1990; Reinhardt, 1999).

Two caveats should be added with reference to this definition of social strategy. First, social strategy normally involves the investment of capital, whether financial or human, in order to achieve social objectives. It is difficult to conceive of social strategy where such investments are not made. Second, although not essential to the definition of social strategy, we are particularly concerned with specific actions or plans for social strategy (Liedtka, 2000). Contemporary intellectual theories treat intentions and plans with considerable skepticism (Lyotard, 1984), with the knowledge that operationalizing intentions and plans is likely to be extraordinarily difficult. Nonetheless, we believe that there is much to be gained by considering the announced social strategies of firms and the plans made to implement them. At this early stage of research into corporate social strategy, we must begin with those firms that deliberately create social strategies and plans so that we can begin the task of building models that can be tested. Moreover, the logical nexus between corporate learning, distinctive competencies, sustainable competitive advantage, and strategic planning is crucial to developing a corporate social strategy concept that provides practitioners with tools to analyze social strategy and motivates them to create and implement such strategies.

Similarities and differences between social strategy and traditional strategy[3]

If we want to speak of corporate social strategy, we are faced with the task of clarifying what we mean by strategy. Strategy, according to military science, is an unambiguous term. Strategy is the science and art of winning at war. Winning at war, it has long been believed, requires planning. "Strategy," wrote von Clausewitz (1976: 4), "makes the plans for the separate campaigns and regulates the combats to be fought in each." Similar military definitions of strategy date as far back as Sun Tzu's *The Art of War* and the Greek writings on the institution of the *strategos* (Cummings, 1993).

Not surprisingly, early definitions of corporate strategy from the 1960s focused on making plans to compete successfully in business. Two classic definitions were those of Chandler (1962) and Harvard Business School's "Business Policy and Strategy" Program (Andrews, 1971). According to Chandler (1962: 13), "Strategy is the determination of the long-run goals and objectives of an enterprise, and the adoption of a course of action and the allocation of the resources necessary for carrying out these goals." Andrews (1971: 14) wrote, "Strategy is the pattern of objectives, purposes or goals and the major policies and plans for achieving these goals, stated in such a way as to define what business the company is in or is to be in and the kind of company it is or is to be." Both definitions incorporate the four principal elements of what has come to be known as the "rationalist" or "design" school (Mintzberg, 1990): strategy is long term, requires the setting of specific goals, implies the development of a plan, and involves the commitment of resources.

All these elements can be found in the definitions of corporate and business strategy provided by Ansoff (1965), Bower *et al.* (1995), Daft (1995), Grant (1995), and Hax and Majluf (1996), as well as in most strategic management textbooks used in universities in the United States and Europe.

---

[3] Some of this discussion can be found in Bryan W. Husted and David B. Allen, 2000. "Is it ethical to use ethics as strategy?" *Journal of Business Ethics*, 27(1): 21–31.

In this book, strategy refers to the plans and actions taken to achieve both economic and social competitive advantage and superior performance. We use the term *business strategy* when we refer to economic issues and *social strategy* when treating social issues. *Corporate strategy* encompasses both the economic (corporate business strategy) and non-economic (corporate social strategy) objectives of the firm. This approach modifies current strategic management terminology in consonance with the advances achieved by the resource-based view. Traditionally, the terms business (business unit) strategy and corporate strategy have been used to identify different levels of analysis: *business strategy* has been defined as the search for economic rents via the achievement of competitive advantage(s) in specific customer-product-market segments, and *corporate strategy* the selection of which industries to compete in (Andrews, 1971; Porter, 1980; Grant, 1995; Hax and Majluf, 1996; Segev, 1997).

The resource-based view effectively eliminates this distinction by defining competitive advantage as the creation of unique resources and capabilities (Peteraf, 1993) that leverage organizational routines (Nelson and Winter, 1982) that may cross various business units. In fact, the main objective of Prahalad and Hamel's influential "The Core Competence of the Firm" (1990) was to warn against the limitations of business unit strategy in favor of the development of firm-wide, frequently intangible, *competencies* that most strategic management researchers now believe are the cornerstone to sustainable competitive advantage. As a result, strategic management research has turned once again to the challenge of investigating "soft" behavioral issues that are difficult to operationalize (Papadakis *et al.*, 1998), including those of corporate values and ethics central to our definition of corporate social strategy.

This shift toward a systemic (organic) view of strategic behavior is especially relevant to social and ethics-based strategies. There is, we believe, a significant coincidence between the approach to strategic behavioral and social issues implicit in the resource-based view and the traditional concerns of the design school. From the outset, the Harvard Business School model has included among its four key elements of strategy formulation "corporate social responsibility." This concept, with its roots in Puritan, New England philosophy (Bercovitch, 1986) runs through much of the twentieth-century management literature, in works as diverse as Taylor's *The Principles of Management* (1911) and Chester Barnard's *The Function of the Executive* (1938) (both of whom taught at Harvard) as well as the standard strategic management college texts referred to earlier. The lesser weight given to social responsibility in strategic management research in the 1980s and 1990s is not a reflection of its lessening importance, but rather an indication of the difficulties faced in doing research on the core concept of the discipline: competitive advantage. The re-emergence of more socially oriented research, and its linkages to the resource-based view, provides a vital continuity between the social orientation of the pioneers of strategic management and the possibilities opened by the resource-based view.

However, it would be a mistake to argue that the resource-based view is simply a sophisticated update of the design school. The design school's orientation toward strategic planning is not a main research interest of the resource-based view. This is understandable given that the emergence of the resource-based view coincides with strategic management's ongoing incorporation of theories and concepts from anthropology, sociology, psychology, etc., in an effort to explain the less rational (or, at least, less transparent) elements of strategic behavior within business firms. The impact of the social science approach to strategy is clearly evident, for example, in Prahalad and Hamel's editorship of a *Strategic Management Journal* special issue, "Strategy: The Search for New Paradigms," including articles anchoring strategic management in ethics (Hosmer, 1994a), corporate epistemology (von Krogh *et al.*, 1994), core competencies (Markides and Williamson, 1994), and chaos theory (Levy, 1994).

Repositioning strategic planning in strategic management

For more than a decade now there has been consistent criticism in strategic management of the design school and strategic planning (Mintzberg, 1990, 1994) due to weak conceptualization and inadequate measurement of constructs. Empirical research has failed to demonstrate that current constructs of strategic planning explain the decision to plan and its usefulness (Venkatraman and Grant, 1986; Montgomery *et al.*, 1989; Boyd and Reuning-Eliot, 1998). In other words, not only are the constructs that define strategic planning (design) in disarray, we do not know why some firms plan and others do not, nor do we know why planning sometimes works and sometimes fails.

In short, the dominant view among academics is that the planning-oriented, design school has done a poor job of explaining corporate behavior (Mintzberg, 1987a, 1991; Mintzberg and Waters, 1985), and that strategic planning systems trap firms into unrealistic strategic "designs" that are overly dependent on "rational," non-adaptive implementation (Mintzberg, 1994).

Whatever the merits of Mintzberg's arguments, the attack on strategic planning as a management tool is confusing to practitioners, who see themselves as largely dependent on rational systems to achieve change (Argyris, 1993) and now find themselves wondering whether strategy is useful (Kay, 1993); moreover, given the current paradigm crisis, we see a logical reluctance on the part of many practitioner-oriented academics and writers of strategy textbooks to align themselves with any school (Kay, 1993; de Wit and Meyer, 1994).

Nonetheless, strategic management texts continue to try to define strategy. Many provide multiple definitions of strategy. Mintzberg and Waters (1985), for example, offer eight types of strategy, only one of which is "the planned strategy" consisting of "clear and articulated intentions;" while Hax and Majluf (1996: 13) offer practitioners "a unified definition of strategy" based on nine strategy *dimensions* that "addresses the controversy between the 'industry structure-competitive position' paradigm and the 'resource-based view' of the firm."

In addition, strategy has been subject to redefinition through the launching of a variety of root metaphors (Brown, 1977) intended to give a new focus to the top management activities associated with leading firms to winning in competitive markets. Thus practitioners are learning that strategy is really about *emergent strategy* (Mintzberg and Waters, 1985), *dominant logic* (Prahalad and Bettis, 1986), *strategic intent* (Hamel and Prahalad, 1989), and even the *absence of strategy* (Inkpen and Choudhury, 1995).

Nonetheless, a practice-oriented theory of strategy reminds us that top management still need tools to help them to decide the most basic question of all: "how are we going to win in the future?" Strategic management seeks to provide a framework for creating the best possible answer(s). Finding the best possible answer usually requires top management's commitment to the firm's business and social objectives as well as its direct participation in the formulation and implementation of strategic plans to achieve those objectives.

This vigorous defense of the design school approach to strategy will be evident throughout the book. We treat strategy as a rational process that seeks two enormously valuable and rational ends – economic value creation and social value creation. To reach these ends, firms must search for competitive advantage via both business strategies and values-based social strategies. This, once again, is how we define social strategy.

Summary

The aim of integrating social strategy with the CSR and stakeholder research traditions coincides with the historical mission of strategic management to build a more comprehensive theory of the firm that accounts in a richer way for firm behavior. Our specific contribution is to develop a better account of how firms may create economic and social value through integrating business and social strategy; we explain how social strategy may assist in improving corporate social performance and corporate financial performance concurrently.

We are aware that treating social action within corporate strategy presents additional challenges to the firm. Some stakeholders may find the idea offensive, arguing that one must do good for its own sake and not to improve firm financial performance. To these objections, the only appropriate answer is to respond that developing corporate social strategy is likely to help firms focus on the social change activities best suited to the firm's continued success: in this way, we improve corporate social performance by taking fuller account of the complex, competitive field on which firm behavior is played out. This approach is probably the best guarantee we have that firms will make a sustained commitment and contribution to solving social problems.

A second difficulty is that social strategies are more complex than "pure" business strategies. Social strategies usually carry with them a perceived commitment to remedying social ills through specific social change activities by the firm. If the firm's social action programs do not contribute to meeting business goals and the firm decides to alter its social strategy, the firm must demonstrate to the affected stakeholders that it is changing social strategies and not abandoning its social commitments. In sum, changing social strategies may be more

difficult than changing business strategies. This situation is a reflection of the increased complexity that results from linking business and
social strategies. If firms do not formulate social strategies jointly with
their business strategies, they may develop competitive disadvantages
in which what was a resource-based advantage becomes a core rigid-
ity for the firm (Zajac *et al.*, 2000; Arend, 2003). We would argue,
nonetheless, that the competitive opportunities created by managing
business and social strategies together are far greater than the poten
tial disadvantages.

An additional powerful argument in support of social strategies
is that social strategy more clearly reflects the reality of corporate
stakeholders. We have come from a theory of the firm in which shareholders and stakeholders were treated as enemies to one in which
"enlightened stakeholder management" is said to be the answer to
the single objective function of the firm (Jensen, 2002). We believe
that it is necessary to take one further step and recognize stakeholder
complexity. Neither shareholders nor stakeholders are 100 percent
oriented towards profits nor 100 percent oriented toward social benefits. Nearly all stakeholders would like to see a profitable firm that
also makes a contribution to society. Finding the right balance is the
real challenge. Our contribution lies in proposing a theory of the firm
in which the varying perspectives can be reconciled. Building a model
of social strategy formulation is a first step.

Road map

Part I of the book is focused on fundamentals, and the very first concern is one of ethics. In Chapter 2, we examine whether pro-social
business behavior should be exploited as a form of competitive advantage for the firm. The "CSR conundrum," as we have termed it, turns
on the following problem: how do we respond to the charge that if the
motivation for social action is profit, then it is not social action but
simply good business? We seek to resolve the "CSR conundrum" and
eliminate much of the current, unproductive debate over what CSR
is and why firms should help solve social problems. We argue that
our theory of the firm sets out clearly the difference between social
strategy and corporate altruism and permits firms and stakeholders
to understand when and why businesses may engage in either or both
activities. Finally, we also discuss the imperative of not neglecting

fiduciary and even moral obligations to stockholders by engaging in social strategy.

We then present in Chapter 3 our understanding of the theory of the firm. This chapter will show how a strategic approach to social action will tend to produce both greater value for the firm as well as greater social impact than more altruistic or coerced approaches. We demonstrate how social strategy reconciles Milton Friedman's requirement that social responsibility maximize return to shareholders, with R. Edward Freeman and others who argue that the needs of stakeholders must be brought into the strategy equation. The chapter addresses the long-standing concern that managers, and MBAs in particular, have been trained to understand that making money inevitably conflicts with doing good, despite the vocal support given to social programs by CEOs. Given the CSR backlash, especially in the US and UK, it is fundamental that a realistic, well-argued approach to how social action and profits go together is developed. The exponential growth of business and civil society organizations insisting that CSR is good for business may be doing more harm than good.

In Chapter 4, we present an overview of the social strategy model. The chapter discusses the design of corporate social strategy via the logic of a business development plan for a new product or service. Consistent with the objective of creating competitive advantage, corporate social strategy involves the management of social issues and stakeholders via projects that build on critical firm resources, e.g., social capital and corporate identity, that are difficult to imitate and/ or lead to creation of new products and services that provide additional value for current or new customers.

We then compare and contrast the development of social strategy with the development of traditional business strategies and social activities. One key difference is that business strategies first measure financial performance (ROI and ROE) as well as secondary benefits of activities (trust, reputation, commitment, values, identity). Proponents of the benefits of social action cite as the key benefits what business strategies consider secondary (trust, reputation, commitment, values, identity) while arguing that these lead to improved performance. We argue that social strategies must measure all the benefits cited by both business strategists and CSR proponents. Moreover, social strategies ought to provide measurable social impacts.

Finally, in Chapter 5, we review the core arguments for considering economic and social value creation as the strategic output of social action projects. In so doing, we provide managers with a framework for analyzing the expected success of the social strategies. Building on work by Burke and Logsdon (1996), we will discuss five strategic dimensions of social action projects: centrality, visibility, appropriability, proactivity (first-mover advantage), and voluntariness. Managers can evaluate the fit of social projects with their businesses and the probability of success by considering the extent to which the projects meet these fundamental criteria. The purpose of the chapter is to place social strategy in a framework that is intuitive and can be presented clearly to others within the firm. The chapter serves as a bridge to Part II where we provide how-to examples.

While Part I sets the conceptual framework, Part II of the book focuses on the "how to" of developing corporate social strategy. We begin in Chapter 6 with an analysis of the competitive environment. The purpose of the chapter is to demonstrate the strategic advantages available via corporate social strategy. We explain the market dynamics that permit CSR to create competitive advantage. We also look at recent advances in the modeling of competitive environments within the strategic management literature that allows us to conceptualize that environment along three dimensions: dynamism, munificence, and complexity. We explain how each of the dimensions affects social strategy opportunities. For example, in low munificence environments where resources are scarce and competitive advantage hard to achieve, social strategies may provide competitors with unique opportunities.

Chapter 7 deals with the role of stakeholders in the development of social strategy. On the one hand, stakeholders refer to nonmarket stakeholders including community groups, NGOs, and governmental bodies and agencies that should be considered in the social strategy formulation and implementation process. Such stakeholders can often provide a threat to the firm's welfare, but may become powerful allies in the development and execution of social strategy. These "mixed-motive" stakeholders have often been shunned in the past by firms as unmanageable; social strategy treats them as high potential partners. We examine the relationship in the context of political strategy, and present the (ia)[3] model for assessing the nonmarket environment.

At the same time, we take care not to forget the stakeholder who most influences the success of the firm and who, in turn, is most dependent on the firm: the employee. We review the vital role of employees in social strategy and the potential positive effect of participative decision-making.

We then take a step back from modeling social strategy to look at the resource-based view of the firm and its contribution to our understanding of the elements upon which social strategy is built. There is considerable evidence that firms that have achieved capabilities for continuous innovation, stakeholder integration, radical transactiveness, social embeddedness, and higher-order learning are especially well equipped to reconfigure resources in ways that will allow the firm to create value through social projects. In Chapter 8, we set out what those resources are, where they come from, and why, though it all sounds quite easy to do, it is really rather difficult. This is, of course, a plus. Only those firms that are willing to make a sustained effort to develop resources will be successful in the long term.

Chapter 9 closes out Part II by examining the role of organizational identity, as defined by corporate culture and values, in the development and success of social strategy. Social strategy asks more of firm members than traditional business strategy; strong identification with the firm's objective of integrating business and social action projects is a must. In most cases, a new corporate identity emerges that energizes employees. In the best case scenario, firm processes change at all levels, across functions, in response to the new way of doing things. Based on empirical research done by the authors, social strategy is more likely to be successful in those firms that are committed to social responsibility as part of their identity. In addition, we argue that participative management is vital to social strategy. Much lip-service is paid to employee participation and commitment. In this chapter, we continue the discussion begun in Chapter 7 and demonstrate the benefits that these management practices bring to social strategies. With this chapter, we cement the argument that corporate social strategy really makes a difference and set the stage for Part III and the implementation of social strategy.

In Part III, we deal with issues related to implementing social strategy. Our purpose here is to explore some of implementation's more problematic aspects. In Chapter 10, we work through how firms

choose the appropriate organizational involvement in the management of the chosen social strategy. Building on the make or buy decision, we explain that social projects can be organized as in-house
projects, outsourced as charitable contributions, or developed in alliances with non-governmental organizations (NGOs), governments,
and even other firms. We examine the attributes of each kind of
social governance and discuss the drivers that lead to one alternative
or another.

Chapter 11 discusses how multinational firms organize social
action, using the well-known typology of multidomestic, transnational, and global firms. Once again, we apply basic strategic management theory to the specific case of social strategy exploring how
firms may benefit from managing astutely the globalization/ localization decision. Working from exploratory field research, we explain
how some firms have elaborated strategies that support firm business
strategies. Among the examples, we include Caterpillar and MTV. We
also examine some of the special challenges for implementing social
strategy in an international context where nonmarket factors create
opportunities and risks.

We then turn our attention to the long underdeveloped issues related
to measurement and evaluation of social strategy. In Chapter 12, we
examine the methods for measuring the economic value of social
action, such as conjoint analysis, hedonic pricing, and contingent
valuation. Given the limitations of net present value methods, we
present real options as an especially useful method of evaluation of
the economic value created by social projects. Finally, drawing from
the project management literature, the chapter summarizes some of
the many methods available to evaluate the social impacts of social
projects. Surprisingly, many companies have been unconcerned about
carefully evaluating the impacts of their social projects. A strategic
focus requires the careful evaluation of the costs and effectiveness of
social projects. Cost-benefit analysis and impact evaluation, among
other methods, can be applied to the small-scale social projects of
the firm.

Finally, Chapter 13 concludes the book by asking: where do we
go from here? It discusses the future of corporate social strategy. We
begin by focusing on the future of CSR. On a very practical level, the
business community is being called on to participate in the development of CSR legislation in Europe and the Americas. As CSR demand

grows and regulation is implemented, top management will inevitably spend more, not less, time on social issues, underscoring the emerging role of social strategy within corporate strategy.

What, we ask, will be the social strategies of the future? We discuss the likely creation of new markets for virtue and set out what we believe are the coming challenges and opportunities for social strategy.

Fundamentals

2 | *Is corporate social strategy ethical?*

The differential characteristic of corporate social strategy is the objective of pursuing both social value creation and economic value creation through social action projects. Moreover, we go so far as to argue that when social action projects achieve both ends, firms will be encouraged to make additional social investments and that economic value creation is positively correlated with sustainable social action.

We also believe that corporate social strategy and corporate social responsibility are compatible. This belief is by no means shared by many business and society academics. The traditional definition of CSR precludes the pursuit of profit when firms engage in social action projects. This is an important point that should not be obscured by the research of a number of authors arguing that corporate social performance is positively related to business performance (Cochran and Wood, 1984; McGuire *et al.*, 1988; Hosmer, 1994b; Waddock and Graves, 1997; Margolis and Walsh, 2003). This positive relationship is understood as an unintended yet felicitous outcome. All of us with some experience in CSR have heard repeatedly from The Global Compact, Business for Social Responsibility, The Caux Roundtable, the US Chamber of Commerce, etc., that doing good is good business. Who, on the other hand, has sighted a CEO jumping up to declare that the reason to do good is because it is profitable?

While the former sounds noble and the later rings ridiculous, neither view makes much sense. Like all corporate activities, social action may or may not be profitable. This is a point we will repeat a number of times, as it is essential to the efficacy of social strategy. Social strategy states that specific conditions must be met for social action projects to create economic and social value.

This chapter is a modified version of Bryan W. Husted and David B. Allen, 2000. Is it ethical to use ethics as strategy? *Journal of Business Ethics*, 27(1): 21–31. Permission to use this article was granted by Springer.

This is a description of how social strategy works. It is not normative, for firms are not required to pursue social strategy. Nor, however, does this free social strategy from being examined in terms of its
intention and ethics. Given that social strategy claims to address and
ameliorate social ills, evaluating its ethics is fundamental. Accordingly,
in this chapter, we attempt to answer the question: is it ethical to use
social action as an instrument of competitive strategy?

Intentions and strategy

Before we address the question of the ethics of social strategy, a brief
review of our approach based on the behavioral or social sciences and
the field of strategic management will help to provide the context for
the discussion.

In our work, we have taken up the emergent view in contemporary
cognitive psychology and philosophy that individuals (and organizations) behave intentionally and undertake plans to meet those intentions (Dennett, 1987; Searle, 1996).

This is in opposition to much of contemporary European philosophy and culture theory that has treated intentions and plans (master
narratives) with great skepticism (Lyotard, 1984). What we now call
post-modernism and deconstruction directed much of its considerable
intellectual arsenal against rationalism. The term "logocentric" was
used to explain how Western society forged the ideological under-
pinnings necessary to maintain colonialism and sexism (Derrida,
1976). Whatever the merits of this argument, late twentieth-century
European philosophy and social theory was decidedly suspicious
of power and knowledge, and rejected positivism in favor of severe
relativism.

Part of deconstruction's legacy in the social sciences is the now
widely held view that stated intentions (and the plans developed to fulfill them) are a cover for other objectives, often unconscious. (Freud's
influence is evident – and openly acknowledged by post-modernists.)
The "facts" or the "truth" are, we learn, a form of subjective legitimization, socially constructed (Berger and Luckmann, 1966).

What, you may ask, does this rarefied discussion of contemporary theory of knowledge have to do with strategic management? The
answer, in a nutshell, is that business schools are not as isolated from
the rest of academics as their critics often suggest. A good example

of the influence of other disciplines can be found in a 1994 *Strategic Management Journal* special issue, "Strategy: The Search for New Paradigms," edited by C. K. Prahalad and Gary Hamel, that included articles anchoring strategic management in ethics (Hosmer, 1994a), corporate epistemology (von Krogh *et al.*, 1994), and chaos theory (Levy, 1994). It is customary for business journals to insist that articles demonstrate contributions to theory; most often theories are adopted from prior work in psychology, sociology, and economics. Methodologies and statistical models are drawn from psychology and economics.

Institutionally, as business schools prospered in the last quarter of the twentieth century, larger, more diverse, and better trained faculties were built at top-ranked universities, many of which had previously considered business a second-class citizen. Academics from "core" disciplines such as sociology, psychology, and economics "invaded" business schools where they found vacancies and superior salaries. They brought with them the theories, methodologies, and concerns of their academic fields. Business school professors made the transition from practitioner-oriented to scholarship-oriented, with the pluses and minuses that go with that change.

One change, aligned with objectives and ideology of deconstruction, is the questioning of the legitimacy of business by a significant minority of researchers with a strong social orientation. These researchers engage in "critical discourse" that exposes the "dark side" of business. (We will have more to say about this later on.) Critical discourse has had a minor impact compared with the influence of liberal economic theory, which fostered the ascendancy of the institution of business, and provided powerful ideological support for the growth of the financial services industry. Philosophically a case was made for equating rationality with doing what was good for oneself, which in turn would be good for everyone. They assumed that the sum total of individually rational behaviors would be collective rationality.[1] This makes about as much sense as betting that in the old game of telephone the last person in the line would actually replicate what the first person had said.

---

[1] In the current crisis, writers are having a field day with this ancient philosophical problem which we do not pretend to resolve here. This will have to wait for our next book.

A second change has to do with the nature of scientific research itself. The post-World War II "how to get this done" orientation of business school professors had to learn to coexist with researchers concerned with "what doesn't work and why." From here has come the insistent critique that MBAs either don't know anything useful or that they finish the MBA with a worsened moral character. Apparently neither the MBA students nor the employers seem to have gotten the message, as MBA applications are up in the recession, considered by many to be the best shot for getting a good job.

Most importantly for our discussion, these changes have influenced how the field of strategic management treats basic tasks like strategic planning, and helps to explain how we arrived at the following anomalous situation: while businesses make strategic plans and no entrepreneur can raise a cent without a business plan, academics in strategic management question the value of strategy and strategic planning. Henry Mintzberg, author of the groundbreaking *The Nature of Managerial Work* (1973) and *The Structuring of Organizations* (1979), went so far as to claim that strategic planning is dead, e.g. *The Rise and Fall of Strategic Planning* (1994). Once again, it appears that the men and women charged with managing firms, listen attentively to what the scholars have to say and then do what they have always done.

Another striking example that will be familiar to most of our readers is the widespread rejection by strategic management academics of Michael Porter's Five Forces and his generic strategies matrix as gross simplifications, though MBA strategy textbooks continue to feature Porter's work and consulting firms still include the models in their field work and presentations.

Finally, in the MBA classroom, students are taught cases that present firms as if the information had come from a "neutral" source when, in fact, the document they are reading has been vetted by the corporate communications department, which has dutifully made sure that the firm is presented in the proper light.[2]

With these examples in mind, we would like to suggest that the field of strategic management is unclear about how to treat what we

---

[2] Several of the cases written by one of the co-authors of this book were written with this process. In the course we teach, we inform students of the conditions under which cases are written and provide supplementary material to provide other possible points of view.

discover in our research and equally uncertain about how to incorporate that knowledge into our teaching and management practice.

A large part of the problem lies in not being very good at explaining the decisions made by firms nor interpreting what managers say. Too often, the choice is between simple acceptance or outright dismissal. In other words, the declarations of the CEO are either taken at face value or they are treated as outright deception. (We note that the November 10, 2009 acquittal of two former Bear Stearns hedge fund managers in a multi-billion dollar fraud case rested on the jurors' rejection of the prosecution's interpretation of emails sent between the two defendants.)

In so doing, we missed out on the one truly important point made by Rorty, Foucault, and Derrida – those with the power to drive the conversation determine the rules of the game. We have no reason to take what anyone says, least of all the CEO of a powerful multinational, at face value. Our expectation is that he or she is representing the interests of a business firm, whose members individually and collectively exhibit ethics that are no better, nor worse, than their neighbors.

The conversation about the meaning of action, according to the deconstructionists, can go on as long as we wish to continue playing the game. We disagree. While conversation and interpretation is inevitable, it is not endless. At some point, the jury must speak. We must decide that some claims are true and that others are false. Of course, mistakes will be made. Sometimes, we will get the facts wrong or make erroneous interpretations, damage companies, and badly skew reputations. But with vigilance, the facts and reputations can be set straight. Following Dennett and Searle, we argue that there is an objective reality of social facts and behaviors. The belief in an objective reality does not preclude human beings from doing good and bad, nor does it prevent individuals and groups within companies from behaving both responsibly and irresponsibly.

Objective reality is not a synonym for simplicity. Nor is a radical subjectivism the antidote to the simple-minded rationality that some very smart people, among them Alan Greenspan, assumed would make a financial bubble impossible.

What does this mean for social strategy? To start, social strategy is not about separating out the good guys from the bad guys. This is difficult to do even with good information; most often our information

about companies is extremely limited. Accordingly, firms that engage
in social strategy should be less concerned with making sure that
everyone thinks the company is a paragon of virtue than with earning
the support of vital stakeholders and then keeping it. This, of course,
is not meant to be an excuse for managers to behave badly as long as
it doesn't hurt the firm. It does mean, however, that making ethical
judgments, particularly about the aims and intentions of organizations with thousands of people, is an uncertain enterprise at best.

Unfortunately, as we have argued, neither strategic management
nor business and society scholars have been very good at this. While
strategists with a strong economics orientation mostly consider CSR
a cost and an opportunity for managerial self-indulgence (Friedman,
Jensen), business and society academics seek to insure that firms do
the right things for the right reason. On the one hand, the intentional
pursuit of gaining strategic advantage via socially responsible and
ethical behavior is considered a high-minded fantasy (Vogel, 2005);
on the other hand, it may be condemned as unethical. A third point
of view, held by critical theorists, is that large firms – multinationals – are powerful and defend their power without regard for ethical
criteria.

Social strategy rejects all three points of view. Our starting point
is to think strategically about social strategy: it works when firms get
it right, just like other strategies. Next, social strategies also pursue
social benefits. If it is ethical to create wealth, and it is ethical to create social goods, in order to conclude that social strategy is unethical, we would have to be convinced that there is real damage done
by pursuing these two ends jointly. This argument must be qualified. Large multi-product multinationals may pursue social strategy
in some product markets and not others. This qualifier is necessary
to distinguish social strategy as pursued in large, diverse multinationals from the social entrepreneurship movement. It is worth noting,
here, that even within the social entrepreneurship movement there
is debate over the ethics of profit. Compartamos, the Mexican mic-
rolender, which began as an NGO and then was transformed into a
publicly traded company, has been severely criticized by Nobel prize
winner, Muhammad Yunus, for its wide profit margins and balloon-
ing share price (Schmall, 2009). Yunus is sufficiently annoyed that he
has announced a non-profit joint venture with billionaire Carlos Slim
to compete with Compartamos. We should note that Wal-Mart has

also entered the microcredit market through its 1,356 banking out-
lets across Mexico. Mr. Yunus opposes Wal-Mart's entry as well; he
believes that only the non-profit model can truly serve the poor.

For our part, we do not claim to know who can best serve the poor,
just as we do not claim that we are in a position to evaluate the ethical status of intentions and plans of Compartamos, Wal-Mart, or
the alliance of Mr. Yunus' Grameen Bank with Mr. Slim's Inbursa.
We are unable to make any claims, either, as to the ethical superiority
(inferiority) of for-profit and non-profit organizations. We are, however, quite certain that we will find ethical and unethical behaviors
across the board, and that there will be both estimable for-profits and
non-profits as well as reprehensible for-profits and non-profits. The
confluence of ethical and unethical behavior within a single organization is, we believe, the norm.

Perhaps we should summarize our argument so far. Social strategy is an activity that falls within the field of strategic management.
Strategic management, institutionally, is subject to influences from
other academic areas. Two competing philosophies (or ideologies, if
you prefer) have influenced the discipline. The dominant position is
held by liberal economic theory and the belief that the pursuit of self-
interest (profit) is the most efficient and most moral way to organize
economic and social life. The weaker contestant, critical theory (a
descendant of deconstruction and post-modernism) holds that large
firms, especially MNEs, hold power and do whatever is necessary to
defend their privileges; the result is more bad than good; the best way
to fix this is to force firms to do good.

In this context, three ethical positions regarding the intentional
use of social action in the pursuit of profit have emerged. The liberal
economist suspects that social strategy is self-delusional and doomed
to failure. The critical theorist argues that only regulation that restricts
firm behavior can stop some, not all, of the harm done. A third view,
though adhered to mostly by business and society academics, rather
than strategists, states that stakeholders have inherent rights and that
firms have an ethical responsibility to respect those rights, irrespective of either cost or benefit. In addition, many argue, following Kant
(Bowie, 1991), that only those actions undertaken with the intent of
doing good can be considered moral.

In the next section, we take up this third view and the different
approaches to firm ethical and social behavior that have developed

in the management literature. In Chapter 3, we take a closer look at liberal/classical economy theory of the firm and economic and social objectives and outputs. In the several chapters on multinationals, we will revisit the concerns raised by critical theory and discuss ongoing efforts to regulate corporate misbehavior.

Current approaches to social strategies

Social strategies embrace a large number of approaches that relate the firm to its social environment. Hosmer (1987: 3) explains that ethical problems in management "represent a conflict between an organization's economic performance (measured by revenues, costs, and profits) and its social performance (stated in terms of obligations to persons both within and outside the organization)." He defines ethics in terms of social obligations or responsibilities. However, technically, ethics tends to focus on personal choice; social responsibility is about meeting generally agreed public expectations of firm behavior. From the point of view of corporate social responsibility, a socially responsible firm (and its members) would behave ethically as part of being socially responsible. In utilitarian philosophy, the concept of the greatest good for the greatest number tends to conflate ethics and social responsibility, but this need not always be the case. The terms are not used here in a precise way to distinguish between two different approaches, but rather as a way to describe a certain kind of strategy, which has not yet received a generally accepted name.

In the management literature, ethics and social responsibility have been linked to corporate "objectives" in various ways. As we indicated earlier, social responsibility and ethics (including personal values) have been an element of management discourse from its inception. In this section, we shall briefly review some of the efforts by management researchers to understand the role of corporate responsibility and ethics in the firm and the research streams that have been developed.

Corporate social responsibility and responsiveness

In the 1950s, business leaders began to debate widely the social and ethical responsibilities of corporate enterprise. Not only in the strategic management literature, but also in the social sciences (Riesman *et al.*, 1950), part of the scholarly effort in the United States was directed to understanding more fully the implications of the triumph of US corporations following World War II. In this context, the corporate social responsiveness literature emerged as a reaction to the corporate social responsibility literature, which was seen as failing to provide managers with tools for managing social responsibility (Frederick, 1994). Corporate social responsibility only spoke of the obligations corporations should fulfill in order to improve their social environment, rather than how they should respond.

Corporate social responsiveness was concerned with the ability of the firm to "respond to social pressures" (Frederick, 1994: 154) in an apparently antagonistic environment with the "firm" on one side and the "stakeholders" on the other. Corporate social responsiveness can be understood as a way of protecting the firm's strategy from the social issues affecting the firm.

Corporate citizenship

In popular usage, the concept of corporate citizenship is closely related to corporate social responsibility and responsiveness. These latter concepts emerged from the sociological literatures, while the concept of citizenship comes from political science. It tends to focus not only on the legal responsibilities of the corporation, but also on those actions that aim "to enhance the quality of community life through active, participative, organized involvement" (Tichy *et al.*, 1997: 3). It moves beyond philanthropy to include projects undertaken by the firm and its employees. Citizenship differs from corporate social responsiveness, by calling upon the firm to engage its social environment proactively (Matten and Crane, 2005). Although its aim is not strategic, supporters of corporate citizenship defend its positive consequences for the financial performance of the firm.

Stakeholder approaches to strategy

Proponents of stakeholder management have characterized the firm as a set of identifiable interest groups to whom management has responsibilities; activities undertaken by the firm vis-à-vis stakeholders are seen as reflecting values and ethical principles. Stakeholder management treats strategy in at least three different, though related, ways: it speaks of the concept of enterprise strategy (Schendel and

Hofer, 1979; Freeman and Gilbert, 1988), outlines generic strategies for managing stakeholders (Freeman, 1984; Savage *et al.*, 1991), and deals with specific stakeholder strategies (Freeman, 1984). Together, the three concepts represent the outline of a theory of the firm in which governance is distributed according to the inputs into and impacts on the stakeholders. Chapter 7 is devoted to a closer look at the contributions of stakeholder theory.

Strategic CSR: the CSR conundrum

CSR is strategic when it is designed to create value for the firm (Burke and Logsdon, 1996). A burgeoning literature has begun to examine the concept of strategic CSR. Unfortunately, strategic CSR leads to a problem. The "CSR conundrum," as we have termed it, turns on the following problem: if the motivation for social action is profit, then it is not social action but simply good business. If the motivation for social action is doing good, then the firm is not doing business but simply charitable work.

One attempt to resolve the "CSR conundrum" is the concept of social entrepreneurship. The goal is to provide business services to solve social problems and make money doing it. However, several issues have arisen. In addition to the issues surrounding competing with non-profits raised by Muhammed Yunus, social entrepreneurs frequently are supported by charities and governments. This raises questions regarding management salaries and profit distribution. Though obviously at a much smaller scale, the basic issue is the one troubling Americans regarding salaries of executives of banks that received money in the bailout. Moreover, the business practices of social entrepreneurs may also come under question. When problems arise, social entrepreneurs inevitably come under attack just as more traditional forms of CSR have, and stakeholders again seek disinterested corporate altruism, including demands for returning the value created to the poor or other stakeholder groups.

One benefit of social strategy is that it resolves the "CSR conundrum" and could eliminate much of the current, unproductive debate over what CSR is and why firms should help solve social problems. We argue that our theory of the firm sets out clearly the difference between social strategy and corporate altruism and permits firms and stakeholders to understand when and why businesses may engage in either or both activities. (See also Chapter 3.) At the same time, social strategy defends the fiduciary and even moral obligations to stockholders.

Corporate social strategy

In the traditional language of strategic management, corporate social strategy is the firm's plan to achieve long-term social objectives and create a competitive advantage. By placing social objectives first, we indicate that what distinguishes social strategy from other types of strategy is this social dimension. In other contexts, we have defined social strategy as a plan to create both social and economic value, emphasizing the inseparability of the two ends. In either case, it is imperative to keep in mind that social strategy differs from previous conceptions of corporate strategy in that it converts the social role of the firm into a potential starting point for strategic planning. Large multinationals plan strategically around markets and products. They focus on the value chain and where value can be added. They ask what can we do new and better. Social strategy operates in the same way. How can social action help create new products and services for our customers? How can social action add value to what we already do? Social strategy looks at the customer decision equation (xPrice + yDifferentiation + zReputation = Choice) and asks, how can social action increase the weight of our reputation for our customers when it comes to time to decide between us and someone else?

Ethical analysis

Let us turn to ethics proper and examine the utilitarian and deonto-logical criticisms that have been leveled against social and ethics-based strategies. As we indicated earlier, it is essential that social strategy meets our ethical as well as business standards.

Utilitarianism requires us to evaluate the ethics of social strategy in terms of its consequences. Although utilitarian philosophers disagree over the correct standard (whether we should maximize average or total happiness), those consequences which maximize happiness are considered ethical (Smart and Williams, 1973). At least five objections may be made to the use of corporate social action as strategy because of its unfavorable consequences.

First, ethically inspired standards may be used to create a competitive advantage by imposing the ethical conventions of one firm on an industry through the public policy process (Reinhardt, 1999). In effect, business ethics creates a monopoly for those firms already in compliance with respect to those that are not, similar to the kinds of monopolies created by professional licensing requirements (Abbott, 1983). Although nothing prevents a firm from complying with specific ethics standards, the firm that already complies with those standards has a cost advantage and thus a short-term competitive advantage with respect to firms that do not comply. An example is that of Toyota, which lobbied the California government to grant an array of privileges to hybrid vehicles (including the right to the prized multi-passenger lane on the Los Angeles freeway for hybrids with just one passenger). By establishing the same standards for all competitors, the new policy created a real competitive advantage for Toyota thanks to its commanding position with the Prius. Donna Wood's (1985) study of food and drug manufacturers in the Progressive Era found that many of them supported the 1906 Food and Drug Act as a way to obtain a competitive advantage with respect to domestic competitors and enter foreign markets. Strategies to impose ethical standards may be used without regard to whether they are really helping or hurting society. In the Prius case, permission to use the multi-passenger lane had to be rescinded thanks to overcrowding. Some social strategies are better described as anti-competitive practices.

However, social strategies are not limited to the construction of ephemeral entry barriers that benefit one firm in detriment of a larger, stronger rival. Though industry ethics codes may acquire a semi-mandatory nature, the ability of a specific firm to compete with respect to lower cost compliance than its competitors does not prevent other firms from innovating and learning so as to compete on an equal footing or even surpassing the performance of first movers. All firms are welcome to find a unique niche within the panoply of social projects that are available to business. In fact, social strategies require firms to think carefully about their own unique capabilities to craft strategies that respond to the competitive configuration of markets, stakeholders, resources, capabilities, and values.

A second objection raised against social strategies is that business is ill-equipped to solve social problems. Few firms have the expertise necessary to attack such problems as poverty, illiteracy or AIDS.

Like the proverbial bull in a china shop, many firms are insensitive to social realities (Peel, 1998) and make a muddle of their excursions into the task of helping remedy social ills (Christian Aid, 2004).

The response to this concern lies, as Porter and Kramer (2006) argue, in the recognition that a firm is more likely to create value from social projects that are highly related to its value chain impacts and competitive context than from projects that are not. If a firm is involved in a project that is closely related to its value chain impacts and competitive context, what Burke and Logsdon (1996) earlier called "centrality," then it is more likely to have the knowledge necessary to solve a particular problem. We argue that firms that do not have a strategic perspective are more likely to become involved in problems that are only loosely tied to their business objectives – where they have neither the expertise to make significant contributions nor the commitment to work through problems should they arise. Nonstrategic approaches, although well intentioned, are thus more likely to fail to achieve any real improvement with respect to a given social problem.

A third difficulty is that social strategies may subvert ordinary democratic processes. Nobel laureate Milton Friedman (1962: 133–134) asks pointedly:

If businessmen do have a social responsibility other than making maximum profits for stockholders, how are they to know what it is? Can self-selected private individuals decide what the social interest is? Can they decide how great a burden they are justified in placing on themselves or their stockholders to serve that social interest? Is it tolerable that these public functions of taxation, expenditure, and control be exercised by the people who happen at the moment to be in charge of particular enterprises, chosen for those posts by strictly private groups?

As companies become involved in social problems, the argument goes, they begin to make decisions that may not be in the best interests of society as a whole. Only freely elected representatives should be involved in decisions that affect the public interest. For example, in many countries corporate philanthropy is tax deductible. Instead of directing resources to areas that will most benefit the public good through government, tax-deductible philanthropy allows the firm to decide where to direct those resources in terms of its own interests.

Yet the involvement of firms in social projects does not leave the government without means to influence the direction of private investments to serve the public interest. Fiscal policy can still be used to motivate corporate social investments in areas that are particularly important to a nation – drug abuse, racism, poverty, support for the arts, etc. Elected leaders can provide the signals for the kinds of social investments to be made by firms and let firms work with competitive NGOs to achieve their social goals. The US experiment with tax breaks for business development in enterprise zones in inner cities is an example of how government can provide positive incentives for specific kinds of social investments made by the private sector. The development of mandatory carbon markets in the European Union is another way in which government can establish social and environmental goals and allow firms the flexibility to meet those standards creatively so as to generate revenue streams.

A fourth question revolves around the strategic use of ethics and corporate social responsibility. Given the fact that strategies must produce value for the firm, corporations tend to be conservative and direct funds toward popular and politically correct causes. Controversial causes do not receive support. Estimates are that 80 percent of corporate philanthropy is directed toward "safe issues" (Peel, 1998). The result is a lack of differentiation and little strategic advantage. This suggests that supporting unpopular, even controversial causes may be advantageous in some cases. We would argue that the utilitarian should be concerned with the net increase in strategic social projects, rather than the distribution of causes. It may well be that companies that have been risk averse in their choice of social projects will be even more inclined to choose safe projects if strategic social strategy were to be widespread. On the other hand, social strategy will probably cause an increase in the total number of social projects, overcoming negative outcomes from projects that are perceived by the majority of the population to do social harm rather than good. Those firms that are willing to seek support for unpopular or controversial causes risk becoming involved in issues that may be highly distasteful to some sectors of the public. Tom Monaghan used Domino's Pizza to pursue pro-life causes, subjecting the firm to a boycott by the National Organization of Women. It may be better, some may argue, to have companies meet the statutory minimum ethical standards, and let people as individuals decide important public issues for themselves.

However, pursuing "unpopular" causes may provide both utilitarian social benefits as well as profit to the firm. Moreover, there may even be a positive relationship between the two.

One way to look at this surprising result is to consider the utilitarian benefits of social strategy in conjunction with action theory (Argyris, 1993). The commitment to social involvement in a democracy implies action. *Intentional* social strategies, rather than emergent ones, permit firms (and firm members) to extend and focus the already considerable impact they have on the communities to which they belong.

Moreover, those firms that pursue social strategies directly linked to their product offerings and customer base, are actively pursuing the creation of competitive advantage and additional value-added for the customers. As a result, effective social strategy enables competitive success that in turn enables social action.

In such cases, the separation between social strategy and business strategy tends to disappear. For social scientists such as Argyris, Lewin, and Drucker, the contemporary firm can best be understood as a purposeful social institution that responds as fully as possible to the needs of its stakeholders, increasing, in utilitarian terms, the total good created for those stakeholders. Of course, this good (or value-added) may not be understood as such by the *entire* society. In fact, the social value-added pursued may even raise controversy. The value-added, however, must be measured in function of the relevant financial and value chain stakeholders (shareholders, employees, customers) who find themselves happier.

Both action theory and stakeholder theory remind us that we must measure the greatest good in function of the importance given by those who consider themselves directly affected. This helps us to understand cases like Domino's Pizza (socially conservative) and Benetton (socially liberal). While offending some, they defend their social practices and positions, apparently satisfying those primary stakeholders essential to the company's profitability and continued survival. If all firms were to pursue social strategies under this dictum, we could then sum the value-added of all firms' social strategies with the expected result that we would achieve a new kind of competitive behavior in which the total "social value-added" is greatly increased. It is possible that there may be more cases of negatively perceived "social value-added," but given that the vast majority of firms

look for value-added projects that present low risk, our hypothesis
would be that the more firms view social strategy as a positive contribution to overall corporate strategy, the more social value-added they
are likely to create – a result confirmed in our own studies of large
Spanish firms (Husted *et al.*, 2003) and MNEs operating in Mexico
(Husted and Allen, 2007b).

As regards the argument that social action should be the domain
of individuals rather than firms, it is difficult to see the difference
between support by an individual for a cause (radical or otherwise)
and support by a corporation. Some may object that the latter case
involves the use of stockholder funds, but, provided the board is presented with complete information about the firm's social activities, it
can always decide to suspend those it opposes. This holds equally for
privately held and publicly traded companies.

In conclusion, the strategic focus should increase ethics and social
projects of all kinds, increasing the likelihood that some of these
projects will be greeted with approval by certain people, while others
are greeted with disdain. A true utilitarian analysis would measure
the benefits of "agreeable" projects as well as the disadvantages of the
"disagreeable" projects. Overall, the strategic orientation satisfies the
utilitarian requirement that seeks to maximize total happiness (Smart
and Williams, 1973).

Deontological ethics is concerned with a different kind of problem that may plague social strategies – the issue of motives. Doing
the right thing for the wrong reason is still morally objectionable.
Kant (1964) argues forcefully that good actions that arise out of self-
interest or immediate inclination are not morally praiseworthy. Only
those actions done from the motive of duty are morally laudable.
Corporate intentions with respect to social projects are questionable
at best, and outright self-interested at worst. By its nature, a strategy
seeks to increase value for the firm through the creation of competitive advantages. If an action does not seek to create value for the firm,
it is not strategic. By definition strategy requires actions in the interest
of the firm. Thus, a social strategy would by definition be incompatible with the condition of moral motives required by Kant to evaluate
the moral praiseworthiness of a particular action.

Certainly, the firm has a duty to maximize earnings for its owners.
It also has duties to other stakeholders such as its customers, suppliers,
creditors, the community, and the natural environment (Freeman,

1984). These duties are often in conflict and thus provide the crux of ethical dilemmas for managers (Hosmer, 1987). Social strategies seek to reconcile these contrasting duties, in order to create an inclination (in the words of Kant) to do good. To the extent that such motives are not founded on duty, although complying with duty, such motives lack moral content. This is not to say that they are immoral or unethical, only that they are not morally praiseworthy from a Kantian perspective. This limitation is one that social strategies will have to accept.

Nevertheless, social strategies may very well be an expression of a desire to comply with duties owed to owners as well as to other stakeholders. Thus the problem of good deeds, but questionable motives is not inherent in social strategies. The strategic orientation only reminds those managers with desires to be socially responsible (or the desire to pursue social actions of their choosing) of their duties to owners. The problem of the moral acceptability of corporate social projects depends upon the motives of the actors behind the social project, not upon the nature of social strategy itself. However, we should remember that we only tend to judge the motives of those who offend rather than those who please; nor do most stakeholders have the information necessary to make reasoned judgments regarding the motives of those who propose social projects. In general, the stakeholders are constrained by limited time and information to either accepting or rejecting the social projects (and strategies) of business firms.

Furthermore, it is decidedly difficult to attribute intentions to a firm. When Ford Motor Company began to pay its workers the US$5 a day wage, Henry Ford proclaimed that the new higher wage was simply a question of fairness, while James Couzens supported the policy due to its impact on the firm's reputation and ability to attract the best workers. Was Ford Motor Company motivated by altruism or strategic gain? Assuming that both were factors, does the weight given to each matter? Even if it did matter, we don't have the necessary information to make a determination.

Finally, there is concern about what happens when a particular social strategy no longer provides the company with a competitive advantage. If management is committed to social projects as a question of duty, it is likely that the firm will continue to support them, putting aside the consequences to competitive advantage and, ultimately, profit. Those corporations that participate in social projects for reasons of competitive advantage may decide to discontinue support.

Still, the difficult position of the business manager is that she or he owes duties to both owners and other stakeholders. If a particular social strategy loses its competitive advantage, thus failing in its duties to stockholders, a Kantian response to those duties may be to drop the social strategy and develop new strategies that do comply with the obligations of duty to owners and other stakeholders. Once again, there is no easy decision calculus. The recent, ongoing tribulations of General Motors (GM), though not a case directly of failed social strategy, illustrate the complexities. Maintaining the commitments made by GM to its workers, past and present, and to the city of Detroit, consumed much of top management's and the federal government's attention as the company's competitive position deteriorated. Among the strategic options open to GM was social strategy. GM could, as the authors of this book have argued for several years (D. B. Allen, 2007, 2008), commit to an environmental strategy and only manufacture automobiles that met very high mileage standards. The sales strategy would combine the benefits for the environment and for America in buying GM. Every customer that walked into a GM showroom would know that every car on sale would help America end its dependence on foreign oil, combat global warming, and provide jobs for Americans.

GM's "new" strategy is not a social strategy, but rather one designed to keep critics quiet and allow the US government to defend its decision to bail out the company. If the firm has an ethical obligation to pursue a strategy that will enable the government to recuperate its investment and keep manufacturing jobs in Detroit, the chosen strategy is not likely to meet that standard.

Conclusion

In this chapter, we have positioned social strategy within the field of strategic management, defined strategy within its institutional context, and examined whether social strategy is, in fact, ethical. From a utilitarian perspective a number of objections were answered. Complaints about the inability of firms to solve effectively most social problems may, in fact, be tempered by the strategic nature of social projects that will limit firm involvement to areas where they do have competencies. Moreover, the contribution of business to solving social ills does not inhibit governments from either directing private action in the public interest nor from undertaking their own projects. With regard to the range of social action taken by firms, a strategic focus may augment the likelihood of low-risk and non-controversial social projects, but the overall number of social projects, including more controversial ones, is expected to increase. Given the private nature of the social projects undertaken, there will be projects that are offensive to a majority of the population and may thus constitute a negative social benefit. Nonetheless, the increase in the overall number of social projects will surely outweigh the damaging effects of a few extreme ones. Moreover, action theory indicates that the commitment and involvement that accompanies social strategy, including those that are controversial and unpopular, is a significant public good.

The deontological approach questions the motives of social strategy as inherently self-interested and not based on a sense of duty. Yet social strategy emerges from a sense of the conflicting duties that managers owe to both asset owners as well as other stakeholders. Social strategy is only a tool to comply with conflicting duties and is not itself a motivation. The motives of actors will still have to be judged independently of the strategy in order to determine the moral acceptability of a given strategy.

Social strategies provide new and exciting opportunities to reconceptualize the role of the firm in society. Certainly, such strategies are not without pitfalls, but they have the potential of increasing overall social welfare. The motives behind such strategies are often mixed, but no particular set of motives can be attributed to the strategic focus other than a concern to take into account the impact of a program on the firm. As with any instrument, social strategy can be used in ways consonant with the demands of ethics. It is in this spirit that we urge business people to look at social strategies as a legitimate and ethical option for their firms.

3 | *Theory of the firm and corporate social strategy*

The theory of the firm is ultimately concerned with the purpose of the firm itself. Neoclassical economic theory has generally taken profit or shareholder value maximization as the appropriate objective of the firm (Jensen, 2002; Sundaram and Inkpen, 2004). A strategic approach to corporate social action does not dispute this basic objective. Now some may claim that firms should maximize both profits and social performance. Although social strategy is focused on understanding the conditions under which profit maximization and social performance are congruent, we face an important constraint noted by Jensen (2002: 238) who indicated that it is "logically impossible to maximize in more than one dimension at the same time unless the dimensions are monotone transformations of one another." This constraint implies that profits and social performance cannot be maximized simultaneously. In other words, there is a trade-off between profits and social performance, except in the special case where they mutually reinforce each other. Jensen's exception points to situations in which it may be possible to achieve both objectives at the same time – investment in corporate social projects needs to contribute to profit maximization. Our challenge is to determine the conditions that this requirement imposes upon social projects.

The discipline of economics has looked at these questions in terms of the private provision of public goods (Demsetz, 1970; Keim, 1978; Thoreen, 1981; Baron, 2001). McWilliams and Siegel (2001) have recently discussed the supply and demand conditions that would lead to optimal investment in social projects by the firm. Using the tools of microeconomic analysis, this chapter explores the conditions under

This chapter is a modified revision of Bryan W. Husted and José Salazar Cantú, 2006. Taking Friedman seriously: Maximizing profits and social performance, *Journal of Management Studies*, 43(1): 75–91. Permission to reprint here has been granted by Wiley-Blackwell on February 14, 2008 and by José Salazar Cantú on February 13, 2008.

which firm investment in social initiatives is consistent with shareholder value maximization, and in so doing points to an avenue for research and practice that may in fact be quite promising. It also sketches some ideas about the advisability of the firm making investments to solve social problems and about the optimal amount of social output to be produced by the firm. We develop this argument by looking at three different cases: the firm as altruist, as coerced egoist, and as strategist. In each case, we consider both the benefits obtained by the firm from its social projects as well as their costs.

The altruistic firm

Investment in social projects by a firm, as with any individual, may arise from two types of motivations: altruistic and egoistic. In the economics literature, the theory of rational behavior and the theory of the firm have treated altruism in different ways. For the theory of rational behavior, the altruistic individual receives utility from the consumption of others as well as from one's own consumption. In the egoistic case, utility is derived solely from one's own consumption. Becker (1976) and Jensen (1998) have formally demonstrated that self-interested behaviors and altruism are not inconsistent for utility-maximizing individuals. Becker (1976) shows that given equivalent incomes, the altruistic individual can obtain greater utility from that income than the corresponding egoist. Based on the theory of the firm, Friedman (1962) and Baumol and Blackman (1991) have both attacked different forms of corporate altruism such as social responsibility and corporate citizenship. Given their relevance to the firm, let us examine with greater detail the arguments of Friedman and of Baumol and Blackman and then look at the decision of the firm to make investments in corporate social responsibility (CSR) projects,[1] which produce social goods that are not readily valued by markets.

Economists have offered two kinds of arguments against CSR – a political argument and an economic one. In terms of the political argument, which we reviewed in Chapter 2, Milton Friedman (1962) questions the ability of business managers to pursue the social interest.

---

[1] Whereas in Chapter 2, we discussed social action projects, here we speak of CSR in order to be consistent with the terminology used by Friedman and successive critics.

Instead, he argues that business managers should maximize corporate value for shareholders in free competition without fraud or deception. Issues that go beyond this narrow mandate fall within the purview of freely elected officials who seek to promote the collective interest.

Baumol and Blackman (1991: 51) echo the threat to democracy that would occur if business people were to use corporate resources to solve social problems. There is simply no way that business executives can know what is ultimately in the public's best interest. Unfortunately, these authors take a somewhat naive view of the efficacy of government and ignore the possibility of governmental and regulatory failure, due in part to the capture of regulatory agencies by business firms (Bernstein, 1955; Breyer, 1979, 1982; Carman and Harris, 1986; Reagan, 1987).

The economic argument emphasizes the competitive threat to the firm presented by corporate altruism due to the waste-preclusion property of perfect competition and contestability (Baumol and Blackman, 1991). In perfectly competitive markets or those in which freedom of entry makes imperfect markets perfectly contestable, an incumbent firm will lose market share to more efficient rivals if it engages in wasteful activities.[2] As Baumol (1991: 13) explains: "[T]he market automatically interprets any expenditure by the firm that is undertaken only as a matter of good works as an act of unmitigated wastefulness." Such wastefulness reduces the firm's competitiveness and would lead eventually to either bankruptcy or takeover by a more efficient firm. The ability of the firm to voluntarily make investments in social projects not oriented toward profit maximization is necessarily due to some form of market power, which it enjoys.

Certainly, examples of what appear to be corporate altruism can be found in the real world. Merck announced in 1987 that it would donate Mectizan, a drug to combat river blindness, to people in third world countries affected by the disease. The Merck decision has provided some benefits such as increased employee pride as well as community recognition. However, at least ten years later, it was still unclear how to measure the overall impact of Mectizan for Merck (Bollier, 1996; Dutton and Pratt, 1997).

---

[2] Contestability refers to a market with a single dominant firm, but with low entry and exit barriers so that a competitive price is maintained.

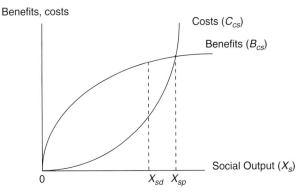

Figure 3.1: Optimal social investment in the case of altruism

We can see the case of the altruistic firm graphically in Figure 3.1. Let us say that a firm seeks to improve its social performance or output (X_s), represented along the horizontal axis, which is an objective measure of the firm's contribution to society. This social output refers to the social impacts of corporate behavior (Wood, 1991) and consists of the production of public goods, or the elimination of "bads," which benefit the community (environmental quality, education, etc.) (Buchanan, 1968; Keim, 1978). A public good is characterized by two attributes: non-excludability and joint consumption. Non-excludability refers to the fact that, as in the case of national defense, the benefit provided to one citizen cannot be excluded from another citizen. Joint consumption, sometimes referred to as the non-rivalrous condition, simply means that a person may consume the good without reducing its availability for consumption by others. Social output has been conceptualized both as units of public goods produced and as units of stakeholder satisfaction with the production of these goods (Preston, 1988; Clarkson, 1995). The measurement of social benefits will be discussed in greater detail in Chapter 12.

The firm faces both a social cost curve and a social benefit curve. The corporate social cost curve (C_{cs}) represents the total amount spent by the firm at each level of social output. The social cost curve indicates the cost to the firm of providing additional units of a public good (social output) to society. The vertical axis represents the firm's social investment – the value of resources expended by the firm to produce social outputs. Following common assumptions in the microeconomic analysis of decisions, we assume that the social cost curve is characterized by decreasing marginal returns and that production occurs in the long run. Generally, we expect that the first units of social output, those where the returns to the factors of production used in the project are marginally more productive, are relatively inexpensive. These activities are the low-hanging fruit that can be captured by minimal effort. This situation is quite common in the case of environmental protection. There are some projects that firms can undertake to improve their environmental impact that are relatively inexpensive (Walley and Whitehead, 1994; Hart, 1995). For example, Wal-Mart Canada announced a plan to replace its 1.75 million bulbs with higher efficiency light bulbs in order to reduce carbon emissions by 17,000 tons and save C\$5 million a year (CNW, 2007). Part of the effort involves replacing storefront signs with LED bulbs. However, generally speaking, the cost of successive units of social output are increasingly expensive, until one reaches a point of maximum potential social output (X_{sp}) (McWilliams and Siegel, 2001). This point might correspond to zero carbon emissions or 100 percent literacy. Beyond this point, the firm could spend more and more on environmental pollution abatement or illiteracy alleviation, without seeing any improvement in social output.

The corporate social benefit curve (B_{cs}) represents the benefits captured by the firm from additional increases in social output. It reflects the change in the total income the firm receives as a result of its social expenditure. The dimensions of this benefit will depend on each case and, once again, *ad hoc* methods will be needed to measure the benefits. It should be noted that this "social benefit" curve is not the social benefit of welfare economics, but is the private benefit to the firm for its production of public goods. These benefits might include increased sales, the ability to extract a price premium, or reduced production costs, all of which are due to the firm's social projects. At first, even the altruistic firm that participates in social programs may be expected to receive additional benefits in terms of increased sales and employee commitment due to its attractive corporate image. However, as the firm's social output increases, this output is less likely to produce the same kind of impact on its image, sales, etc. At some point, additional improvement in social output will provide no additional benefits for the firm. Depending on the type of social project in which the firm invests, the point of maximum possible benefit for the firm is likely to occur either before or at the point where the maximum potential social output occurs. In the case of the altruistic firm, the goal would be to reach the level of X_{sp}, in which the amount corresponding to the difference between the total costs and total revenues is zero. In fact, if the firm continues spending on the resolution of some social problem after that maximum potential output has been reached, it is likely to be viewed negatively and benefits for the firm will decrease.

Given the high cost of reaching the maximum potential social output (X_{sp}), the optimal quantity of social output from the perspective of society is not necessarily that which eliminates all pollution, poverty, social instability, illiteracy, etc., but that which permits a society to maintain at least a minimal desirable state that permits and promotes economic activity (X_{sd} or desirable social output). Thus, X_{sd} may lie somewhere to the left of X_{sp}, if it is not coincident with X_{sp}. The measurement, definition, and scope of the objective level of X_{sd} is one toward which researchers should work (Paul *et al.*, 1997; Reinhardt, 1999). This determination will vary in different contexts and the desirable level of social output could be more ambitious in developed countries than in developing countries, for example.

Just as an economic profit (π) is measured by the difference between revenues and total costs, a firm may calculate its social profit (π_{cs}) as the difference between the benefits it receives (higher prices, increased sales, or decreased administrative and production costs) and the costs of producing a certain level of social output. Given that an altruistic firm is not concerned about optimizing its benefits with respect to the costs of social action, it has no intention of maximizing social profits. Since it is less concerned about the impact of spending on its reputation, it would thus spend up to X_{sd} in order to achieve socially desired goals. A level of output to the left of X_{sd} would fail to eliminate social risks faced by the firm and a level of output to the right would indicate that the resources could be invested in another, more productive activity without creating undesirable risks for the firm due to social ills. It is theoretically possible, although highly unlikely, that an altruistic firm could choose to produce social output that may lie between X_{sd} and X_{sp}, but it would in no case produce social output beyond X_{sp}, where the social profit ($B_{cs} - C_{cs}$) is clearly negative. If the maximum benefit for the firm does not coincide with X_{sp}, but rather occurs before the maximum potential social output, then the altruistic firm may incur negative social profits at X_{sp}. Altruistic firms may move beyond maximum corporate benefits, but would foolishly attempt to move beyond X_{sp}.

The case of the coerced egoist

The firm as an economic agent has as its primary objective the maximization of its profits. In order to achieve this goal, it takes resources from society: land, labor, and financial capital. The form in which the firm uses these resources and administers them determines the scope of its primary objective because its subsistence and growth is conditioned by the stability of the society in which it operates. In the egoistic case, the firm recognizes that its economic activities may have positive or negative externalities that affect the welfare of third parties (Olsen, 1979). When these externalities are negative, the resulting economic, social, environmental, or political problems require the intervention of an independent regulator, who works toward an efficient solution for both the firm and the collective. The most common example of this type of problem is environmental pollution in which the government may impose taxes on energy consumption or require that firms meet certain emission standards so that the firm will internalize the costs of pollution borne by others.

Many environmental and social problems have a direct impact on the firm's welfare (Porter and Kramer, 2006). If it pollutes, the firm can be fined and shut down. If it is indifferent to the poverty that may surround it, the consequent social instability may increase country risk and thus increase the firm's financial costs and reduce its profit margin. If the firm is not concerned with training, which is necessary for its employees, or with the quality of education in the community, from which it draws its workforce, this indifference will affect its productivity, which in turn reduces its competitiveness and profits. Consequently, the firm, in many cases, may be coerced into investing in public goods in order to survive or grow. This case corresponds to the "defensive" firm on Clarkson's (1995) scale of social performance – one that does the least that is required either by law or by social expectation. For example, in a study of US *maquiladoras* (assembly plants) located in Mexico, researchers found that the principal motivation for these firms to invest in environmentally clean technologies was to comply with regulation (Vasquez and Cueva, 2002). These firms are coerced egoists.

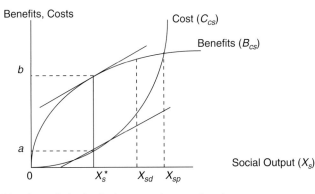

Condition for optimization in the case of coerced egoism:

$$MB_{cs} = MC_{cs}$$

$$\frac{\partial B}{\partial X_s} = \frac{\partial C}{\partial X_s}$$

Where:

MB_{cs} is the marginal benefit of one additional unit of social output; and

MC_{cs} is the marginal cost of one additional unit of social output.

Figure 3.2: Optimal social investment in the case of coerced egoism

In this case, the decision of how much social output to produce depends upon a comparison between the reported benefits for this level of output versus the costs implied by the same output (McWilliams and Siegel, 2001). Corporate benefits for complying with minimal social expectations include not being fined, sued, or subject to consumer boycotts and decreased sales. In Figure 3.2, we illustrate the decision regarding the level of social investment that the egoistic firm will make. For this firm, the optimal level of social output is X_s^*, where it maximizes the return on its social investment (a). X_s^* is that point at which the slopes of both the cost and benefit curves are equal. In other words, the increase in benefit of an additional unit of social output just equals the increase in the cost of that unit. At this point, the firm maximizes its social profit ($\pi_{cs} = b - a$). Both the firm and the regulatory authority may consider this solution to be optimal. The firm will seek this point in order to obtain greater benefit or suffer the lowest net cost from its social expenditure. The government will design regulations that promote private social investment at this point in order to produce the maximum social benefit or lowest net social cost.

The strategic case

The prior case reflects the situation of the coerced corporate social investor, which, in the absence of some form of coercion, makes no investment. Let us now consider the strategic social investor, that is, one who upon making a social investment also obtains an additional benefit (good reputation, differentiated products that extract a premium, more highly qualified personnel) by design and thus obtains greater profitability. Such design may involve either the positioning of the firm with respect to its competitors (Porter, 1980) or the leveraging of unique resources and capabilities (Barney, 1991).

The strategic case provides an important exception to the waste-preclusion property of perfect competition and contestability. Baumol (1991) recognizes that firms may engage in a form of enlightened self-interest to the extent that social investment improves their own productivity and leads to higher profits. Burke and Logsdon (1996) argue that social projects can provide economic benefits when they are central to the firm's mission, highly specific, proactive, visible, and voluntary. As we will discuss further in Chapter 6, there are at least three circumstances under which a firm may engage in activities that benefit the environment or society and also increase the expected value of the firm: where the possibility exists of strategic interaction based on governmental intervention; where opportunities exist to differentiate products; and where cost reduction may occur within the firm (Reinhardt, 1999). Strategic interaction is particularly relevant because many social and environmental innovations increase costs relative to competitors. Governmental regulation can significantly help firms with cost advantages in regulatory compliance to compete against rivals that do not enjoy such advantages (Shaffer, 1992).

An interesting example is the case of the corporate average fuel economy (CAFE) regulations. The CAFE standards were originally legislated in response to the 1973 OPEC oil embargo and raised fuel efficiency requirements for automobile fleets by setting a standard of 18 miles per gallon (mpg) for the 1978 model year. The rules provided a significant competitive advantage for many Japanese manufacturers, which had an average fuel economy of 33.7 mpg in 1976 compared to General Motors with an average of 16.0 mpg in 1976 and 19.0 in 1978. The Japanese were further along the learning curve in terms of increasing gas mileage for their cars. Shaffer (1992: 203) found that "producers of less fuel efficient cars opposed imposition of fines for CAFE violations and special taxes on 'gas guzzlers.'" In 1985, in light of a proposed rollback of the CAFE standards, Chrysler joined environmentalists in opposition due to its focus on smaller cars. Its fuel efficiency was generally better than that of General Motors and Ford. Chrysler argued that the rollback would be unfair because it had complied with the law.

Another example of corporate social strategy is the case of the business that decides to support the community by giving scholarships for training in technical programs. In this case, the firm's reputation in society improves, but in the long run, it will enjoy additional benefits such as the greater availability of a qualified labor pool with higher levels of productivity. These benefits are augmented when the type of training program provides the trainee with abilities and knowledge where their most valuable use is precisely inside the sponsoring firm. At first, as the business invests resources, the marginal returns of the resources will tend to be quite productive given the improvement in the firm's reputation with the community and the increase in qualified labor. An enhanced reputation may translate into the willingness of some consumers to pay a price premium, while a more qualified workforce may reduce labor costs and thus production costs.

For example, Danone's "Let's build their dreams" program in Mexico was a cause-related marketing program in which it made a charitable contribution of 5 cents per yoghurt sold to organizations involved in childhood cancer. Within three months in 1997, the company raised 5.9 million pesos, just shy of their goal of 6 million pesos. In 1998, they raised the contribution to 6 cents per yoghurt and raised 9.5 million pesos, above their goal of 7 million pesos. By 2001, the donation was 10 cents per yoghurt and Danone raised over 17 million pesos. Additionally, sales of yoghurt increased 20 percent in 1998 over 1997. In company-wide surveys of organizational morale, the Mexican subsidiary came out at the top in all surveys after 1995. In 1998, 1999, and 2000 market share always increased significantly during the campaign (Lozano, Moxon, and Maass, 2003).

Nevertheless, as the social investment reaches more people, the marginal improvement in reputation will decrease, and so will the benefit of increasing the availability of qualified labor, since the firm will have hired sufficient employees. In addition, for society as a whole, there will occur a point at which more new technicians may create a labor glut and thus no longer be beneficial for society (X_{sp}). At this point, the firm would also be unable to obtain additional benefits.

Certainly, it is not easy for firms to increase profits for stockholders at the same time that they comply with responsibilities to society and other stakeholders by measuring their social output. Nevertheless, the experience of many companies indicates that more and more firms are seeking ways to achieve both profitability and improved social performance (Tichy *et al.*, 1997; Porter and Kramer, 2006).

Corporate social projects may act as a catalyst for innovation (Kanter, 1999). For example, BankBoston, later a part of the Fleet Boston Financial Corporation and now the Bank of America, developed the First Community Bank (FCB) as a way to reach groups in low-income areas that had traditionally been marginalized by consumer banking. FCB successfully brought new clients into the banking system and grew to 47 branches with over US$1.5 billion in deposits. Not only did FCB contribute to regional economic development in these areas, but became a profitable institution within the Fleet Boston group. In addition, it provided a laboratory for the bank in the development of such innovations as multilingual ATMs, products for newcomers to banking, equity investments in the inner city, and community development officers (Kanter, 1999: 131–132). This example is especially interesting because it indicates that social investment by firms can serve as a driver for technological and managerial innovation (Marcus and Geffen, 1998; McDonough and Braungart, 1998; Hart and Milstein, 1999; Kanter, 1999) and for building new capabilities (Russo, 2001).

Graphically, we can see the following: Figure 3.3 shows that in the strategic case, there are additional benefits that the firm extracts from a given level of social output, not available to the coerced egoist or to the altruist, precisely because the firm has designed a strategy so as to appropriate such benefits. As in the altruistic case, benefits may occur through the differentiation of the product, which allows the firm to charge a price premium (Reinhardt, 1999; McWilliams and Siegel, 2001), or to increase sales, or to reduce costs. Costs may decrease, for example, because of the firm's ability to attract more highly qualified employees and thus increase the firm's productivity (Russo and Fouts, 1997; Kanter, 1999). Unlike the altruistic case where these consequences may occur as a happy coincidence, in the strategic case, these results occur by design.

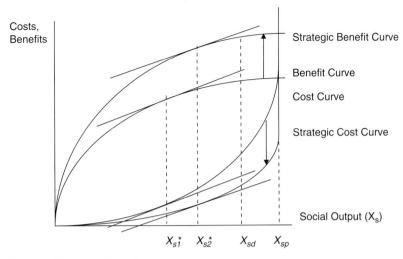

New condition for optimization:

$$MSB_{cs} = MSC_{cs}$$

$$\frac{\partial SB}{\partial X_s} = \frac{\partial SC}{\partial X_s}$$

Where:

MSB_{cs} is the strategic marginal benefit of one additional unit of social output; and

MSC_{cs} is the strategic marginal cost of one additional unit of social output.

Figure 3.3: Optimal social investment in the strategic case

A number of studies are beginning to show that there are specific benefits that accrue from corporate social activity, which may improve firm financial performance, either directly or indirectly (Cochran and Wood, 1984; McGuire *et al.*, 1988; Hosmer, 1994b; Burke and Logsdon, 1996; Russo and Fouts, 1997; Waddock and Graves, 1997). In addition, studies in the literature on instrumental stakeholder theory have also confirmed that a strategic approach to stakeholder management is necessary in order to generate benefits for the firm's financial performance (Jones, 1995; Berman *et al.*, 1999; Ogden and Watson, 1999; Hillman and Keim, 2001). Thus, as social output increases, the marginal benefit of the output will be reduced in both the aspect of the advantage gained from avoiding problems as well as the aspect of improved profitability.

In addition, the cost curve may also shift because of the firm's ability to innovate and reduce the cost of producing social output. Again, we expect the strategic cost curve to become vertical at X_{sp}, because at this point the firm reaches the maximum potential social output, which is the same for the altruistic, egoistic, and strategic cases.

The optimal amount of social output occurs when the slopes of the new strategic benefit curve and the strategic cost curve are equal. To the extent that the benefits of social investment increase (the strategic benefit curve moves up) and the costs of social investment decrease (the strategic cost curve moves down) due to a well-designed social strategy, the optimal amount of social output will increase. It is also clear that the same social investment of the firm produces a greater benefit for it in the strategic case than in the case of coercion. For this reason, given the possibility of suffering a loss of social acceptance and support – a very common situation in many commercial and industrial activities – it is better to design strategies of social investment from which the firm can obtain benefits beyond avoiding fines and lawsuits or developing a reputation for minimal compliance.

In addition, the strategic firm will always produce a greater social profit than the coerced firm. These results could be useful in verifying how the profits derived by the firm as a result of its social participation develop. Consequently, the firm can modify its strategy by comparing social projects to other projects within the firm or projects of other firms, the government, or civil society organizations and thus make a decision to redefine the social project, increase investment in it, or cancel it. In particular, the firm interested in a strategic social investment, rather than a coerced one, will seek, *ceteris paribus*, to undertake projects that shift the strategic cost curve down, for example, by reducing costs associated with producing a given level of social output. Additionally, the firm will seek to shift the strategic benefit curve up, possibly by increasing publicity of its social project. The regulatory authority, in its desire to increase the level of social welfare, could help firms implement this kind of project through appropriate fiscal policy, based on the argument that the strategic social project will enable the firm to produce more public goods as well as social profits. Such results would motivate a more permanent participation by private firms in the alleviation of social problems. In addition, the strategic case provides a justification for being proactive in planning even before starting a new business.

Now in the altruistic case, there may or may not occur shifts in the benefit and cost curves. Undoubtedly, such shifts are less likely for the altruistic firm because it has neither the intention nor the motivation to shift these curves. Unlike the strategic firm, the altruistic firm does not seek a maximum return on the dollar spent, but seeks to reach a level near or even equal to X_{sd}. Approaching X_{sd}, the firm will have achieved its goal, without reference to its particular social profits. Although the altruistic firm achieves greater social output, it does not intend to maximize profits from social projects. Nevertheless, there may exist circumstances in which the profit-maximizing level of social output coincides with the socially desirable level of output, which the altruistic firm seeks to produce. Since such a situation is not likely, the altruistic firm is less likely to maximize social profits compared to the strategically oriented firm, although it is not impossible.

Conclusion

Several lessons can be drawn from the theoretical sketch provided in this chapter. First, it appears that it is to the advantage of the firm to act in a strategic manner, rather than react to a coercive political and social environment. Second, it also appears that a strategic focus increases the social output of the firm compared to the case of the coerced egoist. Clearly, the strategic case is superior to the case of the coerced egoist in terms of benefits to both the firm and society, but what about the altruistic case?

Some business ethicists have argued in favor of corporate altruism in which the firm is managed for the benefit of stakeholder groups other than the traditional stockholders (Evan and Freeman, 1988; Bowie, 1991; Donaldson and Preston, 1995). We have seen that such an approach results in greater social output, although in lower social profits for the firm. We suggest, however, that the overall social output by the entire business community will be greater under the strategic case. Under this case, incentives will be aligned so that the firm will be motivated to improve its social performance and increase its social output. Substantial evidence exists that managers do in fact respond positively to such incentives and take an instrumental approach to social responsibility and stakeholder management (Fry *et al.*, 1982; Navarro, 1988; Agle *et al.*, 1999; Berman *et al.*, 1999; Ogden and Watson, 1999). As a result, we believe that many more firms will be motivated to produce public goods under the strategic case, than by appeals to corporate altruism. If that is indeed the case, although the average social output per firm may be less in the strategic case than in the altruistic case, the total social output of all firms in the aggregate is likely to be greater. Consequently, the focus on corporate altruism would probably result in a lower overall social output by the business community than a focus on social strategy. Given the potential benefits available to both the firm and society by taking a strategic approach to social action, this book focuses its attention on the conditions under which such programs will generate profits for the firm.

Now there are a number of caveats that should be made in interpreting these conclusions. First, the above analysis assumes that strategic decision-making results in the shifts of the benefit and cost curves as predicted. In reality, in a highly complex and uncertain world, these shifts may not always occur this way. Second, strategic and altruistic behavior may coincide at times. As noted in Chapter 2, it can be very difficult to sort out altruistic and strategic motivations. Third, this model assumes that the firm operates in a legal environment in which property rights are well defined and protected. In environments where this is not the case, it may be that the predicted shifts in the benefit and cost curves may not occur. Finally, altruistic decisions may also shift the benefit and cost curves in ways that exceed the shifts from strategic decision-making. Thus, this model must be taken as a way of understanding many important cases, but there may be exceptions that it does not cover.

An important implication is that much of the research into the relationship between corporate social performance (CSP) and financial performance may be misguided. Studies that have looked at this relationship have obtained mixed and inconclusive results (Griffin and Mahon, 1997; Waddock and Graves, 1997; McWilliams and Siegel, 2000; Margolis and Walsh, 2001). The different approaches that firms take to social investment suggest that CSP would drive financial performance only in the strategic case. In the case of the altruist or the coerced egoist, the relationship between CSP and financial performance could be positive, negative, or mixed – as confirmed by the current literature. Future research into the social-financial performance link needs to examine not only whether firms make social investments, but also whether and how these investments and projects are designed strategically to enhance profits. It is also necessary to develop methods that will allow us to measure adequately the costs, benefits, and levels of social output. Although the concepts and tools developed in the field of cost-benefit analysis could be useful in this sense, rarely have they been applied to the relatively small-scale projects contemplated in this book (Riddell and Robinson, 1995).

Some may argue that the approach taken in this chapter represents a step backward in our thinking about corporate social responsibility and stakeholder management. Instead of looking at social responsibility as a strategic opportunity for the firm, we must look at the firm's duties and obligations to society in general and stakeholders in particular (Donaldson and Preston, 1995). As we argued in Chapter 2, regardless of duties owed to stakeholders, firms still owe duties to stockholders. A commitment to fulfilling obligations to both can only be achieved in creative and innovative ways that do not sacrifice shareholder value. By helping firms to find ways to achieve these goals jointly, strategic management will make a major contribution to both business and society.

4 | *How do we build corporate social strategy?*

Introduction

The sagacious management of firm resources has been at the core of strategic management theory for half a century (Penrose, 1959). In fact, if strategic management scholars agree on anything, it is that firm success rests on how firms develop and acquire, organize and deploy resources in competitive market environments.

Accordingly, strategy rarely focuses directly on wealth creation or profit, but rather on the intermediate or proximate goal of competitive advantage. Profit, in this scheme, is the end result of having a competitive advantage and leveraging it (Porter, 1980, 1985). Create competitive advantage, get your products and services to the market, and the profits should come.

In our work on social strategy, our approach to creating competitive advantage focuses on resources as well. However, unlike many in strategy, we treat external and internal resources as equally vital to firm success. In the model developed in this chapter, we consider the external environment in terms of resource dependence (Pfeffer and Salancik, 1978), and the internal firm environment from the perspective of the resource-based view of the firm (Barney, 1991).

Though intuitively resource dependence and the resource based view (RBV) would seem to be an obvious pairing – external and internal resource matching – in management research this is rarely the case. The reason is a recurring theme in academics; the theories come from separate disciplines. Resource dependence comes from a sociology tradition, whereas RBV was developed by strategic management microeconomists (Popp *et al.*, 2006). Furthermore, resource dependence is a macro-level concept initially designed to describe how populations of firms deal with the external resource environment, whereas RBV focuses on the unique internal resources of individual firms that give rise to competitive advantage.

Disputing academic camps are not particular to strategy management. However, the conflict in the 1980s and 1990s between Michael Porter's industrial organization approach to strategy based on choosing the right markets, and RBV's emphasis on unique firm resources, ripped apart an integrated and more accurate concept of strategy that the field is still struggling to restore. In developing social strategy, we have chosen what we believe is a more open, inclusive, and balanced approach to strategy in which it is possible to explain why RBV is compatible both with resource dependence and industrial organization economics. Social strategy is, in this respect, a throwback to earlier strategy models that take into account the firm's internal environment (resources and values) and the organization's reliance upon and interaction with an external environment composed of both market and nonmarket factors.

This integrated approach to strategy, market or social, is also much more in line with how managers work. To begin with, no self-respecting CEO can afford to think of her or his firm either as just an actor in a competitive environment or as the owner of unique resources swimming in vast blue oceans. Rather, effective management treats with equal weight what the world is like out there (less or more stable, dynamic, munificent, etc.) and the firm's resources (better or worse or unique talent, products, finances, social capital, etc.). We should not forget, nonetheless, that the resources required by social strategy are broader than those needed for traditional market strategy. Whether acquired from the external environment or developed internally is circumstantial, though the addition of social strategy-based resources and capabilities often requires investing in relationships with non-market stakeholders absent in traditional market strategy formulation. As we have argued earlier, social strategy extends competitive strategy to include a broader range of inputs and, in turn, expands the possibilities of achieving new and unique strategic positions.

This, we trust, provides a fair explanation of our understanding of the raw materials of social strategy. With this in hand, we now turn to a more practice-oriented discussion of how firms may choose to develop and implement a social strategy.

Social strategy as business development

This chapter discusses the design of corporate social strategy via the logic of a business development plan for a new product or service.

The raw materials of corporate social strategy are social issues and stakeholder positions on those issues. From here, firms develop social action projects that acquire key resources from the environment and build on critical firm resources which, in combination, are difficult to imitate and lead to the creation of new products and services that provide additional value for current or new customers.

The following seven-step model of corporate social strategy provides a more structured explanation of the story we have just told.

Step 1: Analyze social issue opportunities, competitive environment, and nonmarket stakeholders (environmental analysis) including potential creation of competitive advantage.

Step 2: Analyze firm resources and capabilities to see whether the firm can take advantage of those opportunities.

Step 3: Evaluate firm identity (corporate culture, values, etc.) in terms of social needs and opportunities. Most firms initiate values projects first; we suggest that they first consider the social context.

Step 4: If the firm does not have the requisite resources and capabilities, determine the means and cost of acquiring them. Frequently, alliances and other forms of collaboration are necessary.

Step 5: Create a plan integrating issues, stakeholders, identity, resources, competitive environment and expected outcomes.

Step 6: Implement the plan.

Step 7: Measure and evaluate performance.

The rest of the chapter will be devoted to reviewing the seven steps. Most of our effort will be spent on Step 1. The issues central to Steps 2, 3, 4, and 7 each have a chapter devoted to them. In our discussion of Steps 5 and 6, we will limit ourselves to discussing only those aspects particular to social strategy.

Step 1

Step 1: analyze social issue opportunities, competitive environment, and nonmarket stakeholders (environmental analysis) including potential creation of competitive advantage.

Identify social opportunities

Too often firms engage in social issues that are tangential to the firm's business. It is no wonder that corporate initiatives based on these issues do not create value for the firm. Michael Porter and Mark Kramer (2006) have developed an approach for how firms can identify relevant issues central to the firm's business. The firm should first look "inside-out" by examining its own value chain (Porter, 1985). Each element of the value chain has significant social and environmental impacts. The primary activities of inbound logistics, operations, outbound logistics, marketing and sales, and after-sales service all provide clues as to the potential impacts of the firm on society. In addition, support activities of firm infrastructure, human resources, technology development, and procurement provide additional opportunities to affect the surrounding social and natural environment. Thus, Porter and Kramer (2006) recommend that within the universe of all possible social causes a firm might take up, the obvious candidates are those causes that relate to impacts of the firm's value chain.[1]

Firms should then examine those aspects of the firm's environment that impact the firm's activities. This is the so-called activity of "looking outside-in." Porter's (1990) diamond model provides one way of identifying these social impacts. The diamond model examines the context for firm strategy in terms of competitive rivalry, factor (input) conditions, local demand, and the strength of related and supporting industries. The diamond represents a subset of the firm's stakeholder map, but focuses on those elements of the stakeholder map that affect a firm's competitiveness (Hillman and Keim, 2001). Thus, as we will explain in greater detail in Chapter 5, social strategy acquires high levels of centrality when firms focus on those issues that either affect its value chain or are affected by some element of the firm's value chain. It is this subset of social issues that presents strategic opportunities for the firm.

Market environment

The market environment has been conceptualized in two very different ways. On the one hand, strategy has examined the impact of managerial perception on decision-making; given bounded rationality, it is inevitable that managers across firms have varying understandings

---

[1] Porter's value chain is not the only model available. Grant's (2009) *Contemporary Strategy Analysis* provides an excellent up-to-date review of the value chain with detailed segments on both cost analysis and differentiation.

of the market environment. Drawing from industrial economics, strategy scholars have also examined markets in terms of industry structure, often using game-theoretic techniques. In this chapter, we focus on perceptual analysis and its importance to social strategy. In Chapter 6, we will also take up game-theoretic models of industry structure.

The market environment affects the success of firm strategies (Dess and Beard, 1984; Sutcliffe and Huber, 1998) as well as the development of capabilities that permit successful implementation of those strategies. The market environment can be grouped around three fundamental constructs: dynamism, munificence, and complexity (Dess and Beard, 1984; Keats and Hitt, 1988; Amit and Schoemaker, 1993; Sutcliffe and Huber, 1998). These three dimensions, derived from the environmental analysis literature, are indicators of the relationship and dependence that competitors in an industry have upon suppliers and customers, and other primary stakeholders, and are key to managerial *perception* of opportunities for engaging in social strategy.

Why the emphasis on perception rather than factual data? There are two main reasons. One, the three constructs describe features of the environment that the firm does not control and for which timely data collection can be difficult – a textbook case of bounded rationality. Second, and perhaps more importantly, different managers will interpret the same data as more or less dynamic and so on. Managerial perceptions of the environment are similar to perceptions of risk; much depends on how individuals and collectives selectively respond to and, in effect, enact their environments (Weick, 1995).[2]

With this in mind, we describe the three constructs.

Dynamism. Dynamism measures the difficulty in forecasting external events that may affect the competitive environment (Aldrich, 1979). In dynamic market environments, the availability of resources

---

[2] Weick's landmark articles, "Toward a model of organizations as interpretation systems" (Weick and Daft, 1984) and "Collective mind in organizations: Heedful interrelating on flight decks" (Weick, 1993), provided theoretical and empirical support for studying collective decision-making with the same rigor and interest as individual decision-making. Like John Searle, Weick explained how action flowing from perceptual acts can be examined as part of objective reality. Allow us to recommend Weick's "The collapse of sensemaking in organizations: The Mann Gulch disaster" (Weick, 1993); the article is a beautifully told and moving story that explicates his key theoretical concepts.

upon which the firm depends is unpredictable. Complexity indicates the number and variety of environmental influences and their impact on the competitive environment (Duncan, 1972; Dess and Beard, 1984). Complex market environments are characterized by heterogeneous resources. Munificence refers to the relative abundance or scarcity of resources to support sustained growth in a given competitive environment (Staw and Szwajkowski, 1975; Dess and Beard, 1984).[3]

Increased dynamism in an industry leads managers to take more risks and implement innovation strategies in an attempt to overcome uncertainty and minimize the effects of environments they find hard to understand (Miller, 1987; Buchko, 1994). In this context, the incorporation of social change activities into the firm's business strategy enables the firm to break away from established industry practices and organizational routines. For example, social strategy may be a viable alternative where there are abundant nonmarket resources and the availability of market resources is unpredictable. In this way, such firms avoid the pitfall identified long ago by the American jurist, Oliver Wendall Holmes, with respect to the law when he wrote, "To rest on a formula is a slumber, which prolonged means death." In dynamic environments, firms that have not yet explored the possibilities of social strategies may find them to be a singularly adaptive mechanism when faced with unforeseen market changes.

The Body Shop is a classic example of the firm that took advantage of market dynamism. As a new market entrant, The Body Shop understood that a significant customer segment had rejected traditional beauty products. In an environment of new social trends and emerging lifestyles, The Body Shop pursued innovation through social strategy. Integrating social change initiatives of women's liberation, fair trade, and animal rights, Anita Roddick's firm configured a social strategy embracing market and nonmarket activities in the pursuit of inter-related, competitive advantages in stakeholder integration, perceived product safety, closeness to women customers, etc. Anita Roddick was nearly alone in perceiving dynamism in this way in the sector and in understanding how social strategy might be used to build competitive advantage.

---

[3] In Chapter 6, we will add hostility and controllability to the mix of variables. Together the constructs provide us with a basis for analyzing market opportunities for social strategies.

The Body Shop extended the concept of "natural" to encompass all firm activities within the value chain, including raw materials procurement via fair trade and eliminating animal testing of cosmetics. Within the dynamic environment in which increased opportunities for innovation occurred, secondary stakeholders were able to benefit, among them indigenous peoples' rights groups, animal rights activists and environmentalists. Thus, environmental dynamism, through the innovation that it fosters, increases the likelihood that social change activities will actually satisfy stakeholders and improve their perceptions of corporate social performance, while inducing customers to pay a price premium for social value-added.

During the period of its success in the 1980s and early 1990s, The Body Shop sought to eliminate the difference between its business strategy and its social strategy. As The Body Shop has since learned, the two strategies are not identical, however great the degree of integration. When competitors responded to The Body Shop's natural product line, the firm found both its social strategy advantage undermined and its cost structure untenable. The double shock led to Ms. Roddick's dismissal as CEO and the firm's sale to L'Oreal, an organization better prepared to manage, and integrate, a reformulated business strategy with The Body Shop's trademark social strategy. As The Body Shop case poignantly pointed out, even the most successful social strategy must be properly integrated with business strategy.

Complexity. Complexity impels managers to take into account a wider range of environmental factors and resources and therefore to pursue more complex strategies (Hart and Sharma, 2004). Among the factors are new competitors, new market segments, changing government regulations, eroding margins, globalization, and new technologies. Environmental complexity provides opportunities for firms to respond with social strategies that reconfigure relationships with stakeholders, converting nonmarket needs into new market-based products and services. One unexpected place where social strategies may be especially useful is following success in complex environments, when it is normal for rigidities to set in and restrict innovation (Howell and Avolio, 1992; Miller, 1993); social strategies can motivate management to incorporate within the planning processes the requisite variety needed to understand and respond more effectively to such environments.

For example, Leche Ram in Spain was faced with a fragmenting dairy market in which store brands, a powerful market leader, and strong regional players had boxed it into a shrinking, unprofitable segment. Through a joint project with UNICEF, "Ni un niño sin leche" ("No child without milk"), the firm relaunched the brand, returned to profitability, and became known as a CSR-focused firm. Soon it became a favorite of NGOs and embarked on a number of other social projects with the support of its employees (Martínez and Allen, 2000). In a complex environment, Leche Ram was able to forge a competitive advantage and create economic and social value.

Munificence. Perceived munificence has been related to the ability of a firm to diversify into new markets (Keats and Hitt, 1988). In industries where there is high munificence, there are general patterns of diversification and innovation (Miles and Snow, 1978). Ordinarily, we would expect that innovative social strategies would more likely be found in high munificence environments. Given a munificent environment, we would expect many firms in the industry to grow successfully.

However, there is a counter-situation, *hostility* (Miller and Friesen, 1983), in which aggressive competition and severe demand fluctuations provide an opportunity for firms that seek to differentiate themselves from their competitors in low munificence environments. It is here, we believe, that social strategy offers greater opportunities to create competitive advantage through the innovative conversion of nonmarket environmental factors into firm resources. For example, the Spanish package transportation company, MRW, was faced with a hostile environment in which UPS, Federal Express, and powerful local competitors were cutting prices as they offered increased services. Undersized and underfunded, MRW's founder and CEO, Francisco Martín Frías, decided on a social strategy that consisted of hiring handicapped workers to do routine tasks, for which MRW received government subsidies and earned plaudits for its social programs. MRW was able to convert an undervalued resource – handicapped citizens – into a firm resource, creating a competitive advantage in cost and reputation, in addition to achieving strong employee loyalty in an industry plagued with high turnover. Though the same aid is available to all firms that hire handicapped employees, MRW is the only firm in its industry that has hired significant numbers of the handicapped, invested in training, and adapted their installations and work schedules to turn what most believe is CSR into a competitive advantage.

MRW did not stop there. In the last ten years it has engaged in eighty-five social action projects, and maintains thirteen aid programs for soldiers, students, families, and other groups to send packages at a discount. Yearly since 1993, MRW has given 1 percent of gross sales to social action. MRW's marketing program consists almost exclusively of its social action programs for which it wins numerous awards and nearly constant press coverage.

For MRW, low munificence or resource scarcity created an opportunity for social strategy to create a competitive advantage. Through consistent innovation, it has nurtured this advantage and has come about as close as possible to creating a sustainable competitive advantage. In an industry driven by costs and price competition, MRW has achieved remarkable customer loyalty.

It is possible that in the future we will see more of this type of social strategy. Wayne Visser (2008) has argued that while philanthropic CSR will be hurt as a result of the Great Recession, an environment of low munificence, strategic CSR will expand.

With regard to social performance, i.e., the amount of social action engaged in by firms, the relationship to munificence is difficult to determine *a priori*. In the case of high munificence, we would expect firms to have additional resources to devote to social programs; however, we would not expect them to feel the necessity to innovate through social strategy. In the case of low munificence, only those firms that perceive that there is an opportunity to create competitive advantage through new and innovative social programs are likely to increase their social performance. In low munificence environments, firms frequently cut back on social programs. On balance, it is difficult to predict the impact of munificence on social performance.

Nonmarket environment

We conceive of the nonmarket environment as consisting of all those relationships between the firm and its stakeholders that are not mediated by prices. Freeman's (1984: 46) now classic definition of the stakeholder broadly includes all persons or groups that "can affect or [are] affected by the achievement of an organization's objectives." Although his definition is widely debated and numerous other definitions have been offered (Mitchell *et al.*, 1997), it is generally agreed that stakeholders, many of whom are nonmarket stakeholders, form the fabric of the social structure in which firms operate and determine to whom the firm must respond.

At the core of stakeholder theory is the need to manage "potential conflict stemming from divergent interests" (Frooman, 1999: 193). The interaction of stakeholders with divergent interests creates the issues, which provide the opportunities and threats with respect to which firms may then position themselves through their social change activities. Strategic choices must be made; not all stakeholders can receive the same attention from firms because attention is a limited resource that must be allocated efficiently (Simon, 1947). A firm's attention and response to a stakeholder will depend largely on that stakeholder's salience (Henriques and Sadorsky, 1999).

Salience, or the "degree to which managers give priority to competing stakeholder claims" (Mitchell *et al.*, 1997), is a function of the power and legitimacy of the stakeholders as well as of the urgency of the claims made by stakeholders upon the firm (Mitchell *et al.*, 1997). As is the case with suppliers and customers, the power of stakeholders is directly related to the firm's dependence on the stakeholder for valuable resources (Pfeffer and Salancik, 1978; Frooman, 1999), but with the additional factor of the structure of stakeholder networks that give stakeholders their legitimacy (Rowley, 1997). Empirical research has confirmed that a high correlation exists between power, legitimacy, and urgency on the one hand and stakeholder salience on the other (Agle *et al.*, 1999). Highly salient, "mixed-motive" stakeholders represent both a potential opportunity for cooperation and a potential threat to the firm (Savage *et al.*, 1991; Frooman, 1999).

By definition, the firm depends upon mixed-motive stakeholders for specific resources. Given their capacity and disposition to cooperate as well as to threaten the firm, these stakeholders play a fundamental role for social strategy. Scholars have observed that in the presence of mixed-motive stakeholders, firms tend to develop a collaborative strategy in which they work jointly with the stakeholder to develop integrative, mutually beneficial solutions (Freeman, 1984; Savage *et al.*, 1991; Frooman, 1999). A social strategy provides a mechanism to enable cooperation in ways that contribute to competitive advantage. Because of the complex and path-dependent nature of relationships with mixed-motive stakeholders, competitors will find it difficult to imitate this kind of relationship.

For example, Autopistas del Sol (AUSOL), an Argentine highway construction company, faced considerable opposition to a project for a northern access road to Buenos Aires, which would run through both wealthy and poverty-stricken neighborhoods (Austin *et al.*, 2004). As opposition gathered, AUSOL quickly launched a strategy to meet the concerns of these groups, transplanting trees in the wealthier neighborhoods and relocating a school and providing assistance to help legalize property claims in poorer neighborhoods – both actions taken despite contract provisions that made the government responsible to resolve these issues. The effectiveness of this strategy depended upon the close relationships developed with local activists and community leaders. By acting swiftly and fairly, AUSOL was able to turn the presence of mixed-motive, nonmarket stakeholders into a catalyst for the social strategy, enabling the firm to achieve its social and business objectives. Additionally, as in the MRW case, social approval increased employee commitment to the firm's mission and helped boost productivity. Social strategy is especially likely to create competitive advantage precisely when firms are able to help highly salient stakeholders with mixed motives meet their objectives.

Mixed-motive stakeholders represent a special and complex element of social strategy. Dependence on highly salient mixed-motive stakeholders is a powerful motivation for firms to respond to their needs and demands (Mitchell *et al.*, 1997). At the same time, mixed-motive stakeholders often have resources that can be used in collaboration with the firm to carry out social action programs (Husted, 2003). Thus, the likelihood that social strategy will achieve stakeholder satisfaction is greater when salient mixed-motive stakeholders are involved. Returning to the AUSOL example, its social strategy fulfilled the demands of local organizations and thus created high levels of satisfaction in the community, which provided it with the ability to continue with the construction project.

Step 2

Step 2: analyze firm resources and capabilities to see whether the firm can take advantage of those opportunities.

Once again, we turn to consider firm resources and capabilities. The RBV of the firm asserts that competitive advantage depends on firm resources, which, according to Barney include "all assets, capabilities, organization processes, firm attributes, information, knowledge, etc. controlled by a firm that enable the firm to conceive of and implement strategies that improve its efficiency and effectiveness," (Barney, 1991: 101). Resources encompass physical, human, and social capital. Social capital is of special interest. First, social strategy, as it often rests on relationships with mixed-motive stakeholders, frequently depends on building strong social networks. Second, when social capital can be converted into a competitive advantage it is likely to be enduring, due to its causally ambiguous nature, which makes it difficult to imitate (Dierckx and Cool, 1989). Third, social capital is also an integral component of knowledge management (Nahapiet and Ghoshal, 1998).

Clearly, there are many resources and capabilities that may have a positive impact (Russo and Fouts, 1997), but here we discuss only continuous innovation and stakeholder integration (Hart, 1995; Sharma and Vredenburg, 1998; Klassen and Whyback, 1999), both of which we believe have a significant relationship to social capital.

Continuous innovation. Social strategy often involves the introduction of needed products and services to underserved and poorly understood markets (Prahalad and Hammond, 2002) as well as the development of new products and services with social attributes (Kanter, 1999; McWilliams and Siegel, 2001). The ability to generate solutions for such underserved markets or the development of social products and services depends largely on the firm's capability for continuous innovation (Hart, 1995; Sharma and Vredenburg, 1998). Such a capability may already exist on the business side of a firm, but must be redeployed in order to facilitate the development of social strategies that create appropriable benefits for the firm as well as benefits for the community. Such innovation can be incremental or even disruptive to the extent that it breaks with current development trajectories and ways of thinking about social problems (Christensen *et al.*, 2006).

For example, Cemex, the largest cement manufacturer in Mexico, decided to target the problem of housing among low-income Mexican families where the quality of construction tends to be substandard. The *Patrimonio Hoy* project involved helping low-income families save in order to take a more rational approach to self-construction projects as well as provide access to specialized technical assistance. The only way in which the project would be successful from both a business

and social point of view was the development of culturally appropriate
mechanisms to motivate reliable participation. In order to develop those
mechanisms, Cemex sent two anthropologists to study self-construction
practices among the poor. They identified the *tanda* – a type of savings
program used among neighbors in Mexico – as a culturally consonant way to develop self enforcing agreements to foster savings. The
successful use of the *tanda* mechanism permitted Cemex to provide
construction materials and technical assistance in a way that benefited
both the company and its communities. The firm benefited from sales
in an underserved market and the community benefited from better
quality housing. Without Cemex's capability for continuous innovation, *Patrimonio Hoy* would probably have remained another well-
intentioned project to help the poor. Instead, Cemex was able to extract
economic value and achieve its social objectives at the same time.

Stakeholder integration. We have discussed already the vital role of
mixed-motive stakeholders. Recognition of their importance must, of
course, be accompanied by gaining their participation through stakeholder integration. Sharma and Vredenburg (1998: 735) define stakeholder integration as "the ability to establish trust-based collaborative
relationships with a wide variety of stakeholders – especially those
with non-economic goals." Jones (1995) recognized that firm-stake-
holder relationships based on mutual trust enable the firm to create a
competitive advantage.

In addition to high-level relationship, social-capital advantage,
there are also practical advantages to working closely with stakeholders. For example, incorporating stakeholders into product-design
teams drives innovation (Harrison and St. John, 1996) and collective
learning, which benefits both the firm and its stakeholders (Heugens
et al., 2002).

In classic RBV terms, stakeholder integration contributes to competitive advantage because the required skills are valuable, non-
substitutable, and rare (Barney, 1991). Moreover, they are complex,
causally ambiguous and therefore difficult to imitate (Teece, 1987;
Winter, 1987). Finally, stakeholder integration is a dynamic capability, which can be redeployed to solve other social problems as well as
business challenges (Grant, 1996; Teece *et al.*, 1997; Eisenhardt and
Martin, 2000).

Dynamic capabilities are particularly valuable, increasing the likelihood that social strategy will generate new resources that, in turn,

lead to competitive advantage. Dynamic capabilities can arise from apparently quite simple social action programs, provided that they integrate nonmarket stakeholders into firm activities. For example, the Chilean drugstore chain, Farmacias Ahumada, SA (FASA) engaged in a program of strategic philanthropy with an NGO dedicated to caring for impoverished senior citizens. FASA cashiers were trained to ask for a small donation to the NGO at the checkout counter. This practice strengthened the firm's business because they found that their employees became better sales people as they developed their fundraising skills (Austin *et al.*, 2004).

Often, the social capital and social networks of the firm (or members of the firm) are vital to forging alliances and with nonmarket stakeholders with specialized skills and social networks. Such stakeholder integration also permits collective learning and dialogue that can improve the ability of social projects to achieve their objectives and thus improve stakeholder satisfaction. For example, the Brazilian healthcare and cosmetic products company, Natura, had a longstanding collaboration with the Matilde María Cremm School, located in a marginalized neighborhood on the outskirts of Sao Paulo. The school was concerned about the low quality of education it provided. Natura's management believed that its relationship with the school was paternalistic and decided to reshape the relation by entering into an iterative cycle of dialogue with the school's leadership and other community groups. Eventually, Natura and the school transformed their relationship into a more balanced and productive collaboration that helped Matilde María Cremm became one of the top five in the state (Austin *et al.* 2004). Stakeholder integration made this success possible. Natura expects to benefit from its developing capability for stakeholder integration in future business and social action programs.

Step 3

Step 3: evaluate firm culture, corporate values, identity, and ideology, etc. in terms of social needs and opportunities. Most firms initiate values projects first; we suggest that they first consider the social context.

Corporate culture is a complex subject that has proven difficult for management researchers to get a handle on. No one doubts its importance, but it's hard to know where to start. Do values drive behavior, or is it ideology? Do firms have an identity, or are there multiple identities? How do corporate identities take shape, change? To what extent can a specific type of corporate culture be a competitive advantage or handicap?

Many of us would, if we could, avoid the complex and troubling issues of corporate culture. However, when a firm decides to engage in social strategy its success or failure inevitably depends on firm characteristics and behavior that we recognize as corporate culture.

In Chapter 7, we will deal with a broad range of corporate culture variables. In this section, we focus on one key firm resource – corporate values – which has been on the agendas of large firms around the world.

Interest in corporate values is not new. Andrews (1971) originally included corporate values as one of the fundamental pillars of corporate strategy, alongside the market environment and firm strengths and weaknesses. This focus on values was then lost in Porter's (1980, 1985) work with its emphasis on industry structure, which came to dominate the field of strategic management in the 1980s. However, Barney (1986b) argued that corporate culture is a firm resource and can be a source of competitive advantage. As components of firm culture, values and business philosophy are potential resources of the firm and are essential to its identity (Albert and Whetten, 1985) and in the decision of the firm to include non-economic objectives within its mission and purpose.

All managerial decisions include a values component (Simon 1947). According to Kluckhohn *et al.* (1952: 395): "A value is a conception, explicit or implicit, distinctive of an individual or characteristic of a group, of the desirable which influences the selection from available modes, means, and ends of action." The shared values, both explicit and implicit, of a sociocultural system constitute an important part of its culture. Explicit values are captured, in large part, by the concept of ideology, which is a key element in all sociocultural systems (Geertz, 1973; Pettigrew, 1979). Implicit values are associated with universal beliefs that are customarily expressed through more explicit values. Together, these beliefs and values, explicit and implicit, form the bedrock of a company's identity – how the members of the company see the organization.

Corporate identity affects strategy by helping to channel available firm responses to opportunities and threats. This identity affects managerial decisions based on their understanding of the firm's goals and objectives, and beliefs and values about how the world works (Prahalad and Bettis, 1986; Simons and Ingram, 1997) and thus, properly understood and managed, identity, too, can be a source of competitive advantage for the firm.

Similarly, corporate values may coalesce into a strong ideological support for or rejection of social action. Undoubtedly some value systems and ideologies are more likely to produce a commitment to social action than others. Research into corporate ideology systems has provided evidence that there are at least three relevant dimensions: progressive or participative decision-making, social responsibility, and organicity (Goll and Zeitz, 1991; Goll and Sambharya, 1995). Participative decision-making emphasizes a proactive search for opportunities, based on the use of analytic decision tools, open communication channels, and participative consensus-based decision-making. Social responsibility refers to a company's commitment to participating in the solution of social problems. Finally, organicity deals with the firm's ability to adjust to new circumstances (Goll and Sambharya, 1995). This framework is certainly not exhaustive, but provides a useful place to begin to examine the relationship between specific values and their impact on social strategy and corporate social performance. Given the conceptual similarity between the resource for continuous innovation and the organicity dimension of ideology, we will forego a discussion of the organicity dimension and focus on the other two dimensions.

Social responsibility orientation. Social responsibility orientation (SRO) clearly channels the kinds of responses that managers make to social threats and opportunities. Research indicates that managerial values act as a frame for recognizing and evaluating the importance of social issues (Kahneman and Tversky, 1984; Sharfman *et al.*, 2000) and the salience of stakeholders (Agle *et al.*, 1999). These managerial interpretations of social and environmental issues directly affect the selection of social strategies (Sharma *et al.*, 1999; Bansal and Roth, 2000; Sharma, 2000). The ability of a social strategy to create these benefits depends, in part, upon the genuine commitment of top managers to social responsibility. Jones (1995) argues that firms must demonstrate a sincere concern for ethics and socially responsible behavior in order to obtain competitive benefits from its stakeholder strategies. Socially minded consumers, for example, are unlikely to pay a price premium for social products unless they believe the firm has a sincere commitment to its social responsibilities (Menon and Menon, 1997; Maignan, *et al.*, 1999). A strong commitment to social responsibility is evidenced in the firm's application of significant resources to innovative, new social change activities. It is to be expected that this innovation will lead to the development of new resources that are valuable, rare, and non-substitutable (Barney, 1986b; Barney, 1991; O'Reilly and Pfeffer, 2000). However, given the explicit nature of an SRO, it is a resource that is imitable and therefore may only provide a competitive advantage in the short run. Nonetheless, firms such as MRW, which combine SRO with continuous innovation, can develop such a strong program and reputation that its competitors will believe the strategic position is unassailable.

Perhaps the greatest risk of social strategy is that it is seen as insincere. Mixed-motive stakeholders may be quite vocal when the firm's social strategy appears to be characterized by pure self-interest, rather than a social responsibility orientation. For example, after Nike was criticized for the labor practices of its overseas suppliers, the company hired Andrew Young to monitor and report on its CSR activities. Nevertheless, the firm's past history and the perceived lack of conviction by its CEO harmed its attempts to improve its social performance and led to consistent distrust and disapproval (McCawley, 2000; Dunne and Dolan, 2004). Long after Nike had resolved the sweatshop labor issues, activists and other stakeholders continued to point to Nike as the classic example of social irresponsibility. Only after almost ten years did Nike's reputation return to levels it enjoyed prior to the crisis.

Participative decision-making. A participative decision-making (PDM) orientation is especially relevant to social strategy because this orientation includes a commitment to involving employees in decision-making. It shares many of the characteristics of what Miles and Creed (1995: 361) call a "human investment philosophy," because of its focus on the development of the self-governance capability by employees in order to create a learning organization. PDM appears to be positively correlated with financial performance (Goll and Sambharya, 1995). This orientation increases the likelihood that managers will select decision-making processes and practices that foster employee participation.

Theorists argue that the involvement of employees is the key to effective environmental strategy because it fosters process innovation (Sharma and Vredenburg, 1998). Similar to the SRO, participative decision-making is related to competitive advantage because it is valuable, rare, and non-substitutable. For example, from its inception in 1850, the Levi-Strauss family promoted social values associated with caring for employees. Without progressive human resource practices, such as employee participation in decision-making, these values would rightfully be considered paternalistic. Moreover, maintaining employee benefits when a firm is growing and creating wealth is relatively easy. As we have once again been reminded during the severe recession, the first people to be hurt by declining profits are employees. Levi-Strauss faced its first serious economic difficulties in more than half a century in the 1980s when foreign imports and changing fashions resulted in severely reduced revenues and losses. They had to cut one-third of the workforce. Robert Haas, CEO, insisted that the firm ground the process in the company's core values; employees steered the process themselves, deciding on the criteria for who would be let go; outplacement and support programs were set up to aid those who lost their jobs (Howard, 1990). While many other clothing manufacturers failed in this period, Levi-Strauss managed to survive and later prosper once again (Mares-Dixon *et al.*, 1999). Employee participation provided the company with the ability to make difficult decisions that were vital for the company's economic wellbeing and to ameliorate the negative impact on employees.

Admittedly, Levi-Strauss is an unusual case; in most cases, corporate values are off-the-shelf products that those at the top have convinced themselves the rest of the firm believes in. Of course, this is precisely why a firm's values and human resource practices consistent with those values can be a firm resource and a competitive advantage.

Step 4

Step 4: if the firm does not have the requisite resources and capabilities, determine the means and cost of acquiring them. Frequently, alliances and other forms of collaboration are necessary.

One of the main arguments of this book is that social activities can be managed for competitive advantage and value creation just as we customarily do with value chain activities. Accordingly, the acquisition of needed resources and capabilities for social action programs can and should be managed within the framework of the traditional make-or-buy decision. This decision, to incorporate activities within the firm's value chain or buy from a supplier, is at the heart of corporate strategy. Recently, a third alternative, alliances, has become an increasingly important option. Within social strategy, firms then have the option either to outsource social action through charitable contributions, to internalize social projects by undertaking them in-house, or to collaborate with NGOs and other allies. In Chapter 10, we discuss the conditions under which these options are likely to occur so as to produce the greatest benefit and we offer examples of how firms have taken these decisions as well our survey research on how firms make these decisions.

By way of introduction, a brief look at two firms that we have already discussed. In deciding to go ahead with an alliance rather than develop a social action program on its own, Leche Ram accurately assessed the necessity of having a partner, like UNICEF, which could establish who should receive milk and provide the legitimization for such a program. In the 1980s, Anita Roddick at The Body Shop established alliances first with Greenpeace and then with Friends of the Earth that failed. Roddick had a clear idea of how she wanted to integrate environmental issues into the firm's activities and found neither partner willing to accede to her approach. The Body Shop set up and staffed its own environmental affairs department, took stands on issues, and designed and implemented a strategy on its own. We should add, here, that most large firms engage in traditional philanthropy, in effect outsourcing their social action programs.

Steps 5 and 6

Step 5: create a plan integrating issues, stakeholders, identity, resources, competitive environment and expected outcomes; and step 6: implement the plan.

We will be brief. We have combined steps 5 and 6 because the strategic planning process, formulation, and implementation for social strategy is largely identical to strategic planning for any other type of strategy, though the content may be different. We have introduced the key elements of social strategy in the previous sections, nearly all of which we return to in a later chapter. The only item pending for this section is a brief discussion of the one key difference that separates social strategy planning from traditional market strategic planning.

As the objectives include both business and social value creation, top management will need to have a good understanding of both. This involves knowledge, values orientation, and experience with social strategy. In relating the story of The Body Shop, we saw a CEO who had sufficient knowledge of environmental issues and experience in managing alliances with NGOs to chart out the firm's environmental action program and its implementation. Levi-Strauss's Robert Haas did much more than lead the downsizing of the firm in a manner consistent with the firm's traditional values. Working with company employees, most of them from underprivileged backgrounds with limited education, he developed the "Aspirations Statement." Unlike most corporate values statements that merely set out general principles, Levi-Strauss's "Aspirations Statement" was applied in defining occupational roles and responsibilities, performance evaluations, employee training, and in deciding key business decisions with employee participation. Haas' knowledge of the impact of corporate values on Levi-Strauss required years of experience as he learned about the industry, the firm, and the people in it.

The social capital required to talk convincingly about values does not come easily. This we have seen at firms like Enron that prattled on about their outstanding values and people, but in practice fomented unethical and illegal practices from the top down (Gladwell, 2002). The recent severe recession is, in large part, a consequence of the failure of firms that had "committed" CEOs, but no real commitment to anything other than growing revenues, profit, and compensation.

Social strategy, we believe, requires a much more solid, long-term investment in values, including participative management practices. A strategic plan for social strategy is not for a year or even two, but must be undertaken with the idea in mind that values that drive the strategy are enduring, though the specific social action programs may change. As we have insisted from the outset, one of the distinguishing characteristics of social strategy is that once a commitment is made, the firm will be expected by stakeholders to honor it.

Step 7

Step 7: measure and evaluate performance.

One key difference between business strategy and social strategy is the differing ways in which they measure performance and order activities. Business strategists first look at measures of financial performance (ROI and ROE) before considering secondary benefits of activities (trust, reputation, commitment, values, identity). Proponents of social action often cite as the key benefits what business strategists may consider secondary (trust, reputation, commitment, values, identity), while arguing that these lead to improved financial and social performance. In effect, social strategy interposes intangible performance measures between strategic behavior and financial performance and social performance.

We argue that neither approach fully captures how social strategies ought to measure and evaluate performance. Direct measures of both business performance and social performance (or impact) are required. One is not of a higher order than the other. Measures of intangible benefits for the firm are important, but this is entirely different from monitoring the economic effectiveness of social action projects where the beneficiaries are external stakeholders. Measurement of social action is relatively new and not widely extended. There are, nonetheless, a number of methods for measuring the economic value of social action, such as conjoint analysis and hedonic pricing techniques. In addition, real option methods of evaluation are especially relevant to the valuation of social projects. Yet, the evaluation of social impacts is often neglected. Firms without a strategic focus have generally been uninterested in the actual effectiveness of their efforts, being content to be engaged in good social causes. A strategic focus requires the careful evaluation of the costs and effectiveness of social projects. Cost-benefit analysis can be applied to the small-scale social projects of the firm. Firms can apply and adapt techniques used in risk management, project management, and marketing analysis.

While it may be argued that as long as economic performance is satisfactory there is no need to measure social performance, we would insist that over time, if social action projects do not provide significant social benefits this will become clear to stakeholders and the firm will lose their support, damaging the social strategy and the firm's reputation and profitability.

In Chapter 12, we provide an extensive review of evaluation and measurement of social action projects.

Conclusion

Our purpose has been to provide an overview of the seven-step model to help companies build social strategies that will have a positive impact upon both financial and social performance. We have drawn upon the literatures of strategic management, stakeholder management, corporate social responsibility, and environmental management to create a model of social strategy formulation. Certainly it is not the only approach, but it represents one avenue that social strategy research ought to explore if it is to make a greater contribution to the theory of the firm and the practice of management. Nor is the model exhaustive. It can be extended by incorporating additional aspects of industry structure, stakeholder relationships, firm resources, and corporate identity.

The chapter serves, as well, to introduce many of the issues and concepts that we will look at in great depth in coming chapters.

5 | Elements of successful corporate social strategy

Corporate social projects vary greatly in terms of their scale and scope. The economic impacts of these initiatives also differ significantly. In this chapter, we ask: what is the relationship between the nature of these projects and their economic impact? In 1996, management scholars Lee Burke and Jeanne Logsdon wrote a seminal article, "How corporate social responsibility pays off," that made a significant contribution to our understanding of how companies derive economic benefits from social projects. They developed a model that details in five dimensions how social action projects can create both social value and economic value: centrality, appropriability, proactivity, voluntarism, and visibility.

Burke and Logsdon's model was based on their understanding of the US business context. Our research, conducted in Spain and Mexico, has found empirical support for four of these five dimensions (Husted and Allen, 2007a; 2007b; 2009). The strongest support was found for visibility and voluntarism. Some support has been found for centrality and appropriability, while no support has yet been found for proactivity in either Spain or Mexico. In this chapter, we will define and examine each of the five dimensions and their relationship to value creation from a global perspective. Let's begin by looking more carefully at the meaning of value creation.

Value creation

Value refers to the worth of something for someone. Value can be divided into two types: use value and exchange value (Lepak *et al.*, 2007). Use value is a "specific quality of a new job, task, product, or service as perceived by users in relation to their needs, such as the speed or quality of performance of a new task or the aesthetics or performance features of a new product or service" (Lepak *et al.*, 2007: 181). This approach navigates a middle way between the Marxian notion of use value as lying in the product itself and the neoclassical idea of utility, which is concerned with the satisfaction or pleasure that consumers experience upon using a certain product or service. This definition is broad enough to incorporate value derived from the social and environmental attributes of goods and services.

Exchange value is the amount that buyers pay the creator of value to use a product or service. Value is created when a target user experiences satisfaction of a need and is prepared to offer an amount of money in exchange for the value received. The amount exchanged "is a function of the perceived performance difference between the new value that is created (from the new focal task, product, or service) and the target user's closest alternative (current task, product, or service)" (Lepak *et al.*, 2007: 182).

The evaluation of use and exchange value depends upon the users' perception of the novelty and appropriateness of a product or service. According to Amabile (1977, 1997), novel products are those which provide new and original solutions to problems or opportunities. However, "original" does not mean peculiar or outlandish. Solutions need to be appropriate, that is they are relevant or meaningful to the problem at hand and the context in which the problem or opportunity occurs.

Sometimes there is a significant difference between use value and exchange value. This difference is called "value slippage." Value slippage occurs when value is created, but is partly captured by other interested parties. Value can be lost to competitors who imitate the original task, product, or service and offer similar versions on the market thus driving price down. This process of imitation can be limited by isolating mechanisms that create barriers to imitation, such as intellectual property rights, etc.

Value itself is created in multiple ways. New tasks, products, or service can be introduced. New markets can be developed. Value can be created by undertaking tasks, inventing new products, or providing services in less costly ways. In some cases, customers will pay a price premium for this novel and appropriate task, product, or service. In other cases, customers will purchase greater quantities at the same price. Economists, beginning with Joseph Schumpeter, have long associated value creation with new combinations of resources (Gobeli *et al.*, 2002). Strategists have described the process in terms of competitive advantage through differentiation or cost or some combination of the two.

Corporate social projects can also create value – both use value and exchange value. This value is usually created through innovation, whether product innovation or process innovation. Product innovation refers to the incorporation of socially or environmentally desirable attributes into a task, product, or service. For example, the Toyota Prius is a classic case of product innovation involving the development of new technologies that lead to cleaner and more fuel-efficient combustion. Nescafé Partners' Blend, a Fairtrade-certified coffee, is an example of process innovation. This brand is produced in ways that are environmentally sustainable (no pesticides) and in which farmers and farm workers are paid what has been agreed to be a fair wage for their labor. In addition to the usual cup of instant coffee, the consumer trusts that the product neither damages the environment nor harms workers. A segment of consumers will perceive novel and appropriate value not available in alternatives. In both cases, value has been created through the recombination of resources. The challenge we face is to understand why certain social projects are more likely to create value than others. Let us analyze this question from the framework of the five dimensions proposed by Burke and Logsdon.

Centrality

Centrality refers to the extent to which a specific social project is aligned with the firm's core business mission. As we set out in Chapter 4, Porter and Kramer's (2006) identification of strategic social issues in terms of a firm's value chain impacts and the environmental diamond analysis essentially deals with centrality. After the Indian Ocean tsunami disaster of December 2004, Federal Express used its logistics expertise to help move huge quantities of in-kind donations to the affected areas. This type of aid is highly central to Federal Express' core business capabilities. Federal Express is also a sponsor of the March of Dimes, a non-profit organization dedicated to reducing birth defects. This second initiative is much less central to the business mission of Federal Express. Though the March of Dimes is a worthy cause, Federal Express has no special healthcare expertise to contribute.

We argue that greater value is created by social projects that are related to the core business mission of the firm. Value is first perceived by a segment of customers. The magnitude of this perceived value depends on the novelty and appropriateness of the new product or service. In this case, we are referring to the social attribute of a given product or service. The social attribute may be tied to a product the firm sells, as in the Nescafé example, or part of a social action program the firm participates in, as with FedEx's post-tsunami logistics support. The Nescafé example weds social value creation directly to economic value creation, while FedEx's logistics contribution to aid relief demonstrates its capabilities. By mobilizing its resources to assist victims, it earned kudos in the eyes of stakeholders, in particular customers, who found novelty and appropriateness in the deployment of FedEx's assets to assist the victims. Such social action may even assist the firm in developing new capabilities, while enhancing reputation and pointing the way to future innovation and value creation.

When social projects are directly related to the firm's business mission and capabilities, the benefit to all parties is clear. The firm can more easily deploy and recombine its resources and capabilities in new ways that are relevant to resolving social issues.

In contrast, the links between FedEx and the reduction of birth defects are quite tenuous and thus unlikely to shape perceptions of performance quality by FedEx customers. FedEx has no special health industry capabilities to offer to March of Dimes and thus no reason for current or potential FedEx customers to believe that the company has anything new for them. They can appreciate that FedEx supports a worthy cause, but it is likely that their competitors do as well.

Centrality is related to novelty given that it is able to recombine resources in new ways. In the case of the tsunami, FedEx recombined resources of human capital, technological prowess, and political acumen in ways that helped victims receive needed supplies under very adverse circumstances. Donations to the March of Dimes involve relatively limited resources – largely financial capital – that is not combined with other resources in new ways, but are transferred in fairly conventional ways as charitable contributions. In addition, centrality enhances the sense of appropriateness of the social initiative by the target community. FedEx's engagement with the delivery of supplies to tsunami victims will be perceived as fitting its mission in logistics management. There is an alignment between the firm's business

Table 5.1: *Recent studies of the Burke and Logsdon dimensions and their impact on value creation*

Dimension	Burke and Logsdon (1996)	Study 1: Spanish firms Husted and Allen (2007a)	Study 2: MNCs in Mexico Husted and Allen (2009)
Centrality	+	Not significant	+
Appropriability	+	+	Not significant
Proactivity	+	Not significant	Not significant
Voluntarism	+	–	–
Visibility	+	+	+

mission and its tsunami response that is absent from support for the March of Dimes.

By engaging in social projects that are highly central to their mission, firms are more able to create value from these initiatives. The Pfizer Global Health Fellows Program (Vian *et al.*, 2007) was created in 2002 to pair Pfizer employee volunteers with local health personnel in developing countries in order to develop healthcare industry skills among the Pfizer volunteers or fellows. The fellows are given assignments of between three to six months in the field. Typically fellows are involved in improving purchasing, marketing, and drug management systems. Some write grant applications. Clearly the project is central to both the skills and capabilities of Pfizer as a pharmaceutical company as well as of its employees. In turn, employees developed valuable skills in leadership, awareness of conditions in third-world countries, self-confidence, flexibility, communications, project management, contacts, and problem solving (Vian *et al.*, 2007).

In our research, we found that managers of multinationals in Mexico related higher levels of centrality of social projects to greater value creation. However, managers of large Spanish firms did not make this link (see Table 5.1).

At this point, our understanding of why we found confirmation in Mexico and not in Spain for centrality is preliminary and must be somewhat speculative. Nonetheless, we believe it worthwhile to share our initial hypotheses. We believe part of the explanation for the negative result in Spain may lie in the distinction between explicit

CSR and implicit CSR made by Matten and Moon (2008). They argue that in Europe, many social institutions take care of the issues included within CSR in the United States. Social institutions, such as public healthcare systems, form the background in which firms make decisions about the kinds of social issues they will engage in as part of their social action portfolio. The CSR movement has been much more vigorous in the United States, given the lack of support institutions to protect workers when compared to Europe. Spanish firms may be less concerned about their value chain impacts or competitive context than US firms and thus may engage in social issues that are less central to their business mission.

The confirmatory case of Mexico is more complex. Although in theory, the Mexican system is closer to the Spanish than the American approach, in practice, Mexico's social safety and regulatory system is often unreliable, as the government lacks resources and skills for a broad range of tasks. Given these two factors – demand for social services and a shortfall of government resources and capabilities – companies are likely to find that there are numerous direct links between their value chain impacts, the economic and social environment, and the firm's ability to create economic value. Stakeholders, including employees and customers, are likely to look to large firms, especially multinationals, to use their specialized skills and resources in social action programs. Firms that do so may be rewarded with committed employees and loyal customers. Management in Mexico apparently realizes this. In our work with Mexican firms and executives over the last two decades, managers have consistently expressed their concern that their firms' success translates into significant improvements in quality of life and the environment for the less privileged.

Appropriability[1]

Appropriability refers to the ability of a social initiative to extract or capture value. As indicated previously, use value can be created but then lost through value slippage. Imitation by competitors can quickly lead to slippage. Indeed this danger may be even greater in the arena of social actions. Although isolating mechanisms such as patents can

[1] We have substituted "appropriability," the term used in microeconomics and strategy, for capturing value for Burke and Logsdon's "specificity."

prevent such slippage to some extent, the value generated by social projects is designed to be shared by the firm and its stakeholders. In fact, a key dimension of a catalytic social initiative is its scale and replicability (Christensen *et al.*, 2006). A social project is meant to be copied and spread on a large scale – not to be inimitable!

Isolating mechanisms can be based on knowledge as well as physical and legal barriers. Legal barriers such as patents and copyrights are somewhat difficult to invoke in the case of the development of social product attributes. For example, an environmental certification is intended to be adopted by different companies. Legal barriers cannot be created against certification, which is replicable on purpose. Certifications, however, can provide consumers with confidence that firms are observing responsible business processes. Fairtrade and the Forest Stewardship Council are among the many kinds of certification available to firms in order to provide consumers with assurance that companies are in fact doing what they say they are doing. It provides a signal to consumers in order to overcome problems of adverse selection, which often plague efforts to engage in socially responsible behavior given the inability of consumers to verify such socially or environmentally responsible behavior. In addition some certifications can protect their "brand" by sanctioning *ex post* opportunism (non-compliance) – a kind of moral hazard problem after the certification has been granted (Potoski and Prakash, 2005). By making certification subject to periodic auditing with the application of sanctions in the case of non-compliance (e.g., removal of certification or financial penalties), the certification can protect its brand.

Knowledge creation is an isolating mechanism that can help firms capture value from their social projects. Although specific initiatives may be imitated, the knowledge created by developing and implementing a project can generate resources and capabilities for the firm that are not easily copied by competitors. Moreover, as we explained in the MRW case, the capability for innovating in social action projects, just as in any other firm activity, may be superior in one firm, as may be the firm's CSR reputation.

Often the resources and capabilities developed in a social action project can be redeployed to the business areas of the firm and can be difficult to replicate. For example, Reuters lent some employees to assist in a charitable house-building project in India. One of the by-products was the development of teamwork, which assisted the firm in its core business activities (Baxter, 2007). In the process of building houses, employees are obliged to work together in new ways. So the initiative not only accomplishes a social objective, it also generates capabilities that are neither easily developed nor imitated. Certainly other firms can develop teamwork skills, but teamwork depends upon the specific members of the team and each one needs to acquire these skills. Julia Fuller, the corporate responsibility manager at Reuters, explains the value of the project this way: "It challenges you more than a one-day course, as it takes you out of your comfort zone. And it is a great way of getting people to talk, listen, and understand," (Baxter, 2007: 12).

Location can amount to a significant isolating mechanism. Opportunities are often only discovered on the basis of intimate, local knowledge of a situation (Hayek, 1945). For example, Eastman Kodak is based in Rochester, New York. Most of its community outreach is directed to the cities and towns where it has operations. In Rochester, its "Images in the Curriculum – A Kodak Partnership with the Rochester City School District" provides digital cameras and printer docks to local schools, and trains administrators and teachers, who then teach students to use the equipment. By focusing social projects on the communities where it is located, the company generates social and moral capital, which is available later when the company may need it, as if it were a kind of insurance (Godfrey, 2005). When social and environmental issues are local, they are more likely to capture the attention and interest of employees and local stakeholders, and thus are able to capture greater advantages (Andersson and Bateman, 2000).

Some types of product and process innovation can be protected through legal means, such as patents. GE's Ecomagination program has led to the development of numerous green products, which have been protected from imitation through patents. These patents permit the company to help others by licensing technology. GE is licensing patents for its wind turbine control technologies to suppliers in order to enable them to become more environmentally friendly. Through the patent, GE protects its technology and is able to capture benefits as it licenses the technology to other firms (Aaer News, 2007). Although these examples are oriented towards environmental problems, GE's new Healthymagination initiative will also develop more socially oriented products, which can and will be protected by patents. Thus through knowledge, geographic, and legal barriers, firms can reduce the amount of value slippage and capture more of the value that they create through social and environmental initiatives.

Complementary products and services can also help the firm extract benefits from a social "loss leader." For example, instead of securitizing sub-prime mortgages, low-interest rate loans to help the poor purchase a house could be quite specific to the financial institution lending assistance. Such loans would result in the client opening other accounts with the same bank. American Express's collaboration with the National Academy Foundation in the development of the Travel and Tourism Academies strengthens the industry by training qualified travel professionals, some of whom may work for American Express. In addition, the firm receives positive publicity, which benefits its public image. The benefits of Benetton's 1993 Clothing Redistribution Project were highly specific, as clothing donors had to enter a Benetton shop to participate, thus increasing the chances that the donors would become customers. In each case, social activity helps to build the loyalty of consumers to a specific company.

Finally, the benefits of social projects can be appropriated through the unique configuration of resources and capabilities and external factors, which shape the competitive environment of the firm. Initiatives that arise as a result of a careful identification of social issues that impinge uniquely on the value chain of a firm are less likely to be copied by other firms than those "generic" social issues that do not specifically affect a particular firm's competitive context or are influenced by a firm's unique value chain. Marcus and Geffen (1998) have studied how managers assign meaning to their environmental strategies in idiosyncratic ways, thus making proactive strategies more difficult to copy.

Take the recent interest in base-of-the pyramid (BOP) ventures. These initiatives often involve disruptive innovations as firms and social enterprises seek to serve populations that have hitherto not been served by competitors. However, BOP initiatives cannot easily be imitated as they are not generic social issues. For example, Cemex's *Patrimonio Hoy* program, which targets the sale of cement and related products to low-income consumers, really could only be imitated by the two other cement producers in Mexico – Apasco, a subsidiary of Swiss based Holcim, and Cruz Azul, a workers' cooperative.

Cross-nationally, we found that appropriability was related to value creation in Spain, but not Mexico (see Table 5.1). Undoubtedly, the extent of social action by a given nation's companies as well as the sophistication of their projects will be related to the ability to appropriate benefits in that country. Certainly, as a Mexican company, Cemex's *Patrimonio Hoy* is a sophisticated project, yet by and large most firms fail to think about ways to extract economic value from their social projects. Furthermore, where competition based on social attributes is in a nascent stage, as in Mexico, appropriability is probably not as relevant. As competition increases, and the likelihood of imitation does as well, creative ways of capturing value will also become more important.

Proactivity

Proactivity refers to the ability of the firm to anticipate social trends through its initiatives. Aragón-Correa and Sharma (2003: 73) define a proactive environmental strategy as "proactive postures involve anticipating future regulations and social trends and designing or altering operations, processes, and products to prevent (rather than merely ameliorate) negative environmental impacts." In the social arena, social responsiveness, which is the capacity of the firm to respond to social demands, has similarly been evaluated on a scale ranging from reactive to proactive (Clarkson, 1995). In this approach, a firm is an industry leader when it anticipates its responsibilities and does more than is required by law or industry practice.

The connection between proactivity and value creation has been studied in a number of ways. Dean and Brown (1995) found that first movers created barriers to entry competitors by going beyond regulatory compliance. Chad Nehrt (1996) found that first movers who invest in clean technologies do achieve greater financial performance than do second movers. According to Nehrt, several factors – learning effects, time compression diseconomies, and asset mass efficiencies – link proactivity to competitive advantage.

Learning effects include the learning that companies acquire as they develop and implement new environmental technologies. Since much of this knowledge is tacit, late movers are unable to acquire this knowledge and lose the opportunities that first movers have by arriving to the market first with their time-dependent technologies. For example, Swedish firms obtained a great advantage in environmental technologies in part because of forward-looking, innovation-oriented governmental regulation that required superior environmental performance from national pulp-and-paper firms. Having acquired that kind of learning, many of these firms were able to obtain price premiums for their chlorine-free paper (Porter and van der Linde, 1995).

Time compression diseconomies refer to the idea that some activities require considerable amounts of time to complete and that speeding things up is very expensive in terms of both human and financial resources. Many of the new base of the pyramid initiatives involve considerable interaction with local communities. Take Cemex's *Patrimonio Hoy* program again. The schema was developed only after anthropologists studied local communities and their spending and savings habits. The knowledge acquired is not readily accessible through a market survey, but only through careful, often labor-intensive and time-consuming interaction with local communities.

Finally, asset mass efficiencies refer to a "minimum investment in a technology in order to fully understand it and gain from it" (Nehrt, 1996: 537). If management fails to invest in an adequate level of training, for example, the implementation of new pollution reducing technologies may be hindered. *Patrimonio Hoy* required minimum investments in the training of personnel who would be able to target appropriate groups and deploy the savings technologies of the traditional Mexican savings club – the *tanda*. MRW's workforce initiative with the handicapped required significant redesigning of installations and work processes and scheduling.

Proactivity is related to value creation precisely because of the element of novelty, which requires a firm to do things differently than in the past. By "designing or altering operations, processes, and products to prevent ... negative environmental [and social] impacts" (Aragón-Correa and Sharma, 2003: 73) proactivity is likely to create this perception of novelty.

Interestingly, our surveys do not find a link between proactivity and value creation in Spain and Mexico. Our questions investigated the firm's ability to anticipate future social trends and regulation, but being first does not lead to value creation. Although we did not specifically examine the novelty component through our questionnaire, in some sense what is novel in one setting may be quite ordinary in another. Mexico is a country that has a tradition of corruption and weak institutional structures (Husted and Serrano, 2002). In an emerging economy where compliance with the law is seen as highly socially responsible, beyond-compliance behavior has not become part of the discussion. Although first-mover investments may be useful for creating insuperable barriers in knowledge, our preliminary research among both large Spanish firms and multinational firms in Mexico indicates that an ability to anticipate social trends and respond is not essential to social value creation. Although being a first mover in social strategy does not in and of itself create value in some countries like Mexico and Spain, such a premise would be practically inconceivable in the context of other countries like the United States and Canada.

Voluntarism

Voluntarism is defined as the degree to which social initiatives are carried out free of legal or social constraints. The strategic management literature has, until recently, taken voluntarism as a given. Business firms freely seek to exploit market opportunities in order to create a competitive advantage. Now, firms and scholars are beginning to pay attention to the opportunities offered by nonmarket activities – playing within a system of rules and regulations in order to create competitive advantages.

Burke and Logsdon, writing from a US context, suspected that only initiatives free from constraints would be perceived as value creating. However, among the large Spanish firms and multinationals located in Mexico, it appears that legal constraints are in fact associated with the perception of created value. Part of this discrepancy may be due to some controversy regarding the definition of social responsibility. Frequently, CSR is defined as social behavior that goes beyond legal compliance (McWilliams and Siegel, 2001). Yet as mentioned in connection with proactivity, in some emerging markets simply complying with the law is considered socially responsible. In the USA and many other developed countries, compliance is seen as a minimum.

In some countries, however, compliance is seen as an aspiration. So these counterintuitive results appear to say that greater legal constraints do, in fact, create value and a willingness on the part of consumers to pay a price premium. Strict regulation can be seen as a vehicle to create value for firms, if some firms meet them and others don't, or if some can do it more efficiently than others (Porter and van der Linde, 1995).

It is difficult to understand how the case of Spain fits into this category, though if viewed from a historical perspective a plausible hypothesis emerges. In the 1980s and 1990s, Spain's remarkable transition to democracy created new political institutions alongside spectacular economic and social development. Among the keys to this success were the tax code, fair and efficient tax collection, and a strong central bank, which together permitted the reconversion of a good part of the underground economy and spurred the creation of strong multinationals (Telefónica, Santander, Inditex, etc.), which were hailed as national champions. These firms were vocal in their support of the new institutions, regulations, and the country's commitment to meet the criteria to be among the founding nations adopting the euro. We would expect that the status of CSR will change quickly in the next decade to become much more similar to its status in the United States and other countries that have had developed economies for a longer period.

The Mexican situation is clear, but explaining what it means and how to move ahead is anything but obvious. Firms that simply comply with legal requirements to provide employees with housing, healthcare, and training are viewed as responsible, given the many firms that do not comply with these regulations. Very often paying one's fair share of taxes or not paying the bribe is unusual and even surprising! Thus, the nature of voluntary social action depends on the institutional context. What may constitute voluntary behavior in one context due to a weak institutional infrastructure (weak enforcement), may be considered obligatory social behavior in another. The message from our research is clear – the institutional context for value creation is vitally important to understanding when a firm's social action, voluntary or not, will create social and economic value.

Visibility

Visibility deals with the extent to which social action projects and their benefits are known by stakeholders. There is a wide range of corporate attitudes regarding the publicity given to these projects. HEB, a Texas-based grocery chain, has for many years chosen not to publicize its social activities (Lozano, Romero, and Serrano, 2003). HEB has been active in developing a number of community programs in Monterrey, Mexico in collaboration with the Roman Catholic social agency, Caritas. In the case of HEB, the reason for not publicizing social initiatives is the religious principle, as enunciated in the New Testament: "But when you give to the needy, do not let your left hand know what your right hand is doing."

A quite different and practical reason that companies may hesitate to go public with their good deeds is the possibility of a backlash should they set themselves up as corporate do-gooders, only to be exposed later as hypocrites when some shortcoming is uncovered. The examples of Enron, Siemens, BP, and other firms with highly visible CSR profiles are unpleasant reminders of the misuse of CSR in duping stakeholders.

However, the religious and practical arguments against publicizing social action are counterbalanced by equally strong arguments in support of firms making known their good deeds. Holy Writ also says that one should light a lamp and put it on a stand so that others can see it. The HEB–Caritas alliance, although intended to be of "low visibility," catalyzed contributions from other donors who inevitably became aware of the relationship (Lozano, Romero, and Serrano, 2003). On the practical side, as we set out in Chapter 2, our expectation is that the amount of social action programs and, on balance, the summed social welfare produced, should be greater where social strategy is pursued as an ethical and legitimate corporate strategy. Visibility of social action projects is fundamental to this objective.

Visibility is most importantly linked to value creation and competitive advantage through corporate reputation. Scholars have observed that a firm's reputation is closely tied into stakeholder perceptions of a firm's social responsibility initiatives (Fombrun and Shanley, 1990). Some research has demonstrated that a good corporate reputation has a significant potential for value creation and is, moreover, difficult for competitors to imitate (Roberts and Dowling, 2002; Sanchez and Sotorrio, 2007).

Reputation can provide various sorts of advantages. First, in terms of employees, research indicates that firms with reputations for social action are more able to recruit highly qualified employees. In terms of customers, reputation can serve as a way to differentiate a corporation and its products in the minds of consumers (Thompson and Thompson, 2006). Thus, although social action is important, firms also need to invest in the targeted disclosure of those programs in order to create advantages in terms of their employees and customers (Branco and Rodrigues, 2006) and other stakeholders with whom a reputation for social and environmental responsibility can benefit the firm (Toms, 2002). Unfortunately, firms do not always choose to make their projects as visible as they could be. In the Pfizer program already mentioned, surveys of external stakeholders revealed little awareness or knowledge about the impacts of the program (Vian *et al.*, 2007).

One effective means of making a social project visible is through certification programs. For example, coffee sold with the Fair Trade certification provides customers with trustworthy information about an otherwise hidden process. There is no way for consumers to ascertain whether fair labor practices are used in the cultivation and harvesting of coffee beans. Certification is an astute mechanism for overcoming asymmetric information and inspires confidence that ethical and responsible business practices are being followed (Husted, 2007). Certification serves as a signal that companies comply with specific standards – thus making social and environmental projects and, most importantly, the quality of those projects, more visible to consumers.

Yet, while certification is good for consumers, capturing value is uncertain because firms must rely on collaboration from competitors to put certification infrastructure in place and legitimize the process. The link between certification and value creation can also be uncertain. Forest certification improved the reputation of Finnish forest companies, but did not increase financial performance (Toshiaki *et al.*, 2006). Generally speaking, certification serves as a way to capture benefits of social and environmental investments by making them more visible to consumers, however firms must find a way to encourage consumers to translate awareness into a willingness to buy certified products and pay a premium for them (Kilbourne *et al.*, 2002).

In many cases, not just certified products, visibility may be the deciding factor for customers. Visibility of social action projects may facilitate a firm's product differentiation, increasing market share or obtaining a price premium from consumers. For example, Danone Mexico, a subsidiary of the French Groupe Danone, used the "Let's Build Their Dreams" campaign to make donations to charitable organizations with a mission to help needy children, based on the quantity of their products purchased by consumers (Lozano, Moxon, and Maas, 2003). As a result of the campaign, the public image of the company moved from "cold and unfriendly" to "warm and involved in the community." This change is credited with helping Danone maintain market share and pricing at a time when the competition was offering deep discounts of up to 40 percent (Lozano, Moxon, and Maas, 2003). The high visibility of this social program was instrumental to Danone sustaining its differentiation strategy.

The strong relationship between visibility and value creation was clear in both the Spanish and Mexican studies. It is important to note, however, that visibility is not related directly to novelty and appropriateness. Rather, visibility's role appears to be essential precisely because it assists consumers to see the novelty and appropriateness of social and environmental innovations. Without a means of making social projects visible through certification and/or publicity, many efforts would remain unknown. Although altruistic firms may quite legitimately seek anonymity, a strategic focus requires that stakeholders, especially consumers, know about the social project.

Conclusion

Our aim in this chapter has been to describe how social strategy creates economic value using the model proposed by Burke and Logsdon. Their five dimension model is one of the very few attempts made to create constructs that posit the components (independent variables) of social strategy and how they contribute individually, and collectively, to economic value creation.

Taken as a whole, we find that the five strategic dimensions of social projects are a useful instrument. However, there are significant challenges for future research. A model developed in the USA was tested in Spain and Mexico with positive, though inconsistent results. Proactivity was found to have no impact in either study. Visibility and voluntarism were both found to be significant, the first positively, the second negatively. The other two dimensions, centrality and appropriability, were also found to be significant, but to a lesser degree.

We believe that these results are an essential first step in testing social strategy models. Mixed results are not surprising; in fact, confirmation of all hypotheses in an exploratory exercise might justifiably be interpreted as a sign that we were looking for easy answers.

What matters is that there are significant findings from which we can draw preliminary conclusions and propose new directions. This we have tried to do in our analysis. For example, in the discussion of voluntarism, we found that analyzing the historical and institutional context in both Mexico and Spain was fundamental to providing a plausible explanation for the surprising result that voluntarism was negatively associated with value creation. Based on this finding, in two very different contexts, we should be able to develop and test richer hypotheses about the role of voluntarism in other countries and regions of the world.

It is clear that the application of social strategy models in varying institutional contexts will need to take into account the nuances and textures of regulations, culture, and the evolution of social-attribute markets and even in those settings. Specific firm attributes also need to be taken into account. Consider the following from MarketingWeek.co.uk in which Sharon Greene, managing director of ethical business consultancy, Risc International, comments on the low visibility of an innovative Procter and Gamble (PrG) scheme to provide clean water to children in emerging markets: "Greene was 'astounded' by its brilliance. 'Why wasn't P&G talking about the initiative?,' she asked. 'Because we are P&G. When we put our head over the parapet, we get knocked down. So we just get on with it and do what we can,' came the reply."[2] It is hard to believe that P&G, a world marketing leader for more than a century, a pioneer in segmentation, market research, and self-cannibalization, has not figured out how to give the right visibility to its social action projects.

Curiously, if one looks at P&G's website, there are numerous testimonies to the company's corporate responsibility, but they come from third parties. For example,[3] it displays an image of Rosabeth Moss Kanter's latest book, *SuperCorp*, and explains that Kanter cites P&G as a positive example. Management at P&G, we learn, has apparently decided that when a firm is a giant multinational, serving nearly four billion customers, it is best to let others praise you. The communications strategy makes good sense, given the nearly ubiquitous presence of the firm, consistently high rankings in polls such as *Fortune*

---

[2] Accessed by internet at www.marketingweek.co.uk/presentation-is-the-lifeblood-of-csr/3004762.article on November 26, 2009.
[3] See www.pg.com/news/kanter_super_corpnes.shtml.

magazine's "Most Admired Companies," and the myriad social action programs P&G has run worldwide for years. P&G has demonstrated the advantages of a long-term approach to social action.

In the firm's website, the presentation of social and sustainability programs and the language used to describe the firm's values could easily have been taken from any one of dozens of other multinationals. Below, as an example, is an excerpt from a recent speech by CEO A. G. Lafley, posted in the "News" section of P&G's website.[4]

What has enabled P&G to thrive – not just survive – so many challenges for so many years?

We are purpose driven, values and principles led. Our purpose is to touch consumers and improve their everyday lives. Right now, we're serving about 3.8 billion consumers. We are committed to serve 5 billion by 2015. Our values include integrity and trust, leadership and ownership. Our principles guide us to do the right thing for the greater good and the longer term health of the business and the institution.

We believe business in general and P&G in particular touch and improve more lives every day in our increasingly interconnected and global economy. When we are at our best, businesses, including P&G, are a consistent force for economic growth and a passionate force for a better society.

Professor Kanter understands quite well that many talk about values, but only a select few come even close to their declared aspiration. There is, she remarks, a "vanguard" of firms that integrate serving society into their businesses (Kanter, 2009: 2), which includes Banco Real, CEMEX, IBM, ICICI Bank, Omron, PrG, Publicis Groupe, and Shirshan Bank, among others. As the title of her book *SuperCorp: How Vanguard Companies Create Innovation, Profits, Growth, and Social Good* clearly states, supercorps create economic and social value and do it in ever larger quantities. Each supercorp has an inspirational, transformational leader who makes it happen and committed management and employees prepared to keep the story going when the firm's leader (often the founder) steps down.

We do not doubt that the firms Professor Kanter praises have created economic and social value; in our work, we, too, cite examples of

---

[4] A. G. Lafley acceptance speech upon receiving the Peter G. Peterson Award for Business Statesmanship by the Committee for Economic Development on Tuesday, October 20, 2009 in New York. www.pg.com/news/exemplary_leadership.shtml.

firms that have achieved these objectives. We share the case of Cemex. Such examples provide essential anecdotal evidence for how to get it done.

However, they do not provide evidence that any specific values, or combination of values, is positively correlated with economic wealth creation, nor that any other value or set of values is more or less correlated with economic wealth creation. Neither do these cases demonstrate that social action programs are correlated with economic wealth creation, nor that firms that do not engage in social action programs are more or less profitable than those that do.

Professor Kanter's insistence that social action foments innovation and the assertion that altruism and good deeds are correlated with profit builds on the argument she made a decade ago in her *Harvard Business Review* article, "From Spare Change to Real Change" (1999), an argument which must still be confirmed by research.

Professor Kanter's work over the last decade made a valuable contribution to the literature on social strategy. Our work has another objective: we seek to create a theory and models of social strategy that can be tested empirically. We need to know how social strategy stacks up against other strategies. We wish to learn when social strategy is advisable and when not. We want to figure out what configurations of environmental factors are most likely to lead to success. We have questions about what firms should do when social strategy falters or fails and a firm must abandon some of its most gratifying social action projects and commitments.

These are the reasons why we are developing social strategy theory and models and why testing them is so vital.

Burke and Logsdon's model, first proposed in 1996, was untested until we did our exploratory studies. The results were sufficiently rich and complex for us to conclude that there is much to be done, and that Burke and Logsdon's model must be overhauled in order to account for institutional differences across societies and for specific characteristics of firms. Otherwise, it is unlikely that this model (or any other) will accurately explain how social action projects in a given context create economic value for the firm and social value for all of us.

PART II

The process of developing corporate social strategy

6 | *Competitive environment*

Introduction

Following the presentation of our model for developing social strategy, we now turn to considering the competitive conditions conducive to corporate social strategy having a positive impact on firm performance. As should be clear from our presentation of the model, social strategy is not amenable to a one-size-fits-all approach. Rather, the formulation of social strategy must take into account both the competitive context and the unique resources and capabilities that a firm brings to the task. Scholars have argued that the development of market-based advantages is useful in less dynamic environments, while the development of capability-based advantages is vital to moderately dynamic and high-velocity environments (Grant, 1996; Teece *et al.*, 1997; Eisenhardt and Martin, 2000). In this chapter we will focus on how firms can achieve an advantageous market position through social strategy in different environments; in Chapter 8, we will take a closer look at resources and capabilities.

The task of characterizing the competitive environment is especially challenging due to the varying ways scholars have taken up the issue (Boyd *et al.*, 1993). Two approaches stand out. The first is based on industrial organization economics and uses the tools of game theory to model social investment under different competitive assumptions. This approach is often applied to the macro-environment and the study, via mathematical measures, of strategic decision-making and firm behavior under norms of rationality. The second approach (introduced in Chapter 4 in our analysis of the market environment – Step 1 of Corporate Social Strategy), develops qualitative evaluations

We thank José Salazar Cantú, who contributed significantly to the development of the game-theoretical models in this chapter, which are drawn from Husted and Salazar Cantú (2002), and for his consent to use them.

of the competitive context at multiple levels, both for the industry, and for the individual firm. This methodology depends on perceptual measures that describe the corporate decision-makers' evaluations of the competitive environment.

Each branch of the literature has advantages and limitations.[2] The first, primarily of interest to economists, is useful in developing inter-industry comparisons. The second, employed by strategic management scholars, is helpful in understanding intra-industry variation. In the following section of the chapter, we investigate both branches in order to analyze how the competitive environment, differently understood, influences the effectiveness of social strategy.

Industry structure – the economist's view

Although firms may make decisions to engage in social strategies, it is impossible to determine the competitive impact of those decisions in isolation as their rivals are also making competitive decisions, including whether to participate or not in social strategies. Thus, it is not enough to analyze a specific social project, but we must also take into account the projects of competitors in order to understand their impacts on business and social performance (Sethi and Sama, 1998).

Competitors in perfectly competitive markets are unlikely to demonstrate much interest in matters of business ethics or social responsibility (Baumol, 1991). In models of markets characterized by intense competition, scholars have shown that social investment is likely to be quite low (Fernández-Kranz and Santaló, 2007). Consequently, most interest in strategic forms of social action has focused on oligopolistic markets as the relevant arena. In this chapter, we examine specific kinds of competition within oligopolistic markets and develop the implications of these kinds of competition for social strategy. In so doing, we use the tools of game theory, which are appropriate for the analysis of decisions in oligopolistic markets (Tirole, 1988).

---

[2] Game theory has been attacked for presenting too simple and rational a view of behavior. Perceptual measurements of managerial behavior are criticized for making assumptions about the meaning of what managers say about their perceptions and intentions in interviews and on structured survey instruments. We will not spend much effort defending the two methodologies. Rather, we are interested in the contribution each can make to our understanding of social strategy's potential value.

Game theory is well suited to modeling firm decisions relating to investments in social projects. The extent to which such an investment is advantageous with respect to other oligopolistic competitors depends upon their decisions regarding similar investments. A collateral benefit of using game theory is that it highlights the difference between social strategy and cases where social action is a product of either corporate altruism or societal coercion. In these latter cases, firm social action is, by definition, independent from behavior by competitors.

The literature modeling oligopolistic markets is extensive and quite complex. In order to simplify our work, we will focus first on markets that involve homogeneous products. Our objective, once again, is to determine under what market conditions investment in social projects will be profitable. Assuming that more than one firm seeks to increase profits via social investments (McWilliams and Siegel, 2001), competition will ensue in which the firms do not cooperate[3] (make binding commitments) when selecting a specific strategy. These cases thus fall squarely within the arena of non-cooperative game theory.

Before turning to our analysis of the non-cooperative games, a brief comment on social investment/spending (CSR) and firm profitability is necessary. As we explained previously, the available evidence on the effect of CSR on firm profits is not conclusive (Griffin and Mahon, 1997; Waddock and Graves, 1997; McWilliams and Siegel, 2000; Margolis and Walsh, 2001; Orlitzky *et al.*, 2003). For our work in this chapter, this finding is crucial. In the case of non-strategic social investment, this inconclusive evidence limits the possibility of predicting the impact of such decisions on profitability. In other words, non-strategic social action is not an investment, because there is no competitive intent; furthermore its impact, regardless of intent, is uncertain. This is consistent with our conclusions at the close of Chapter 5, where we argued against the continued insistence by influential management writers and public figures (e.g., Rosabeth Moss Kanter) that CSR not only leads to profit, but that altruistic social action is superior to strategic social action because only the former will build the corporate values of commitment and innovation that lead to profit.

---

[3] Such cooperation is customarily unlawful – i.e., collusion.

This leaves us with the task of evaluating the strategic case, which we began in the penultimate paragraph. In the strategic case, we propose that social investment will lead to competitive advantage and profit, but that this positive effect could be diluted, or even eliminated entirely, when other firms from the same industry also make strategic social investments or when there is no demand for social action projects.

Below, we will apply game theory to strategic social investment, including this proposition about competition and several variants.[4] We begin the analysis by examining first the case of the prisoner's dilemma and its relationship to strategic social investment. We then relax the assumptions about information in the prisoner's dilemma model to develop a more general *ad hoc* model. Finally, we explore the impact of market structure on the profitability of social investment using Bertrand and Cournot models of oligopolistic competition.

Prisoner's dilemma model

The prisoner's dilemma model will serve as a baseline for comparison. The prisoner's dilemma will help us identify the different agents involved and propose results for less complex situations, in order to then think about those more complex, and more realistic cases. The prisoner's dilemma model involves a non-cooperative strategy, with symmetric, imperfect, complete, and certain information. Information is symmetric because each player (firm) has the same information, but imperfect because the players move simultaneously. Information is complete because all participants know the rules of the game. Finally, the game is characterized by certainty because no new information is revealed after the move of the first player. These information conditions are quite stringent and unlikely to occur in the real world.

In this case, if neither firm makes social investments, both obtain zero profits. We expect the greatest benefits to be obtained by a firm when it makes a social investment, but its rival does not. However, when both firms decide to make social investments, then both are

---

[4] Game theory employs its own vocabulary and notation system. We have restricted our use of technical terminology, keeping in mind that while most of our readers are familiar with game theory, few are everyday users of the methodology.

Table 6.1: *Results of strategic social investment in a*
prisoner's dilemma model

	F2	
F1	Invest	Do not invest
Invest	−1,−1	2,−2
Do not invest	−2,2	0,0

Payoffs: (F1, F2)

likely to suffer losses. Let's assume that the demand for investment in
social causes is not zero, and consider two firms (F1 and F2) that make
a decision to invest (I) or not invest (NI) simultaneously and knowing
beforehand the results of their decisions. We can depict the possible
strategies of the participants and their respective payoffs in Table 6.1.

In this case, we see that the game has a dominant-strategy equilibrium, where each firm's dominant strategy is strictly its best response
to any of the choices of the rival firms. If we consider the result of "2"
as the one which represents the best improvement in profits and "−2"
as the worst impact on profits, the best strategy for F1 regardless of
any choice of F2 is "Invest" and the same for F2, so that we would
expect that the most likely payoff for this game would be (−1, −1). In
other words, in a situation where both firms decide to make social
investments, they both suffer a net loss. This result is also a Nash equilibrium, because if F1 invests, F2 faces the choice between a payoff of
−1 upon investing and a payoff of −2 if it does not invest, therefore F2
decides to invest. If F2 invests, then F1 faces a choice between a payoff of −1 if it does invest and of −2 if it does not invest, so that F1 also
decides to invest. Likewise, a combination of strategies is a Nash equilibrium if neither player has an incentive to deviate from its strategy
assuming the other player also does not deviate (Rasmussen, 1989).
Clearly, in this case, neither player has an incentive to deviate from its
strategy, given that the other party does not change its strategy.

Note that the dominant-strategy equilibrium is Pareto inefficient
for the players. Pareto efficiency refers to an equilibrium in which
any change that improves the position of one of the players necessarily worsens the situation of the other player. In this case, the payoff
to one of the players can only improve without worsening the payoff

of the other when the combination of strategies moves from (Invest, Invest) to (Do not invest, Do not invest). In a prisoner's dilemma world, repeated play would lead to a situation in which neither player makes social investments (Axelrod, 1984).

Ad hoc *model*

Given the highly unrealistic assumptions about information in the prior model, let us consider a model that more closely approximates the case of social investment by firms. A more realistic model should focus on the non-cooperative situation in which information is asymmetric, imperfect, incomplete, and uncertain. Information is likely to be asymmetric in a real social investment decision since local firms often have access to information about unique social needs in the communities where they operate. Also, such information will be imperfect because each manager will probably know only part or perhaps nothing of competitors' social action programs. Information will be incomplete because the environment customarily changes during the course of the game, and the information will be uncertain because the players do not know much about the expected payoffs derived from a given social investment strategy.

Let's analyze the case of firm F1, which does not currently make social investments (NI), but does participate in a market where its competitor, F2, seeks to differentiate its product by making social investments (I). If F1 decides not to invest, then F2 obtains a profit of 2, but if F1 does invest, then F2 may either stop investing, which will lead it to suffer a loss of –2 or continue to invest with three possible outcomes, each with a probability of one-third: both firms receive some benefits (1, 1), both firms receive zero benefits (0, 0), or both firms suffer losses (–2, –2). The game tree of this situation can be illustrated as in Figure 6.1.

The expected profit ($E(\pi)$) of F2 upon investing, given that F1 also invests is:

$$E(\pi) = 0.333(-2)+0.333(0)+0.333(1) = -0.333$$

and if F2 does not invest at the time F1 invests, then it loses –2.

These results are similar for firm F1. If one firm begins to invest, then the strategic equilibrium combination would be that both end up

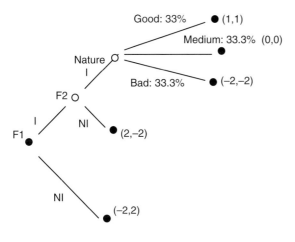

Payoffs: (F1, F2)

Figure 6.1: Social investment game characterized by asymmetric, imperfect, incomplete, and uncertain information

making social investments and having an expected loss of −0.333. In such a case, it becomes attractive for the two firms to agree, overtly or tacitly, that neither one will undertake social investments.

Bertrand and Cournot competition

However, the way in which the competition behaves and whether one firm is a first mover can lead to different results. By obtaining a first-mover advantage with respect to products with social attributes – what we referred to as proactivity in Chapter 5 – the firm is more likely to obtain private benefits from the investment (Clarkson, 1995; Burke and Logsdon, 1996; Nehrt, 1996). However, if all firms follow the same strategy, then the financial benefits will probably diminish and social investment will become unsustainable.

Suppose that the firm, which does not make social investments, decides to imitate the proactive firm. Typically, we would expect that the proactive firm would incur a certain extra cost due to the risk of implementing a novel, unknown strategy that may be imitated by competitors at a lower cost. We also assume a Bertrand market structure, or one in which firms respond to competition by adjusting their prices, assuming the rival does not change its prices. In Table 6.2, we

Table 6.2: *Results of a social investment strategy in a game with imitation and Bertrand competition*

	F2	
F1	Innovate (Proactive)	Imitate (Reactive)
Innovate (Proactive)	−1,−1	−1,0
Imitate (Reactive)	0,−1	0,0

Payoffs: (F1, F2)

illustrate this case in which the firm that moves first incurs a cost of 1 (payoff = −1), but the imitation is less expensive (payoff = 0) and results in a kind of Bertrand competition.

In a Bertrand market structure, prices are equal to the competitive market price because, whichever player charges a price higher than its marginal cost, loses the entire market, assuming the player does not face capacity constraints (Tirole, 1988). If both players set prices equal to the marginal cost, they split the market in half. Thus, there is a strong incentive to charge the competitive market price.

The dominant-strategy equilibrium in the Bertrand case is to imitate (be reactive) on the part of both firms, which would lead them to avoid incurring additional marginal costs. This would explain why, in many markets, there is so little social investment and why in most cases social investment is non-strategic, in effect a social cost, a result either of coercion by the government or of top management's altruism (Sethi and Sama, 1998). This outcome also explains why, as discussed in Chapter 5, proactive social projects may not always be relevant to value creation. We now see that proactivity may be moderated by market structure.

In a Bertrand market, firms set prices and sell all they can at this price. This game has only one Nash equilibrium, where the prices charged by each firm are equal to the marginal cost, which is the competitive price. Consequently, the price premium for social attributes in this market would have to be equal to zero. No other pair of prices would be an equilibrium, given that a firm would have the entire market, if it were to set a price slightly below the other. The only pair of prices where this incentive does not exist is where the price equals the marginal cost. Each firm would end up with no above-normal profits and would thus make no social investments.

Table 6.3: *Results of a social investment strategy in a game with imitation under a Cournot market structure*

	F2	
F1	Innovate (Proactive)	Imitate (Reactive)
Innovate (Proactive)	1,1	1,2
Imitate (Reactive)	2,1	0,0

Payoffs: (F1, F2)

Under different assumptions, proactive social investment or innovation can occur even with the lower cost implicit in imitation. The key is what happens in the product market. Let's suppose that there exist two firms that agree to Cournot-type rules – a quest for market share rather than price competition. In this case, the firms fix their production quantities simultaneously, assuming that the production levels of their competitors do not change. In this case, the firm that innovates pays the cost of innovation, but obtains half of the benefits (payoff = 2 – 1 = 1) with the imitator receiving the other half of the benefits without paying the costs of innovation (payoff = 2 – 0 = 2). Where neither firm innovates, there is nothing to imitate, thus the payoff for the imitation (reactive) strategy for each firm is zero. Table 6.3 illustrates the possible payoffs.

In this game, imitation is no longer the dominant strategy. Without taking into account the advantage that could derive from being a first mover in this game, this case has two Nash equilibria (innovate, imitate) and (imitate, innovate) and a Nash equilibrium that is symmetric in mixed strategies in which each firm innovates with a probability of 50 percent.

This case is particularly interesting because it suggests the possibility of a sequential form of social investment in which one firm first innovates and the other imitates. The benefits received by the second induce it to innovate, causing the first to imitate and so on iteratively. In the long run, it would be a sustainable situation because at worst, no one wins, but no one loses – neither the firms nor society.

Conclusion

By taking into account the impact of industry structure on social investment, we are able to predict in which industries proactive social investment is more likely to be an effective strategy. Market structure appears to play a key role in understanding why social investment sometimes affects firm financial performance positively. Specifically, it appears as though firms that face Cournot-type competition are much more likely to publicize social investment in order to capture benefits from such projects than firms that face Bertrand-type competition. Bertrand competition is based on price and approximates the conditions of a highly competitive market with many firms. Cournot competition is based on market share. By increasing market share, firms are able to reduce costs through economies of scale. Given disappointing survey results in Spain and Mexico for the relationship of proactivity to value creation, these results suggest that social strategy research needs to take into account market structure.

Anecdotal evidence provides some support for the intuitions developed through the analytical tools of game theory. A useful example of Cournot competition is the Mexican cement industry, where competition has been based on market share over the last hundred years. Mexican leader Cemex has progressively bought out local competitors and accounts for 55.4% of production in the Mexican market (Hargreaves *et al.*, 2005). It has been able to drive down costs through scale economies. Its principal competitors are Holcim Apasco and Cruz Azul with 21.5% and 10.6% of the market respectively. The smallest of the three, Cruz Azul has a strong presence in the central and southern part of Mexico. It is an employee cooperative and has had an overtly social mission since its founding. Holcim Apasco is part of the Swiss conglomerate controlled by the Schmidheiny family. Stephan Schmidheiny has expressed a longstanding interest in sustainable development (Schmidheiny, 1992). Of the three, Cemex and Holcim also compete internationally.

Cemex has both initiated and responded to its competitors with programs such as *Patrimonio Hoy*, which is a social initiative aimed at combining microfinance with cement sales to the poorest strata of Mexican society. It participates in high profile public projects, including a recently announced joint venture with Spanish energy company, Acciona, to operate what will be Latin America's largest wind farm in Oaxaca (Milenio, 2009).

The cement business in developing countries is plagued with social/community issues and environmental concerns. Like its competitors worldwide, all three Mexican cement companies have been criticized at one time or another for different aspects of their social or environmental performance. What makes the Mexican competitive environment so unusual is that all three companies have sought to position themselves through highly visible social action projects. Cruz Azul's sports club and cultural center is famous throughout Mexico; the firm does an excellent job reminding stakeholders that Cruz Azul is a cooperative and that its community programs are as important as its business projects. Holcim Apasco leverages its environmental projects from its companies worldwide and proclaims its commitment to sustainability. The marquee project in Mexico is its preprocessing cement waste program. Cemex has focused on expanding into environmental sustainability (e.g., alternative energy) and on its commitment to bringing those at the base of the pyramid into the Mexican economy.

The social and environmental activity of the three firms makes a great deal of sense in light of the Cournot competition based on market share that characterizes the cement industry in Mexico. The three cement companies appear to make sequential investments in social and environmental projects as they respond to each other's moves.

The Mexican cement industry case is an example of how managers may find game-theoretic approaches useful to understanding the nature of competition in their industry, and assist them in making decisions on social investments.

Market dynamics – managerial perception

The game-theoretic approach to understanding the market environment is effective for comparing industries and visualizing inter-firm rivalry. Nevertheless, modeling industry structure raises difficult questions that have vexed strategy researchers for the last two decades (Eisenhardt and Martin, 2000). We are faced with firm heterogeneity, permeable industry boundaries, dynamic capabilities, and managerial perceptions of industry structure (Sutcliffe and Huber, 1998), which raise important challenges for understanding industry impact on firm business and social strategy. Strategy scholars have argued that industry structure is a dynamic construct by which firms define product markets and competitors (Sampler, 1998). As product markets and competitors shift their domains, so do managerial definitions of the industries in which their firms compete. For social strategists, under-standing and measuring dynamic industry market structure requires a wider view of firm environment than that provided by industrial-organization economics. Additional instruments and measures are needed so that managers can assess their ability to build competitive advantage and create value. As we argued at the outset of this chapter, managerial perception of the industry environment is a key driver of firm decision-making.

In this section, we look at top management perceptions of industry structure via five fundamental environmental variables: dynamism, munificence, complexity, hostility, and controllability (Sutcliffe and Huber, 1998), four of which we reviewed in Chapter 4. These five dimensions of firm environment are indicators of the perceived rela-tionship a firm has with both its principal competitors and principal market stakeholders (suppliers and customers). Resource depend-ence theory holds that managers develop strategies in response to their relative power as they compete for scarce resources (Pfeffer and Salancik, 1978; Dess and Beard, 1984). How managers perceive the terrain of the competitive industry environment (dynamism, munifi-cence, complexity) as well as their ability to respond (hostility and controllability) are key indicators of managerial understanding of opportunities for engaging in social strategy and the likelihood of success.

One possible limitation of the perceived firm environment approach to industry structure is the dependence on managerial percep-tions rather than objective data external to the firm (Robinson and McDougall, 1998). These objective measures include industry con-centration, growth rates of markets, stage in industry lifecycle, etc.

This problem is mitigated in two ways. First, managers within and across firms in the same industry tend to have closely aligned per-ceptions regarding objective data (i.e., market growth rates) that are external to the firm and can be easily measured (Boyd *et al.*, 1993; Sutcliffe and Huber, 1998). In short, managers differ little in their perceptions regarding easy to obtain objective data: e.g., product sales growth in stable and mature industries. The most significant differences between managers emerge in their perception of how to employ their firm's resource base and capacity to respond in the per-petual search for strategic competitive advantage. This is of crucial importance to social strategists.

Second, if managerial perceptions are the most important driver of strategic decision-making (Hambrick and Mason, 1984; Carpenter and Golden, 1997), then we ought to take into account the full range of influences on top managers. We can then propose a social strategy framework for how firms determine their strategies within specific industries (product markets and competitors), linking managerial perceptions of objective market conditions – munificence, complexity, dynamism (Keats and Hitt, 1988) – to managerial perceptions of possible strategic action – hostility and controllability (Sutcliffe and Huber, 1998).

The five dimensions are derived from the environmental analysis literature (Dess and Beard, 1984; Keats and Hitt, 1988; Sutcliffe and Huber, 1998). As is the case in many areas of management research, there are no standard definitions for the specific variables (Boyd *et al.*, 1993). For each construct, we have chosen what we believe is the best definition available. We discussed the three environmental dimensions in detail in the overview of the model provided in Chapter 4. Let's briefly review these dimensions and add the other two dimensions related to the perceptions of possible strategic action.

The constructs are defined as follows: *dynamism* measures the perceived degree of difficulty in predicting external events that may affect the competitive environment (Aldrich, 1979). *Complexity* indicates the number and variety of environmental influences and their impact on the competitive environment (Dess and Beard, 1984). *Munificence* refers to the availability of resources to support growth in a given competitive environment (Staw and Szwajkowski, 1975). *Hostility* measures managers' beliefs regarding the degree to which the environment is more or less favorable to their firms (Sutcliffe and Huber, 1998). *Controllability* concerns managers' beliefs regarding their ability to influence outcomes given a specific level of environmental hostility (Sutcliffe and Huber, 1998).

As we indicated above, dynamism, munificence and complexity are constructs based in large part on managerial perceptions regarding real data on sales and income growth, capital expenditures, consumer demand, competitor behavior, etc. Given a specific competitive industry understanding, managerial perceptions of hostility and controllability influence the approach managers will take as they seek the best possible fit between their strategy and the environment (Sutcliffe and Huber, 1998). It is likely that only those managers capable of interpreting the industry environment as less hostile and more controllable than their competitors will choose a social strategy.

Generic social strategies

Managers must then select the most effective social strategy, given the industry structure. Building on the insights of industrial organization economics, Michael Porter (1980) identified two generic strategies to achieve a competitive advantage: differentiation and cost leadership. Forest Reinhardt (1999) applied Porter's framework to environmental strategies and added a third generic strategy – strategic interaction. Although originally developed with respect to environmental strategies, Reinhardt's approach applies just as well to social ones. It should be pointed out that these three generic social strategies are not mutually exclusive, and firms may use them in combination, simultaneously or sequentially. In this section, we discuss each of these three generic social strategies and the market dynamics where they will best operate. We summarize the three strategies and corresponding market conditions in Table 6.4.

A social strategy based on differentiation is successful when customers are willing to pay a premium for social products (McWilliams and Siegel, 2001). The opportunity for a differentiation strategy

Table 6.4: *Generic social strategies for market-based advantages*

Generic social strategy	Environmental conditions	Examples
Differentiation	High dynamism High complexity Low munificence	Patagonia The Body Shop Fox News
Cost leadership	Low dynamism Low complexity Low munificence	Canadian oil industry Grameen Bank Aravind Eye Care
Strategic interaction	Low dynamism Low complexity Low munificence	Honda Telefónica

exists because of demanding consumers who are willing to make purchases based on the social performance of the firm (Zalka *et al.*, 1997; Menon *et al.*, 1999). However, in markets where there is high dynamism and/or high complexity, and where munificence is low, few firms have been prepared to meet those social needs. Hence, the significant opportunity.

Creating sustainable competitive advantage in dynamic and complex competitive environments is difficult and expensive (Miller, 1988). In low munificence environments, firms may lack resources to engage in traditional product differentiation strategies. In these cases, a product differentiation social strategy may provide an important alternative. Patagonia provides an excellent example. In the 1980s Patagonia took advantage of a clothing and sports equipment sector that had not reacted to social trends and emerging lifestyles (increasing dynamism and complexity) to carve out a niche in the clothing market. However, in 1991 industry growth stalled (low munificence), and Patagonia was forced to lay off 20 percent of its workforce. Patagonia responded by increasing its commitment to environmentalism and its social values, decided to limit the firm's growth and borrowing while at the same time bolstering employee benefits including child care, healthcare, health food cafeteria, flexible work time, and weekend group sports activities. Patagonia's managers thus converted what could have been a hostile environment into something they knew well – a smaller, less hostile competitive environment that took the opportunity to reconfirm and maintain the firm's integrated business and social strategy based on technology-driven development of patented, environmentally friendly products for their loyal customer base (high controllability). In effect, Patagonia was able to enact its environment.

Generally speaking, advantages based on market position succeed more often in less dynamic and complex environments (Grant, 1996; Teece *et al.*, 1997). The use of social strategy differentiation in dynamic and complex environments is of special interest for this reason. It provides an alternative that we believe can be quite effective even where firm access to resources is limited.

With this in mind, a quick look at what will be a controversial example. Fox News was launched by Rupert Murdoch in 1996 with CEO Roger Ailes, former Republican media consultant to Presidents Nixon, Reagan, and George H. W. Bush. From its inception, Fox News has taken a conservative stand on public issues and has proclaimed itself to be the defender of "true" and "real" Americans through its news broadcasts and commentators such as Bill O'Reilly and the recently incorporated Glenn Beck. In little more than a decade, Fox News has become the United States' largest cable news network, growing from its initial base of 10 million subscribers to over 100 million, surpassing CNN.

Despite Fox News' clear ideological orientation, its trademarked slogan is "Fair and Balanced." Curiously, accordingly to an October 2009 Pew Research Center Poll neither the channel's critics nor its supporters believe Fox News to be "fair and balanced." (Poniewozik, 2009). Apparently, what Fox News viewers want is to have their point of view aggressively represented. Fox News CEO Ailes and Fox News broadcast personalities consistently maintain that Fox is the only real alternative to the "liberal" news media and that Fox provides an invaluable social good – namely, the truth. In an astonishingly dynamic and complex television news industry environment, Fox News has adopted a social strategy based on, to quote the title of Glenn Beck's bestseller, "The Real America: Messages from the Heart and the Heartland" (Beck, 2005). Fox News and its social strategy is a success. The men and women who run Fox News don't care that you, Al Franken, or even President Obama can demonstrate that Fox's facts are wrong, the arguments demagoguery, etc. Fox has a mission, business, social, and political that it pursues irrespective of other voices, or stakeholders who believe they have been damaged.

Let us shift our attention from social differentiation strategy to examine the two other generic strategies based on market and segment selection where social strategy may be useful for comparatively less dynamic markets.

A cost leadership social strategy may emerge where firms discover that cost savings are available through process innovation (Hart, 1995; Porter and van der Linde, 1995). Although much debate exists as to the possibility of such "free lunches" (Palmer *et al.*, 1995), there exists evidence of the capacity of firms to innovate in response to social opportunities and threats (Kanter, 1999). Such cost leadership may occur through the ability of a firm to attract and maintain an effective labor force based on its commitment to the firm's social products (Greening and Turban, 2000; O'Reilly and Pfeffer, 2000). Other mechanisms for cost savings may occur through the wise management of relationships with suppliers (Husted, 1994; Dyer and Singh, 1998) who are committed to similar objectives.

One area where it appears that cost leadership social strategies have been undertaken by firms is environmental standards (Orsato, 2006). In a study of the Canadian oil industry, Sanjay Sharma and Harrie Vredenburg (1998) found that firms that proactively sought process improvements designed to exceed environment standards may achieve lower process costs than those that simply sought to meet regulatory standards. Such process innovation may also be related to the development of unique, inimitable organizational capabilities that emerge within the framework of social action and may give rise to socially desirable products as well.

Another area where cost leadership social strategy has grown is the "base of the pyramid" (BOP) – the four billion people who earn less than US$2,000 a year and thus cannot afford most products and services offered by multinational corporations (Prahalad, 2005). These BOP markets have usually been less complex, less dynamic, and far less munificent than markets at the top of the pyramid. Through radical process innovation, companies have been able to develop and commercialize products that are appropriate for this enormous market (Prahalad and Hammond, 2002).

With this in mind, let us look again at an example of two competing microfinance institutions we discussed briefly in Chapter 2. The Grameen Bank of Bangladesh was designed by its founder, Muhammad Yunus, to deliver banking services to the poor. It began the concept of microcredit and innovatively reduced the costs of providing financial services to the poor through solidarity lending. Through this technique the bank bundles individual loans and allows a small group of women to share responsibility and manage relationships, thus reducing costs of assessing, managing, and collecting loans. Nonetheless, microcredit banking is labor intensive with agents visiting customers frequently. It has been found to be particularly effective in rural settings in underdeveloped countries.

Though there is no doubting Grameen Bank's success and enormous contribution to fight poverty, the bank is not a for-profit organization. It is best described as "self-sustaining," as it depends on investment and support from individuals and other organizations that are willing to accept below market return on labor and capital.

Compartamos Bank, however, is a for-profit microfinance bank. Begun in 1990 as a non-profit funded by other non-profits, over the last decade, with the support of World Bank's International Finance Corporation (IFC), Compartamos made a progressive transition to become a for-profit entity trading on the Mexican Stock Exchange. In press releases and public forums, the IFC has described how it has assisted Compartamos:

The partnership between IFC and Compartamos began in 2001, when IFC provided financing and equity to help it develop from a nongovernmental organization to a commercially viable entity, facilitating access to market-based funding and expanding services. In 2004 and 2005, IFC provided a 34 percent partial credit guarantee to the two tranches of a local currency five-year bond (rated locally as AA by Standard and Poor's and Fitch), the first ever for a microfinance institution in Mexico. (Gómez, 2008)

Compartamos now has 327 offices, and has expanded its business from women's group microcredit, based on a solidarity guarantee, to other segments of microfinance. It has lower costs than non-profit microcredit organizations thanks to investments in technology (Gómez, 2008) and to its larger customer base, which allows agents to travel less distance between customer visits than its competitors.

A widely discussed example of BOP innovation is Aravind Eye Care. The hospital focuses only on ophthalmological problems. Its founder, Dr. Govindappa Venkataswamy, was able to reduce costs of procedures like cataract surgery by making such surgery more efficient. With almost assembly-line efficiency, Aravind surgeons perform 1,500 cataract surgeries per year compared to about 200 for the normal ophthalmologist. They were able to reduce the costs of lenses by producing them in-house and reducing cost to only US$7.00. Finally, fee-paying patients subsidize the costs for non-paying patients. Note that in these cases, the market environment may be conducive to cost leadership, but the development of specific innovations requires resources and capabilities, which we will discuss in greater detail in Chapter 8. We should add that, like Grameen Bank, Aravind Eye Care is a "self-sustaining" organization, not a for-profit. In the concluding chapter of this book, we revisit the question of BOP companies and social strategy.

In contrast to the differentiation and cost leadership social strategies, the strategic interaction social strategy specifically incorporates nonmarket actions in creating rent-seeking opportunities through the use of regulation and/or industry standards. However, nonmarket actions may also include activities such as social network development, political contributions, and community service (Shaffer *et al.*, 2000). Researchers have demonstrated that firms can use the public policy process to enact regulation as a means to obtain competitive advantage with respect to other firms that are less well positioned to comply with such standards (Leone, 1986; Shaffer, 1995; Schuler, 1996). Where compliance with a standard, such as fair-trade practice or zero-carbon emissions, may increase costs, regulation may be a way for a firm with a particular cost advantage relative to competitors to exploit that advantage. Without invoking some sort of regulation, such cost advantages might not be sustainable.

For example, throughout the privatization and market deregulation process of the telecommunications industry in Spain, Telefónica was able to persuade government regulators that, because it provided service to unprofitable but needy customers, the new regulations should include restriction on entrants and permit infrastructure pricing that would allow the incumbent, Telefónica, to maintain its cost advantages based on economies of scale. Telefónica employed the same strategic interaction social strategy in Latin America, offering exceptional service to rural areas and the poor in its bid for contracts. Telefónica's long-term, market consolidation strategy was made possible in large part to its astute strategic interaction social strategy. Spain's governments, regardless of the party in power, defended its "national champion."

Nowhere was the success of Telefónica's strategy more evident than in the 3G mobile telephone license frenzy of 1999–2001. Where Telefónica paid just €130 million for its home market license, British Telecom paid £4.03 billion for its British license (BT Annual Report 2000; Eguía and Allen, 2004).

Throughout the entire industry restructuring process, Telefónica's European and global competitors, Deutsche Telekom and British Telecom, received far less favorable treatment from government. Where British Telecom was done in by the UK government's 3G licensing auction, Deutsche Telekom was victim of the German government's insistence on creating a "level playing field" following privatization. Government regulators decided that Deutsche Telekom customers would be free to purchase telephone calls from other providers on a per call basis; customers were provided with a number to call free of charge to find out which company offered the lowest price for that call. The caller then dialed direct, using the preferred service provider's code. The service provider received the phone call charges from Deutsche Telekom, which continued to bill the customer, and, in turn, paid Deutsche Telekom an infrastructure fee as stipulated by the new regulations. In addition, Deutsche Telekom was required to maintain approximately 25,000 employees with government-guaranteed contracts for whom the company no longer had work. In a matter of months, Deutsche Telekom's fixed line revenues fell sharply, as did its share price, and it has since suffered a series of management shake-ups.

Telefónica's astute strategic interaction social strategy and political savvy helped to open up resources for the firm, allowing it to pursue an aggressive international strategy. Today, Telefónica is the world's fifth largest telecommunications company in revenues, third in profits (Fortune, 2009), and is considered a model to follow by its competitors.[5] As in the case of cost leadership social strategy, strategic interaction social strategy is most likely to be effective in key moments of change (e.g., market re-regulation, government contract bidding) in less dynamic and less complex markets where product differentiation is difficult and price competition is intense. In utilities – telephone, gas, electric – where various stakeholder groups usually have strong influence on corporate behavior and government contracts are required, the market structure is usually an oligopoly, even with restructuring, and competitors are required to provide environmental and public-service attributes. One essential factor in these markets is that cost differences between competitors in compliance may be considerable with significant effect on margins and market share. Many other industries are also characterized by measurable cost asymmetries that provide one firm with a cost advantage in providing social products that comply with higher environmental or social standards than its competitors. Important differences can arise, for example,

---

[5] The discussion of the telecommunications industry is based on work the authors have done with the industry and from conversations with industry executives.

due to economies of scale in record keeping, reporting, and assurance staff (Shaffer, 1995; Reinhardt, 1999).

An opportunity for strategic interaction social strategy may arise when a firm with high social and environmental standards detects free riders who are doing less without damage to their businesses; at this point, the firm can seek to influence public policy so that the regulator imposes its high standards on the entire industry. Often, through lobbying, the firm provides policy-makers with information or builds constituencies to support new regulation at higher standards (Hillman and Hitt, 1999). After the new regulation is enacted, the firm may then exploit its advantage with respect to its competitors, first by going public with having been the leader in the sector, and later by the cost advantage it will have as its competitors invest to catch up.

Conclusion

This chapter examines the positional advantages available to firms via social strategy in different competitive environments. We first examined industry structure through the lens of industrial-organization economics and game theory before turning to recent advances in modeling the competitive environment based on perceptual approaches used in strategic management.

Game-theory modeling permitted us to reinforce the argument that there is support in economic theory for making a case for social strategy. From there, our concern was to demonstrate that a typology of social strategies may be formulated consistent with managerial perceptions of the competitive market.

We proposed three generic social strategies – differentiation, cost leadership, and strategic interaction. Like all generic strategy typology, there is the risk of over-generalization. Typologies, we must keep in mind, represent ideal types and we should not expect firms to fit perfectly into one of the categories (Doty and Glick, 1994). In presenting the generic social strategies, and what we believe are quite interesting examples, we have sought to demonstrate that social strategy is a real and viable strategic alternative, at times the most effective.

7 | *From stakeholder management to social strategy*

A stakeholder in an organization is (by its definition) any group or individual who can affect or is affected by the achievement of the organization's objective.

Freeman, *Strategic Management:*
A Stakeholder Approach, (1984: 25)

The social strategy decision

Thanks to Professor Freeman's considerable efforts, the term stakeholder is now a standard part of the business lexicon. Unfortunately, despite Freeman's insistence that shareholders and stakeholders are on the same side, the term stakeholder is used most often in an adversarial context:[1] shareholders and their CEO hired guns are pitted against the stakeholders – i.e., everybody else. Freeman's core argument – that in the long term the firm's success depends on satisfying legitimate non-economic as well as economic stakeholders – has not convinced microeconomists and strategic management scholars. Legitimacy is the crux of the issue. In a series of Academy of Management Review articles, Thomas Jones (Jones, 1995; Jones and Wicks, 1999; Jones *et al.*, 2007) has made a laudable effort to reconcile normative and instrumental stakeholder management theory by demonstrating that both are necessary and possible. In his most recent paper, he builds on Phillips' (2003) work on normative and derivative legitimacy to defend, via the former, meeting the ethical demands of stakeholders,

---

[1] Walsh and Nord (2005) describe in detail how Freeman's stakeholder concept, predicated on voluntarism and the intrinsic strategic benefits of what has come to be known as "enlightened stakeholder management," became part of the challenge to shareholder control and a call to firms to fix the world's problems.

and, by the latter, acceding to the demands of powerful stakeholders that may harm the organization and/or other legitimate stakeholders (Jones *et al.*, 2007: 142).

Nonetheless, there still remains the quarter-century-old problem of stakeholder theory when it comes to navigating conflicting normative (ethical) and instrumental objectives. In response, Jones *et al.* (2007) define a typology of organizational ethical cultures and provide propositions on how each type will respond to stakeholder groups under different conditions of stakeholder salience. The model is descriptive, predicts when a particular type of ethical culture will pay attention to specific types of stakeholders, but it cannot claim to advance the prospect of firm ethical behavior or of stakeholders benefiting from firm responsiveness to their needs. As has often been the case in stakeholder research, the authors suggest that creating trust through ethical behavior will redound to the firm's benefit. However, they cannot make an economic case for ethical stakeholder management, nor explain how stakeholder management creates competitive advantage and economic value.

The choice facing managers when addressing stakeholders has not changed since Thrasymachus proposed interest group theory in Plato's *Republic*: either the owners of firms and their agents treat stakeholders as interest groups, some hostile and some not, or the firm is managed in function of an ethical theory, be it utilitarian, Kantian, virtue ethics, the ethics of care, and so on.[2] If we may simplify a bit, after twenty-five years of research, stakeholder management theory remains stuck on the same two problems: Do firms have an ethical obligation to meet the demands of "legitimate" stakeholders when it hurts firm performance? If yes, what then constitutes a "legitimate" stakeholder?

Most microeconomists and many strategists believe the answer to these questions lies in the application of law and corporate governance regulations which, historically, have privileged shareholders and profit. They argue that stakeholder theory simply muddles what has already been decided. Among the most influential supporters of this view is Nobel laureate Oliver Williamson, whose transaction cost economics

[2] In fact, those responsible for decision-making at firms end up doing both. Sometimes, they behave instrumentally, sometimes normatively. On occasion, the two get mixed in together.

(TCE) model has found wide-ranging application in explaining organizational and managerial behavior. Despite Williamson's repeated claim that TCE is solely concerned with how "corporate governance structures align with transactions" (Williamson, 2000: 597), he has carefully positioned TCE to explain how competing forces, market and institutional, influence managerial and firm behavior. Within a fundamentally rational system that responds to incentives and costs, there are three well defined groups struggling for control of the firm. The first two are, in fact, part of the firm: (1) shareholders and other suppliers of financial assets who are legitimate profit seekers; and (2) top management, legally the shareholders' agents, but prone, like all of us, to "self-seeking with guile" (Williamson, 1985: 65) and hence capable of pursuing its interests at the expense of shareholders. Group 3 includes broadly everyone involved in making the rules of games, mostly institutional nonmarket players, notably regulators, who inevitably complicate market transactions, often increasing costs as they pursue social ends. (There is a fourth group of stakeholders left out of Williamson's picture – the large repository of other nonmarket players, most prominently civil society organizations, keen to change corporate behavior and/or appropriate value, but with no financial or legal relationship with the firm.)

Williamson does not pretend that aligning the interests of the three groups is either possible or a good idea. This is due to problems of "credible commitments," as well as "unavoidably incomplete contracts" and a horde of additional contractual hazards that make economic transactions inherently messy and difficult (Williamson, 2000). For these reasons, Williamson has consistently opposed inclusion of any stakeholders on corporate boards other than those with financial ownership interests. In "Strategizing, economizing and economic organization" (1991: 86), he wrote: "the first and simplest lesson of transaction cost economics is that corporate governance should be reserved for those who supply or finance specialized assets to the firm. Large numbers of nonspecific groups with which the firm has contracts are thus eliminated from potential stakeholder status immediately."

Williamson's objective is efficiency. Increased stakeholder participation at the board level is, in his view, inefficient, because specialized asset stakeholders pursue objectives incompatible with those of non-financial stakeholders. In Chapter 4, we too argued that multiple stakeholder participation on boards is unproductive, but for quite a different reason: information asymmetry. CEOs and top management are insiders; independent board members are outsiders and inevitably depend on the CEO's presentation of information. In other words, increased stakeholder board participation is not especially inefficient; it's just ineffective (Surowiecki, 2009).

We realize that many academics and civil society organizations feel strongly that broader stakeholder board representation is necessary to ensure that business firms meet their social as well as economic obligations. However, we do not believe that restructuring corporate boards is the best way to create wealth, reduce negative externalities, and increase social benefits. Instead, drawing on John Dewey's concept of democratic pragmatism (1998), social strategy suggests that if we focus on employees and participative decision-making we may find innovative ways to create and sustain economic and social value. We will set out this view later on in this chapter. However, first, we must continue our discussion of conflicting stakeholder objectives and how social strategy addresses this fundamental issue. Social strategy, as we model it, seeks to resolve part, not all, of the conflict among stakeholders groups that wish to appropriate firm economic value by focusing on those specific contexts in which the interests of financial stakeholders, other economic stakeholders, and social stakeholders may coincide.

This effort is anchored in the *strategic decision* to engage in social strategy. Unlike Williamson, we do not treat the transaction as the fundamental unit of firm behavior. Individual transactions acquire meaning as part of an activity – just as a wave of the hand may either be part of saying hello, saying goodbye, or warding off an intruder.[3] Depending on the context, we determine what we take to be the appropriate activity that best explains "how things work." With respect to business organizations, we believe that activity to be strategic decision-making. The decision to select one strategy from a set of alternatives – i.e., a group of economic and social programs with economic and social impacts – embarks management on a concatenation of decisions regarding organizational structures, processes, and transactions. Neither separately nor collectively can we say that the

---

[3] This example follows the form of Gilbert Ryle's famous example of the multiple meanings of a wink of the eye in *The Concept of Mind* (1949).

transactions, the processes, and/or the structures explain firm behavior. Putting aside the epistemological objections of relativists, we will argue that strategy drives behavior and that transactions and transaction costs are just one factor among many that strategic decision-making takes into account.

The strategy decision (deliberate or not) is an ideal. No strategy dictates 100 percent of all action. Nonetheless, in large firms, we expect to see a clear strategy that commits the organization members to specific programs and activities (Andrews, 1971; Grant, 2009). In a best-case scenario, strategy is a set of coherent, integrated and coordinated programs and activities chosen with deliberation by top management and implemented in accordance with a plan that even takes into account crucial contingencies. However, strategy may also turn out to be mostly a melee of actions to which we give sense retrospectively (Weick, 1995). Strategists, since Sun Tzu, have been clear in their preference for the former and its superior results; however, as we discussed in Chapter 4, there are those who believe all explanation is, at best, *post hoc* rationalizing.

We are giving close attention to strategic decision-making, emphasizing the intentional, or purposive, dimension in our efforts to explain the transition that some firms may choose to take from stakeholder management to social strategy. We do not claim that all firm behavior is intentional nor that it even could be – Herbert Simon effectively decided that question in the 1940s. However, we do insist, following Dewey, Weick, and Searle, that collective agents (e.g., top management) have intentions, and that such agents have strategies for acting with respect to other agents (e.g., stakeholders).

In order for one group to have a strategy for action with respect to another group, it must be able to identify what it believes to be the intentions and the strategy of the other group. One of the difficulties firms have in formulating a stakeholder strategy is the diversity of stakeholder groups, including objectives, strategies, and patterns of behavior. We believe that stakeholder management theory, despite the laudable efforts of researchers, has not been able to provide a practicable model in which they can properly define stakeholders, stakeholder legitimacy and aims, and how corporate strategists can and ought to respond. For this reason, we repeat, Jensen, Williamson, and many others have made repeated attacks on stakeholder theory.

We may now return to our discussion of the social strategy decision itself. In addition to all that enters into deciding for or against social strategy, we must add here one additional level that Williamson, too, has considered fundamental to any understanding of firm behavior: the institutional environment. Modern society is best understood as a society of institutions. Formal institutions, such as government, are directed through organizations. Even institutions such as marriage and family are sustained by law, regulation, and other formal institutions and organizations. Business is no exception. Firms are legally constituted with the institutional role of wealth creation. Wealth creation is, like all other organized human action, a social activity; hence, firms are social actors (Dewey, 1926; W. T. Allen, 1992; Searle, 2005). All corporate strategies include both economic action and social action programs. All parties to economic value creation are social actors whose behavior is regulated by social institutions. This is an ineluctable social fact. Or, as John Searle, succinctly states: "Economics as a subject matter, unlike physics or chemistry, is largely concerned with institutional facts" (Searle, 2005: 1). The immersion of economic activity in social facts and social institutions does not mean, however, that all firms pursue a social strategy. On the contrary, most engage in economic (market) strategies which seek to segregate value chain activities both from negative externalities and firm social action programs. Often this is done under the umbrella of corporate social responsibility; and though firms insist that their CSR is strategic and aligned with their business mission and objectives, our research does not sustain this view.

Corporate social action is similar across firms, rather than differentiated, as it would be if social action were truly strategic. This is not surprising. It may just be a straightforward case of what sociologists call institutional isomorphism (DiMaggio and Powell, 1983). Firms behave similarly because "that's just how things are done." Within this isomorphism, the role of strategy is to find competitive advantage through some form of differentiation. For example, organizational routines, such as the strategic planning process, may be quite similar across firms in an industry; nonetheless, it is possible, despite the similarity of the process, that each firm develops a unique strategy. In other cases, where differentiation is not an objective, processes and outcomes will look quite alike. Nike's competitive position in the athletic shoe business does not depend on who manufactures its shoes. In fact, the same factory may work for Nike and its competitors. In our research, we have found that what firms themselves call CSR is not often a source of differentiation. The social action programs of multinationals tend to have similar objectives and organizational structures. Firms engage in CSR because it is expected. Social strategies are exceptional. When successful, they end up becoming the subject of much attention – MRW in Spain, Patagonia in the United States, Cemex in Mexico, and so on.

Unlike CSR, which in its current vogue is overwhelmingly isomorphic, social strategy is likely to follow a deliberate decision to pursue economic value creation and social value creation jointly, to wed efficiency and profits to social benefits. Because social strategy is uncommon, different from what others are doing, it will, as we have argued, customarily emanate from a conscious decision-making process.

The economic and social intentions of social strategy are evident in the divergence of the objectives and programs of social strategy from those of CSR, Freeman's stakeholder management theory, and even social entrepreneurship. Where most definitions of CSR require that the firm meet society's ethical and social demands irrespective of their impact on the firm, social strategy selects specific social issues to work on with the aim of creating economic and social value. Social strategy narrows down the range of stakeholders, and economic value and social value are quantifiable and limited requisites. For its part, stakeholder management theory proposes that firms must first meet the legitimate demands of stakeholders if they hope to be profitable and sustainable. Responding to legitimate stakeholder needs is not, in itself, a guarantee of profitability, but non-response is understood to be a deterrent to success. Stakeholder management theory does not leave it up to the firm to decide which stakeholders are legitimate, and though researchers have labored to explain when different kinds of stakeholders can harm or help the firm, the ethical obligation to respond to legitimate stakeholders does not leave the firm much choice in the matter.

Social strategy selects which market and nonmarket stakeholders the firm can satisfy profitably and organizes social action programs to do so; questions of ethics and other social contributions are managed as well, both inside the social strategy program and as part of general management. Social strategy alone cannot answer all the ethical issues facing a firm; it does indicate, nonetheless, a commitment to social value creation, and may well, independently of the motivations for the commitment, inculcate habits of mind and behavior conducive to ethical and socially responsive action.

Finally, social entrepreneurship has quite a different approach to stakeholders and economic and social value creation from social strategy. While social entrepreneurs who market to the poor often depend heavily on aid from governments and NGOs as well as on investors willing to accept below-average returns (Karnani, 2007), social strategy pursues a defined social good for a stakeholder or group of stakeholders as well as improved firm performance vis-à-vis competitors.

The source of the distinctions between social strategy's approach to stakeholders and CSR, stakeholder theory, and social entrepreneurship is grounded in the strategic decision to treat social action in the same way as the firm would any other source of competitive advantage. Social strategy is a strategic option, not an obligation. Like other forms of strategy, social strategy is not a response to stakeholder demands or ethical concerns, but rather looks to business opportunities that are aligned with some stakeholders' social preferences. Stakeholders' rights do not depend on the firm's strategy, but are granted by law and social institutions. The decision to engage in social strategy neither limits nor changes stakeholders' rights. Of course, it is hoped that by satisfying a stakeholder group with social action that the ethical and legal scales will be tilted in favor of social good, but there is no guarantee that this will be the case. Social strategy is intended solely for those stakeholders for whom management can develop social action programs that help the firm meet *both* the economic value and social value criteria set out in the corporate strategy. The firm, we repeat, may also choose to engage in other social activities (e.g., philanthropy unrelated to the firm's business mission) for the benefit of stakeholders that create social value and provide no economic gain. The same managers that decide in favor of social strategy may also choose not to pursue businesses and opportunities they believe unethical. Given that social and ethical concerns are often a key reason for managers to select social strategy, we believe it is probable that the same managers are more likely to reject unethical opportunities. One crucial question remains regarding our discussion of the social strategy decision and stakeholders: "which stakeholder(s) defines what constitutes a social attribute, social good, or benefit?" Without a clear definition, we cannot determine whether or not social value has been created. In Chapter 12, "Measurement and evaluation", we discuss how this critical task can be done.

Perhaps a brief summary of our argument up to this point would be useful. Aligning the interests of shareholders and other financial stakeholders, value chain stakeholders, and nonmarket stakeholders is a challenging and complex task. Transaction cost economics rejects such alignment as inefficient and, hence, unnecessary. Numerous management scholars disagree with Williamson on this point. They do not believe that shareholder value maximization necessarily leads to the most efficient and best outcomes. Neither do we. At the same time, however, we cannot assent to the principal contending view – stakeholder management theory – which seeks an enlightened collaboration between interested parties, but has yet to demonstrate why and how it will occur (Jensen, 2002).

Accordingly, our goal in this chapter is to offer, through social strategy, one way of aligning more (not all) of the various interest groups with a legitimate concern in what business firms do. We recognize that our approach will not satisfy many management scholars, and that social strategy is not the answer to all the negative externalities that arise from business behavior, nor can it resolve many of our most pressing social problems. We do, however, believe that the way social strategy models strategic decision-making and its encouragement of employee participation in firm decision-making processes will make a significant contribution to ameliorating social ills, meeting the legitimate concerns of both market and nonmarket stakeholders, and to organizational justice.

We have divided the work of presenting this case into several sections. First, we review Sumantha Ghoshal's sociological approach to stakeholders, and make some preliminary comments on how firms can work effectively with nonmarket stakeholders. We then engage in an extended discussion of nonmarket stakeholders, including defining who they are and explaining the relationship of social strategy to political strategy. In so doing, we flesh out the central role of employees and their participation in social strategy. In the final part of the chapter, we present a model for nonmarket analysis.

Sumantha Ghoshal's social capital approach to stakeholder management

Many multinationals operate in industries that affect all of us, everywhere in the world, making them the target of continual attention and demands. In the pharmaceutical, finance, and energy industries, the institutional arrangements, the rules of the game, are often challenged. In order to defend the firm's and/or the industry's interests, firms and industry organizations are required to ally with and/or confront multiple parties. For example, in the United States, recently much of the federal government's time and energy has been spent in myriad versions and multiple rewrites of healthcare legislative proposals that will directly affect the pharmaceutical industry. Firms, industry lobbyists, regulators, NGOs, and other interest groups press their respective causes. In addition to market forces, institutional history, law, custom, political power, and a host of other factors get thrown into the mix. Finding common ground has become close to impossible.

Stakeholder theorists have long argued that political dispute and acrimony destroy value and that corporations are largely at fault. If firms would only assess the public good and then strive to align legitimate interests, they would find that trust and cooperation would ensue to everyone's benefit, including the firm's shareholders. The conciliation of conflicting interests and groups through trust and cooperation has found enthusiasts in multiple academic fields, among them evolutionary biology (Nowak, 2006), sociology (Fukuyama, 1995) and, of course, game theory (Axelrod, 1984). In management, the most influential proponent has been Sumantha Ghoshal.

Ghoshal, best known for having developed with Christopher Bartlett their influential typology of MNE organizational strategies, devoted much of the later part of his work to remonstrating against the doleful influence of "amoral" theories such as agency theory and transaction cost economics on management practice (Ghoshal and Moran, 1996; Ghoshal *et al.*, 1999; Ghoshal, 2005). He called for the development of a new management theory and practice that reflected the vital role of social capital and social networks in firm success; he sought to reconstitute governance and value appropriation in accord with what he believed was the real contribution to value creation of the various participants in the firm. He argued that management theories, particularly in strategy, ought to reflect a more broad and realistic notion of human nature than that offered by liberal economics and transaction cost economics (TCE).

As a strategic management professor, Ghoshal pursued a similar agenda to stakeholder theory without using the term; he seemed apprehensive about his work being tossed into the business and society sack and labeled "not serious." Be that as it may, Ghoshal's objections to TCE were grounded in what he believed was the theory's self-fulfilling prophecy in which corporate governance was founded on the principle of defending shareholders from management's "self-seeking with guile" (Williamson, 1975: 26). Once distrust is institutionalized in corporate governance, Ghoshal argued, and self-seeking behavior is assumed to be the norm, then inevitably we find such behavior. In arguing that moral conduct by individuals was no less likely than self-interest seeking, Ghoshal wrote (2005, 83): "If both common sense and empirical evidence suggest the contrary, why does the pessimistic model of people as purely self-interested beings still dominate management-related theories? The answer lies not in the evidence, but in the ideology."

The ideology at fault, he argued, was liberalism, and he placed the blame squarely on Milton Friedman and Oliver Williamson for insisting that the role of ethics in human behavior be left out of economics in favor of strict reliance on self-interest. In place of self-interest, Ghoshal offered social capital. As firms, through their managers, build social capital, and earn the confidence and trust of market and nonmarket actors, the possibility of success is enhanced. This, as Ghoshal wrote in one his last articles, "Bad management theories are destroying good management practices" (2005), was a more accurate picture of how firms actually behave than Williamson's TCE.

Social strategy is sympathetic to the legitimate concerns raised by Ghoshal. In the design of organizational arrangements, we agree that TCE's assumption of self-interest seeking with guile is too narrow, as is the view that efficiency is the only proper objective of management. We are hardly alone in arguing that neither self-interest nor efficiency operates as theorized. Granovetter (1985) rejects both under-socialized (e.g., TCE) and over-socialized models of economic behavior in favor of embeddedness. TCE is an under-socialized explanation because it assumes that firms simply exist because they are efficient. Granovetter cites

the remarkable fact ... that in Oliver Williamson's work ... *how* firms come to exist receives no attention. Instead, it is assumed that firms emerge when needed to reduce transaction costs. In the functionalist style of the New Institutional Economics, this emergence is taken to be automatic.

But economic institutions do not emerge automatically in response to economic needs. Rather, they are constructed by individuals whose action is both facilitated and constrained by the structures and resources available in social networks in which they are embedded. (Granovetter, 1992: 6–7)

Institutional theory and embeddedness help to explain why the transaction is not the proper unit of analysis, and why strategy is. Strategy is the collective statement of intentions and a pattern of behavior by a group of individuals, members of an organization whose legitimacy, or right to exist, is socially determined. At some level, which we call strategy, firm intentions and behavior must be coordinated, consciously or not. Strategic decision-making and behavior are complex because first, the members of the firm will have multiple and often conflicting objectives; and, second, because the firm is embedded in various social networks (of stakeholders) that make multiple and often conflicting demands.

Ghoshal intuitively understood this. However, in offering an over-socialized view of the firm, he grants trust and cooperation too smooth a path. In fact, we believe the potential for both conflict and cooperation to be broader and more complex than either Ghoshal, Freeman's stakeholder theory, or TCE has tackled.

If we are to analyze cooperation and conflict in greater depth, we will require a careful enumeration of the actors and the interests they defend. Herbert Simon, in *Administrative Behavior*, uses a deceptively simple issue, like the opening of a new street to demonstrate the multiple questions of values and interests raised by actors (Simon, 1947: 6). Firm decisions on issues as small as who gets a parking space and as large as a merger, provide exponential opportunities for parties to negotiate, bargain, buy, sell, appropriate, make, and unmake alliances and even to take ethical decisions that benefit their parties rather than themselves. In contrast to the public administration organizations that Simon studied, business firms are not bound to serve all the population, and therefore may choose not to take into account the claims and needs of stakeholders who dislike the firm's values and products. Not only may the satisfaction of one stakeholder's desires conduce to the offense of another stakeholder, the success of some products – those targeted to teenagers, for example – may actually feed on the fierce opposition of stakeholder groups. Such stakeholder groups are part of the complex social networks firms are embedded in. Understanding how those networks function, assessing all the players and their interests, is essential to the practice of social strategy. The environment in which firms operate can be neatly divided into market and nonmarket. Obviously, the nonmarket part of the world is far larger, with more numerous and more diverse stakeholders. We now turn to the nonmarket environment; much of our discussion will focus on examples.

Working with nonmarket stakeholders

In Chapter 3 we acknowledged the attractive clarity of economic value creation (profit = income−costs) as opposed to the uncertainties inherent in the day-to-day management of firms, in which managers wrangle to control assets in the pursuit of multiple, competing, and often hard-to-measure objectives (Simon, 1947; Thompson, 1967). We also recognize that the discipline of putting profit first can be the right medicine when firms lose their way and money. In such circumstances, no one will fault a CEO for dropping everything else to focus solely on the profit equation, slashing costs and eliminating unprofitable units, with discretionary spending the first to go. Moreover, as we have learned once again in the Great Recession (low munificence accompanied by profound hostility), CSR starts with jobs.

When working with nonmarket stakeholders, the managerial perception of risk is enhanced by the hard work that must go into aligning objectives (e.g., Leche Ram and UNESCO from Chapter 4). However, once this obstacle is overcome, the support acquired from stakeholders in the nonmarket environment can acquire a powerful sense of commitment and purpose. As an example, we can take a case of strategic sponsorship: the famous Texaco Metropolitan Opera broadcasts. Texaco (ChevronTexaco as of 2001 and Chevron after 2005) sponsored live radio Saturday programs of the Metropolitan Opera over 63 years (1940–2004), carried by over 300 stations in 40 countries, with more than 10 million listeners. The broadcasts received over 60 awards, including 9 Peabody Awards as well as a Presidential Arts and Humanities Award from President Reagan in 1983. When ChevronTexaco terminated its participation in 2004, thousands wrote to the company and to the Public Broadcasting Service in protest.

An initial one-year agreement was approved by Texaco's board in 1940 following the storm raised in New York by the forced resignation of Texaco President Torkild Rieber over his relationship with Nazi Germany.[4] In 1941, the board gladly renewed the agreement, convinced that in a hostile and complex war environment Texaco needed all the goodwill it could get.

Texaco soon discovered that it was good business as well. Forty years later, in declarations to the press in 1981, Kerry King, Texaco's senior vice president for public affairs, boasted that in the four decades of the partnership, Texaco had spent the extraordinary sum of US$55 million on the opera broadcasts. King explained why. "The opera audience is a very loyal one. We've made studies over the years that show purchases of Texaco products are directly related to our sponsorship, although the broadcasts carry no commercial product messages. Besides, many of our 400,000 shareholders own stock precisely because they love opera" (Turner, 1981).

During the course of its sponsorship of the Metropolitan Opera, Texaco decided that there was the potential for a social strategy that included nonmarket stakeholders (civil society organizations, the government, the general public) as well as shareholders and customers. By the 1950s Texaco began to measure the economic value created by the project, using the most fundamental market indicators – shareholder and customer satisfaction – as well as general reputation and government relations indicators. Once Texaco saw that the project was creating economic and social value, management increased the investment, with the "Met in Schools" program. Texaco also funded new sound technology for the Metropolitan Opera and launched in 1960 the "Independent Texaco Metropolitan Opera Radio Network" to expand the Saturday radio broadcasts across the United States. Live telecasts from the Metropolitan Opera began in 1977 with Puccini's *La Bohème*, conducted by James Levine and featuring Luciano Pavarotti and Renata Scotto (Metropolitan Opera Guild, 2008). But in 2004, with the decline in opera attendance and ChevronTexaco in financial difficulties (high hostility), the firm pulled out. The consumer gasoline business had changed, customer loyalties had shifted and, just as importantly, the shareholder relations argument had vanished along with the idyllic concept of lifetime investment in blue-chip companies. Patricia E. Yarrington, ChevronTexaco's vice-president for public and government affairs, announced the company's decision in a polite,

---

[4] *Time* magazine, August 26, 1940.

but unflinchingly direct statement, "As our business has evolved, we believe it is important to focus more of our resources directly with the countries and markets where we do business."[5]

What began as a public relations necessity and became a profitable social strategy ended when ChevronTexaco saw that the mutually reinforcing business and social benefits had expired. While opera lovers were disappointed, ChevronTexaco shareholders did not protest. The process was handled correctly by ChevronTexaco. To assure that New York politicians and powerful community decision-makers were not offended, the company funded in perpetuity its popular "Met in Schools" program and its classical music scholarship program. As we have insisted from the outset, undoing a social program is not the same as discontinuing a product or service.

The logic of social strategy and the nonmarket environment

The Texaco-Metropolitan Opera sponsorship began as a textbook example of crisis management and social action predicated upon strategic necessities: an angry and powerful nonmarket stakeholder had to be assuaged. However, the straightforward public relations element was transformed into social strategy. At the same time, the Texaco Metropolitan Opera became embedded in institutional arrangements common to large sponsorship projects. Inevitably, the expectations of management and employees, customers and nonmarket stakeholders (including the management of the Metropolitan Opera), begin to exert significant influence on decision-making. In just a few years, the enormously successful sponsorship effectively became part of the corporate landscape. The Texaco Metropolitan Opera Broadcast itself was now an institution with a life of its own, resistant to change and demanding of its resource provider.

Decades later, the 2001 merger shifted the institutional structure on which the sponsorship depended, and with the post-internet downturn, the new ChevronTexaco management team felt free to undo the commitment. In other words, the resources allocated to the social action program that had become part of normal operations – i.e., the Metropolitan Opera sponsorship and the additional programs that

[5] www.nytimes.com/2003/05/21/arts/chevrontexaco-to-stop-sponsoring-met-s-broadcasts.html.

had emerged during the six decades of the relationship between the organizations – was only terminated by a shock to the system. We are not surprised by this. We do not need a "theory of attention" to understand that most firm activities are taken for granted because management does not have time for everything; for ChevronTexaco, the Metropolitan Opera sponsorship had been an insignificant investment with a prudent, measurable return for decades.

Obviously, not all sponsorships, nor all nonmarket stakeholder relationships go as smoothly as Texaco Metropolitan Opera. Insight into more common complex stakeholder situations can be had by considering perhaps the most frequently employed generic differentiation social strategy: "buy local." The logic presented to the consumer is that though the price for the local good may be higher than the comparable "imported" good, the local producer/vendor is providing something extra to the community, town, nation, etc., not to speak of the lowered carbon emissions from reduced distances for transportation. Let us take as given that some consumers are convinced and buy local, while for others "buy local" is just an excuse for less efficient enterprises. The inefficiency objectors are irrelevant for the buy-local social strategy so long as there are enough customers.

Until quite recently, buy-local campaigns have had trouble attracting customers in the United States, most notably in the auto industry. However, buy-local campaigns associated with additional product and service features – e.g., the eat-local movement – are beginning to have more success. Customer segments are defined much more precisely; government support is available (e.g., permitting the establishment of farmers' markets in town squares and other desirable locations); and certification processes of local product origin and quality (e.g., smaller and more specialized wine growing regions in France, Spain, and Italy) have been put in place, and so on.

In social strategy, as in all forms of strategy, segmentation plays a central role. Texaco's social strategy targeted well-educated, liberal New Yorkers. There was no obvious downside to the strategy other than an assumable investment. This may, however, also limit the upside when compared to more aggressive social strategies that deliberately displease selected stakeholder groups while pleasing selected customers. Consumer goods companies have been practicing this form of social strategy for several decades. Benetton's famous "Enemies" campaign and Mel Gibson's *The Passion of the Christ* offended the religious beliefs of millions of Christians, Muslims, and Jews. It might be fair to say that many more were offended than pleased. This, however, was part of the plan.

Both the Benetton ad campaign and Gibson's movie were successes. Success is measured by two indicators. First, sales. Benetton's ad campaign was consistent with the firm's strategy of drawing attention to its renegade provocateur image essential to bringing into the store its target customer group. Gibson's film grossed over US$600 million worldwide, making it the highest box office R-rated film, an incredible achievement for a movie that was made in Aramaic, Latin, and Hebrew and distributed with subtitles. The second indicator is how much (or little) damage was done by the offended stakeholders. As regards the *The Passion of the Christ*, offended stakeholders helped to hype the movie and, with its success, assured Mr. Gibson that he would find ample funding for his next film, the equally controversial *Apocalypto*. With regard to Benetton, the potential threats included consumer boycotts or local movements to close stores. Neither happened, and for the clothing franchise, the campaign was a plus. Interestingly, a different Benetton ad did serious damage in the United States. Prisoners on death row were featured in the campaign. Families of prisoners and civil rights groups were outraged; the backlash was sufficient to move Sears to close down its line of Benetton clothes. Benetton was unrepentant, and interpreted Sears' action as a demonstration that Sears had never been the right venue for the company. In other situations, offended stakeholders may take recourse to legal action, lobbying for regulation, etc. For the most part, however, boycotts and lobbying tend to be unsuccessful when the firm's customers enjoy the difference that is implied by using the product. One of the more intriguing elements of consumer marketing is precisely the playing off of a desired customer segment against other stakeholders.

For consumer goods firms like Wal-Mart or P&G with a customer base that embraces most market segments, social strategy presents far greater complications. Wal-Mart has found that environmental action programs, which reduce environmental impact and at the same time reduce costs, are extraordinarily effective, while even seemingly uncontroversial social action projects – e.g., the decision to ban or censor selected music CDs – have offended consumers and been criticized by free speech NGOs and the media (Ostroy, 2009).

When this happens, the answer is not simply to back down immediately. Neither customers nor employees are anxious to see that the firm's social commitments and values will be tossed aside at the first sign of dissent. Before taking action, management must evaluate whether it agrees with the criticism. If so, the response should be a gracious acknowledgment of error and announcement of the adjusted policy. If management believes it is right, it must then evaluate the net effect, long term, on revenue, reputation, and stakeholder relationships. When the expected outcome is negative, management must then consider that cost in terms of the importance of the social policy to key internal stakeholders and other loyal customers.

Sorting out the upside and the downside where there are many market and nonmarket stakeholders may not be easy. Wal-Mart continues to come under pressure for its decisions regarding what books, music, and movies it features, censors, and even sometimes bans. However, the firm has decided that it wants to be in the position to decide what popular culture entertainment it will carry, and does not see a threat to its business. In the same way, Wal-Mart continues to sell weaponry and ammunition despite criticism. Loving to hate Wal-Mart and shopping there at the same time has become a normal part of US culture.

Other stakeholder situations can be far more difficult to work out. Michael Eisner's famous decision at Disney to cancel distribution of Michael Moore's *Fahrenheit 9/11*, produced by Disney's Miramax unit, was engulfed in a morass of stakeholder conflicts.

The story begins with brothers Harvey and Bob Weinstein, Hollywood superstar producers of independent films who had sold Miramax to Disney and remained on to run it. The Weinsteins funded Moore's film, looking both to create economic value and social value. (The social contribution of the documentary was to be a serious appraisal of the US's involvement in Iraq and Afghanistan; though much of it turned out to be insinuations regarding the Bush family's relationship to the Saudi Arabian ruling family (Stewart, 2005)).

During filming Eisner advised the Weinsteins to shut the film down; later, in post-production, Eisner angrily told the Weinsteins in April 2004 that Disney would not distribute the film. The Weinsteins wisely entered the film in the Cannes Film Festival, and when in June *Fahrenheit 9/11* won the Golden Palm Award for best film, they felt sure that they had Eisner trapped and that he would concede defeat.

Media conglomerates spend millions every year promoting their movies at Cannes, Venice, and the Oscars in the hope of gaining artistic and institutional legitimacy. Not distributing a Golden Palm Award winner would be unthinkable.

But not for Michael Eisner. He was personally offended that the Weinsteins had gone ahead with production of *Fahrenheit 9/11* despite his direct order in 2003 to shut the project down. But personal issues alone would not have been enough for Eisner to refuse to distribute a film that he knew would make money. Disney's relationship with Florida Governor Jeb Bush was at risk as well; Disney World is a Florida company and the film was a direct attack on the Bush family. Disney executives were also worried that the movie would anger key customer segments (Stewart, 2005).

Though Eisner said no to Disney distributing the film, he did not finally shelve *Fahrenheit 9/11*. That would badly damage Disney's reputation with key players in the film industry. The press in the US and Europe had already begun to portray Eisner and Disney as crude censors. Eisner's decision not to distribute the film had been leaked by Miramax, and on May 5, 2004, *The New York Times* had run a front-page headline: "Disney is Blocking Distribution of a Movie that Criticizes Bush" (Stewart, 2005: 520).

Eisner's way out was to permit Miramax to buy back the distribution rights to the film, and *Fahrenheit 9/11* was released via Lions Gate. *Fahrenheit 9/11* grossed nearly US$250 million worldwide, making it the highest-earning documentary in the history of the film industry. Total revenue for the film, including DVD sales, went to well over US$500 million.

Despite the criticism and the lost revenue, Eisner probably made the right decision. There was no easy calculation for him to make. Taking the right decision required first making an accurate reading of Disney's multiple and complex relationships with powerful market and nonmarket stakeholders, and then finding a solution that would protect these relationships without serious financial damage and that would also be consistent with Disney corporate values and strategy. In "DisneyWar," James B. Stewart (2005) describes Michael Eisner as angry and frustrated by the demanding task of managing a battery of market and nonmarket stakeholders, each with their own interests. Eisner's difficulties in the *Fahrenheit 9/11* affair pointed the way for Roy Disney to press ahead in his ongoing challenge to Eisner's leadership. In March 2004, Eisner was forced to give up his board chairmanship. On March 13, 2005, he was removed as CEO.

Michael Eisner was a strong CEO who had taken over a company in bad shape, fixed it up, and increased shareholder value. Eisner was proud that he knew what the market wanted, and that he knew how to deliver. He felt comfortable dealing with the market. Like many CEOs, he believed that first and foremost he had to grow the business. He saw that the motivations and objectives of value chain stakeholders such as suppliers and employees (Hillman and Keim, 2001) are customarily aligned with shareholders and management in growing the business. In this "business as usual" scenario, conflicts between value chain stakeholders are mostly about price and wages – the mechanics of wealth creation and appropriation – and not about what businesses to be in, nor how to run those businesses. When firms grow, everyone is happy. Or almost everyone. Roy Disney wanted a Disney like the one he grew up with, but he lost control of the company to Eisner, was stripped of all operational responsibilities, and was only able to strike back at Eisner after he floundered. Eisner thought Roy Disney was an old fool. He could not understand what he was doing. Roy Disney behaved like a nonmarket stakeholder.

Nonmarket stakeholders present a much more complex, less understood challenge than market stakeholders. Nonmarket stakeholders are moved by motivations and objectives quite different from market (value chain) stakeholders. They rarely share management's concern for growing the business and have their own social and political objectives and agendas to manage. We should keep in mind here that individuals may have conflicting objectives. The classic example, once again, is the customer of Wal-Mart who, when queried, confesses to being "anti-Wal-Mart" and may even be a member of an organization that is fighting Wal-Mart on issues such as store location and HR policy. This is true, as well, for Microsoft, Telefónica, and other market-dominant firms whose persona in the world is sufficiently complex to create conflicting sentiments even in its own customers ... and perhaps even in its founders and owners. Roy Disney had no qualms about putting the company values before profits. If Disney was worth saving, it was only to make sure that it was the company he thought his uncle would have wanted.

Having analyzed a simple stakeholder situation (the Texaco Metropolitan Opera that lasted for sixty-three years and came to an amicable close) and an usually complex one (the Disney–Miramax battle that undid Eisner's support in the film industry and paved the way for Roy Disney to win their bitter dispute), we would like to make some preliminary conclusions. In both cases, market and nonmarket stakeholders were important. For Texaco, it was important to demonstrate that the sponsorship created economic and social value; the firm took care with both market and nonmarket stakeholders. Eisner did a good job with market and nonmarket stakeholders except for one group – industry stakeholders. These industry stakeholders are not quite market stakeholders, but not quite nonmarket ones either. Influential producers, directors, writers, agents, and columnists, most of whom had no direct economic relation with Disney, could have had an enormous impact on Eisner's and Disney's legitimacy. When Eisner's legitimacy was attacked, it made it possible to attack him in the name of defending Disney's legitimacy.

This description of stakeholders is intended to underscore the complexity of the relationship between market and nonmarket environments as depicted in "The integrated view of business and social strategy" (Figure 1.2). As we have seen, firms generally feel on firm ground in the market environment, but when it comes to the nonmarket environment, managing the multiple and diverse objectives and behavioral norms of nonmarket stakeholders demands resources and capabilities that many firms have not invested in sufficiently. Among the most obvious shortcomings are the compartmentalization of tasks in organizational units and insufficient coordination.

Often, managing nonmarket stakeholders is divided up into community relations, which handles NGOs and local authorities; investor relations, responsible not just for shareholders, but also for keeping investment bankers and rating agencies happy; government relations, in charge of lobbying and negotiating with government lawmakers and regulators; a CSR unit that manages ethics and compliance; and a foundation that distributes money to worthy causes. Corporate-level responsibility for these functions can rest in corporate communications or strategic planning; the chief corporate counsel may add some of this work to the legal department's duties; and so on.

In highly regulated basic service industries, the government relations department has sometimes been located in the CEO's office by a top-level direct report. The prominence of lobbyists during the Bush Administration and the growth of European Union bureaucracy in Brussels over the last decade gave additional incentives for CEO involvement in political strategy. Government intervention in the financial crisis and the recession accentuated what was already a trend toward far greater involvement of large firms in the political arena.

Researchers in management have been attentive to these developments, and firm political strategy has become an active area of research (Hillman *et al.*, 2004). One innovative approach is to model politics, in democracies, as a market in which firms and stakeholders measure where, when, and how to compete (Bonardi *et al.*, 2005).

Unfortunately, as we have explained, many firms still lack the organizational structure, resources, and capabilities to coordinate management of diverse nonmarket stakeholders. This presents a serious challenge for MNEs that may be considering social strategy. For large firms, the market for politics should be integrated with the market for social action projects as part of the firm's competitive strategy. In this way, the firm will increase the prospects for pleasing customers as it satisfies nonmarket stakeholders.

Clearly, more effective management of stakeholders will benefit all firms, not just those that decide on social strategy. With this in mind, we take a step back from our general discussion of stakeholder management to look at a fundamental question that must be answered: which individuals, groups or organizations merit the label of nonmarket stakeholder?

Who qualifies as a nonmarket stakeholder?

We are all nonmarket stakeholders when it comes to multinationals. The same person who works for a large multinational and believes that the firm is, on balance, a good corporate citizen, may also claim to be shocked by the way multinationals behave. Though we are all nonmarket stakeholders, only some of us are involved in organized stakeholder activity. But that number has increased as the number of nonmarket stakeholder organizations we belong to has grown. As we have mentioned on several occasions, NGOs, local, national, and transnational, have become far better organized, more professional and aggressive. In centers of political power, e.g., Washington and Brussels, NGOs have become a significant lobbying force, often working against what are termed "the interests of big business." Multinationals are accustomed to having their social and environmental projects dismissed as a cover-up for their dastardly deeds by NGOs, whose press units have learned how to get their stories onto television and in the newspapers. The blogosphere has intensified the anti-business, anti-multinational campaign as well.

Leaving aside the markedly negative portrait of multinationals, empirical research on multinational corporate responsibility turns out, unsurprisingly, to reveal that most firms engage in both good and bad behavior, and that behavior across divisions and departments of multinationals is hardly uniform (Strike *et al.*, 2006). At the same time, the reasons management at multinationals give for choosing to engage in social action are varied and complex (Basu and Palazzo, 2008). As in the Texaco Metropolitan Opera case, the first impulse may come from a simple crisis-management stimulus-response. More often, however, strategic opportunity, institutional expectations, and market structure (Diamond, 2009; Fernández-Kranz and Santaló, 2007) influence firm decision-making. And, of course, ethics and values may be key motivators.

Nonetheless, in the press, in the popular culture, it is standard fare to treat top management at multinationals as if they were motivated by such greed that profit is debased. The distinction between profit and greed is essential to social strategy. Profit is the result of value creation; it is both an economic and a social good. Greed is a personality trait which drives human beings to pursue wealth with scant regard for the law, ethics, or harm inflicted. Profit is an economic success indicator, in itself a positive event; greed, however, is deplorable, always.

It would be fair to say that firms and management are more suspect today than in 1976 when Silk and Vogel lamented the sad state of business ethics. This is not to say that overall behavior is actually worse, though it seems clear that stakeholder perception has worsened. From a social strategy point of view, this is an opportunity for those multinationals that can take the heat, understand the current environment, and have the will to innovate.

The stakeholder environment

Researchers in stakeholder management theory over the last quarter-century can justly claim that their work is founded on solid ethics and irrefutable evidence of negative externalities. They argue persuasively that the hundreds of millions of poor who have not benefited from economic wealth creation and, in fact, have often been victims of development, merit redress and assistance in attaining a better life. Stakeholder theory, moreover, stepped in when economists and strategists did not respond either with sufficient interest or compassion.

In the last two decades, in addition to Sumantha Ghoshal's sociological approach, there have been a number of efforts to describe the firm as a participant in a social contract. Donaldson and Dunfee's (1999) integrative social contract theory situates the firm within a network of universal standards, much like the UN Global Compact. This work is notable for its insistence on combining a strong philosophical foundation with applied ethics. Often such Rawlsian approaches are criticized for glossing over the difficulties of implementation; Donaldson and Dunfee avoid this error, though, on occasion, the examples chosen don't hold up. Scherer and Palazzo (2007) go a step further and embed multinationals in a reconfigured network of global democratic institutions, though it is difficult to see how their model could work.

On the table there are many other new ideas on how to reconstruct the rules of capitalism in pursuit of greater procedural and distributive justice (Husted, 1998). Nonetheless, despite academic work, despite recurring financial crises and the severe recession, the vastly superior position of shareholder interests with respect to other stakeholders has not been shaken. Though President Obama may call firm behavior shameless, and George Clooney may win an Academy Award for his portrait of a corporate villain in "Up in the Air," the rules of the game do not appear to be in question. Activists and Hollywood superstars may portray multinationals as economic Medusas, loyal to no nation, corrupters of governments, bound by no law, squeezing the blood out of workers, bowing to the god of efficiency ... and it makes no difference.

And why should it? The portrait itself is neither real nor representative. It is a pastiche of the worst among us and the worst consequences. It is the worst of all worlds. Even the winners in the game take their shots at "the system." One frequent argument, made by George Soros (1998), among others, is that the economic and media power of multinational corporations inundates public space and truncates effective dialog, experiment, and change. It is difficult to resist a touch of sarcasm when Mr. Soros, one of the world's wealthiest men, distances himself from what he has helped devise and made him rich; nonetheless, inadvertently we can read his work as a reminder of the difficult predicament multinationals are in. First, they are asked by their shareholders *and by their home governments* to create wealth. Their great success, in turn, becomes evidence for their complicity in the world's social ills. Accordingly, they are asked to do penance by tacking on to their corporate mission the task of fixing the world's problems. CEOs have little choice but to agree and announce that their firms are paragons of virtue and are spending millions on CSR.

In all this noise, is there any good news, any worthwhile proposal? The answer is, fortunately, yes. Perhaps the most promising idea is an old one that fell out of favor as the markets became enamored of the CEO as savior and of transformational and charismatic leadership, while at the same time labor union affiliation declined, job mobility increased, and each individual began to be seen as his or her own small enterprise. We are speaking of participatory management.

Multinationals headquartered in democracies in the developed world are being asked again to reorganize their decision-making processes to empower employees: in a democracy, key institutions should be run with democratic principles in mind, including business firms (Bennis and Slater, 1964; Mintzberg, 1983; D. Collins, 1997).

Earlier, we argued that increased board representation for non-financial stakeholders, including employees, has been found ineffective. One reason may be that democratizing the organization at the board level is too little, too late; and it is not a substitute for the lack of participation in decision-making in those areas that directly affect employees. We know that firms devote an inordinate amount of time on what is called "our most important asset" and "the source of competitive advantage" and so on. This is not participatory management, or to use our preferred term, participatory decision-making. In our research, we have also argued that social strategy is more likely to be adopted by companies with greater participative decision-making. We also believe that social strategy is more likely to be successful in firms in which participatory decision-making is practiced. Testing this hypothesis is a significant challenge, and a key element in our research agenda. But as we move ahead on that work, in the interim we can provide the reasoning behind the proposition that participatory decision-making is positively correlated with the adoption of social strategy and with its success.

First, the quite rational desire not to be perceived as a mere instrument of greed is a strong motivator. Instinctively, CEOs and corporate communications departments take an upbeat approach as they try to convince the world that as they create wealth, they look out for those who are less fortunate. Today, in the standard CEO interview on CNN, Bloomberg, etc., the CEO first defends the firm's business strategy before launching into the obligatory CSR and corporate values speech. This would be fine, but the approach is neither strategic nor convincing because of the annoying problem of all CEOs saying the same things and firm after firm applauding itself for the same social programs to build housing, to educate the poor, and to eradicate hunger, AIDS, cancer, and illiteracy – and all of it made possible by committed company employees who dedicate thousands of hours of their time, some of it even paid for by the company, etc.

When we tell top management that their own employees don't buy it, they respond by showing us their own in-house studies that "prove" that their employees are generally content, committed, and proud of the firm's CSR programs.

And we tell top management that the employees are telling them what they think they want to hear. There is ample evidence to support this argument. A recent Wyatt Watson report on employee satisfaction across the US is titled "Looking toward Recovery: Realigning Rewards and Re-engaging Employees" (WorldatWork, 2009). Among the most telling indicators of the disjunction between what employers believe and say and what employees believe and say involves what is called EVP (or Employee Value Proposition). EVP encompasses all those things that employers offer to employees, including pay, training, benefits, workplace environment, promotion, etc. It seems that 73 percent of US employers believe EVP to be *informal* (implicit and evolving) while 74 percent of employees take EVP to be *formal* (articulated, documented, and communicated). Bluntly stated, employers and employees are in two different worlds.

The data is not bad just because of the recession. Another Watson Wyatt (2007) report in 2006, at the height of the boom, found that 45 percent of employees did not believe that management behaved in a manner consistent with the company's core values.

This US data from a global consultancy finds an illuminating complement in a 2004 study published in *Organization Science* "Guanxi Practices and Trust in Management: A Procedural Justice Perspective"

(Chen *et al.* 2004). Using a combined survey and experimental methodology with 140 Chinese Executive MBA students in Shanghai, researchers Chen, Chen, and Xin found that the Guanxi HRM (human resource management) practices were negatively related to employee trust in management. In other words, *informal* Guanxi practices provoked distrust, and, moreover, this distrust could be mediated by perceived procedural *(formal)* justice measures. Among the key findings is the importance given to trust and honesty at the institutional level. Employees are pleased to have good personal relationships with their bosses, but also would like to believe that those at the top mean what they say. Employees realize that their CEOs know the language of good corporate citizenship. CEOs speak of stakeholders as "partners," and that success without the support of the firm's stakeholders would be unthinkable.

One thing employees don't know is that top management, too, are not happy. In the annual CEO surveys of McKinsey and PriceWaterhouse, CEOs complain year after year of having to do more and more politicking and PR and that they long to spend more time on "just doing business." For most CEOs, satisfying ever more demanding shareholders is more than enough to do. Stakeholder management is perceived mostly as demanding, unrewarding work that is fundamentally handholding to assure annoying interested parties that the firm cares about them. Significant differences between stakeholders are glossed over, starting with the conflicting objectives of shareholders, employees, suppliers, regulators, NGOs, community groups, and so on.

For those CEOs and other top management executives who would like this to change, employee participation in decision-making is the right place to start. We should not underestimate the repercussions. Step 1 will not sit well with many. Top management privileges (including pay, though pay is not the most critical factor) must be stripped down. When CEOs and top management live the kind of privileged lives formerly restricted to royalty and the few who built their own businesses, talk of shared values and teamwork is an insult to the intelligence of ordinary workers whose real pay has not increased in over a decade. Real employee participation begins with HR decisions. Employees are perfectly capable of participating in the selection of the firm's CEO and working with (more likely fighting with) the board's "independent" compensation committee to decide on remuneration. The current system, based on professional HR compensation consultancies, has failed. Operating on the principle that the new CEO of firm X must not make less than the average of the CEOs of similar firms, the result is compensation inflation, applauded by the board, many of whom are top management themselves, dependent on "independent" committees to decide their compensation. Inflation is good for all of them.

Few firms depend on employee participation to decide on top management positions and compensation. Cooperatives like the Mondragon Group in Spain's Basque region have demonstrated how this can be done successfully. Of course, cooperatives are different from shareholder controlled firms, and we do not recommend that firms convert themselves into cooperatives. We are suggesting, however, that there are real opportunities for innovation in corporative governance and that employees are central to taking advantage of those opportunities. Moreover, such innovation in corporate governance may be linked to further democratization in the workplace that social philosophers, such as John Dewey, esteemed essential to developing a more just, creative, and productive society (Dewey, 1927).

This appeal to Dewey's pragmatism will not satisfy those who are already certain that no such transformation of corporate governance is necessary, and who, moreover, believe that any attempt to build sustainable business on democratic practices is as foolish as running a military force by popular vote. Perhaps they will turn out be right, but the risks involved in experimenting with democratic or participatory decision-making in firms are not those of war, and the potential rewards are great.

With this in mind, we briefly discuss Dewey's theory of social action, its extension to business firms, and the potential benefits for stakeholders, specifically employees and nonmarket stakeholders.

Dewey termed his philosophy pragmatic, in the tradition of Pierce and James, for its insistence on always looking at the consequences of a philosophical theory on human action. Human behavior, he decided early on, was only understandable within the context of the behavior of others, and that human beings had a choice: remain ensconced in moral and legal traditions and institutions based on coercion and class struggle or progress through education and democracy. His conception of education shares with Rawls' work, half a century later, the conviction that justice is only possible when all members of society have equal opportunity to share in basic goods of life, and this is only possible when all have access to a proper education.

Up to this point, Dewey's philosophy is a straightforward combination of the natural rights of human beings and social contract theory. His next step, however, is to argue against the priority of conflict over cooperation and against individualism. In *Liberalism and Social Action* (1935), Dewey claims that knowledge is socially constructed and must be subject to scientific and public scrutiny. Democracy provides the political and social structure for resolving conflict of interest – or, what we call in management, stakeholders. Dewey explains:

> of course, there *are* conflicting interests; otherwise there would be no social problems. The problem under discussion is precisely how conflicting claims are to be settled in the interest of the widest possible contribution to the interest of all – or at least the great majority. The method of democracy – insofar as it is that of organized intelligence – is to bring these conflicts out into the open where their special claims can be seen and appraised, where they can be discussed and judged in the light of more inclusive interests than are represented by either of them separately. There is, for example, a clash of interests between munitions manufacturers and most of the rest of the population. The more the respective claims of the two are publically and scientifically weighed, the more likely it is that the public interest will be disclosed and be made effective. (Dewey, 1935: 331)

Dewey's conviction that progress and cooperation are possible is based on historical evolution and the shift in the human condition from scarcity to plenty, the emergence of the scientific method, and the opportunity these achievements offer us to rearrange our legal and social institutions so that cooperation trumps conflict and not the other way around.

> To say that all past historic social progress has been the result of cooperation and not of conflict would be also an exaggeration. But exaggeration against exaggeration, it is the more reasonable of the two. And it is no exaggeration to say that the measure of civilization is the degree in which the method of cooperative intelligence replaces the method of brute conflict. (Dewey, 1935: 332)

How remarkably alike are Ghoshal's and Dewey's respective views. The task, as both see it, is to potentiate conflict resolution and cooperation through the public institution of democracy, which is not merely a set of political institutions, but a way of behaving. Dewey's ideal was that all institutions would be run democratically. He called this a "radical change" both in his academic papers and his essays that would require decades to come to pass.

Dewey's radical change encompasses two factors that Amartya Sen has considered essential to social welfare (1970). First, for democratic decision-making to work, men and women must have the necessary capabilities; second, the empirical evidence must be examined without prejudice. Neither Dewey nor Sen argued that achieving either would be easy or rapid. However, at many firms, the conditions for implementing participatory decision-making are far more favorable than Dewey encountered in the 1930s when the Great Depression had given impetus to communist and fascist totalitarianism; and prospects for success infinitely greater than in the developing world societies Sen sought to benefit.

The members of large multinationals begin with the simple advantage that they are gainfully employed. Most often they have strong general educations as well as specific training. In short, their lives are more secure and their training better than average. As we have argued, they should be top management's most supportive stakeholder. Yet, far too many employees see management as a threat. Instead of allies, they have become mixed-motive stakeholders who share some of the concerns of nonmarket stakeholders.

It is possible that this situation could be turned around through participatory decision-making. Social strategy and participatory decision-making, formerly the province of cooperatives and social entrepreneurs, often a subject of derision among those serious about making money, are strategic options potentially too valuable to ignore. Multinationals and top management feel ever-increasing pressure for social performance, but don't quite know how to achieve it. For the most part, they depend on proclamations of values and increased visibility for higher profile CSR and environmental programs. Unfortunately, employee confidence and consumer confidence continues to decline, while the press, NGOs, governments, and other nonmarket stakeholders express their lack of trust in harsher terms.

Some time ago, we suggested a social strategy for General Motors (GM). When the government took over the firm from management, the job was handled by "The President's Task Force on the Auto Industry," which included no union representatives. The Task Force fired Rick Wagoner and picked another GM executive, Fritz Henderson, to put things right. Henderson spent eight months downsizing and was fired on December 1, 2009, and replaced by the Board Chair.

We believe that the Task Force took the wrong approach. An opportunity was missed to reconstitute the firm, not just rearrange the broken pieces into a smaller, slightly less ugly, less costly mosaic. GM's best chance, as we have argued, was a social strategy, committed employees, and a nation that believed in what GM was trying to achieve. Perhaps serious employee participation in the decision-making process might have helped; perhaps creative commitment might have saved GM. Unhappily, mere downsizing is not the answer.

Finally, we should point out that GM in the United States is one specific case. In Germany, where innovative business-government collaboration has kept workers on the job despite the recent recession, we shall see if firms are able to convert this commitment to stakeholder number one into new competitive advantages in the marketplace and the continued support of nonmarket stakeholders. The German response to the recession has been widely, and deservedly, praised.

A model for nonmarket strategy

In the previous sections of this chapter, we have outlined the factors that have contributed to making stakeholder management a demanding task for firms. We have argued that a commitment to employee participation in decision-making can be the key to opening up the firm to new approaches to collaborating with market and nonmarket stakeholders in search of economic and social value creation.

We turn our attention now directly to political strategy and nonmarket stakeholders. The modern pursuit of political strategy as a means of achieving business goals is an invention of Cosimo de Medici (1389–1464), who built the first true multinational, advised his heirs "to stay out of the public eye," and served in public office solely to protect the family's business. Cosimo de Medici ran his banking business to make money. Like contemporary CEOs of multinationals, he realized that diverse, powerful stakeholders needed to be satisfied. He did not believe that it was the bank's mission to make the world a better place by lending to popes and kings. In lending to the most powerful, there was profit but also inordinate risk. For losses from the very top of the political world, there was no recourse. Moreover, from time to time, operations were undertaken that were deemed necessary though unprofitable. Under Cosimo de Medici and Lorenzo de Medici, the Medici Bank pursued a corporate social strategy that integrated business and social activities that included serving in the Florentine government, philanthropy to the arts and religious institutions, and funding large public celebrations. The people of Florence, as well as Europe's kings and Rome, were courted. The Medici Bank's strategy endured a century, and failed only when later generations of the Medici decided that their mission was either to lead the church or frivolity, rather than the seemingly unexciting affair of risk management.

The principles of nonmarket strategy and stakeholder management have not altered in the last 600 years, and in many places in the world, e.g., Russia, neither have the risks associated with inordinate success. In our analysis, we focus on nonmarket strategy under the assumption that corporations are legal entities that must obey the law while benefiting from its protection.

Nonmarket strategy takes a different approach from CSR.[6] The focus is on strategic issues rather than stakeholder legitimacy and firm obligations. Invariably, multinationals face a daunting array of issues, often paralyzing firm action until either crisis or an unavoidable market problem emerges. The proper approach is to decide on the handful of social and political issues that really matter, preferably before the competition figures it out. At this point, an (ia)³ analysis should be performed for each critical issue (see Figure 7.1 below).

The (ia)³ framework is built around the analysis of *issues, actors, interests, arenas, information,* and *assets.* As always in strategy, we start with the market. The first objective is to identify those issues – and only those issues – that are salient for the firm's ability to create and appropriate value. Starting with the issues, we ask the following six questions.

1. *What is the* **issue?** The *Oxford English Dictionary* defines "issue" as "a point in controversy on which interested parties take

---

[6] This discussion of the (ia)³ framework is adapted from David Bach and David Bruce Allen, 2010. Beyond the market: What every CEO needs to know about nonmarket strategy, *MIT Sloan Management Review* (2010).

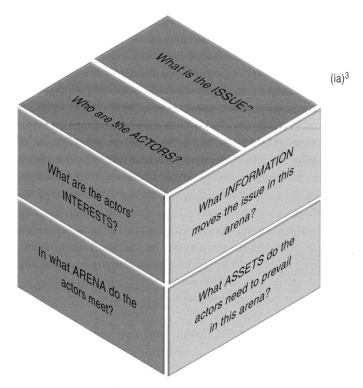

(ia)³

Figure 7.1: The (ia)³ framework
Source: Figure of (ia)³ framework in David Bach and David Bruce Allen, 2010. Beyond the market: What every CEO needs to know about nonmarket strategy. *MIT Sloan Management Review.* Spring, copyright © 2010 by *MIT Sloan Management Review.* Reprinted by Permission of *MIT Sloan Management Review.*

affirmative or negative positions." A firm's nonmarket environment is organized around issues. A firm should take a position on an issue if its resolution could significantly affect the firm's ability to create and/or appropriate value.

2. *Who are the actors?* Identifying the issue highlights the importance of "interested parties" and the potential conflict among them. The next important task is identifying the actors who care about the issue, which are generally those with an economic or ideological stake in it. Take the example of the much-desired landing slots in the principal international airports, especially those in the airports

closest to the world's largest cities. Besides the various airlines, one can assume that airport operators, providers of airline services such as catering, residents living in the vicinity of airports, municipal governments, and environmental groups concerned about air and noise pollution will sufficiently care about the issue to try to influence how many are awarded and to which airlines. Not all actors are equally powerful. Money and headcounts are important, but often not decisive. In politics, what matters most is organization. Organized groups – such as farmers demanding agricultural subsidies – are often more powerful than unorganized consumers who have to foot the bill via higher food prices or taxes, even though the latter outnumber the former.

3. *What are their* **interests**? Building on the identification of actors who care about an issue, the next critical question is what these actors actually want. What motivates them? What makes them tick? What do they hope to achieve and how critical is this issue for them really? Also, how homogenous is a particular actor in terms of their interests? Do all members feel the same way about the issue or is there a degree of heterogeneity – an internal split – that provides an opening for engagement? Probing every identified actor in this respect permits the drawing up of a strategic map, a landscape of political constellations that is critical for the identification of potential allies and key adversaries.

4. *In which* **arena** *do these actors meet?* Nonmarket issues can play out in multiple settings, from courtrooms and regulatory proceedings to parliamentary committee hearings and industry forums all the way to the news media, the public domain, or the blogosphere. Knowing in which arena actors with a stake in the issue meet matters greatly because the rules of the game vary greatly across settings. An asset in one domain can often become a liability in another. Shell lost the battle over the future of the abandoned Brent Spar oil rig because it failed to appreciate that Greenpeace had shifted the arena – away from the realm of British environmental regulation where the company's scientific arguments had proved compelling and into the public domain where Greenpeace's emotional appeal was far more effective than Shell's insistence on science and reason.

5. *What* **information** *will move the issue in this arena?* If money is the currency of markets, information is the currency of the nonmarket

environment. But the kind of information that can influence the resolution of an issue varies across arenas. Public opinion data will be more effective in lobbying critical members of a congressional committee, for example, than in a courtroom or a regulatory hearing. Owners of critical information often have a decisive advantage. One reason why US pharmaceutical firms were so influential in shaping the intellectual property-related agenda for US trade negotiations in the 1990s is because they could provide policymakers with hard-to-get information about the alleged losses to foreign piracy US firms suffered.

6. *What* **assets** *do the actors need to prevail in this arena?* Lastly, while having the right kind of information for a given issue and arena is critical, other assets matter as well. A firm's reputation and its perceived trustworthiness are essential if it wants to influence an issue in the public domain. Here, the example of Wal-Mart once again is appropriate. No firm has worked harder to build an image of an organization committed to reducing environmental impacts while saving the consumer money. In some situations, a broad network of contacts and the ability to quickly assemble and mobilize coalitions can be critical assets. There is no better example than the work of Goldman Sachs in putting its considerable networking talents in play during the recent financial crisis.

An (ia)^3 analysis sets the stage for proactive as opposed to reactive nonmarket management. With the analysis in hand, a firm can plot what steps, including social action programs, it should take in order to favor its business interests.

Among all the steps that a firm may take, perhaps the most difficult decision is whether to engage in political action alone or in concert with others, including industry partners and civil society organizations. On issues with large economic impact, such as climate change, alliances can shift rapidly. For example, in fall 2009, several companies, including Apple, resigned from the US Chamber of Commerce in opposition to the Chamber's lobbying position on global warming. Nike resigned from the Chamber's board. Much more telling was the resignation of utility companies with comparatively low carbon emissions – Pacific Gas and Electric, PNM Resources, and Exelon – with high-carbon-emission utilities receiving support from the Chamber in their quest to weaken and delay new regulation. Other areas of disagreement, even between companies in the same industry, include information protection (Google, Yahoo, etc.), consumer protection (banking), gasoline mileage requirements (automobile industry), the use of plastics (packaging), and so on.

It is vital not to get trapped on the wrong side of a political issue or be associated with the wrong partners. Once again, the best answer is to have firm political strategy integrated with business strategy. Firms that pursue social strategy and are already integrating nonmarket issues into the strategy process have a head start.

Connecting nonmarket stakeholders to social strategy

Having selected the issues and partners to work with, the next step is to decide how to incorporate nonmarket stakeholders into social strategy. Given the wide range of options, our discussion here is necessarily suggestive, rather than definitive.

For example, a product differentiation strategy is particularly effective in situations characterized by a high salience of NGOs and community stakeholders. In these situations, groups that represent a variety of interests in the community or society at large make demands upon the firm. Such demands create additional constraints on firm performance. Such constraints, in and of themselves, imply additional costs for the firm (Palmer *et al.*, 1995). The best option for the firm is to flip these constraints on their head by using them as the basis for innovation, creating social attributes that command a price premium from customers. The firm thus differentiates its products and creates new markets as did the often cited The Body Shop, in its agile responses to the demands of animal rights groups.[7]

However, a product differentiation strategy by itself may not be enough to create a sufficient price premium to pay for the social attribute. In such cases, it may make sense to engage in political strategy or what we referred to as a strategic interaction social strategy in Chapter 6, petitioning (lobbying) the government to mandate the constraint through regulation. As we indicated above, strategic interaction of a firm with regulators depends on the firm's relations with

---

[7] In an intricate turn of the screw, The Body Shop later suffered attacks from animal rights activists for having used substances in its products that had earlier been tested, by others, on animals.

regulators, with industry competitors, with industry lobbying groups, as well as on the relations of their competitors with regulators. The firm's social capital and social networks are essential to success and to avoiding potential gaffes that can seriously damage important relationships.

An additional caveat is that governments are frequently subject to regulatory failure (Breyer, 1982). Sources of regulatory failure include technical and information shortcomings, jurisdictional mismatches, and public distortions (Esty, 1999). One common cause of regulatory failure, although certainly not the only one, is corruption, which undermines the ability of governments to monitor effectively and enforce public policy (Abaroa, 1999). A strategic interaction social strategy will only function where the government is an effective and, therefore, powerful stakeholder.

Conclusion

The shift from managing stakeholders to social strategy comes with the risk of being accused of putting profits before ethics. As we discussed in Chapter 3, the discourse of CSR requires firms to maintain activities directed towards making the world a better place. Any deviance from this standard was deemed inappropriate. Should these activities prove profitable, these must be merely a pleasant, positive externality. This, we have argued, makes little sense, but we would remind managers that they should not try to convince their stakeholders that the firm's social action programs are first and foremost about making money.

The catch-22 which says that you can make money out of social action just so long as you don't say so has deterred serious discussion of how social action can be strategic. Tack on the ethical obligation to satisfy stakeholders and it is easy to understand why social strategy is underdeveloped.

We have argued from the first page of this book that the CSR mess is an opportunity, particularly for corporations under pressure on multiple fronts, for innovative social strategies that create economic and social value. In this chapter, we shift the discussion from the ethical obligation of providing social goods and satisfying stakeholders to a practical analysis of how firms can jump-start the process toward social strategy through employee participation in decision-making and thus effectively opening up corporate governance to the first, primary stakeholder. The next step is a realistic evaluation of the nonmarket environment and the importance of developing political strategies in conjunction with social action programs. The $(ia)^3$ framework is a starting point for this work. With a realistic assessment of the market and nonmarket environments and with employee support, firms are more likely to accurately assess the potential for social strategy and develop and implement social action programs that create social and economic value.

To conclude this chapter, permit us an additional comment regarding the difficulties of developing a model of social strategy given the terminology and the conversation we have inherited. Interest group is a more accurate term than stakeholder. Nonmarket strategy is an infelicitous term, as it may suggest that nonmarket strategy and market strategy are opposing strategies or even mutually exclusive. Furthermore, we have the task of making sure that it is always clear that nonmarket strategy is not the same as social strategy. Social strategy seeks economic value creation and social value creation through social action projects joined to firm products and services. Nonmarket strategy is a general term for a firm's plan for managing nonmarket issues. If we limit our discussion here to multinationals, it is obvious that not all firms should pursue social strategy; however, all do need to have a well-developed nonmarket strategy.

8 | *Resources and capabilities*

Introduction

In Chapter 6, we began with a discussion of why social strategy must account not only for industry structure and the nonmarket environment, but also firm resources. Despite the frequently vexing debate in strategic management over the influence of industry (external) and firm resources (internal) on corporate performance, there is little question that a theory of the firm must account for both (Barney, 1991), just as a theory of human behavior must account for environmental and individual factors.

Social strategy must then answer the question: how do these factors, separately and in their interaction, influence corporate success and under what conditions? In Chapter 6, we defined a framework for industry structure, and set out propositions for creating competitive advantage via generic social strategies in differing industry contexts. In this chapter, we define firm resources (and capabilities), describe the features of social-action-based resources, and explain the development of dynamic capabilities for social innovation (Russo and Fouts, 1997; Sharma and Vredenberg, 1998).

The resource-based view (RBV) defines competitive advantage as the creation of unique firm resources and capabilities (Peteraf, 1993) that leverage organizational routines (Nelson and Winter, 1982), crossing various business processes. RBV presents two significant advances on previous approaches to competitive advantage. First, it eliminates the need to define industries, and in its place substitutes competitive domains in which firms choose to compete. Second, the integrative nature of core competencies (Prahalad and Hamel, 1989) or activity systems (Porter, 1996) is highlighted, offering a picture of how firms organize to meet market demands.

The resource-based view and social strategy

The RBV theory argues that firm-specific, intangible assets are a more likely source of sustainable competitive advantage than tangible assets (Barney, 1991; Peteraf, 1993; Rao, 1994). This finding is essential to much of current research in areas such as organizational learning, intellectual capital, knowledge management, and is the link between industrial-organization economics and the cognitive sciences supporting much current research.

Traditional economic theory emphasized "the importance of external market factors in determining firm success" (Hansen and Wernerfelt, 1989). RBV theory, however, grounded in the work of Selznick (1957), Penrose (1959), and M. Polanyi (1967), among others, argues that organizational competitive advantage depends on the dynamic relationship between innovation and managerial behavior by which organizational capabilities are developed. Adapting concepts from economics, sociology, and cognitive psychology, RBV attempts to systematize causally ambiguous (Rumelt, 1984), path dependent (Nelson and Winter, 1982; Rosenberg, 1990), and socially complex (Barney 1986a) processes by which companies develop firm-specific competitive advantages that are "imperfectly imitable."

While there are numerous classification schemes describing the key constructs of resource-based competitive advantage (Peteraf, 1993; Ginsberg, 1994) and categorizing resources and capabilities (Hall, 1993; Grant, 1995; Miller and Shamsie, 1996), perhaps the most complete is that of Barney (1991) shown in Figure 8.1.

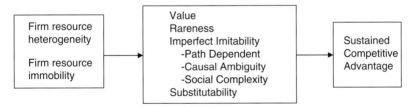

Figure 8.1: Relationship of resource heterogeneity to sustained competitive advantage
Source: Figure 2 of Jay B. Barney, 1991. Firm resources and sustained competitive advantage, *Journal of Management*, 17(1): 99–120, copyright © 1991 by *Journal of Management*. Reprinted by Permission of SAGE Publications.

Quite simply, Barney refocuses traditional internal analysis of strengths and weaknesses under the prism of how firm resource heterogeneity and immobility generate the potential for creating "value," "rareness," and "imperfect imitability" that are difficult to be substituted with similar resources by competitors.

Defining firm resources has itself proved contentious (Priem and Butler, 2001). In this chapter, we adopt Barney's definition from his influential 1991 article: "firm resources include all assets, capabilities, organizational processes, firm attributes, information, knowledge, etc., controlled by the firm that enable the firm to conceive of and implement strategies that improve its efficiency and effectiveness ..." (1991: 101).

Though criticized as excessively broad (Priem and Butler, 2001), Barney's definition makes patent the extraordinarily rich set of resources (a.k.a. *assets*) firms may employ in the search for competitive advantage. Traditionally, firms have measured and managed tangible assets – capital, building, stock, etc. These resources are well understood, with the logical result: competitive advantages based on rare and socially complex intangible resources are more difficult to imitate and hence more valuable (Itami, 1987; Peteraf, 1993. Moreover, firm resources are dynamic in the sense that firms may deliberately choose to build, manage, and reconfigure resources in order to create and sustain competitive advantage (Teece *et al.*, 1997).

Research on firm resources has had a significant impact on how we regard firm resources and capabilities. Among RBV's contributions has been its ability to refocus strategic management on "organizational advantage" (Ghoshal and Moran, 1996). Possessing a resource does not mean that a firm has a competitive advantage. Strategic deployment is required. Customarily, a battery of resources must be joined together to create and take advantage of the industry factors (Porter, 1980) where it is possible to achieve superior economic rents (Penrose, 1959). Frequently, those resources and capabilities are co-determined and linked together in larger themes (Sharma and Vredenburg, 1998). This is especially vital for social-action-based competitive strategies that inevitably draw in both market and nonmarket participants (Baron, 1995).

Properly defining resources and capabilities is essential to creating a rigorous model that explains how resource and capabilities may be the source of competitive advantage. Grant (1995) provides a solid framework for explaining core assets that may be developed, dividing these into tangible, intangible and human. In part, we follow his framework, substituting identity for culture. As regards capabilities, the work is much more difficult. Collis (1994) argues that there are an unlimited number of potential capabilities, while others have grouped lists of capabilities known to be sources of competitive advantage. In a recent article, Sharma and Vredenburg (1998) provide a case-based approach in which they find first, second, and third order capabilities specific to the competitive environment under study. In our work, we have opted for Sharma and Vredenburg's approach as we seek to develop a taxonomy of capabilities that embraces both firm market and nonmarket activities.

Moving beyond the challenges of working with the RBV, we would emphasize the positive results stemming from renewed attention to the challenging behavioral issues and intangible assets (Bernard, 1938; Selznick, 1957; Penrose, 1959; Andrews, *et al.* 1965), including those of corporate values, ethics, and human capital central to our definition of corporate social strategy.

In formulating and implementing social strategies, the role of intangible resources is paramount. Many of the advantages to be obtained by social action are linked to product and process advantages dependent on firm reputation, employee motivation, and stakeholder commitment. Each of these intangible resources is a dynamic social relationship that we can classify as a species of capital (e.g., human capital, intellectual capital, organizational capital, social capital, reputational capital (Hall, 1993; Grant, 1995; Nahapiet and Ghoshal, 1998). Each is developed over time as the firm interacts with all market and nonmarket stakeholders. The application of these resources to both market and social opportunities represents for each firm a unique, dynamic positioning (Eisenhardt and Martin, 2000).

Social competitive advantage will emerge where firms create strategies and build resources in specific industry contexts. In all cases, there will be opportunities to create competitive advantage through the more effective use of superior resources and capabilities. In all cases, it will be possible to develop superior resources and capabilities though strategic decision-making and implementation. In some cases, firms will already possess excellent social resources and capabilities. In other cases, firms will seek to develop them.

In terms of social strategy, how might such behavior play out? For example, in the case of Levi Strauss, social strategy included a commitment to building reputation capital (intangible resource) as the basis for a sustainable competitive advantage (Howard, 1990). This reputational capital was necessarily tied to social activities with a number of stakeholders, many of them related to their labor force, mostly minority workers with limited education: outstanding employee benefits, community action programs, outsourcing practices that prohibit child labor. In developing reputational capital, Levi Strauss built competitive advantages in human resources management (high commitment, excellent retention rates, high productivity), supply chain management (stable supplier relations, absence of bad publicity from child labor problems), and quality management (low turnover and employee commitment vital to TQM – total quality management – processes). The development of this reputational capital required a specific social strategy tied to the firm's business strategy.

The reputation capital developed by Levi Strauss is frequently termed "credibility" (Kouzes and Posner, 1993). Credibility is a particularly important social resource needed for the development of a differentiation social strategy. For example, credible information is essential if customers are to pay premium prices for social products (Reinhardt, 1998). Such credibility is an essential element of a corporate reputation that is only developed through consistent long-term effort and contributes to the firm's financial performance (Fombrun and Shanley, 1990; Fombrun, 1996; Miles and Covin, 2000). The development of credibility lies in part on the willingness of a firm to disclose information about environmental and social impacts (Hart, 1995; Szwajkowski, 2000). Levi Strauss announced publicly that it was necessary to lay people off and that it would do so in accordance with corporate values it had developed over the last century. It proceeded to develop, in concert with employees, an open and consensual program of staff reduction, retraining and outplacement.

Such activity is quite rare. Sharma and Vredenburg (1998: 740) explain that "trust and credibility developed by proactive companies … is a path-dependent strategic capability that cannot be easily imitated by competitors." In addition, a consistent policy of credibility, implemented over time and across issues, requires discipline to maintain when corporate performance is poor or worse than expected.

Credibility and loyal employees were not enough to prevent Levi Strauss from having to close plants and lay off workers as the firm confronted competitors manufacturing overseas at lower cost. The lesson, as Lynn Sharp Paine (2003) notes, is that social responsibility (even for firms that do not compete via social strategy) is part of the total package that makes up a competitive market position. This need for integration highlights the role that social strategy can exercise in fostering innovation and vice versa. If Levi Strauss had been able to extend its social strategy advantage beyond its employees and find new ways to bring its customers to see the additional value created by buying products made in the United States by committed Levi Strauss employees, it could have avoided the layoffs. As we saw in our previous discussion of "buy local" social strategies, often two or more advantages are required to make a social strategy effective. This is where innovation and dynamic capabilities come in.

Disruptive and catalytic social innovation

Within the RBV, a central theme has been innovation (Schumpeter, 1934) and the creation of dynamic capabilities to innovate effectively (Teece *et al.*, 1997; Teece, 2007). A firm's capability for disruptive innovation is crucial to its ability to maintain competitive advantage over the long run. The concept of disruptive innovation was originally applied to technological innovations, where innovation simply referred to a change in technologies. Christensen and Bower (1996) distinguished between sustaining and disruptive innovations. The former maintains "an established trajectory of performance improvement," while the latter "disrupts an established trajectory of performance improvement, or redefines what performance means," (Christensen and Bower, 1996: 202). The concept of disruptive innovation has since been extended to include both business model innovation and radical product innovations (Markides, 2006).

In fact, often social problems themselves are disruptions in that they change social, environmental, and demographic trajectories. Climate change presents extraordinary and severe threats to contemporary civilization. Social inequities, most prominently poverty and unjust wealth distribution, induce political and economic instability. AIDS has reconfigured the demographics of many African nations as it has underscored the deprivation of health services in poor nations.

Capabilities in understanding, seizing, and reconfiguring assets are vital if firms are to convert social problems into opportunities for innovation.

The discussion among large corporations about the base of the pyramid is precisely about converting social problems into opportunities (Prahalad, 2005; Hart, 2007). However, the solution to many social problems involves significant changes in current trajectories; without disruptive innovation, solving multiple social problems is not possible (Christensen *et al.*, 2006). Christensen *et al.* (2006: 96) refer to these innovations as catalytic innovations – a subset of disruptive innovation, "distinguished by their primary focus on social change, often on a national scale." Such innovations are characterized by:

1. Scaling and replication in order to create system-wide social change.
2. Meeting needs that are either over-served because current solutions are too complex or largely ignored.
3. Radical simplicity and cost reductions by focusing on products and services that are perceived as "good enough."
4. Ability to attract resources, such as charitable contributions, grants, sweat equity, or intellectual capital, which are initially unappealing to existing competitors.
5. Filling voids created by current competitors for whom the business model or market segment is uninteresting (Christensen *et al.*, 2006: 96–97).

Let us now examine in some detail catalytic innovation from two businesses located in Mexico: Corporación Proteina Americana (Quali) and Amanco. Such efforts represent the types of projects necessary in developing countries to achieve sustainable economic growth and social change.

Case 1: Corporación Proteina Americana (Quali)

Corporación Proteina Americana (American Protein Corporation – not to be confused with the US corporation by the same name) is organized as a cooperative in Mexico with thirty-five employees and annual sales between US$100,000 and US$250,000 per year. Although this social enterprise is quite small, it illustrates how organizational capabilities can be unleashed to develop catalytic innovation in the social arena. Corporación Proteina Americana, also known as the Quali Group because it manages the Quali[1] brand, is a project of the NGO, Alternativas, operating in the states of Puebla, Oaxaca, and Hidalgo. More than 1,100 rural families comprise cooperatives organized in the 80 villages where they live. The families consist primarily of Mixtec, Popoloc, and Nahua Indians. The Quali organization seeks to help rural workers by generating employment and fostering fair trade and ethical consumption through the production of food products based on amaranth.

The Mixtec region of Mexico faces a number of serious problems of underdevelopment. It is a very poor region, with low levels of education, high malnutrition, and recurring droughts. The climate is semi-arid with soil hostile to the cultivation of many crops. Young people, mostly men, often migrate to other parts of Mexico and the United States in search of job opportunities.

In response to these conditions, Alternativas sought to stimulate economic activity in the region. Although the NGO had undertaken several initiatives that introduced innovation, Alternativas now decided to reconfigure its programs in search of much greater change. Previously, it had experimented with the amaranth plant, native to the area. They found that certain species of amaranth were more resistant to drought conditions than others. This research was initially oriented toward improving the local diet. However, a major conceptual breakthrough occurred with the idea using amaranth as the basis for a variety of new food products, especially "junk food" that could be sold outside the Mixtec region. The plan was to invent healthy amaranth snacks.

As is often the case, an innovative product was not sufficient for success. A significant organizational innovation was also necessary. In its earlier projects, Alternativas worked out of a dual structure, creating a separate unit for the Mixtec operations. This structure, though typical of many social enterprises in Mexico, was inappropriate for the business challenges it faced. Accordingly, three cooperatives were created to handle the cultivation, manufacture, and commercialization of the amaranth food products. Thus the value chain was covered

---

[1] The word "quali" means good in Nahautl. The web page for Quali is www.quali.com.mx and for Alternativas it is www.alternativas.org.mx

by this vertical integration of the entire agro-industrial process. This organizational restructuring was then supplemented with additional, specific financial and technical innovations.

Financing cultivation was critical. Obtaining bank financing was out of the question. So Quali extended the *campesinos* a line of credit in order to cover costs during the period of cultivation. They were allowed to repay their loans with payments in kind – in the equivalent of kilos of amaranth grain for the debt owed. Such an innovation proved especially useful during the Mexican financial crisis of 1995, which caused skyrocketing interest rates and inflation. Despite the high interest rates, real rates offered by the commercial banks were actually negative. By making in-kind payments, the *campesinos* paid positive, real rates of interest so that the costs of financing were fully covered and this permitted refinancing – benefiting both the *campesinos* and Quali.

There were also numerous technical innovations that were vital to the success of the social venture. For example, since many women were involved in cultivation, the group's Technology Center developed three-wheel wheelbarrows and double-handled shovels. Given the scarcity of energy resources for pumping water from vertical wells, horizontal wells were drilled in hillsides in order to avoid the costs involved in electrical pumping, so that water could be extracted with gravity. Hand-powered tortilla machines were developed to avoid burning scarce trees for energy. In each of these cases, the Technology Center faced specific problems and overcame them with solutions that were appropriate for the Mixtec context.

One of the important elements of a catalytic innovation is its replicability. Replication of innovative projects where many elements had to come together to achieve success is often difficult. The Quali project was reproduced through Eficoop (or Escuela de Financiamiento Cooperativo – School of Cooperative Financing). A careful selection of eight NGOs was undertaken in order to facilitate the reproduction of the project in other regions. Unfortunately, differences in organizational cultures and the inability of some of the participating NGOs to comply with the technical guidelines led to several failures.

Case 2: Amanco

The Amanco case provides a significant contrast to Quali. It is a multinational, acquired by the Mexican group, Mexichem, in 2007, with more than 7,000 employees operating throughout Latin America. It specializes in the production and marketing of pipes and accessories for the transmission of fluids, including water, electricity, and natural gas. The firm's markets include residential and commercial construction as well as agriculture and infrastructure. In Mexico, irrigation is one of its most important businesses.

Irrigation projects are usually designed for a minimum of 10 hectares (24.7 acres), although 20 hectares (49.4 acres) is more common. Unfortunately, small farmers usually have plots that range from half a hectare to two hectares (1.2 to 4.9 acres). Ordinarily, it would not be profitable to sell irrigation systems for such small areas. However, Amanco has developed a way to provide irrigation to small producers. It offers the same product to low-income customers that it offers to regular customers by grouping small farmers. Amanco then develops the project for a total of 20 hectares. Amanco helps the group of small farmers to work together, even though these producers are not accustomed to collaborating. In addition, the irrigation technology is adapted for small farmers.

A key capability has been Amanco's skill in developing intersectoral alliances with government, NGO, and private companies. In order to reach the small farmers, Amanco collaborates with NGOs that have a local base and have greater experience in activities like microfinancing that help ensure the project's success. In the Mexican states of Oaxaca and Guerrero, Amanco works with well-established foundations like Ashoka, Atoyac (a local NGO), and INSO (Instituto de la Naturaleza y Sociedad de Oaxaca [Institute for Nature and Society of Oaxaca]) to improve production. These groups also joined with RASA (Red de Agricultores Sustentables Autogestivos [Network of Self-managing Sustainable Farmers]). Amanco provides the equipment and advice, Ashoka helps to identify leaders in marginal rural communities and, together with Amanco, obtains the backing of the Mexican government and NGOs.

In order to increase the demand for the products of its customers, Amanco has multiplied the impact of the project through a deal with Wal-Mart, which agreed to sell lemons harvested in these communities. Wal-Mart benefited by sourcing through small producers instead of large producers, who frequently forced small producers out of business only to later raise prices.

In addition, Amanco assisted in the development of alliances with government organizations for financing. Right now 50 percent of the project is funded through the Comisión Nacional de Agua (National

Water Commission) and 30 percent is covered by a soft credit payable in one year through the Fundación Mexicana de Desarrollo Rural (FMDR [Mexican Foundation for Rural Development]). The remaining 20 percent is financed by the producers themselves who also take charge of installing the irrigation systems on their own with the supervision and advice of Amanco.

The prospects for replication throughout Latin America are excellent – including the opportunity to leverage financial support through international development organizations such as the World Bank and Inter-American Development Bank. In 2005 Amanco developed such a project for 620 small farmers covering 464 hectares in Guerrero and Oaxaca.

One organizational innovation that was fundamental to success was to fine-tune incentives for distributors and sales people who ordinarily work with larger customers with commensurate commissions and earnings. In order to make the market for small farmers more attractive to its distributors, Amanco is now offering them discounts on the products for this segment.

Both Amanco and Quali illustrate the concept of catalytic innovation. First, they create systemic social change through scaling and replication. In the case of Quali, the project is now spreading across the entire Mixtec region. Quali has attempted, although not entirely successfully, to replicate the program in other NGOs. As regards Amanco, the project promises to expand throughout Latin America. Second, both projects meet the needs of populations that were not being served. The Mixtec region had been largely neglected as a serious sourcing opportunity by large agri-business firms. *Campesinos* were overlooked by irrigation equipment manufacturers because of the small scale of their operations. Third, they offer radically simpler or less costly alternatives. Amanco is particularly interesting because it offers irrigation equipment that is less expensive than existing alternatives by taking advantage of the manual labor of the same *campesino* customers who purchase and then install the equipment.

Fourth, both ventures have been effective in generating resources from grants, volunteers, and networking. Both Quali and Amanco have been able to harness the manual labor equity of local inhabitants as well as leverage social capital through alliances with NGOs and governmental institutions. Finally, the *campesinos* were ignored by existing players. In the irrigation industry, the parcels that were to be irrigated were thought to be too small to be profitable. In the case of Quali, the development of products from amaranth was initially seen as undesirable. However, both initiatives have broken mental paradigms. The results have been profound and the changes disruptive. Both projects promise to create further change through a chain reaction created by design.

Dynamic capabilities for social innovation

David Teece (2007: 1319) defines dynamic capabilities as "the capacity (1) to sense and shape opportunities and threats, (2) to seize opportunities, and (3) to maintain competitiveness through enhancing, combining, protecting, and when necessary, reconfiguring the business enterprise's intangible and tangible assets." Social problems frequently provide disruptive opportunities for the firm that require new configurations of resources (Gilbert, 2005).

The Quali and Amanco cases point to the importance of several closely related dynamic capabilities discussed in the literature as necessary for social innovation: stakeholder integration, radical transactiveness, social embeddedness, native capability, and institutional influence capability. A word of caution is due – the meanings of some of these capabilities and their distinctions are not always crystal clear. Nevertheless, they do describe a cluster of capabilities that are essential to many kinds of social innovation. Stakeholder integration was discussed in Chapter 4 and refers to "the ability to establish trust-based collaborative relationships with a wide variety of stakeholders, especially those with noneconomic goals. These stakeholders may include local communities, environmental groups, regulators, non-governmental organizations (NGOs), etc." (Sharma and Vredenburg, 1998: 735).

Radical transactiveness takes stakeholder integration a step further by focusing on those fringe stakeholders with whom most multinational enterprises have rarely dealt in the past, and requires crossing numerous boundaries, including social, cultural, and institutional ones (Hart and Sharma, 2004). Both Quali and Amanco engaged stakeholders effectively. But Quali is itself a social enterprise, born of an NGO, in close contact with the people it served. Amanco is a multinational corporation much further removed from the local context, and thus depended upon intermediaries to draw close to the customer group it hoped to serve. By working intensively with various Indian groups of the Mixtec region, groups typically left out in the co-creation of relevant solutions, Quali has been able to develop and reconfigure many innovations to create a project that resolves a number of social, health, and environmental problems. Many of the innovations are low-tech, but effective and at an accessible cost for the Mixtec region.

Quali's radical transactiveness was enabled by consistent effort from management. Top management meets frequently with community leaders; through these meetings community representatives identify and make recommendations to resolve specific problems. In addition, specific attention was given to the perspective of women, who participate both as executives and workers. The top management team maintains permanent, direct communication with the *campesino* groups in order to identify and analyze the needs of families and their villages. Finally, the head of Quali, Raúl Hernández Garciadiego, a philosopher who was awarded a doctorate *honoris causa* from the Iberoamerican University in Mexico City for his leadership, understood the key role that stakeholder dialogue would play in successfully developing disruptive innovations. In most instances, projects that emanate from NGOs require the exceptional commitment and leadership of one or two individuals. The Quali case is a perfect example. Such leadership is unusual. For this reason, replicability is crucial.

Social embeddedness is closely related to radical transactiveness. It has been defined as "the ability to create competitive advantage based on a deep understanding of and integration with the local environment. This capability involves the ability to create a web of trusted connections with a diversity of organizations and institutions, generate bottom-up development, and understand, leverage, and build on the existing social infrastructure" (London and Hart, 2004: 364). Another term for social embeddedness is native capability, which consists of the "skills and competencies needed for firms to become thoroughly embedded in the local context" (Hart, 2007: 195). The distinction between radical transactiveness and social embeddedness or native capability consists in the approach taken by the multinational. The former involves engaging the multinational's competitive imagination, while social embeddedness deals with the ability of the multinational firm to enter into the local context so thoroughly that it is able to co-create solutions incorporating local knowledge and local assets (Hart, 2007). Social capital is fundamental to social embeddedness.

For both Quali and Amanco, there is extensive use of social capital through the development of relationships with local, fringe stakeholders, the co-creation of customized solutions to very specific problems, and local capacity-building (London and Hart, 2004). Quali was dedicated to empowering the *campesinos* from different indigenous groups to find unique ways in which they could insert themselves into the contemporary economic system. By exploiting the properties of drought-resistant forms of amaranth, Quali discovered a grain adapted to the Mixtec region with which the indigenous groups were completely familiar and capable of supplying sustainably. It tied this locally adapted grain into a demand for its products by developing a unique niche within the snack food market – specifically, healthy snack food. Although Quali had trained scientists working on the development of specific strains of amaranth, the Quali team worked closely with the indigenous peoples in finding new ways of obtaining water and developing tools appropriate to the needs of a highly female farming population. There were numerous meetings between Quali, its parent Alternativas, and indigenous families to deal with specific problems as they emerged. At the same time, Quali built capacity in the local populations through training and the development of an organizational infrastructure through the village cooperatives.

The Amanco approach was different because its origins were further removed from the *campesinos*. It worked with local and global NGOs to develop and identify the fringe stakeholders. RASA was instrumental in this endeavor because of its close ties to the *campesinos*. Amanco was able to develop a customized solution to their specific irrigation problems. By joining small plots into a single project and taking advantage of the sweat equity that the locals had to invest in this kind of project, it was able to lower the costs of modern irrigation systems considerably and make them accessible. Amanco was successful in developing both technical and organizational capacity among the indigenous farmers. The key to the success of the project was the ability of the *campesinos* to join together in developing this kind of shared irrigation system.

Embeddedness in the social context also creates the possibility for the effective use of a firm's institutional influence capability, which refers to "the ability to define or shape the norms, standards, and beliefs of an industry or to reframe public perceptions about the social acceptability of a firm's practices" (Oliver and Holzinger, 2008: 511). This capability is related to social legitimacy as the firm works to shape definitions of what is legitimate corporate behavior. It is manifested in lobbying and efforts to shape public expectations regarding socially and environmentally appropriate business behavior. For example, companies like Toyota and General Electric are helping to redefine corporate expectations about carbon neutrality as a legitimate business goal.

Both Quali and Amanco illustrate an institutional influence capability, although at different orders of magnitude. Although a very small venture, Quali is shaping perceptions in a number of ways. First, it is demonstrating the possibility for sustainable regional development in a very arid area largely devoid of valued natural resources. In addition, it has reshaped the perceptions of *campesinos* with respect to conservation and care of the scarce resources, especially water. Its Water Museum has been an important tool to create awareness of the proper care for water resources and how the sustainable cultivation of amaranth can lead to a regeneration of water sources, especially the river basins of the Mixtec region.

Amanco, a multinational enterprise, was involved in reshaping the beliefs and norms of the Mexican federal government, especially the Comisión Nacional de Agua (CNA). Through a partnership of the public, private, and social sectors, CNA and Amanco joined forces to provide irrigation systems for agricultural use to groups that had previously been neglected by the private sector.

Related to the political capability of institutional influence is the capability for developing cross-sectoral alliances (Rondinelli and London, 2003; Austin *et al.* 2004). As a social enterprise, Quali was the brainchild of an NGO; so the partnership existed by design. Other collaborations such as those with local governments, for example, played a key role for its success. In addition, relationships with other local collectives provided the basis for the replication of the Quali model throughout the region.

In the case of Amanco, collaborations with NGOs were critical to innovation in the firm's business model. Ashoka, Atoyac, INSO, and RASA enabled Amanco to identify and collaborate with relevant *campesino* farmers who could benefit from their irrigation program for small plots. These partners possessed the local social embeddedness that Amanco lacked. The NGOs were able to identify potential partners and assist them in training clients to work in groups, thus preparing the way so that Amanco could organize them and thus benefit from the irrigation program. In addition, financing involved creative collaborations between governmental organizations as well as sweat equity from the *campesinos* themselves.

Where do these capabilities come from? Capabilities like stakeholder integration, radical transactiveness, and social embeddedness are slightly different forms of distributed cognition, in which processes like memory, reasoning, and learning are dispersed across individuals. In management, Karl Weick (Weick and Roberts, 1993) has pioneered research on the "collective mind," but there is strong resistance to this kind of work, too often dismissed with phrases such as "people think, organizations do not." Hutchins (1995: xiii) warned that "the emphasis on finding and describing 'knowledge structures' that are somewhere 'inside' the individual encourage us to overlook the fact that human cognition is always situated in a complex sociocultural world and cannot be unaffected by it." These capabilities take the concept of distributed cognition a step further by recognizing that the cognition needed to solve many of our most pressing challenges like climate change and poverty alleviation can be distributed across groups.

Some of these capabilities like stakeholder integration can be facilitated through alliances with NGO, government, and other partners who are more closely located to fringe stakeholders. Nevertheless, social embeddedness requires that the firm itself become truly involved in the local context. Clearly, Quali and Amanco engaged in a number of strategies to develop these capabilities. They had routines to develop social bonds across groups. Quali's regular meetings between staff and *campesino* groups is an example. There was an alignment of incentives in the case of Amanco in order to overcome possible resistance. The linkages between the company and its knowledge sources were fostered through informal relationships as well as formal alliances. Putting people together with such different backgrounds fostered innovation through a new kind of collaborative innovation network (Gloor, 2005).

Some readers may protest that Quali and Amanco are special cases, which focus on the base of the economic pyramid (BOP). Such conditions do not apply to the specific situations of most other firms. Although Hart and Christensen (2002) would argue that the BOP is precisely the best place to incubate radical new technologies like clean technology, we only want to point out that the BOP is interesting because it is provoking firms to rethink commonly held assumptions about who are their target markets and suppliers. There are many "pyramids" that represent social problems all around us. One does not need to go to the third world to find them. The challenges faced by immigrants, differently abled persons, the elderly, the homeless, the mentally ill, and the substance dependent, among others, can all provoke the kind of disruptive innovation that is associated with BOP markets.

Given the novelty of social strategy, it is not surprising that the ability to create above-normal profits and beyond-compliance social performance requires unusual combinations of dynamic capabilities. To date few firms possess all of the resources and capabilities needed to achieve catalytic innovation. Nevertheless, the examples of Quali, Amanco, and many other firms point to the possibilities that exist to harness market forces to solve problems of social inequity in ways that are consonant with robust financial performance. By aligning incentives so that attractive returns are available in the pursuit of social good, firms can mobilize their capabilities to develop and implement effective social strategies. Certainly part of the secret is the ability to identify resources dormant both within the firm and in potential collaborators. As this chapter clearly indicates, private firms, civil society organizations, and governments together possess the resources to solve many problems of social inequity. The capabilities discussed in this chapter are important precisely because of their ability to mobilize these resources for creative problem-solving.

9 | *Organizational identity*

Introduction

We began our discussion of corporate identity as an integral element of corporate culture back in Chapter 4, as we set out the step-by-step model for social strategy formulation and implementation. Step 3, you may recall, is "Evaluate firm identity."

In Chapter 4, we dodged the multiple issues of defining a workable concept of culture, which we must try to make amends for here. While management unflinchingly invokes culture as the reason for doing things in a certain way, and "our culture" is often said to explain what makes the company what it is, culture is a highly contested concept in academics. First, the concept is properly in the domain of anthropology – in fact, so central to the field that it is often simply called cultural anthropology, and so divisive that anthropology habitually engages in definitional turf wars over the term (Geertz, 1973). Cultural anthropology, like its sister science, sociology, has a habit of bumping into psychology and borrows much of its terminology from early twentieth-century work in personality psychology in areas such as identity and values. The concepts of culture, identity, and values are dragged into management research and applied to organizations with questionable results. To be fair to the management field, and the social sciences in general, these concepts are difficult, highly abstract, yet fundamental to all human behavior.

For this reason, we would be remiss if we did not mention two scholars who had a strong impact on our understanding of organizational culture, identity, and strategy – Philip Selznick and Karl Weick. Selznick's *Leadership in Administration* (1957) focused management research on legitimacy, multiple objectives, firm constituencies, and the process of institutionalization; Weick's work, which we discussed in Chapters 4 and 7, gave to the concepts "collective mind" and "organizational sensemaking" the empirical substance they required in order for us to describe the practical role of organizational culture and identity in firm behavior. Neither Selznick nor Weick places his work within corporate culture and identity, though each is essential to our understanding of these concepts.

Unfortunately, corporate culture is rarely treated in management practice rigorously. Corporate culture has become a big money game about what the players involved call *values*. Top management is expected to work with everyone in the firm to agree on the company's values. These values are always auspicious and ecumenical – integrity, partnership, honesty, and so on – but are denatured by pretentious and often ridiculous packaging. It is as if each firm were asked to stick its hand into the bag and pull out three or four or five out of the baker's dozen of celestial values to call its own and proclaim to the world its undying loyalty ... before then throwing them back in the bag for the next company to take its turn. In the end, companies declare allegiance to the same values, the same HR and social action programs, the same feel-good routines. In each company, there are true believers who run around asking how "we" can put "our" values into action, but any person who has worked in more than one company in his life can quickly figure out that it all sounds the same. No wonder, as we pointed in Chapter 7, employees are distrustful of top management.

This is rather sad. Anyone who has sat through a company meeting in which managers discuss whether or not some person or some project or some part of the organization is living up to or believes in the company's values should know exactly what we mean. We have sat through dozens, at many different companies. The meetings are painful, sometimes cruel, sometimes dishonest, and a significant step backwards from the voluntary cooperation invoked by Barnard (1938) and the "inevitability" of organizational democracy Bennis and Slater (1964) foresaw. The use and abuse of values obstructs serious analysis of corporate culture, diminishes identity, and is an invitation to external stakeholders to cynicism.

Often, when we say these things, we, too, are accused of being cynical. On the contrary, we feel strongly that corporate culture – identity, values, behaviors – are far too important to be manipulated and trivialized.

With this in mind, in this chapter, when we use the terms "culture," "identity," "values," "ideology," "image," and "reputation," we will try to use them precisely and carefully. We will set out why we believe corporate culture, and in particular corporate identity, is fundamental to social strategy.

When a firm decides to pursue social strategy, most often management has determined that it wants to change the firm's identity and role in society and that it wants to be in some important way different from its competitors. A business strategy promises a product and service at the right price. A social strategy goes one step further and promises a product and service and a social benefit at the right price. When a firm promises a social benefit with its products and services, it is saying that it has social objectives that it is willing to stake the company's success and perhaps even its survival on. A statement is made about "who we are" (our identity) that goes considerably beyond what a company normally commits to. What we have called a social responsibility orientation (SRO) is likely to be a part of the company's identity when social strategy is successful. This statement is an extension of one of the principal findings of our research and we wish to state it again, at the beginning of this chapter.

There is a strong positive relationship between social responsibility orientation (SRO) and value creation via social strategy planning.

Later on, we will discuss this finding in depth. Until then, we should keep in mind that a firm whose identity includes a strong SRO and decides to engage in social strategy planning has a very good chance of creating both economic value and social value.

The rise of corporate culture

Early writers in the field of strategic management often emphasized the role of values and ethics in strategy formulation (Barnard, 1938; Andrews, 1971). As Barnard (1938: 282) wrote: "high ideals are the basis for the persistence of cooperation." Drawing on his experience as CEO of New Jersey Bell, Barnard argued that sustained success (survival) rests on the voluntary commitment of men and women to the organization's purpose. Barnard reminded us that religious and educational organizations, e.g., the Catholic Church, European and American universities, are far older than businesses or governments, which often fail in their pursuit of profits and taxes, respectively.

Despite the wisdom of his arguments, Barnard's "soft" management approach had far less influence on twentieth-century American businesses than Taylor's top-down efficiency model, which laid out a certain path to profits for owners while winning workers over with the incentive of high wages for increased productivity.

Thus, corporate "follow-the-leader" behavior triumphed in the USA, with most companies first organized pretty much like their neighbors, practicing the same management techniques and promulgating the usual values of hard work and fair pay.[1] If in the first part of the twentieth century, owners and workers battled what each meant by hard work and fair pay, by the 1940s union shops were the norm and management and labor enjoyed mostly stable, mostly prosperous, rule-governed relationships. For example, management and worker expectations and behavior in Ford and General Motors were fundamentally alike, however great the differences in style between family-run Ford and the academically minded Alfred Sloane at GM. For US companies, competition was conceived principally as a race to get out the right products and sell them. Management was mostly about getting workers to do what was needed now, not later.

Firms with highly distinct cultures and identities were nearly always the result of some "eccentricity" of the founder (Whetten, 2006). Management writers in the '80s and '90s frequently extolled the virtues of the founders of Levi Strauss, Hewlett Packard, Johnson and Johnson, The Body Shop, IKEA, Sony, etc., as examples of enlightened or visionary management (Howard, 1990; Joachimsthaler and Aaker, 1997). Moreover, repeatedly, the departure of the founder or competitive setbacks (or both) resulted in the firm stepping back from the most innovative aspects of its distinctive culture.

At the outset of this section, we promised to define our terms. Perhaps we can now give a reasonable first definition of corporate culture. To start with, though culture includes how people feel about themselves and what they do – i.e., identity – when we talk about culture we are going to limit ourselves to observable behaviors. This will bring us close to the concept of routines (Penrose, 1959; Nelson and Winter, 1982) and will permit us to point out those things that make one firm's "way of doing things" different from another's. It will us allow us to discuss identity in terms of feelings and commitments without getting culture and identity confused.

---

[1] The organizational theory literature refers to this process as mimetic isomorphism.

This practical definition of culture is also useful in going back a quarter-century to the 1980s when culture became a vital subject in management. At the time, the United States faced superior foreign competition in manufacturing from the Japanese who were said to have a superior corporate culture.

The sudden concern with corporate culture, including values and identity, was a result of what management gurus would later term "the Honda effect" (Pascale, 1996). In less than two decades, Japanese firms wiped out American manufacturing, a defeat so humiliating that in the 1980s the US Congress had to institute "voluntary quotas" on Japanese car imports.

It was an unimaginable defeat. Taylorized American manufacturers had dominated world markets for more than fifty years following World War I. They had also stopped innovating. Following World War II, as we all know, US firms turned a deaf ear to statistical quality experts, among them W. Edwards Deming and Thomas Shewhart, who preached that product quality would be radically improved by reforming management practices. Nearly all the changes Deming proposed (his famous 14 points) were oriented toward giving the worker greater responsibility and a greater voice in the production process. (Deming was another idealistic proponent of employee participation.) In the United States, neither union leadership nor management thought this was a promising scenario.

And so Deming, stationed in Japan following World War II, offered his services to the Japanese, where his theories of statistical quality control were taken up and converted into a cult of management practice. Over the next three decades, the Japanese created total quality management (TQM), instituted *kaizen* (permanent improvement), empowered workers via quality circles, and integrated design, logistics, and production into a seamless operation that Toyota termed the "Total Production System."

Astonishingly, throughout this entire period, including long after it was common knowledge how the Japanese model worked and how to copy it, Ford and General Motors persisted in doing exactly what they had been doing since Henry Ford had developed assembly line manufacturing. Not even the loss of world leadership and the collapse of the American market could get the American companies to change. Whatever lessons may be drawn from the debacle of the American car industry, we, at least, have the first important message of this chapter: changing corporate behavior, and reinventing a corporate culture and identity is very difficult indeed – even when a company, an entire industry, or a century-long tradition of manufacturing leadership is at risk.

Not surprisingly, the spectacular failure of US companies put into question American management practice. Academics and consultants concluded that Japanese culture and Japanese corporate values and culture were superior (Ouchi, 1981; Deal and Kennedy, 1982). The Japanese competitive advantage consisted, effectively, of a double whammy. Japan produced men "programmed" to cooperate and sacrifice for the greater good. At the same time, each successful company, e.g., Honda, developed its own culture, its own way of doing things, and a unique corporate identity marked by shared values and a powerful corporate ideology that was different from its equally successful competitors Yamaha and Suzuki (Ouchi, 1981; Pascale and Athos, 1981). Alas, Japanese culture and Japanese firms were far better suited to the ideas of Barnard, Deming, and McGregor than American firms.

Perhaps even more odd is how little management actually changed in the United States. The US automobile industry heard over and over that a firm's culture is the unique expression of the identity of the firm (Albert and Whetten, 1985), but did not respond. Traditionally uncomfortable with managing intangibles, automobile industry executives found the whole discussion of culture, values, ideology, and corporate identity daunting and confusing. It was never clear which came first (values or behavior), nor why values always end up sounding like pablum. Expensive consulting projects on corporate values produced, over and over again, the same lists of values, the same sterile values projects, and the same disappointing results. There was lots of talk about CEO commitment and the need for visionary leadership, and then the values project was handed over to someone without profit and loss responsibilities. Given that culture projects were embarked on during downturns, it did not take long before employees figured out that "culture change" was shorthand for "we're downsizing" and "you're fired." The culture fad faded, though not before Tom Peters and Robert Waterman could sell more than 6 million copies of *In Search of Excellence: Lessons from America's Best-Run Companies* (1982), promising us that we could learn from America's leading companies that had made the cultural transition to excellence. In his next book, *Thriving on Chaos* (1988), Peters began with the phrase "There are no excellent companies ..." (1988: 3), perhaps because nearly half of the excellent firms he had praised had either been bought, disappeared, or fallen on hard times.

While Peters and other management gurus offered simplistic recipes (e.g., the famous 7S's) packaged as culture, within management theory, the resource-based view offered a serious discussion of culture and competitive advantage. Internal components of corporate culture – e.g., corporate identity and corporate values (what we think about ourselves) – could be leveraged into corporate reputation (what others think about us). Identity, values, and reputation can be strategic "assets" or "resources," part of a hard-to-copy, sustainable competitive advantage (Barney, 1986b; Downey, 1986). All three resources have their origin in social relationships and, logically, are fundamental to the importance of corporate culture in social strategy. In this chapter, we focus mainly on corporate identity. To this we turn now.

Identity and strategy

On July 17, 2009, Wal-Mart's CEO, Michael T. Duke, announced that the Arkansas multinational will be green-labeling products that go on its shelves, and suppliers will be asked to meet environmental impact standards. Duke stated that Wal-Mart's objective is to reduce carbon emissions by informing customers who may choose to factor into their purchasing decisions environmental impact. Wal-Mart's approach in this case is polite and respectful, as the firm has come to be. There will be no arm-twisting ... because Wal-Mart does not need to. Often, Wal-Mart is the single largest customer of its suppliers. Wal-Mart can, if it wishes, put the Five Forces at work to its advantage. But Wal-Mart has institutionalized another way of talking about itself and how it exercises its large-scale competitive advantages. Of course, Wal-Mart will, as it always does, reduce costs and prices, but it will also win over customers and other, often cantankerous, stakeholders when it demonstrates that what's good for Wal-Mart profits is also good for the environment and good for the consumer. Over the last decade, Wal-Mart has learned to integrate market strategy and social action.

Yet, despite praise from *Fortune*, business and human rights advocacy NGOs such as As You Sow (Gunther, 2008), Wal-Mart's commitment to corporate responsibility is treated with suspicion, and will continue to be for the foreseeable future. Given its status as "the biggest company in the world," a legion of scholars, pundits, and watchdogs track the firm's every move, trying to figure out "who" Wal-Mart really is and why it does what it does. The identities attributed to Wal-Mart are potent examples of the three conflicting, macro-social identities of business firms in the USA. Below, we have set them out in tidy master narratives we believe are fairly close to how we, collectively, talk about the Wal-Marts of the world.

1. Got to give Wal-Mart credit; only they could do it. Remember how they got rid of deodorant packaging and saved millions in plastic and shelf-space. The perfect win-win. I know, that was easy, but this new eco-labeling thing is going to be really big. I admit that I am finally convinced that Wal-Mart really believes in the environment. This is a great firm. After all, who wouldn't feel good about being famous for having everything, selling it cheap, while you clean up the environment and make a bundle of money all at the same time? Wal-Mart is showing us that we can have a consumer society and a healthy environment while they make scads of money doing it ... This is a triple bottom line we can live with: win-win-win.

2. Wal-Mart could not care less about the environment. The eco-labeling scheme is just one more example of how the biggest S.O.B. on the block runs around making up the rules, building an even bigger unfair competitive advantage so we can fill up the world with more and more Wal-Marts. You don't really think that Wal-Mart is doing this to reduce carbon emissions, do you? If "Wal-Mart Watch" and the rest weren't on top of their every move, they'd still be locking up immigrant workers overnight in the warehouses, squeezing out free overtime, and plotting to turn Vermont into a parking lot. Wal-Mart is playing Mr. Environment because it's good business. Wal-Mart is about making money. End of story.

3. We have nothing against Wal-Mart eliminating plastic and rationalizing the supply chain to save fuel. Every little bit helps. But it's up to governments to set up the rules and reduce carbon emissions and stop global warming. Every time we step back and let Wal-Mart decide or we applaud Wal-Mart for doing something good, we forget that the real challenge is *global* warming at a *global* scale

and that we will survive only if our governments finally have the courage to help us change how we live. We don't need Al Gore and the rest of the gurus to explain this to us all over again, do we? Wal-Mart is a business in the business of making money. That's the only thing we can be sure Wal-Mart wants or believes in; and that's OK as long as we understand it and don't expect something else. There must be a separation of government and business just as there is a separation of church and state.

We have heard it all before. The debate hasn't shifted an iota in decades. What has changed, however, is how Wal-Mart executives respond to the issues and how Wal-Mart understands social strategy. There is a clear pattern in the statements and actions of Wal-Mart executives and corporate representatives. First, they make an active effort to find out what different interest groups want from Wal-Mart. Second, in word and action, Wal-Mart seeks to engage in social action that benefits its shareholders and society. Wal-Mart is building a corporate identity that integrates social action into its strategic behavior.

In making this observation, we are not making any pronouncement on the intentions of the decision-makers within Wal-Mart, or on the firm's status as an ethical actor. Divagations on the motivations of Wal-Mart executives are unproductive; we are not privy to their decision-making process.

If we don't have access to motivations, how do we come to an understanding of an organization's identity? Researchers on organization identity, following the work of Albert and Whetten (1985), seem to agree on the following:

Identity at the organizational level refers to insiders' answers to self-reflective questions about what is central to their organization's existence, such as "Who are we as an organization?" or "Who do we want to be as an organization?" ... It represents insiders' central perceptions and beliefs about what distinguishes their organization from others and provides the foundation for presenting the organization to external audiences.

(Corley and Gioia, 2004: 174–175)

The two questions seem to provide a straightforward, direct view into corporate identity, by asking members of the organization about their business objectives as well as personal and group value objectives. Unfortunately, once again, we don't often have access to ask such questions.

The answer lies in behavior – in the "presenting of the organization to the external world" (Corley and Gioia, 2005: 175). Kenneth Andrews' (1971) definition of strategy is as good as any explanation of how firms are presented to the world.

Corporate strategy is ... *the pattern of decisions* in a company that *determines* and *reveals* its *objectives*, purposes or goals, produces the principal policies and *plans* for achieving those goals, and defines the *range of businesses* the company is to pursue, the kind of economic and human organization it is or intends to be, and the nature of *the economic and non-economic contribution it intends to make to its shareholders, employees, customers, and communities.* (1971: 18–19, emphasis added)

Andrews' definition of corporate strategy was taught for more than thirty years at Harvard's MBA in the capstone business policy course; he was co-author of the textbook, Business Policy: Text and Cases (Christensen and Andrews, 1965). Andrews, like Barnard, never questioned that values, identity, and the "non-economic" contribution of the firm was part of strategy and that the proper way to understand these things was to look at "the pattern of decisions in a company that determines and reveals its objectives ..."

The phrase is worth repeating. We believe Barnard and Andrews were right and that Porter and Jensen, and even Williamson, were wrong. Admittedly, our approach is difficult. Among the constraints are the complexity and cost of developing an integrated market and nonmarket strategy (Chapter 3–5), and of measurement and evaluation (Chapter 12). Focusing on the market and shareholder and putting all else in a subordinate role does make life easier. This does not mean that such companies are socially or environmentally irresponsible. Most multinationals, whatever their approach to strategy, make the expected and proper declarations of commitment to social responsibility and environmental sustainability and implement the customary array of CSR and environmental practices. It is also standard practice to speak of the cost of social action programs as "strategic," "part of who we are," etc. This does not change the fact, nonetheless, that management, in fact, considers the expense incurred as a necessary part of doing business, and that there is no strategic benefit from being a "good corporate citizen." Proper behavior is rarely a differentiator in developed countries.

However, though most multinationals seem to have much the same social and environmental approach, negative social and environmental impacts do vary across firms. On occasion, unethical and illegal behavior is systematic, as in the Enron case. When caught, these firms deservedly become cannon fodder for the press and NGOs; they also provide evidence for anti-business and anti-globalization groups who hardly need encouragement.

Much more interesting than Enron are firms that do not suffer a clinical pathology, but earn the label of "bad corporate citizen" through a high-profile environmental accident or an isolated case of malfeasance. In many occasions, it is difficult to ascertain whether a negative event is one that could happen even at a well-run company with a positive and professional social action and environmental program or is part of a pattern of behavior. Below, in our review of the Archer Daniels Midland (ADM) case and the movie *The Informant!*, the issue of who is involved and whether their actions are representative of the company is central to our understanding of what happened. Not surprisingly, the movie's view of the extent of unethical behavior at ADM is quite different from that of the firm.

The ADM price-fixing scandal, as presented by director Steven Soderbergh, addresses these issues through an examination of the impact of corporate identity on corporate behavior and on the personal identities of those involved. The informant, played by Matt Damon, is Mark Whitacre, an ADM executive who goes undercover to expose price-fixing while at the same time getting rich on his own kickback scheme. There is nothing special about either ADM's price-fixing or Whitacre taking kickbacks. The subject of the movie is Whitacre's brilliant, comedic, compulsive lying while his identity and values crumble as his ADM identity is torn apart. When caught, he tries to get off by faking bipolar disorder, inventing a twenty-minute mafia bullying story, and falsely accusing an FBI agent of harassment. Whitacre's personality disorders are contrasted with his ADM colleagues who, though crooks, are played to be completely normal, vulgar, sane, and boring. While Whitacre has neither identity nor values, ADM is depicted as possessing a fully developed and repulsive identity and debased values.

In 1995, as Whitaker went to trial, the Cato Institute wrote a scathing, at times hyperbolic, report on the pernicious consequences of ADM's power and influence.

The Archer Daniels Midland Corporation (ADM) has been the most prominent recipient of corporate welfare in recent US history. ADM and its chairman Dwayne Andreas have lavishly fertilized both political parties with millions of dollars in handouts and in return have reaped billion-dollar windfalls from taxpayers and consumers. Thanks to federal protection of the domestic sugar industry, ethanol subsidies, subsidized grain exports, and various other programs, ADM has cost the American economy billions of dollars since 1980 and has indirectly cost Americans tens of billions of dollars in higher prices and higher taxes over that same period. At least 43 percent of ADM's annual profits are from products heavily subsidized or protected by the American government. Moreover, every $1 of profits earned by ADM's corn sweetener operation costs consumers $10, and every $1 of profits earned by its ethanol operation costs taxpayers $30. (Bovard, 1995)

At the close of 2009, ADM continues to be agro-business's largest recipient of ethanol and other subsidies, and is a highly skilled political and nonmarket strategist. In response to the multiple ethical and environmental scandals that followed price-fixing arrests, ADM's board in 2006 hired Patricia Woertz from Chevron to replace CEO G. Allen Andreas, who had succeeded his uncle, Dwayne Andreas,[2] in 1997. The appointment of Woertz was a surprise, as G. Allen Andreas had proposed that yet another Andreas family member be promoted to CEO. In a *Fortune* article analyzing Ms. Woertz's appointment, "The Outsider" (Birgir, 2006), the title alone was sufficient to tell the story. Ms. Woertz was appointed because she was everything ADM was not: polite, polished, unsullied by scandal, and not an arrogant male. Her charge was to fix the company's reputation. In her first year at work, Ms. Woertz updated the corporate ethics statement and implemented ethics training. She instituted the ADM "Sustainability Steering Committee," which she still leads as "The Corporate Sustainability Priority Champion"; the Committee is given prominence in the ADM corporate webpage, and Ms. Woertz

---

[2] Another of Dwayne Andreas's nephews, Michael Andreas, was sentenced to a three-year prison term in 1999 for the price-fixing scandal.

speaks on issues of environmental sustainability in events around the world. In ADM's 2009 Corporate Responsibility Report, Ms. Woertz informed shareholders of the firm's progress:

To ensure that our energies and resources are focused on areas where ADM can make the greatest possible impact, our Company teamed with Business for Social Responsibility in 2008 to conduct a thorough review and prioritization of the sustainability issues surrounding our business.

This materiality assessment was informed by a review of our corn, soy and palm supply chains, and by interviews with nearly two dozen outside stakeholders, including not-for-profit organizations, think tanks, government agencies, NGOs, foundations and institutional investors.

The assessment revealed that ADM and its stakeholders would best be served by a concentration on supply chain integrity, water resource management and climate change. In response, our Sustainability Steering Committee (SSC) comprising senior executives from throughout the company, formed working groups to drive our activities in each of these key focus areas. Additional workgroups have been established to address energy usage and waste-management. (ADM, 2009)

ADM's webpage, its pronouncements, and the pattern of Ms. Woertz' behavior since she took over as CEO demonstrate, at least, that she can speak the language of CSR. Unfortunately, calling herself "Corporate Sustainability Priority Champion" sounds like it came out of Orwell's *1984* and the Ministry of Truth, and her high profile sustainability persona may be too much of a good thing. In terms of reputation, ADM is a long way off from achieving a turnaround like Wal-Mart.

As regards the firm's identity, we need a good deal more to believe that ADM is a different being, with a different identity or values. Though ADM is a member of the Sustainable Palm Oil Roundtable and has put in place the standard multinational responsibility projects, including "ADM Cares," which targets "up to 1 percent of pretax earnings"[3] for action programs, significant change is difficult to verify. Moreover, Ms. Woertz has remained silent about the negative impact of corn syrup and palm oil on the diets and health of billions of people all around the world.

---

[3] We have been unable to ascertain what commitment the "up to" in "up to 1 percent of pretax earnings" entails.

On the other hand, ADM wisely has not remained silent with regard to *The Informant!* In fact, on the company's homepage, there is a link "About ADM and *The Informant!*" that explains in clear, precise language ADM's assistance to Soderbergh in making the movie. While deploring the price-fixing episode, ADM insists that only a handful of people were involved in the scandal, and outlines the steps that have been taken to ensure that such events do not happen again. In ADM's words:

In response to the illegal activity, we put in place the policies and controls needed. Today, we emphasize achieving the right results, the right way. We have a robust ethics program, with practices and policies that align our actions with our values. We have new leadership. And we now have 28,000 employees around the globe who take great pride in the work we do serving vital needs for food and energy. We value the productive, mutually beneficial relationships we have built with customers, farmers, suppliers and communities.[4]

If ADM's management is able to respond with equal equanimity and intelligence to other social and environmental issues, including those that directly affect business, over a sustained period of time, the firm may construct a much more positive reputation. This will not happen quickly. More importantly, Ms. Woertz must understand that reputation recovery should be treated as an outcome of identity and values reconstruction. Dependence on superficial, prepackaged CSR, ethics, and values programs is especially likely to backfire in an organization that lived through a long period marked by unsavory values and identity.

Reconstructing a firm's identity and values is a difficult task. Setting objectives and measuring and evaluating results, as we commented earlier, is a far less precise exercise than working with financial objectives and measures. In addition to reconfiguring organizational routines, CEOs like Patricia Woertz at ADM must satisfy wary social and environmental stakeholders, while meeting the demands of investors angry at the negative impact of scandals on results. Investors' short-term goals, moreover, often lead them to believe that once all

---

[4] Accessed by internet at www.adm.com/en-US/informant/Pages/default.aspx on December 26, 2009.

the institutional instruments of ethics, CSR, and sustainability are in place, the "doing the right thing" problem is taken care of. To make matters even more difficult for ADM, the firm has two special complications, as well. First, it is dependent on government subsidies; second, palm oil and corn syrup are roundly condemned by nutritionists and blamed for obesity and food addiction.

We conclude our discussion of ADM with some final remarks on the role of the CEO. As has become standard practice, the appointment of a new CEO is meant both to symbolize and enact momentous change. How can a CEO actually live up to such expectations?

On the one hand, it is tempting to dismiss the question and say, "She can't," but that would not be of much help. Instead, we will try to put the strategic role of the CEO in context and see if we can offer a way to think what CEOs can and should do.

ADM's CEO is expected to take decisions that will repair the firm's reputation (external view of the firm). This will be achieved primarily by reconstructing the firm's identity (internal view of the firm). Seen in this light, a CEO's strategic decisions are embedded in a network of institutions and actors. CEOs are expected to respond to legitimacy demands that require them to take decisions that cannot be calculated in terms of profit and loss terms. Selznick (1957) in his descriptions of the adaptation and survival of the Tennessee Valley Authority and other public agencies explains how needs for legitimacy initiate a reformulation of objectives and efforts to co-opt recalcitrant, powerful stakeholders. The end result of the process is a profound change in organizational identity and, when successful, institutional legitimization. Only the few decisions that decide "who" and "what" the organization is going to be are strategic. Strategic leadership, according to Selznick, is required only for those decisions.

When a large multinational has a superior reputation, it is likely that social action projects have something to do with it. Rarely is this a fluke. A superior reputation is generally an accurate reflection of a firm's identity. In other words, we expect a firm's reputation to be a reasonably accurate representation of "who" the firm really is.

Which brings us back to the Wal-Mart case. How can we decide which Wal-Mart story is closest to the truth about "who" the company is? Which story reflects most accurately Wal-Mart's identity and reputation? By extension, we ask which story represents the collective identity of business firms and what we, as a society, want from them?

Answering these questions will go a long way in helping us to understand how corporate identity and reputation may be important to social strategy.

The Wal-Mart case is not unique. BP, Monsanto, Pfizer, Siemens, AccelorMittal, Telefónica, Cemex, Google, etc. – would surely serve just as well to demonstrate that society is divided and unsure about what it wants from business firms. As the 2008–9 economic crisis underscored, we are still at the beginning of a vital debate over the social impact of multinationals.

Though we are at the beginning, we have already discovered one very clearly lit dead end, populated with statements such as "Wal-Mart *decided*" and "Wal-Mart *believes*" and "Wal-Mart *intends*." These volitional statements provide us with what sounds like a meaningful argument, but we soon realize that there's no substance.

As trained observers of corporate behavior, we should recognize that large sophisticated multinationals like Wal-Mart have begun to create social action programs as part of an integrated strategy. Unfortunately, the language used by corporate representatives, the press, and academics often makes a spurious link between corporate intentions and corporate behavior. We read in the business press that company A "intends" B and, therefore, is embarking on C, which will lead to outcome D. The CEO then makes the rounds of CNN, Bloomberg, etc. to explain the firm's great values, great people, great products … not to mention its commitment to sustainable development.

Noble words are sent out in search of a mission to attach themselves to. No wonder there have been few true believers. And then the crisis comes and the questions turn to "How did this happen?" and "How many jobs can be saved?"

In such circumstances, pondering what Wal-Mart "thinks," "believes," "intends," and "wants" may be a luxury. Perhaps what is required is a more measured understanding of, as Charles Fishman has termed it, "The Wal-Mart Effect" (Fishman, 2006). How does Wal-Mart fit into our lives? How would we like Wal-Mart to be in our lives? What can we expect from Wal-Mart in the future?

In answering this final question, we attribute identity to Wal-Mart in order to predict future behavior. We conclude that Wal-Mart's reputation for doing x is a result of who Wal-Mart is.

The three stereotyped "identities" of Wal-Mart that we invented earlier in this chapter all make strong attributions of identity and purpose to the entity called "Wal-Mart". The three caricatures were drawn from the literally hundreds of articles about Wal-Mart we have read over the last decade, many of them quite passionate. They all pretend to "know" Wal-Mart.

Do they? One simple way of demonstrating that we know a person, a company (or any volitional entity) is to predict its behavior. In contemporary social science, there are a good half-dozen theories (rational choice theory; social exchange theory; attribution theory, etc.) that try to explain how this works. We won't put you through a pell-mell recounting of them all. You will recall, however, in our discussion of the theory of the firm and our basic model of corporate social strategy, we did argue that it is customary for us to assume that others attempt to do what is rational (best) for themselves. We argue that intended rational behavior allows us to attach ethical objectives to human action. The coherence and consistency of intended rational behavior is the basis of corporate identity.

From the perspective of the social strategy, the objective is to create a coherent and consistent program of social action that achieves sufficient notoriety, financial and administrative support within the firm that firm employees believe the CEO when he talks about the firm's contribution to society. On this Barnard was surely right. Unless your own people believe, it's not very likely anyone else will.

Identity and social strategy

Social strategy, we have said, is not for everyone. When it comes to identity, our message does not change. Not every company can or should create an identity and culture linked to social strategy. ADM, we suspect, is not a candidate today for social strategy.

Conversely, some companies can and should shape their identity and culture to compete through social strategy. Here's why.

Albert and Whetten (1985) observed that business organizations frequently experience a drift from a single identity to dual or multiple identities. This comes, as we have discussed, with a company's growth. At the same time, success means visibility in the community and increasing demands are made on the firm. Inevitably, business organizations are asked to undertake social projects in the community. Most often, the projects are small, low-cost endeavors that management decides are simply a cost of doing business. The projects have a minor impact on the firm and its understanding of its role in society. It's normal to give back a little.

This is not social strategy, rather the firm's social action projects are a response to society's dual demands for utilitarian and normative behavior (Etzioni, 1961). In other words, the firm maintains its focus on the bottom line, while recognizing it must take into account the impact that it has on the social and natural environment. Social strategy requires two additional steps that go beyond keeping one eye on profit and the other on externalities. First, social action projects are evaluated, approved, and budgeted as part of the strategic planning process. Second, social strategy must become part of *who* the organization is, ultimately affecting the way that the firm responds and adapts to its environment (Dutton and Dukerich, 1991).

While in theory social strategy could simply emerge in the normal course of doing business, this is rather improbable. Jettisoning the idea that "CSR" is an assumable cost and taking up social action as a "strategic investment" is a major cognitive shift. In practical terms, it means competing in a whole new way, reconfiguring markets and reorganizing business units.

Often, the impetus to pursue social strategy will come from a business unit manager who has "seen the light" and can demonstrate that his or her social project was instrumental in getting new business or seeing the market in a new way. This alone is not social strategy. Only top management, beginning with the CEO, can say yes to the resources and organizational changes required for social strategy.

Moreover, implementing social strategy comes with the additional baggage, and cost, of reshaping corporate identity and corporate culture to fit the new strategy. BP found this out when it decided to go green. Months of hard work and the commitment of John Browne to go public with "Beyond Petroleum" were required to convince BP personnel that this was for real. Unfortunately, many remained unconvinced and, as soon as profits slumped, budgets for environmental safety programs were cut, even while Browne was campaigning for BP's rebirth as an advocate for programs to combat climate change (Bach and Allen, 2010). Unhappily for BP, the budget cuts led directly to inspection and maintenance failures involved in the Texas City refinery and Prudhoe Bay disasters, which put an end to BP's social strategy positioning.

In sum, social strategy is not just about putting together a coherent group of social action projects that might be profitable. As with any strategy, here too the right fit with corporate identity, culture, values, etc. will give the firm the staying power needed to make it through the inevitable competitive challenges.

Corporate identity and culture (values and ideology) can affect social strategy formulation because they shape the manager's interpretation of events through processes of selective perception (Goll and Sambharya, 1990). Identity and ideology (values and beliefs that support a social and/or political program) can either strengthen or undermine a firm's commitment to social action. Management values such as social responsibility orientation and participative decision-making are essential to integrating social and environmental impact into decision-making (Goll and Zeitz, 1991).

Social responsibility orientation (SRO)

As introduced in Chapter 4, social responsibility orientation (SRO) refers to a company's commitment to participating in the solution of social problems (Goll and Sambharya, 1995). Not surprisingly, when a firm commits to social strategy, inevitably key members of the top management team have a strong ideological allegiance to SRO.

We knew this when we began our research. We did not know, however, the impact of SRO on firm behavior. As we stated twice at the outset of this chapter, we now know that there is a strong relationship between SRO and value creation via strategic planning.

This is one of our most important findings. The success of social strategy is not accidental, but is mostly likely to be the result of deliberate action – strategic planning – in firms where SRO is part of "who" the firm is. In other words, when a firm's genetic make-up (identity) includes SRO, and when a firm incorporates social strategy into its strategic planning, economic and social value are created. In short, the combination of SRO and social strategy planning works.

The process begins with an SRO identity. Social strategy planning then backs up ideology and values with action. Beliefs are supported with time, commitment, investment. No surprises here. As explained in Chapter 8 on resources and capabilities, just as the credibility of leaders depends on their ability to do what they say and believe (Kouzes and Posner, 1993), so too does the credibility of a firm depend on a match between its values and its behavior.

Moreover, managerial perceptions of the social and natural environment are, of course, shaped by SRO, and accordingly influence the choice of social strategies (Sharma *et al.*, 1999; Bansal and Roth, 2000; Sharma, 2000). Consensus on SRO, including which social and environmental issues to focus on, is a must when customers may be asked to pay a premium for products with social and environmental attributes (Menon and Menon, 1997; Berman *et al.*, 1999; Maignan *et al.*, 1999; Schuler and Cording, 2006).

Participative decision-making

Much of Chapter 7 was devoted to participative decision-making. Here we wish to emphasize that achieving broad organizational consensus on SRO and social strategy can be assisted by participative decision-making (PDM). Though it sounds obvious, the term "social" in strategy implies that the firm is broadening its view of the world and of who and what is important to it. Participative decision-making is an obvious fit, independently of the benefit derived when firm members understand the value of (and are committed to the values associated with) a social project.

We argue that social strategy is more likely to be successful in those firms that promote employee participation in decision-making, creativity, and innovation. So far, however, and contrary to our expectations, our survey research does not support the role of PDM practices in the development of a strategic plan for social strategy. One explanation for this finding is that top management itself does not see the benefit of PDM despite the lip service in favor of it. Another explanation is that PDM may depend upon the cultural context. Our studies took place in Spain and Mexico, while the research of Irene Goll and her colleagues regarding PDM took place in the United States. In some countries where participative decision-making is less common, and respect for authority is greater (Hofstede, 1984), it may be that PDM has a lesser impact on the effectiveness of social strategy.[5]

The argument for PDM was established unequivocally by the success of TQM. There is no question about its essential role in creating

[5] According to Hofstede (1984), respect for authority or power distance (PDI) is greater in both Mexico (PDI=81) and Spain (PDI=57) than in the United States (PDI=40). Although Japan, for example, has a high level of respect for authority (PDI=54), it also has a long tradition of consensual decision-making practices.

employee commitment, vital for effective social strategy. Employee commitment refers to "the extent to which a business unit's employees are fond of the organization, see their future tied to that of the organization, and are willing to make personal sacrifices for the business unit" (Jaworski and Kohli, 1993: 60).

The link between PDM and employee commitment is clear. The link between social strategy and employee commitment is also well established. The research support is extensive. Below, we lay out the research and the logic that puts it together.

US-based research demonstrates that high social performance has a positive impact on employee commitment (Maignan *et al.*, 1999). Also, we know that initial job choice decisions are highly influenced by the image of an organization held by potential job candidates (Gatewood *et al.*, 1993). Firms that are known for environmentally responsible behavior have greater success in recruiting candidates (Dechant and Altman, 1994). In a study of the relationship between a firm's social performance and its attractiveness as an employer, Turban and Greening (1996) found that they were positively related. They specifically asked potential job applicants about the attractiveness of different companies and found attractiveness to be correlated with ratings of corporate social performance (CSP) developed by Kinder, Lydenberg, Domini and Co. (KLD), a stock market research firm, after controlling for profitability and firm size. They suggest that CSP is more important for candidates with many job options than for those candidates with only one job opportunity. In addition, research shows that the fit between an employee and the organizational culture is necessary to job satisfaction, commitment, and the intent to leave an organization (O'Reilly *et al.*, 1991). Behavioral commitment has a significant impact on employee turnover (Kline and Peters, 1991). Thus firms with social strategy are more likely to retain those employees that share similar goals and values. At least in the United States, PDM is essential to the identity of firms that engage in social strategy.

From identity to image and reputation

In our wide-ranging discussion of ADM and Wal-Mart, we explained how identity and reputation are linked. Identity, we said, is the "who" of the firm, whereas reputation is the image others have of the firm.

Over time, with consistent behavior, we claimed, firm management can achieve a fairly good match between the two. If the members of a firm feel good about the firm's identity and reputation, then it makes sense to say that both are firm resources that can be put to work in creating and maintaining competitive advantage. In our discussion, we recognized that identity, in particular, is a difficult concept. First, firm members rarely think or talk about the firm's "identity." Second, large multinationals are complex and diverse, so there is no one identity but rather a dominant or central one.

Reputation, in contrast with corporate identity, has received considerable attention in academic research and even more attention by communications consultants and marketers. With regard to social strategy, reputation, it is often claimed, is the principal competitive advantage acquired via CSR (Fombrun, 1996; Mackey *et al.*, 2007).

Let us consider how this may work in theory and practice in the case of Telefónica in South America. Reputation is a particularly important form of *social capital* because it is related to the question of corporate identity and how stakeholders perceive the firm. Corporate reputation is "the overall estimation in which a company is held by its constituents" (Fombrun, 1996: 37). Reputation creates tangible resources for the firm as it opens doors to other actors in the social and economic environment that may not know the firm's agents personally, but do know the firm's reputation.

Social projects can provide a good way to develop a corporate reputation and generate benefits. Research by Fombrun (1996) indicates that the three factors that companies can proactively manage in order to improve its reputation ranking in the *Fortune* survey are advertising, visibility in the media, and community involvement. Russo and Fouts (1997) have found that high levels of environmental performance are associated with enhanced profitability, in part due to the consequences of a positive reputation for environmental performance. Corporate social strategy systematizes a company's approach to building its reputation by cultivating its involvement with the community through social and environmental projects.

Spanish firms like Telefónica, Repsol, BBVA, and Banco Santander aggressively acquired national firms as a result of privatizations throughout Latin America, mostly in the 1990s. Unfortunately, their work was complicated tremendously by the "neo-colonialist" and "reconquista" labels that were slapped on Spanish multinationals.

These firms needed (and still need) to build social capital through appropriate social strategies that help create trust between the firm and its relevant stakeholders.

However, in order for a reputation to be valuable for a firm, there needs to be a consistency between the firm's identity and the image it projects (Fombrun, 1996). Without consistency between identity and image, reputation will likely suffer. Telefónica's Corporate Reputation Project was created precisely to assure that the image that was being communicated to the public actually matched reality and the corporate identity and ideology that was being professed by top management. César Alierta, president of Telefónica, understood the problem. He said: "Reputation is the consequence of equilibrium between the messages sent and the actions undertaken by all areas of the firm. Consistent messages sent on the basis of each of the aforementioned concepts as well as the relationship between them are essential in order to maintain a good reputation" (Eguía and Allen, 2004: 8). Telefónica invested worldwide in communication programs that focused on the central value of trust internally and with stakeholders. The programs included global corporate identity campaigns, local market identity campaigns as well as global and local social action programs. It based trust on shareholders' expectations of profitability and transparency, the customer's expectation of quality and *"cumplimiento* – fulfillment," the employees' expectation for clarity and career development, and society's expectation of contribution and closeness.

In addition, its communications program involved the development of an ethics code, a corporate responsibility report, and a defined plan of institutional presence whereby it would seek to be included in such programs as the FTSE4Good, UN Global Compact, Foro de Reputación Corporativa ("Corporate Reputation Forum"), among many others. Telefónica also established a CSR master plan built around a series of indicators to monitor relationships with stakeholders and follow up on information required by the Global Reporting Initiative (GRI) and other sustainability measurement initiatives like the Dow Jones Sustainability Index (DJSI), the identification of best internal practices.

Most importantly, Telefónica actively promoted corporate responsibility worldwide. The multi-year project began with reputation workshops in Spain and in each of its subsidiaries to bring employees into the decision-making process. The workshops identified potential reputation threats and resulted in a consensus on ethical, social, and environmental *common minimums*. In addition, the workshops identified concrete projects such as ethical purchasing and a model of the socially responsible office for implementation through the company.

Telefónica carefully linked values and identity with its social action programs and corporate reputation. As a result of its efforts, Telefónica has earned a reputation as a firm that is socially committed to assisting the local communities where the firm operates (Eguía and Allen, 2004).

In the five years since we worked on the "Telefónica Corporate Reputation Project" case, the firm has consistently incorporated new projects and programs, most notably its "Business Principles" employee training and "Proniño," a philanthropic project that provides more than 100,000 Latin American children with schooling. In the recession, Telefónica has emphasized its 257,000 direct employees worldwide and 330,000 indirect jobs in supplier companies.

Telefónica does not describe itself as a firm with a social strategy. Management is also quite careful about selecting which stakeholders to please and under what circumstances. In our discussion of Telefónica in Chapters 6 and 7, we depicted a firm that was exceptionally skillful at nonmarket strategy, and a firm that aroused conflicting responses in its customers, much like Microsoft. Customers complain, the firms get sued by the competition for alleged unfair market practices, but customers keep coming back. Like Microsoft, Telefónica has a strong social responsibility orientation built, in large part, though employee participation.

Conclusion

Curiously, in the 2009 healthcare debate, supporters of US President Barack Obama ended up spending much of their time talking about his personality: does he have the strength to stand his ground on what they consider a non-negotiable, inalienable right to healthcare? Meanwhile, the anti-Obama forces were attacking Obama's identity. Where's his birth certificate proving he is an American eligible to be President? Is he really a Christian? Is he, finally, really an American at all? Does he have true American values? Does he understand, as Sarah Palin challenged in the Presidential campaign, the real America, the real American culture?

The debate was about identity, culture, and values, the same concepts we have been discussing throughout this chapter. Perhaps we may be inflating the importance of social strategy a bit by comparing what we are doing here in this book with the challenges of comprehensive healthcare addressed by President Obama, but with your permission, we would like to push the analogy a bit further.

Many people have been struck by the extraordinary aggressiveness of the attack on President Obama. Some find the statements made by those opposing him astonishing and irrational. Irrational is the label we use for what seems to us the wrong way to do things.

Obama has striven first and foremost to appear to be rational. He defined his identity in a book, *Dreams from My Father: A Story of Race and Inheritance*. Few have understood better than Obama that identity is the "who" that decides what to do. "Doing" happens in a culture, in multiple cultures. An identity must be coherent with culture if one is to cope successfully. In his book, President Obama explained how this works, and how he sees himself fitting in. On March 18, 2008, he used these same concepts to explain race in America in a brilliant and insightful speech entitled: "A More Perfect Union." His aim was, and is, to reshape America in a way consistent with its "true" identity and "truest" values. Not everyone agreed, or agrees now. There are competing interests, competing identities and values. Interest groups defend their ideologies, sometimes offering programs, sometimes simply rejecting competing ideologies and identities. The political process is often ugly, often unfair, objectives are distorted, provisions in laws get twisted; at times democracy looks like anything but. Obama cannot shape America in his image. It is all very, very messy.

Culture, identity, and values are messy in large firms, too. Legally, firms are different from governments in one very important way. There are rules for firms to cease operating. Schumpeter's famous phrase, "creative destruction," aptly explains why firms must die; they are instruments of innovation and economic wealth creation. When others come along that do the job better, the old firm folds because it is no longer profitable.

Try telling this to the founders, owners, and employees of a company that goes bankrupt. Over time, as the members of an organization construct its identity and values, as they collectively develop ways of doing things (a culture) that make our company different from any other company, firms are institutionalized (Selznick, 1957) and we care about what they do and what happens to them. Suddenly, the continued life of the company is far more important than its profitability. For those inside the firm, the social impact of their enterprise on them is more important than economic value creation.

Social entrepreneurs create companies whose first objective is to meet a social need; solve a human problem. Often these companies seek support from non-profits and other governments to stay alive. At some point they either fold, become NGOs, or become companies, like Compartamos, the Mexican bank that started as an NGO, became a business, went public, and now is vilified by microcredit purists.

Perhaps the most important lesson to be drawn from this chapter is that we all want to have it all. Make money, do good, stay in business forever. Recall that the oldest organizations in the world are the Catholic Church and universities. Governments follow and businesses come in next to last, only slightly ahead of social clubs.

Social strategy will not turn a business into a religious organization or a university. The identity of the firm may now incorporate social objectives, but these must be compatible with the business objectives of the company. If the company is a large multinational with a long business tradition, it is probable that long-standing business objectives are more important to the firm's identity than recently acquired social objectives and commitments.

In these companies, social action is a complement to business strategy. Sometimes, those involved in social action would like to see the firm actively pursue social strategy.

It can happen. Get the word out, achieve short-term business successes, demonstrate that social action projects are equally or more profitable than standard market operations. Remember that most of us would rather "do work that is profitable and makes the world a better place" than "make money and do CSR on the side." In time, social strategy may become the dominant strategy and identity of the firm.

Social strategy will flourish only where there are strong advocates. The instigators of social strategy have a strong social responsibility orientation and believe in participative decision-making. The cultural model should be clear: people who care about social problems want to work in firms with participative management. They want to create and market products and services that also create economic and social value. It's a more complex identity than the "single object-ive function" organization posited by the classical theory of the firm (Jensen and Meckling, 1976). It's harder to organize, to manage, and to keep on track when times are tough.

Hard as it may be, social strategy can be achieved within the bound-aries of a single organization. This is a piece of cake next to Obama's challenge of putting together a new identity and social strategy for a divided nation.

PART III

Implementing social strategy

10 | *Organizing for social strategy*

Internalizing social action

To increase a firm's competitive advantage, social projects must be cost effective and produce a clear return on investment. The odds of success are higher when projects are strategically aligned with the business mission of the company, and the costs of implementing social activities are managed as they would be for other business investments. The strategic decisions facing senior managers are twofold: (1) which social activities are right for the company? and (2) how can social activities be managed to reduce costs? For example, stakeholders often ask publicly traded corporations to respond to issues such as AIDS research and homelessness. The decision to focus efforts on AIDS research rather than homelessness (or any number of other social ills) is the company's choice. Once decided, the firm must then determine how it can be most effective. Shall the firm support research by other organizations through charitable contributions? Shall it undertake in-house research to find a cure? Or should the firm collaborate with a university to develop a joint program of research? The decision to outsource social activity through charitable contributions, internalize it, or collaborate with other organizations has important implications for the cost side of corporate social management. These alternatives represent issues of governance – i.e., how the company chooses to organize a particular activity in order to realize mutual gains for itself and its partners (Williamson, 1996).

The problem for senior management is to determine which governance structure or mode is most effective for organizing a particular social activity, e.g., in-house, outsourcing, or collaboration. This

This chapter is based on Bryan W. Husted, 2003. Governance choices for corporate social responsibility: To contribute, to collaborate, or to internalize? *Long Range Planning*, 36: 481–498. Used with the permission of *Long Range Planning* and Elsevier.

decision is important for several reasons. First, to be effective, social activities must be organized and managed to create the greatest social good at the least possible cost.[1] Corporations cannot afford to waste resources, even those dedicated to discretionary, non-strategic activities. Second, the discretionary nature of much CSR activity lends itself to possible abuse, ranging from top management siphoning off money to their favorite causes to outright fraud. According to a report by the Association of Certified Fraud Examiners (2008), corporate fraud was estimated to amount to almost US$994 billion in 2008. Internal fraud is not the only concern. Firms must ensure that the non-profit recipients of donations do their work honestly and efficiently.

Such practical matters of governance are more easily managed when firms pursue social strategy through the alignment of shareholder and stakeholder interests. The objective function is clear: competitive advantage for the firm and social action projects for the community. When it works, economic value and social value are created.

In this chapter, we offer a framework for managers to think about the decision to undertake corporate social activities internally, to outsource them, or to collaborate. Thus, we examine corporate experience in undertaking social activity in order to build a decision-making framework consistent with current thinking in strategic management. In the first section, we describe and compare the three modes of social governance. Using the concepts of centrality and appropriability from Chapter 5, we then build the framework to guide managers in the governance decision. Finally, we develop some of the implications of this framework for management practice and research and explore its limitations. Throughout the chapter, we make extensive reference to cases, chosen from secondary sources, to illustrate the different points we have made.[2] In order to facilitate reference to these cases, they are summarized in Appendix 10.1.

---

[1] In this chapter we use the term "social activities" to embrace a broad range of social action, including everything from a charitable contribution to an in-house project. In keeping with our usage throughout the book, when we speak of projects, we refer to projects that need to be managed by the firm. Some activities, like corporate contributions, require little or no management.

[2] These examples were found through secondary sources, such as N. N. Tichy, A. R. McGill, and L. St. Clair (eds.), 1997. *Corporate global citizenship: Doing business in the public eye*, San Francisco, CA: The New Lexington Press. In addition, a great deal of information was obtained from the annual reports of many of these firms as found on the internet.

Governance for social strategy

Governance structures for social activities

Corporate social action is made concrete through the specific projects or activities that a company implements. A social activity entails the investment of firm resources for the production of social goods and services. As stated earlier, social governance refers to how these activities are organized. Within companies, three types or modes of social governance are most common. Firms customarily either: (1) outsource social activities through charitable contributions; (2) internalize social activity through in-house projects; or (3) collaborate with partners.[3] Figure 10.1 depicts each of these governance modes.

Companies utilize charitable contributions more often than any other form of social governance. Charitable contributions involve the transfer of financial and/or other resources from the firm to non-profit organizations that undertake charitable, social, educational, community, or scientific work. In 2007, corporate charitable giving in the United States amounted to almost US$15.69 billion (American Association of Fundraising Counsel, 2008). As seen in Figure 10.1, there is an independent relationship between the "donor" and the "recipient" of the charitable contribution. Through charitable contributions, a company can direct resources to those community and other social organizations that are experts at a particular problem. The company's involvement in the management of the project is usually minimal. These transfers may be made by the corporation through a corporate foundation, in its own name, or through its employees. For example, through its company foundation, Nokia gives funding to external organizations focused on scientific research and education related to information and telecommunication technologies. Symantec Corporation makes both direct donations of software to non-profit organizations as well as donations through its foundation.

Unlike charitable contributions, in-house projects involve extensive corporate participation in the planning, execution, and evaluation

---

[3] These three modes parallel the three forms of contractual governance postulated by Oliver Williamson (1985): market, hierarchy, and hybrid. Joseph Galaskiewicz enumerates many kinds of CSR activities, but they can all be summarized by these three basic types.

(A) Charitable Contributions

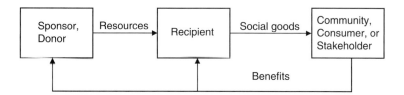

(B) In-house project

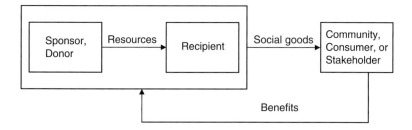

(C) Collaboration

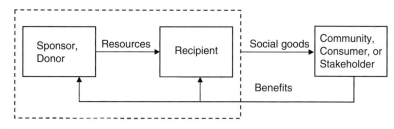

Figure 10.1: Social governance structures

of social action projects. Generally, the company allocates financial and other resources to the project, which is implemented through an organizational unit within the firm. Thus, the solid line surrounding the "donor" and the "recipient" in Figure 10.1 suggests a dependent relationship between the two, i.e., the donor and recipient are part of the same company. Many in-house projects focus on employees as the internal "consumer" or the benefiting stakeholder such as the UK transport company, FirstGroup plc, which includes employee well-being within its social domain. Other in-house projects focus on external stakeholders, such as Vancity located in British Columbia, which provides a whole range of innovative banking products to serve the needs of low-income communities as well as financing environmental improvements. In each case, companies design, develop, and execute the in-house social action project alone, without the assistance of outside non-profit organizations. The greatest advantage of in-house programs is that senior management can strategically target resources to meet specific company and community needs. In the above examples, FirstGroup's employee wellbeing program assists in employee retention, while Vancity targets traditionally underserved markets. In each case, the benefits reaped by the company are more complex than those achieved through charitable contributions. However, the costs of implementing in-house projects can be significantly greater.

Collaborative projects involve a partnership between the firm and a non-profit organization, in which the firm transfers resources to the non-profit partner in order to carry out social activities jointly (Mullen, 1997). In Figure 10.1, the dotted line suggests an interdependent relationship between the "donor" and "recipient," where the donor and recipient partner on a specific project work together and jointly benefit. For example, Johnson and Johnson works with the World Wildlife Fund on issues of environmental health and education. Hewlett Packard works with organizations that support the employment of differently abled people to recruit and support them in technical careers. Google.org, the for-profit philanthropy owned by Google, lends its capabilities in information and technology to partner organizations specialized in such current issues as climate change, poverty, and emerging diseases. In each case both the company and its non-profit partner contribute resources to the development and implementation of the program. Like in-house projects, the benefits of collaborations are multiple, but accrue to both the company and the non-profit partner, while costs may be shared or carried by the corporate sponsor, as in the case of Leche Ram and UNICEF.

Attributes of social governance

When choosing a social governance structure, senior managers need to take costs into consideration, especially those associated with the basic tasks of governance: coordination and motivation (Milgrom and Roberts, 1992). The task of coordination arises because it is often less costly for two different departments or companies to specialize in providing a particular good or service and then exchange those goods or services than for the two parties to produce everything on their own. Thus, there is often a need for companies to coordinate their activities effectively in order to reduce costs. Coordination involves processes such as searching for potential partners, negotiating rights and responsibilities, and making mutually acceptable adjustments to unforeseen contingencies. The company is responsible for the costs associated with these processes and they vary in relation to the governance structure selected by senior management. In the case of charitable contributions, for example, the firm has to search for worthy causes and recipients that will promote its strategic and/or social objectives.

Coordination can either occur autonomously or cooperatively. When the parties to a transaction are able to adjust independently to unforeseen contingencies, this is autonomous coordination. For example, if a hurricane destroys the citrus crop of a region, buyers and sellers can independently make changes in the price of oranges so that the supply and demand remain in equilibrium. Cooperative coordination refers to the capacity of the parties to work together, i.e., interdependently, in responding to unexpected changes, either through bargaining or administrative decisions. Continuing with the same example, if the hurricane leaves a multitude of people homeless, a firm can direct its employees to work with the Red Cross in relief efforts.

The second task of governance – motivation – assures that individuals and/or companies fulfill their agreements. In relation to social activities, motivation costs arise because of the concern that the internal or external recipient of funds will not carry out the interests of the donor company. The effectiveness of motivation depends on the intensity of incentives or the presence of administrative controls. Incentive intensity can be defined as the extent to which economic rewards vary according to performance. In other words, as the performance of a person or an organization increases, compensation also increases. In the business world, the classic example of motivation characterized by high incentive intensity is a sales commission. In terms of social activity, the continued funding of grants contingent upon performance is a good example of high-intensity incentives. On the other hand, where economic rewards are not tied to performance, incentive intensity is low. In the compensation example, a fixed salary provides a salesperson with no economic motivation to increase sales. In the social activity example, non-contingent funding reflects low incentive intensity.

Administrative control refers to the company's systems, which allow it to evaluate the performance of its employees and/or departments, and either reward or punish those employees for behavior that supports or undermines its objectives. For example, firms may use the balanced scorecard, standardized performance measures, and 360-multi-rater performance evaluations of employees to get a more accurate picture of the contributions made by different members of the organization. In the case of social action projects, evaluation systems can also be used to measure the achievement of social goals and objectives. These evaluations are translated into rewards such as salary increases or punishments such as the deferral of job promotions.

Comparisons of social governance modes

Table 10.1 compares the three social governance mechanisms in terms of coordination (autonomous and cooperative) and motivation (incentive intensity and administrative control).

In the case of charitable contributions, the participation of the donor company in the development of social activity is minimal. The donor and recipient have a high ability to adapt independently to unforeseen contingencies because the donor is able to switch funding from one recipient to another depending on current needs and changing social trends. A hurricane in Honduras may require donations to the International Red Cross, while the growing AIDS crisis in India may result in donations to the AIDS Research Foundation of India. The independent, autonomous nature of the relationship between donor and recipient results in a low level of cooperation and coordination. If the donor disagrees with the response of the recipient non-profit organization to unanticipated contingencies, the donor may simply withhold future funding from the recipient; there is no need for the donor and recipient to adapt to each other.

Incentives are intense because the donor is able to tie future contributions to the recipient's performance. Administrative controls over the recipient are low because the donor company is unable to evaluate the non-profit recipient's employees or systems to ensure that the recipient is fulfilling the social activities as agreed.

Table 10.1: *A comparative analysis of social governance structures*

Organizational tasks	Attributes of social governance	Social governance structures		
		Charitable contribution (Odebrecht and Education NGOs)	In-house projects (Vancity and "Our Change Products")	Collaboration (Lafarge and Habitat for Humanity)
Coordination	Autonomous coordination	High	Low	Intermediate
	Cooperative coordination	Low	High	Intermediate
Motivation	Incentive intensity	High	Low	Intermediate
	Administrative control	Low	High	Intermediate

A case in point is the Odebrecht Foundation in Brazil, which provides financial support to non-profit organizations that develop and implement educational programs for adolescents in order to develop capacities that improve the quality of life. The Foundation is a member of the conglomerate Odebrecht Group. Non-profit organizations submit formal proposals to the Foundation and these projects are funded according to their fit with the Foundation's objectives. Clearly there is a high level of autonomous coordination between the Odebrecht Foundation and the recipient non-profits. Odebrecht exercises no administrative control over the non-profits. However, the competitive grant system creates strong incentives to comply with and exceed program requirements in order to obtain continued or future funding.

Do all corporate contributions conform to this logic? No. Certainly, there are long-term relationships between firms and favored non-profits, e.g., IBM's decades-old relationship with the Museum of Modern Art in New York or Telefónica's support for the Prado Museum in Madrid, in which the firms provide unconditional support without regard to performance measures, but these cases do not represent an effort to minimize governance costs and maximize firm benefits.

In-house social action projects require corporate involvement that goes beyond the donation of money or goods. The firm plans, executes, and evaluates the project. Since these projects are developed within the organizational structure of the firm, they are subject to all of the advantages and disadvantages of organizational hierarchies. Cooperation within the firm is high because the recipient submits to the same authority structure. However, autonomous adaptations are minimal because the decisions of the in-house recipient are bound by the objectives of the donor, i.e., the company itself. Incentives are weak because the employees responsible usually receive a fixed salary and the success or failure of the social action project will not directly affect their compensation. However, there is high administrative control as internal company systems provide ways to evaluate employees and departments.

Vancity is a credit union with 57 branches and 360,000 members based in British Columbia, Canada that took CSR from being a core value of the company to being a core differentiator.[4] It is hard to separate the business of Vancity from its social action projects. They are integrated in the core strategy of the company. "Our change products" is not exactly a social action project, or a particular line of services, but represents the way the company conceives of its offering. It is not your traditional banking service segmentation of "open an account," "get a loan," etc. The service categories are "acting on climate change," "social enterprises," "entrepreneurs," "financial literacy and basic banking," and "socially responsible investing." Under each category are the actual products and services sold by the company, such as socially responsible investment funds, or a microloan program tailored for social enterprises doing work in the community and that require small amounts of capital to grow.

Collaborative social activities are characterized by intermediate levels of the governance. Incentives are more intense for a collaborative venture than for an in-house project, but weaker than in the case of charitable contributions. Competition for funds from the donor company is tempered by the donor's greater dependence on the non-profit

---

[4] Presentation given by Sloan Dinning (director, brand and marketing communications for Vancity Credit Union) and Jim Southcott (TBWA Canada) on realigning Vancity's marketing strategies with the CSR strategies of the company at the 2007 " Social Responsibility Forum – Why Doing Good is Good for Business", Toronto.

partner-recipient. This dependence is mutual because the recipient also depends on the resources of the donor in order to carry out the joint social activities. Administrative controls exist, but once again are effective only through voluntary cooperation between the two organizations. In terms of coordination, adaptation to unforeseen contingencies is neither entirely autonomous nor completely cooperative through the exercise of hierarchical authority. Instead, cooperative coordination in the form of bargaining is necessary because the interdependence between the partners requires them to work out disagreements, rather than simply switch partners or order compliance.

For example, Lafarge, a major construction materials manufacturer, and Habitat for Humanity, a non-profit, faith-based organization that helps people build affordable housing, have partnered to build social homes in Romania since 2003. Habitat for Humanity is active in about 7 medium-sized Romanian towns and has helped over 650 poor families build a home.[5] Through volunteer labor, and donations of money and materials, Habitat finances and organizes construction of the houses and sells them at no profit and with affordable loan payment to the participating families. The mortgage payments are used to build other Habitat houses and the new homeowners contribute their own labor to building houses for other families (Habitat, 2008).

Lafarge provides construction materials and volunteer employees to work on Habitat's construction sites. According to the corporation, the value of the Lafarge contribution in terms of materials, equipment, and volunteering employee labor will be approximately €300,000 for the period 2003–12.[6] Cooperative coordination between Lafarge and Habitat for Humanity is far greater than it would be in the case of a charitable contribution, but less than an in house project. Lafarge administrative controls extend only to its employees, but cannot evaluate the performance of other Habitat for Humanity collaborators. The interdependence of this collaborative arrangement allowed Lafarge to contribute in an area where it has relevant resources rather than take on the social housing project alone.

---

[5] This information is from the news section of the website www.responsabilitateasociala.ro accessed October 25, 2008.

[6] "Lafarge si Habitat for Humanity isi prelungesc parteneriatul pentru inca 5 ani" was located in the news section of website www.responsabilitateasociala. ro accessed on October 25, 2008 by research assistant Iuliana Dutkay.

In summary, social action can be carried out as charitable contributions to third parties (NGOs, community organizations, etc.), directly as in-house projects, or through collaborative partnerships and alliances. Each form enjoys different strengths and weaknesses with respect to its capacity for coordination and motivation as well as commitment and investment.

A decision-making framework for organizing social activities

In this section, we examine how two dimensions of social activities – centrality and appropriability – relate to the comparative costs of these governance modes. But before discussing this issue and a brief review of the definitions of centrality and appropriability, we need to deal with a very basic question. What happens to this framework if the company's purpose is altruistic rather than strategic in nature?

Motivation for social engagement

Organizational economics provides the foundation for our approach. However, some may question whether it makes sense to evaluate social action programs in terms of economic theory. Should social activity be evaluated in terms of costs and benefits? Clearly, if the corporate purpose behind social activity is strategic in nature, i.e., to increase the competitive advantage of the firm, then cost considerations play an important role with respect to governance. Activities related to motivation and coordination create costs that need to be considered when choosing governance structures.

It is also natural to question the extent to which concerns about social activities can be reflected in economic theory. This theory assumes that economic actors are self-interested, and sometimes even opportunistic in their willingness to mislead or confuse others (Williamson, 1985). Such an assumption appears to go against the spirit of most social action, which is based on concerns for cooperation and solidarity and seems to emanate from an assumption of altruism. However, the economic assumption of opportunism only requires that some people act opportunistically some of the time; it is not necessary that people always behave opportunistically. This understanding is supported by research demonstrating that self-interest rather than altruism is the working assumption of most firms that participate in social activities (Berman *et al.* 1999).

Opportunism in the form of non-profit fraud can cause actual economic losses in the case of social strategy or goal displacement in some non-strategic social action. Goal displacement occurs when employees seek objectives other than those expressed in the firm's mission and objectives. Even assuming that altruistic motives rather than strategic ones drive social action, there are still concerns about the effectiveness of such projects. Once effectiveness becomes an issue, recipients may then use resources unwisely or for purposes other than those originally agreed upon. Indeed such concerns occur even for non-profit organizations as evidenced by the charges of fraud and mismanagement against officials of US religious and community organizations, e.g., the Episcopal Church, the National Baptist Convention, and the Red Cross (Greenlee *et al.*, 2007). In each case, the problem is: how does the donor motivate the recipient to manage financial and other resources wisely?

In social activities, senior managers act opportunistically when making decisions that benefit their own personal interests rather than corporate interests or social needs. The possibility of opportunism exists for both parties involved in social activities – the donor company and the recipient non-profit organization. In both cases, neither shareholder nor community interests are served. For example, charitable donations from corporations can represent corporate fraud as in the case of John Rigas, founder and CEO of Adelphia Communications, formerly the sixth largest cable company in the United States. He used corporate funds to make generous donations to local and community groups and thus advance his personal charitable causes and interests, rather than those of the company. If donors are more interested in their image than the non-profit's effectiveness, then it is quite easy for funds to be diverted to other purposes.

In the case of non-profit fraud, resources are directed toward activities that further corporate interest, but the non-profit recipient diverts the use of those resources for personal benefit. Although the total amount of non-profit fraud is difficult to estimate, it has occurred in community, religious, and educational institutions as well as NGOs of all types (Greenlee *et al.*, 2007). Fraud may be easier to commit in non-profit organizations because they often lack many of the financial controls and expertise that exist in business firms. Also, without a bottom line, it is often difficult to measure effective performance of a non-profit organization. This results in a situation where some non-profit recipients take advantage of the corporate donors to use funds for personal rather than intended purposes.

Corporate social activity thus occurs in a tension between two worlds: a strategic world in which cost considerations are predom-inant and a non-strategic, even altruistic one in which cost consid-erations are less important, although not entirely irrelevant. To the extent that strategic concerns are less important, one will find greater deviations from the economic logic outlined in this framework and explanations of social governance choice will move to considerations of the institutional environment (Meyer and Rowan, 1977) and the idiosyncratic preferences of senior managers (Andrews, 1971). Thus where strategic concerns are weak, social activity is often a reflection of pressures to imitate other companies as a way to obtain approval from the corporate or local community. As stated from the outset, the extent to which social action is used to pursue strategic opportunities aligned with the economic mission of the company as opposed to non-strategic motives is a basic decision made by senior management.

Dimensions of social activity

If the firm decides to align its social action projects with its economic objectives, then considerations of efficiency or cost effectiveness become paramount. As mentioned previously, governance in social activities takes into account two broad kinds of tasks: motivation and coordination. Both of these tasks are especially relevant in under-standing when the firm internalizes, outsources, or collaborates in order to carry out social activities. The challenges of motivation and coordination in social activities are captured by the concepts of cen-trality and appropriability, discussed previously in Chapter 5.

Centrality. Centrality refers to the closeness of fit between the firm's social activity and its mission and objectives. There is a close relation-ship between the social project and the firm's value chain activities or its competitive environment (Porter and Kramer, 2006). Centrality is high when the firm's social activity is closely related to its core business activity. Conversely, centrality is low when social action is unrelated to the core business. This social dimension is relevant to the governance decision because it affects motivation and coordination costs. To the extent that social activities are closely related to the firm's mission and objectives, the firm has a greater capacity to use its own administrative control systems in order to evaluate social activities. The firm can then reward or punish behavior that is consistent with the firm's mission. In addition, coordination costs are reduced for in-house projects where they are closely related to the firm's core business mission. As social action becomes less central to the firm's mission, administrative control systems are less capable of evaluating performance, and therefore motivation costs rise. Under such circumstances, it makes more sense to tie economic incentives to an easily observable measure of performance in order to motivate managers of the recipient to pursue the social objectives the donor company seeks to support.

For example, Banco Itaú has developed a core competence in the structuring and financing of commercial projects, which it often extends to social action projects. It thus takes few new resources to engage in the same activities as a form of social action. Itaú can easily evaluate the performance of its own personnel in managing low-interest loans for community projects. This would not be the case for either American Airlines, when it donates money to the San Francisco Symphony, or Levi Strauss, when it gives money for AIDS research. Neither of these activities is central to the mission, objectives, and core competencies of either American Airlines or Levi Strauss. In these latter two examples, motivation can be quite problematic because the donor does not have the skills to evaluate adequately the performance of the employees or programs of the recipient non-profit organization.

Sometimes there are significant differences in the centrality of social projects undertaken by the same firm. Banco Itaú of Brazil and Banco Bilbao Vizcaya Argentaria (BBVA) of Spain both have low-interest mortgage programs for the needy. Such programs are highly central to their missions as banks. On the other hand, reforestation in Brazil and the restoration of cathedrals in Spain are less central to their respective missions. As we will see later, these differences in centrality will call for different governance structures.

Appropriability. Social activities are also subject to pressures for economizing on coordination and motivation costs through the variable of appropriability, which refers to the extent to which the firm is able to capture a share of the profit stream generated by its investments in social action. Of special interest is product differentiation, which can be created by endowing a product with social attributes (product innovation) or developing the product through socially responsible processes (process innovation). In either case, the firm creates either a new market for such social products or a willingness by the consumer to pay a price premium for products with social attributes (McWilliams and Siegel, 2001).

Social activities capture private benefits when they are difficult to imitate (Barney, 1986a) and easily exclude competitors from the benefits of social investments (Teece, 1998). Appropriability is high when it is a social activity that is both inherently difficult to imitate and easily excludes others from its benefits. Appropriability is low when social activity is easy to duplicate and fails to exclude others from its benefits because of its nature as a public good (Layard and Walters, 1978). Intellectual property protection such as patents and trade secrets can exclude competitors from the benefit of some social activities such as process or product innovations. However, many forms of social activity cannot be protected as intellectual property. Nevertheless, as explained in Chapter 5, many different kinds of isolating mechanisms, such as location or process innovation, can enable a firm to extract economic and social value from its social products.

The ability to extract benefits through these isolating mechanisms, such as a social loss leader or the creation of knowledge capabilities, requires considerable communication and management between the project sponsor and the recipient and is thus best organized in-house with cooperative coordination, rather than autonomous coordination. The administrative controls of highly appropriable, in-house projects also reduce potential motivation costs and conflicts of interest between the project sponsor and recipient.

Relationship of social dimensions to governance modes

In order to reduce the costs associated with a specific structure, senior managers must select an appropriate governance structure according to the centrality and appropriability of the social activity. Let us now examine the relationships of centrality and appropriability to governance separately, and in the next section we can look at them together.

In terms of centrality, corporate contributions tend to occur in areas of social concern that are less closely related to the core business mission of the firm. As observed in the case of Levi Strauss and American Airlines, neither AIDS research nor classical music are central to their respective missions. Given the fact that the donor organizations are not experts in AIDS research or classical music, each faces a problem of evaluating the performance of the recipient of funds because of a lack of adequate administrative control. Consequently, these firms are involved in unrelated social activities through corporate charitable contributions to non-profit organizations. From the perspective of the donor, the problem posed by its lack of competence is reduced for social issues unrelated to the mission of the firm by outsourcing social action to external non-profit recipients that do have the necessary competence and are motivated through competition for limited corporate contributions.

Social activities in areas closely related to the core business of the firm are usually internalized because of the greater competence of the firm and thus the greater ability to evaluate the decisions and activities of recipients through its administrative control system. For example, Benetton has been involved in a number of publicity campaigns that feature social problems. In 1998, its "Enemies" campaign featured a clothing catalogue of Jewish and Palestinian citizens of Israel with statements about their daily life together. The catalogue sensitively portrayed the humanity of both sides of the conflict. The persons featured in the catalogue were not models, but regular people, all wearing Benetton clothing. In this case, the nature of the social campaign melded seamlessly into Benetton's competence in marketing. Benetton is quite capable of evaluating the effectiveness of such campaigns. Repsol and Boeing are involved in programs to reduce the environmental impacts of their respective production activities. These projects are all closely related to each firm's competence and existing administrative controls. Consequently, the firm can evaluate the effectiveness of environmental process improvements, thus reducing the problem of motivating recipients to achieve the objectives of these programs. So when American Airlines works on increasing fuel efficiency and conservation, it is involved in an activity that is fundamental to its mission as an airline. However, music is not central to its mission, and so contributions to the San Francisco Symphony are appropriate, while the organization of an orchestra is not.

In terms of appropriability, the problem the donor faces is how to capture the benefits from its social activity. There is a tension between appropriability and replication, as we explained in Chapter 5. To a certain extent, social projects are meant to be imitated and so value slippage occurs by design. Given that an external recipient, like an NGO, also receives part of the stream of benefits flowing from a given social activity, the donor firm must decide when it is worthwhile to try to capture those benefits. If the benefits are specific, it makes sense to bring the external recipient inside the firm so that the donor can capture more of the value produced by a given social activity. For example, product differentiation creates dependence of the buyer on the supplier of the social good or service. If the immediate supplier of a social good is an NGO, the donor firm fails to obtain all the potential benefits created by that differentiation. By bringing the immediate supplier within the boundaries of the firm, the donor firm is able to appropriate greater value from the social activity.

In order to understand the relationship between appropriability and in-house projects, let us revisit the case of Vancity and "Our Change Products." Suppose that Vancity decided it would combat climate change by contributing to the Climate Action Network. Certainly, the activism of the network fits into the global effort to reduce the emission of greenhouse gases, but Vancity would not be able to capture the attention of its clients, except only indirectly. On the other hand, through its "Clean Air Auto Loans," it gives members preferential rates if they buy fuel efficient cars that emit less carbon. This program stimulates the purchase of cleaner cars and generates direct benefits for Vancity by directly engaging its members. By only acting as a contributor of resources to an NGO, it would lose many of the benefits generated through the Clean Air Auto Loan program.

In the case of non-specific social action, the lack of benefits does not justify the increased costs associated with bringing the external recipient in-house. For example, a gift by CIT Group to found a university research chair to study the financial services industry benefits the chair holder, students, and the industry as a whole. The donor benefits only indirectly. Since the benefits are non-specific, utilizing charitable contributions as the governance structure to foster research reduces the costs associated with managing tasks inside the firm and thus reduces coordination costs.

Until now, we have been dealing with the conditions that foster two polar forms of social activity: corporate contributions or in-house projects. As previously mentioned, there are also collaborative forms, including strategic alliances and other partnerships. Collaborations allow the firm to participate in social projects outside its core business mission. The firm contributes its resources, such as managerial capacity or the structuring of financial transactions, together with other organizations that have greater expertise with a given social problem.

Intermediate levels of centrality foster collaborative modes of social action. Benetton's collaboration with different non-profits in clothing redistribution is a case in point. Obviously, distribution of used clothing to the needy was not central to the firm's business mission, but at the same time was related to the firm's mission because of Benetton's competence in the design and marketing of clothing. Still Benetton did not attempt to manage the entire redistribution project and thus was capable of organizing those portions of the project within its competence.

Appropriability is moderate either when social action projects are both easy to imitate and competitors can be easily excluded from their benefits, or when projects cannot be copied and others are excluded from their benefits only with great difficulty. These conditions foster collaborative modes of social governance. Cause-related marketing provides a relevant example. Cause-related marketing is a collaborative form of philanthropy "organized around the marketing objectives of increasing product sales or enhancing corporate identity" (File and Prince, 1998). The firm justifies support of non-profit organizations by linking such support to corporate benefits (Varadarajan and Menon, 1988). For example, as in the case of Leche Ram, the firm may tie a donation to a charitable organization (UNICEF in this case) for each product unit sold. Although it is easy to imitate, it effectively excludes others from its benefits, which accrue only to the firm. Thus, cause-related marketing involves a moderate level of appropriability.

Capturing benefits involves collaboration between the company and its non-profit partner. However, the costs associated with this partnership are considerably less than if the firm were to organize the entire project in house. In the case of cause-related marketing, the company does not incur all of the costs of organizing the social activity internally, but is still able to capture significant benefits. Conflicts

Table 10.2: *Choice among social governance structures*

	Low	High
Low	1) Charitable contributions Example: American Airlines and the San Francisco Symphony	2) Collaborative activities Example: Cirque du Monde – Partnership between Cirque du Soleil, Jeunesse du Monde, and Oxfam-Quebec
High	3) Collaborative activities Example: Bettys and Taylors of Harrogate and Oxfam	4) In-house projects Example: Vancity and "Our Change Products"

in a collaborative relationship are managed through bargaining, rather than incurring the full costs of an in-house project, which weakens the intensity of incentives for the recipient and eliminates the capacity for autonomous adaptation by the firm and its partners. Thus, collaborations occur when the firm develops projects characterized by intermediate levels of centrality and appropriability.

Social governance decision matrix

The two key considerations in the decision to internalize social activity, outsource through contributions, or collaborate are centrality and appropriability. The prior discussion treats centrality and appropriability separately, but actually both operate simultaneously. Based on these two considerations, one can develop a matrix that lays out the social governance decision more adequately. Table 10.2 summarizes the conditions of centrality and appropriability that lead to the most efficient form of social governance. This table oversimplifies the decision by treating appropriability and centrality as being only high or low, when in fact they are both continuous. Nevertheless, it is useful to visualize the decision in this way to understand the relationships that exist between these variables.

The matrix is divided into four quadrants. In the first quadrant, both centrality and appropriability are low. The firm is unable to monitor the activity of a recipient and is unable to extract benefits from the activity. In this case, the best option for the firm is to handle its social activities in the form of corporate charitable contributions. In the example of American Airlines and the San Francisco Symphony, we have a clear case of low centrality and low appropriability. American Airlines is not capable of monitoring the performance of the conductor of an orchestra and any benefits to be derived from the investment in an orchestra would be indirect at best. As a result, the best way to organize activities of this type is through charitable contributions.

In the second quadrant, the social activity is characterized by high centrality, but low appropriability. Here the firm can manage the activity because of its close relationship to its core business, but is unable to capture benefits. In this case, collaborative governance is more cost efficient. Cirque du Monde is a program developed by Guy Laliberté, founder of Cirque du Soleil, in partnership with Jeunesse du Monde and Oxfam-Quebec. It is a program "combining circus arts and social intervention" focused on helping at-risk youth. As mentioned in an interview by a company's spokesperson, "it uses the circus arts as an alternative teaching method for youth in difficulty. The workshops are designed to introduce the participants to the perseverance, discipline, respect and mutual support required by the circus arts, providing new tools that will help them develop and achieve self-fulfillment."[7] The initiative resonates very well with the origins of the company. Guy Laliberté himself left home at age fourteen with the dream of becoming an accordion player; so he lived close to the streets and occasionally close to poverty.

The program started in Canada, Chile, and Brazil and is now operating in fifty-five communities throughout the world, reaching "teenage war survivors in South Africa, homeless kids in Mongolia, the aboriginal Atikamekw Nation in Quebec and Crips and Blood gang members in inner-city Los Angeles" (Sexton, 2008). In each community, circus coaches recruited from circuses and circus schools all over the world work with social workers specialized in marginalized youth; Cirque du Monde has a local not-for profit partner – either the local branch of the above-mentioned Oxfam or Jeunesse du Monde or smaller organizations. The initiative is funded out of the 1 percent of Cirque du Soleil's profits – about US$500 million per year – that goes

---

[7] Brigitte Bélanger (for Jean David, VP Marketing) Cirque du Soleil, Montreal, Quebec H1Z 4M6. Interview: April 14, 1999. Internet accessed at www. dfait-maeci.gc.ca/arts/ss_cirque_du_soleil-en.asp on November 24, 2008.

to programs targeted at youth in difficulty (Sexton, 2008). In addition, Cirque du Soleil provides training and guidance. Clearly this is a collaborative initiative involving high levels of centrality for Cirque du Soleil, but there is little business gain for the company, except for the occasional youth who later becomes an acrobat with the Cirque.

The third quadrant represents social activities involving low centrality, but high appropriability. In these cases, the firm is able to extract benefits from activities, which it is not able to evaluate well because they are not closely related to its core business activity. Collaborative activities are appropriate here. Cause-related marketing is a good example because the company is able to obtain benefits from consumers who buy its products in order to support the particular charitable cause in question. For example, the "Trees for Life" program by Bettys and Taylors of Harrogate involved a promotion in which the company donated £1 for tree planting for every six tokens collected from packs of its best-selling Yorkshire tea. As a result of an initial donation of £100,000 and this promotion, its NGO partner, Oxfam, was able to plant 1.2 million trees overseas in 2000. Clearly, tree planting is not central to the mission of Bettys and Taylors of Harrogate, but the promotion helped it to build brand loyalty among its customers. Although such programs are often easy to copy, imitation of an alliance with a high-profile NGO, like Oxfam, would be much more difficult. The alliance with Oxfam allowed the company to participate in social activity outside of its core business, while obtaining specific benefits.

The fourth quadrant deals with social activities that are characterized by both high centrality and high appropriability. The firm can more easily monitor these activities because they are related to its core business, while benefits are extracted for the company. Vancity illustrates this case because it provides investment and credit products that are both socially and environmentally responsible. These products are highly central to the mission of Vancity as a credit union. In addition, Vancity is able to capture value from the underserved markets it is targeting.

This framework has important implications for managers because it can identify mismatches and inefficient forms of social action governance. For example, the Mexican beer company, Cervecería Cuauhtémoc, for many years sponsored the Monterrey Museum. However, during most of that time, the beer market in Mexico was a duopoly with little competition. Efficiency was not an important consideration for a company with an almost captive market. With the opening of Mexican markets to foreign competition in the 1990s, many foreign beers have been introduced and efficiency has suddenly become a very important factor. In this new market environment, the organization and management of an art museum – a social activity characterized by low centrality and low appropriability – was clearly a mistake for the beer producer, since it needed to think more strategically about its operations, including social activities. Cervecería Cuauhtémoc was eventually forced to close the museum. By understanding the drivers behind this kind of decision, senior management will be able to avoid engaging in inefficient forms of social governance.

Conclusion

Senior management will continue to face a variety of challenges when engaging in social activities. First and foremost is the fundamental question of whether the company's social activities should be strategic and support the competitive advantage of the firm. If the response is "yes," then social governance choice also becomes a strategic decision, with the purpose of increasing competitive advantage and greater return on investment. Clearly, social action operates in a tension between two distinct worlds, depending upon the role assigned it by the upper-level management of the firm. If the company's intent in participating in social activity is strategic in nature, cost considerations will play an important role in governance choice. Where the intent is altruistic in nature without concerns about effectiveness, other considerations such as legitimacy and senior management's idiosyncratic values will play an important role in the decision to internalize or outsource. Where the purpose is strategic, our framework provides managers with guidelines for determining whether social activities should be outsourced, conducted in-house, or managed through some collaborative form.

Prior work has examined extensively the relationship between corporate social responsibility and financial performance. This chapter shows how the positive impact of a company's social action on financial performance may be increased by taking into account the costs of coordination and motivation of alternative social governance modes and their fit with the nature of the social activity. By helping senior managers take into consideration the relevant issues in the governance choice decision, the framework helps them to avoid costly mismatches that may undermine the effectiveness of social action.

Certainly, the approach taken in this chapter has a number of limitations. First, organizational economics disregards many social and psychological issues. Economic transactions are embedded in a social structure that relaxes the economic logic (Granovetter, 1985). In addition, this approach neglects cognitive aspects of transactions leading to an unjustified confidence in organizational flexibility (Foss, 2000). Inertial tendencies in organizations inhibit responses to changes in the environment that may necessitate different governance modes. Finally, the focus on costs ignores the role of resources in firm boundaries. Many firm boundary decisions are the result of a decision to either acquire new resources or reduce dependencies on others for firm resources. Such considerations may also be relevant to the social governance decision.

Despite these limitations, this framework has important implications for researchers. First, it asks social strategy researchers to move beyond the CSR-financial performance link in order to examine the specific ways in which CSR and social action, more generally, affect financial performance. Second, it looks at the fit between the attributes of social activity and governance structure in order to determine the impact on competitive advantage. Third, it points out the theoretical usefulness of the constructs of centrality and appropriability, developed in prior work, but not really used until now.

Given these implications, more work needs to be done. The framework developed in this chapter should be examined through more rigorous survey methods.[8] Future research needs to examine more deeply the boundaries between the firm and its corporate foundation. This relationship was left ambiguous in this chapter. For example, is the firm bound to support the corporate foundation or can it support other foundations in competition with its own? When is the foundation more like an external recipient and when is it more like an internal

---

[8] We have published some survey research conducted in Central America with our colleague, Jorge Rivera, which supports the role of centrality in the internalization decision. Husted, B.W., Allen, D.B., and Rivera, J. 2010. Governance choice for strategic corporate social responsibility: Evidence from Central America. *Business and Society*, 49(2). 201–215.

recipient? Finally, collaborations include a wide range of hybrid forms that merit further study. Future work needs to determine under what conditions different collaborative forms are best used.

The pressures for firms to become more competitive continue to increase. Corporate social action is being transformed by the necessity to meet economic and social objectives (Burlingame, 2001). Senior managers will benefit greatly by understanding the comparative advantages and disadvantages of each form of social governance and the key drivers of efficient governance choice. This framework is limited to the issue of social governance choice, and is only a piece of the complete relationship between social strategy and competitive advantage. Nevertheless, by demonstrating the possible mismatches between social governance and levels of centrality and appropriability, this framework enables companies to obtain greater benefits from their social activities. As such benefits become more apparent to other firms, they should be motivated to give social action a more important role in their own strategic planning.

Appendix 10.1: *Summary of cases*

Firm	Recipient	Social project	Social governance structure
American Airlines	San Francisco Symphony	Culture	Contributions
American Airlines	American Airlines	Fuel efficiency programs	In-house
American Express	Travel and tourism academies	Travel education	Collaboration
Banco Itaú	Banco Itaú	Credit assistance for low-income customers	In-house
BBVA	BBVA	Credit assistance for low-income customers	In-house
BBVA	Community	Cathedral restoration	Contribution
Benetton	NGOs	Collection and distribution of used clothing	Collaboration

Appendix 10.1

Firm	Recipient	Social project	Social governance structure
Benetton	Benetton	"Enemies"	In-house
Bettys and Taylors of Harrogate	Oxfam	Trees for Life	Collaboration
Boeing	Boeing employees	Vital Measures	In-house
Cervecería Cuauhtémoc	Monterrey Museum	Art	In-house
Chevron	Chevron	Environmental impacts	In-house
Google.org	NGO partners	Climate change, poverty, emerging diseases	Collaboration
Hewlett Packard	Universities	Minority recruitment	Collaboration
Hewlett Packard	Hewlett Packard	Planet partners recycling	In-house
Johnson and Johnson	NGOs	Environmental health and education	Collaboration
Levi Strauss	NGOs	AIDS research	Contributions
Odebrecht Group	NGOs	AIDS education	Contributions
Repsol	Repsol	Environmental impacts	In-house
Symantec Corporation	NGOs	In-kind software	Contributions
Vancity	Vancity	Our Change Products	In-house

11 | Corporate social strategy management and the multinational firm

Introduction

Though there is a strong body of theory and research on how multinationals organize their market and product strategies across borders, relatively little is known about their global organizational strategies for social issues management (Gnyawali, 1996; Meyer, 2004). We do know, however, that global MNEs often do not respond effectively to issues of importance in their host countries (Logsdon and Wood, 2005). Highly publicized examples of failed cross-border social issues management by multinationals include global protests and consumer boycotts of Nestlé following the baby formula scandal in Africa and of Nike in response to revelations of child labor abuses by its outsourcing partners in Asia.

It is common practice for global MNEs to centralize social issues management and leave local market units with limited functions and small staffs that are then unable to monitor and respond effectively. This problem is not limited to highly publicized crises that go international. In fact, most social issues management failures come from entering new markets with products and advertising that have enjoyed success at home, but when transplanted, may not be properly adapted to local culture and values.

In the sensitive entertainment industry, for example, it is common to transfer formats to other markets. Latin American soap operas, for example, have sold well in North America, Europe, and parts of Asia, as has "Big Brother," the Dutch reality show giant, Endemol's

This chapter was derived from Bryan W. Husted and David B. Allen, 2006. Corporate social responsibility in the multinational enterprise: Strategic and institutional approaches. *Journal of International Business Studies*, 37(6): 838–849. Palgrave Macmillan has granted permission to use this article in this book. The authors would also like to thank Iuliana Dutkay for her valuable research assistance, which contributed to this chapter.

signature hit. But when Endemol launched its "Big Brother" franchise in the Middle East in 2004, Muslim religious leaders and organizations protested and the program was cancelled despite strong audience interest. Though the firm had done solid product strategy work for its target segment, Endemol had simply followed its usual organizational strategy and invested little in local staff and in understanding local religious and political institutions.

Such bellwether cases, like others we have considered, remind us that for multinationals, business and society is, in fact, international business and socie*ties*. As more businesses have gone global, local sensitivities have, in fact, multiplied, and multinationals must take a strategic approach to social issues and abandon the simplistic, market-based product approach so often taken. This does not mean that all multinationals must suddenly shift from market-based strategies to social ones. Rather management at multinationals must not forget about growing social issues management risk. In our response to this concern, throughout this book, we have sought to demonstrate the need for firms to think strategically about social issues and social action whatever their business strategies.

For those firms that decide to compete via social strategy, they will find that it can provide theoretical and practical coherence to firm social action and create economic and social value. In this chapter, we continue the work begun in Chapter 7 on stakeholder management. We dig down to the organizational level as we examine the essential role of MNE organizational strategy in social strategy.

Building on the organizational strategy typology for multinationals developed by Bartlett and Ghoshal (1989), scholars have hypothesized that multinationals should respond to pressures for global integration and local responsiveness with respect to social issues, just as their organizational strategies respond to pressures of integration and responsiveness in their product markets (Gnyawali, 1996; Arthaud-Day, 2005). In some cases, social expectations and stakeholder demands require multinationals to respond to both global issues and local issues; the underlying argument is that diverse stakeholders and conflicting value systems require complex social issues responses (Logsdon and Wood, 2005).

As the prior examples indicate, multinational firms do not always manage social issues strategically. Moreover, social issues management is often subject to strong institutional pressures that undermine strategic thinking. Instead of applying the Barlett and Ghoshal logic in their social issues decision-making process, management often replicates the organizational logic of product markets and applies it mechanically to social issues, as in the case of Endemol. Unfortunately, the failure to manage social action strategically can have serious economic consequences for the firm. On the other hand, effective strategic management of social issues can reduce risk (Husted, 2005); and well-thought-out social action programs may also bring significant benefits (Hillman and Keim, 2001; McWilliams and Siegel, 2001) that go beyond mere reputation-building to the development of valuable organizational capabilities (Sharma and Vredenburg, 1998) and products with social benefits. In short, there are numerous opportunities for engaging not just in strategic social issues management, but in taking the leap forward to social strategy.

The relevance of social strategy to multinational competitive advantage and value creation is fundamental to the argument developed in this chapter. We begin by reviewing the definition of corporate social action introduced earlier in the book and distinguishing local and global social issues. We then adapt the integration-responsiveness typology developed by Prahalad and Doz (1987), Bartlett and Ghoshal (1989) and extended by Yip (1992) to corporate social action. Just as firms select an organizational strategy (e.g., multidomestic, transnational, or global) contingent upon global and local product-market demands, a strategic approach to social action requires that firms select a strategy contingent upon the demands of salient local and global stakeholders. We then consider the challenges institutional theory presents to this approach. The processes of institutional inertia and imitation across business units within the firm will likely result in a single organizational strategy for product market and social issues management even where there is a clear need for distinguishing between the two, as we saw, once again, in the case of Endemol. Moreover, the local subsidiaries of multinational enterprises face conditions of institutional duality, which makes the adoption of effective social action strategy or social strategy even more difficult.

Local and global social issues

Before distinguishing between local and global social issues, a brief review of the definition of corporate social action. As explained in

Chapter 1, given the highly contested nature of corporate social responsibility, we have used the terms "social issues management" and "social action" to describe corporate activities. These terms avoid some of the motivational, intentional, and normative ethical weight so often attached to CSR. As social entities with the status function of economic actor (Searle, 1996), firms inevitably engage in social action as they engage in normal, everyday economic activity. For the most part, it is up to firm management to decide how much of that social action is incorporated within the firm's strategic and operational planning, and to determine whether or not to aspire solely to meet legal and regulatory requirements or to take a more active role in society – global and local.

There is no explicit theory that distinguishes between global and local social issues, though there is a brief discussion in Gnyawali (1996) and more extended consideration in Donaldson and Dunfee's "Toward a unified conception of business ethics: Integrative social contracts theory" (1994). Their work examines issues of business ethics from the perspective of social contracts and has been applied in CSR research (Garriga and Mele, 2004). According to Donaldson and Dunfee (1994: 260), there exists a "set of principles regarding economic morality to which contractors would agree." These universal or global principles can be identified by a "convergence of religious, cultural, and philosophical beliefs around certain core principles" (Donaldson and Dunfee, 1994: 265). Local community norms may differ from each other as long as they do not contradict what the authors term "hypernorms" – i.e., universal standards of behavior. Recent research has found empirical evidence for the distinction between universal principles and local norms (Spicer *et al.*, 2004). Other approaches, such as critical theory, have arrived at similar distinctions between the universal versus the particular responsibilities of corporations (Reed, 2002). These approaches suggest that distinguishing between global and local social issues is possible, and, we believe, desirable.

The key difference between global and local issues as well as global and local social action is the community in which the issue and action occurs. A local community is "a self-defined, self-circumscribed group of people who interact in the context of shared tasks, values or goals and who are capable of establishing norms of ethical behavior for themselves" (Donaldson and Dunfee, 1994: 262). In contrast, universal principles about moral rights and obligations reflect "a set of standards to which all societies can be held" (Walzer, 1992: 9). Thus, "local" social issues deal with the firm's actions based on the standards of the local community, while "global" issues deal with the firm's actions based on those "standards to which all societies can be held."[1]

Let us examine two examples from Mexico of social issues that are clearly local. The first is the legal requirement that companies share profits with their employees. In order to avoid sharing profits, companies will create a "shell" corporation, which has as its sole purpose the provision of human resources to the parent company. Employees work for the parent company, but are hired through the shell corporation and, given that the revenue of the shell company is designed to equal its only expense (the payroll), the shell corporation has no profits and thus no legal obligation to share profits with employees. The profits of the parent company are left intact. A second example deals with discrimination based on medical conditions. Under Mexican law, firms may either provide medical care directly to their employees or pay into the Mexican social security system. There are cases where companies, which decide to provide medical care directly through company-owned clinics, will discriminate against hiring employees with certain medical conditions like diabetes, because of the potential increase in medical costs that the company could incur. Both examples are clearly local issues based on specific expectations created by local laws. These issues are not common to all jurisdictions, though the United States suffers this same problem, and there are multiple variations on the theme of employee rights and discrimination which are of concern throughout the world. In Spain, where it legal to ask prospective employees their age, it is also common practice to query younger women candidates to find out if they planning on having children.

Local issues arise in relation to the needs and circumstances of each community (Reed, 2002). There is no global consensus as to the

---

[1] We are certainly aware of the contentious nature of this claim, rejected by a number of contemporary philosophical schools. On the other hand, universal principles of human rights are well established in the UN Charter and the Universal Declaration of Human Rights, by international law, and by international business organization such The Global Compact (sponsored by the UN as well).

obligation to respond to highly context-specific local social issues, though in local situations where the firm clearly has no direct interest, e.g., a badly designed local development project supported by the ruling party, prudence suggests that the firm should, literally, mind its own business.

Some issues, however, are a little bit less clear in terms of their classification as local or global. Take HIV-AIDS, which is a global epidemic. In South Africa, companies view their active cooperation in the fight against HIV-AIDS as absolutely essential (de Jongh, 2004). Nevertheless, despite the importance of these issues in South Africa, as well as a general understanding that HIV-AIDS is a source of human suffering, it is not part of the social agenda of many firms around the world; nor do these firms generally find their most salient stakeholders demanding social activities related to HIV-AIDs. In fact, as HIV-AIDS has passed from being a terminal to chronic disease in the developed world, stakeholders are now more likely to focus on the most urgent topics on their radar – global warming and unemployment.

In contrast, there are issues that transcend national boundaries and about which considerable consensus is emerging, such as ensuring human rights (de George, 1993) and environmental protection (Frederick, 1991 ; Gnyawali, 1996). These issues appear on the agenda of nearly every multinational and are "global." The prominence of new agreements, such as the UN Global Compact, is evidence of the perceived need to provide an institutional structure for managing the corporate response to global social issues. These agreements share the view that multinationals are uniquely situated to help solve these problems, often in collaboration with governments and NGOs.

Managing social issues abroad

Having identified social issues as global or local in nature, multinationals must then decide how to manage them, first determining which issues are of strategic importance (Ansoff, 1980; Dutton *et al.*, 1983; Mahon and Waddock, 1992). According to Ansoff (1980: 133), an issue is of strategic importance based on its "impact on the ability of the enterprise to meet its objectives." Porter and Kramer (2006) operationalized strategic importance by asking firms to examine the value chain impacts of a company on the community and environment as well as the social dimensions of the competitive context in which the firm operates. Accordingly, a company must both examine its externalities and how social issues, such as healthcare reform, affect the firm's competitive context. New developments that become issues and require managerial attention are then placed on the firm's strategic decision agenda (Mahon and Waddock, 1992).

Given the confusion in academic research regarding the strength and direction of causal links between CSR and firm financial performance, it is not surprising that multinationals take different views on the strategic importance of social action. Some approach social action as vital to achieving financial objectives through the generation of competitive advantages or the control of risk. Others treat social action as strategic by definition, not solely in terms of its relationship to financial objectives. Still others do not place any special importance on social action either with respect to the firm's mission or its business strategy.

We argue that the importance placed on a social issue within the multinational's strategic agenda may vary according to two alternative processes. On the one hand, the firm may engage in a strategic analysis of the issue and stakeholder demands to determine the appropriate response. Alternatively, institutional isomorphism linked to the organizational strategies of multinationals may lead to a "copycat" approach which responds to the social environment in accord with what is considered appropriate or normal. Let us examine how these processes work.

A strategic approach to the analysis of the importance of social issues parallels the Bartlett and Ghoshal approach to organizational strategy. Organizational strategy in the multinational has been conceived as a response to different pressures in its product markets (Prahalad and Doz, 1987). On the one hand, there are strong pressures for integration and coordination between the host-country subsidiary and home-country parent company due to multinational customers and competitors, technological developments, access to raw materials and energy, and the need to leverage investment and achieve economies of scale. On the other hand, pressures for local responsiveness are due to local customer needs and tastes, market structure, and governmental requirements (Prahalad and Doz, 1987). Building on these two dimensions (Bartlett and Ghoshal, 1989), many studies have developed typologies of multinational firms.

Harzing (2000) reviews these typologies and finds empirical support for the multidomestic firm, the transnational firm, and the global firm. The prototypical multidomestic firm combines high responsiveness and low integration. It is organized as a federation of autonomous subsidiaries defined by national markets that modifies products and services to meet local needs and tastes. Bertelsmann, the German media and entertainment company, is a case in point. In each national market, its subsidiaries select from the range of Bertelsmann products and adapt those products to the market, or may even launch new products. In contrast, global firms are characterized by low responsiveness and high integration. The local organizational structures of global firms tend to be lean – frequently restricted to well-developed distribution and sales – focusing on a limited number of products and services to achieve economies of scale and low average unit costs. Some industries seem ideal for global competitors – e.g., telecommunications equipment and pharmaceutical drugs. Finally, the transnational firm attempts to combine the best of both worlds – local responsiveness and global economies of scale and coordination. For example, professional services firms, like McKinsey, have focused on developing transnational strategies to leverage organizational knowledge. This knowledge may emerge in a specific project in a single country that is a leader in an industry, or by a cross-functional, international work team; in either case, the knowledge is then transferred throughout the firm's worldwide network as cutting edge "best practice."

The strategic importance of global or local social issues similarly turns on pressures for global integration and local responsiveness. Integration pressures stem from multinational stakeholders and NGOs, global social problems, as well as from local NGOs focused on global problems, and the need to economize in the provision of social projects. Pressures for response to local social issues stem from differences in stakeholders as well as market structure and the demands of host governments. Table 11.1 compares the key differences between product-market and social-action pressures for integration and local responsiveness.

The principal pressures for a global approach to social action are multinational stakeholders and the need to economize in the provision of social goods and services. Multinational stakeholders include international governmental organizations such as the World Bank, the World Trade Organization, or the International Organization for

Table 11.1: *Comparison of pressures for integration and responsiveness for product markets and social action*

Pressures	Product markets	Social action
Global integration	Multinational customers Global competitors Global trends and tastes	Multinational stakeholders Global NGOs Local NGOs with global focus Need to economize in the provision of social goods and services
Local responsiveness	Local tastes Local distribution channels Availability of substitutes Market structure Host government demands	Local stakeholders Local NGOs Market structure Demands of host governments

Source: Adapted from Prahalad and Doz (1987).

Standardization. These organizations play a vital role in establishing a basic institutional framework within which nations and firms operate. In addition, multinational NGOs increasingly play an important role in raising environmental and social issues to the public's awareness. The footwear industry was transformed when NGOs raised awareness of the sweatshop labor used by suppliers for Nike. Local NGOs, such as Evangelische Kirchengemeinde Duisburg-Neumuhl in Germany, Christian Aid in the United Kingdom, and Agir Ici in France, began boycotts of Nike products in their respective local markets. Local watchdogs can monitor multinationals for violations of labor rights in third-party countries. Local NGOs were joined by multinational NGOs such as Oxfam and Amnesty International. Puma, the German footwear company, fell foul of an alliance of German and Latin American NGOs due to labor problems identified at a local Mexican garment manufacturer in Puebla. Whether the interests of international NGOs and local stakeholders coincide is not always clear (Lohr, 2004). The important point is that the many different groups, demanding action on a similar issue, create pressure for a uniform and standardized response across a multinational corporation, regardless of the organizational structure of a firm as a multidomestic, transnational, or global company.

At the same time, local stakeholders and NGOs also raise awareness of specifically local issues that need to be addressed by multinationals. One need look no further than the many philanthropic initiatives of corporations, which are quite often community-focused in order to derive the greatest benefit from the contribution. The demands of local governments are particularly salient in creating pressures for local responsiveness. The Mexican federal government's Clean Industry certification draws significant attention among multinationals, who certify plants under the program almost as frequently as they certify under the global ISO 14001 standard (Husted and Montiel, 2008). The Clean Industry program assures compliance with Mexican environmental law and protection from unwanted environmental inspections by federal authorities.

Market structure can create pressures for responsiveness to local issues. Global product markets will push firms to pay attention to global social issues; however, local product markets will lead multinationals to focus on local issues.

The pressures for the integration/responsiveness of social action may not correspond to pressures for integration/responsiveness in the product market. In other words, the necessary organization of social strategy at an international level, following Bartlett and Ghoshal, might not correspond to the requisite organizational solution for the product market. For example, a global telecommunications equipment firm may face strong host country demands for black economic empowerment in South Africa. Thus, in the product market, the firm would be organized globally, but in terms of social action, the firm will need to be responsive to local demands. Accordingly, assuming rational behavior, we would expect the organizational strategy for social issues management to be independent from the organizational strategy of the firm in the product market. A firm that handles social action strategically will examine global and local social issues independently of product market pressures; the firm would respond to social issues according to demands for responsiveness and integration by local and global NGOs, host and home country governments, and local market structure. For example, British Petroleum (BP), a global MNE, makes clear the need to detect and respond effectively to local social issues: "Business Unit Leaders are expected to engage in open dialogue and consultation with local communities and their representatives, non-governmental organizations and government at all levels to ensure that potential issues arising from our operations are identified and the risks addressed" (Logsdon and Wood, 2005: 61).

Responding to local social issues

Responding to local issues can be a great challenge for multinational firms. Certainly, some firms seem to be quite responsive. Caterpillar is a transnational firm in terms of its products and markets, facing tremendous pressure to reduce costs as well as share learning across its subsidiaries (Hill, 2007). It has been remarkably effective in developing both local and global social initiatives. One of its most prominent programs is ThinkBig, a two-year technician-training program; the program arose from the company's "growing need for skilled technicians to service its machines" and is now running at eighteen colleges worldwide, predominantly in the USA and South America, with one in China. It is preparing students for technical jobs in the Caterpillar dealerships. According to students' testimonials, the paid internship at a CAT dealership, which is part of the degree, offsets the cost of tuition.[2]

Its 220 dealerships represent Caterpillar's strength at the local level. Almost all dealerships are independent and locally (and some family) owned; contracts are long term to favor trust with customers.[3] Caterpillar's local social projects are undertaken in close relationship with its local dealerships: Caterpillar and its local dealer Haytrac set up a generator in a medical facility in hurricane-hit Haiti; with its Venequip dealer, the company supplied the Venezuelan government with 300 machines to help out in rescue and rebuilding efforts after torrential rains; Caterpillar dealer WesTrack was a partner of the Chinese officials for repurposing land in the Jilin province for use in rice agriculture. In Ecuador, as there was no technical college to host ThinkBig, the local CAT dealership, IIASA, opened a school to run the program, helping to create knowledge and jobs in a country

---

[2] ThinkBig program details accessed at www.cat.com on March 20, 2009.
[3] Accessed at http://csr-news.net/directory/caterpillar on March 24, 2009.

characterized by high unemployment. The dealership system appears to be very effective in responding to local social needs in order to leverage its worldwide expertise.

In contrast to the Caterpillar experience, other multinationals have not felt it necessary to respond to local social issues. One unusually interesting example, again from the entertainment industry, is MTV Networks, a Viacom subsidiary. MTV is a broadcasting conglomerate that has 166 channels and over 400 websites in 33 languages, running in 162 countries.[4] Its best known TV channels are BET, Nickelodeon, CMT, Comedy Central and, of course, MTV. Since its inception in 1981, MTV has created an intricate maze of brands and associated TV channels and websites. MTV has progressively segmented its market. There is MTV2 (with content geared to young males), MTVU (a website for college students mixing student produced music with information about scholarships), MTVTr3s (targeting Latinos living in the USA), in addition to the basic MTV channel with its country-specific interpretations ranging from MTV Denmark to MTV China and MTV Philippines – over 30 country-specific MTV versions in total. In 2005, worldwide MTV reached approximately 340 million viewers, making it the largest television network in the world (McPhail, 2006: 134).

MTV's geographical expansion began in the late '80s with MTV Europe; then MTV Germany was launched right after the fall of the Berlin wall, and later the network expanded across the continent. The ownership models are varied; some are wholly owned subsidiaries (i.e., MTV Latin America), others are joint ventures with local TV channels (i.e., MTV Russia, MTV India), and there are also licensing agreements with other companies that own and operate the service using the MTV name and format (i.e., MTV Romania and MTV Australia) (Wasko, 2005). From an organizational perspective, local stations are grouped under local hubs; MTV Networks Europe and MTV South-East Asia are more of a conceptual hub, as each country has its own physical MTV subsidiary, while MTV Latin America is one large subsidiary headquartered in Miami, Florida, distributing feeds throughout the entire region (except Brazil, which has its own subsidiary). Originally MTV embarked on an international strategy

---

[4] Viacom 2008 Q4 Pulse Report (accessed in the Investor's Section at viacom. com).

built on standard content; however, when strong local competition with local content arose in key markets such as Germany, MTV moved to a multidomestic strategy.

Each country-specific MTV station now has a mix of local and international programming, with local programming progressively becoming more dominant. Between 50–80 percent of the content is now locally produced.[5] MTV India, for example, has 70 percent of the content devoted to Indian film and popular music (Wasko, 2005). US developed content such as the reality shows *Life with Ryan*, *Pimp my Ride*, *The Hills* or cartoons such as *Daria* and *Beavis and Butthead* are seen worldwide.

The issue of local identity is not just a question of the percentage of locally produced content. Most local content follows MTV's "international" (i.e., US) model; for example MTV Music Awards has ten locally produced versions but follows a standard format worldwide. Music must meet MTV international style.

Not surprisingly, MTV's social initiatives are carefully aligned with its professed, international youth culture values, and include awareness campaigns about a whole range of issues from HIV-AIDS, to the environment, discrimination, and the civil war in Darfur. The main awareness campaigns have been branded and are summarized in Table 11.2.

MTV's largest "global" social campaign is *Staying-Alive*, which focuses on HIV-AIDS prevention, which is distinguished by being the only bilingual – English and Spanish – program. All other campaigns, although defined by the company as global in nature, are in English only. *MTV Grita* was conceived as a regional Latin American initiative, but has little current activity.

MTV social projects are built on a marketing-driven construct, like a show brand, with their own logos and ads designed by professional ad agencies and TV/web presence. The awareness campaign "Turn on TV" built for AIDS Day included twenty-four TV spots created by no less than six advertising agencies (180 Amsterdam, Cake, Lowe Worldwide, Ogilvy, Wieden and Kennedy, 12 and Young and Rubicam) (Banham, 2006).

---

[5] "International MTV and Globalization" blog accessed at http://themediamademecrazy.com/papers-projects/mit-cms/mit-cms-internationalmtv on February 22, 2009.

Table 11.2: *MTV social initiatives*

CSR initiative	Description
Think MTV	An MTV owned web "community" and the umbrella for MTV's main social awareness messages related to discrimination, politics, environments, faith, health, substance abuse, relationships and sex, human rights, war, poverty, and crime. The collection of online blogs, videos, and educational messages represents MTV's cooperation with more than forty organizations. The site has an interactive nature allowing youngsters to have a dialogue, upload info, express support, advocate, sign petitions, and get involved. It also serves as a broadcast tool for non-profits that want to post their messages and causes to the website.
MTV Staying-Alive	An MTV foundation, campaign, and website focused on HIV-AIDS prevention. The initiative is built in partnership with several non-profit organizations – the Kaiser Family Foundation, UNFPA, UNICEF, UN AIDS and Y Peer. HIV-AIDS prevention is one of the oldest and most prominent social campaigns supported by MTV. The http://staying-alive.org website exists in English and Spanish and features general educational information, blogs, and a wide selection of videos. The network holds special programming for World AIDS Day, concerts and is lobbying at the UN for better funding and support for AIDS/HIV education, particularly in Africa.
MTV Switch	A website and public service announcements campaign launched in Summer 2007 meant to raise awareness about climate change and advance environmentally friendly lifestyles; the goal of the initiative, as mentioned by the director of MTV International is "to have a 'splash' of multimedia promotional activity two or three times a year to sustain interest in MTV's ongoing global climate change effort."[a] The ads have a youthful, funny tone and are focused on behavioral changes that youngsters can make such as spending less time on the computer to

Table 11.2: *(cont.)*

CSR initiative	Description
	consume less energy and playing more outside, instead of constantly being hooked to video games. Interestingly, it is one of the few corporate environmental initiatives that talk about the need to reduce consumption of stuff, in general, to decrease carbon footprint. The website is available in English and has a blog section in Spanish.
MTV Grita	A Latin-American-specific initiative, launched in 2004, as a "pro-social campaign designed to motivate young people to express themselves and take actions on issues such as sexual health, citizen participation and global warming."[b] The main educational objective of the initiative is focused on sex education. The first campaign under the MTV Grita umbrella was "Sé(x) tu Mismo" (Be Yourself Sexually) and featured true-life testimonials from Mexican and Argentine youths.[c] Currently there seems to be little activity as the latest posts date from mid-2008. *Agentes de Cambio* is an initiative on the same subject of self-expression; it is a MySpace page that acts like a forum for sharing comments, videos, and stories on subjects ranging from sports to human rights, violence, and education. The site has just over 6,000 members and fairly infrequent posts. Links can take viewers to the websites of youth organizations such as Organización Iberoamericana de Juventud and Ashoka.

[a] Ted McKenna, "MTV Intensifies Global Climate Change Efforts", PR Week US, December 24, 2007.

[b] Accessed at www.viacom.com/corpresponsibility/Pages/globalcommunity.aspx on February 23, 2009.

[c] "'Grita' Is the Word for MTV Latin America," Online Staff, *Multichannel News*, September 17, 2004.

The causes selected by MTV (HIV-AIDS, climate change, poverty, citizenship/voting, violence) are major global problems, with little relationship to its broadcasting business, but of major relevance to its youth target. Rarely are these global issues approached in a local context. One notable exception has been the 2006 and 2008 Presidential elections in Mexico and the United States.

In 2006, MTV Latin America prepared a series of half-hour specials – a series of interviews with presidential contenders hosted by "Noticias MTV" – in the run-up to Mexico's presidential election, urging the country's youth to become informed and vote. The project was developed in cooperation with two non-profit organizations, Tu Rock Es Votar ("Voting is Your Rock") and the Todos Participando ("Everyone Participating") Foundation (de la Fuente, 2006). In the USA, MTV has been actively urging youth to vote since 2004 with its *Choose or Lose* campaign and website section on the www.mtv.com/ thinkmtv website. In 2008, the network broadcast a thirty-minute special with Barack Obama answering questions from America's youth, election themed news broadcast segments and concerts to support the go-vote message and assembled a "street team" of fifty-one amateur journalists, one in each state and DC, to file blog reports, photos, videos, and audio podcasts about election issues during the course of the campaign season. Material filmed and written by the journalists was broadcast on MTV's mobile website, social network, and to the Associate Press Online Video Network.[6]

Except for the Mexico and US projects, there appears to be little evidence of local MTV stations being active in encouraging youth voting in other countries that have MTV subsidiaries. The reason may be partly a question of ownership – MTV Latin America is a wholly owned MTV subsidiary, not a joint venture or a licensee, making it easier to design, manage, and implement local initiatives; but more plausibly, it may be a question of simple scale economies. The English speaking audiences of the United States as well as Hispanic youth represent a major percentage of MTV's audience, so it may be that the company is focusing its social projects on its largest markets.

MTV's programming strategy of "localizing" successful international shows is not applied to its social campaigns. The local subsidiaries, although benefiting from administrative autonomy when it comes to content production, often have little or no involvement in the company's social activity. There are few country-specific social projects and the local stations (except in the Latin America region)

---

[6] Accessed at www.readwriteweb.com/archives/mtv_election_coverage_ citizen_journalism.php on February 23, 2009 and "MTV's Choose or Lose Campaign to Air Youth Targeted Political Coverage Across Platforms," New York, October 31, 2008, PRNewswire.

seem to have little involvement in the development or adaptation of social projects.

Perhaps most importantly, the social issue of cultural identity is not addressed from a CSR perspective. Though in many MTV stations local programming is dominant, it is produced within the MTV model. Accordingly, despite this "localization" of content production, MTV is still often accused of "electronic colonialism," of trying to own (and sell to global advertisers) the "mindshare" of young people across the globe (McPhail, 2006).

These accusations are not addressed by MTV. In interviews with MTV personnel in Europe, we found that they are proud of MTV's progressive social and cultural views and believe that the international youth culture and the music the network promotes to be a positive force for tolerance and understanding.

Obstacles to local responsiveness

BP and Caterpillar are unusual. The strategic importance given to social issues usually depends, not upon the rational application of the Bartlett and Ghoshal (1989) framework to social issues management, but rather upon the firm's market-focused organizational structure (Hammond, 1994). As a result, subsidiaries of global multinationals are often constrained in their ability to respond to local social issues. Two institutional factors help to explain this negative outcome. First, significant institutional forces lead to organizational inertia within the firm. Second, multinational firms face challenges stemming from "institutional duality" caused by the competing demands of host country and home country environments. Let's examine each of these.

Organizational inertia

Generally speaking, institutional theorists argue that pressures for the adoption of policies and structures by companies emerge from the coercion of the state, the effects of the organizational field on firm policies and structures, and the internal generation of such policies and practices within organizations (Fligstein, 1991). Of special interest is the internal reproduction of policies due to routines developed to treat specific challenges and problems. These routines are often adopted in the resolution of new problems as a way to reduce search costs (Nelson and Winter, 1982); once in place, these routines will be used over and over again, to be supplanted with great difficulty. Even more difficult to change are the basic structures, imprinted early on in new organizations, which resist change (Stinchcombe, 1965). Although this stability of basic structures and routines may reduce costs, they can also reduce "effectiveness if more efficient ways of organizing are ignored" (Zucker, 1987: 446).

A number of forces play a role in the isomorphism that is typically seen in the area of corporate social action, which contribute to what may be termed "traditional CSR functions" imitating patterns established by the market-oriented areas of a firm: as a staff function, CSR is dependent on other units both for financial and managerial resources. As a cost-center that most often serves the needs of external stakeholders, the CSR function suffers from uncertainty in the relationship between means and ends; in other words, few within the firm may see a clear connection between corporate social performance and corporate financial performance (Hillman and Keim, 2001). As is often the case at cost centers, CSR managers are prone to looking to profit centers for established practices and policies. As a consequence of serving external stakeholders and not providing tangible products or services for customers, the CSR function's goals will seem obscure or ambiguous to others (Meyer and Rowan, 1977), once again motivating the CSR department to model itself after other areas within the firm that are perceived as more successful. In his study of Cemex, the Mexican multinational cement company we have cited several times, our colleague José Salazar Cantú (2006) found that managers leading the company's development of a widely acclaimed social program *Patrimonio Hoy* (Hart and Sharma, 2004) had difficulty in identifying the program's specific economic and social objectives. Unable to articulate clear, impressive goals, managers in CSR departments within firms often look to their peers in production, marketing, and other areas, directly related to value creation, in order to structure their activities.

If market strategy influences social action policies across subsidiaries due to pressures for institutional isomorphism, then we should find a similarity between organizational strategy for product and service activities and the organizational strategy for social activities. Our own survey research suggests that multidomestic firms and transnational companies place greater importance on country-specific social issues than global multinationals, while all types of multinationals place similar importance on global social issues (e.g., environmental conservation) (Husted and Allen, 2006). As a result, we can say that social action seems to conform to the organization strategy established for product market activities of multinationals. This result is consistent with our expectations based on institutional theory. We must clarify that the results of this particular study (Husted and Allen, 2006) must be strictly applied only to multinationals located in developing countries and to the specific social issues examined. Only further research will determine whether the theoretical relationships hypothesized can be applied to other locations and social issues. Nevertheless, the finding of Strike, *et al.* (2006) that multinationals reach an inflection point where increased diversification leads to increased corporate irresponsibility suggests that inadequate international organizational strategy may be a factor in these failures. It is possible that growth brings with it globalization of functions and a loss of contact with local host-country social issues.

One objection to this conclusion is the argument that the logic of institutional isomorphism may be internally efficient, regardless of whether the firm neglects some social issues. The strategic management literature, beginning with the Harvard School (Andrews, 1971), has treated social action within the strategy process, following market strategy and organizational strategy. Nonmarket strategists would prefer to treat market and nonmarket strategies as simultaneous inputs, but recognize that few firms do so (Baron, 2005). Hence, social initiatives are made to "fit in" with firm market strategy. While firms will argue that this is efficient, hence coherent with firm strategy, this is only the case if, in fact, stakeholder demands do not affect strategic outcomes and firm performance. In short, such efficiency, when achieved without taking into account all firm activities including social action, is accidental. The strategic deployment of resources is an intentional act based on assessing strategic needs and outcomes. Such an assessment may lead to the conclusion that a firm may be global in its market strategy, but may need to be multidomestic or transnational in its social strategy, if benefits involved in having differing organizational strategies for products and social issues outweigh the costs. In effect, a more "efficient" organizational strategy that is consistent with firm product strategy must be evaluated in terms of all firm activities – market and social – that may affect firm performance.

Institutional duality

Overlaid on the organizational strategy is the complex institutional environment that subsidiaries face. This condition of institutional duality refers to "distinct sets of isomorphic pressures and a need to maintain legitimacy within both the host country and the MNC" (Kostova and Roth, 2002: 216). Thus a subsidiary faces not only the norms and expectations of the home country of the parent company, but also the norms and expectations of the host country where it operates. These host country norms and expectations are largely transmitted to the subsidiary via its local employees who are deeply imbued with the local culture and institutional framework.

The adoption of an organizational practice by a subsidiary includes both its implementation, in order to comply with external requirements, as well as its internalization, the extent to which subsidiary employees "view the practice as valuable for the unit and become committed to the practice" (Kostova and Roth, 2002: 217). In large measure, the ability of a subsidiary to adopt a social practice of the parent company depends on the compatibility of the practice with the regulatory, cognitive, and normative dimensions of the local institutional environment. These institutions vary widely and form part of what Matten and Moon call "implicit CSR." "Implicit CSR normally consists of values, norms, and rules that result in (mandatory and customary) requirements for corporations to address stakeholder issues and that define proper obligations of corporate actors in collective rather than individual terms" (Matten and Moon, 2008: 409).

The regulatory institutions related to social issues are, for the most part, government organizations that comprise the legal environment in which social action operates. For example, the Mexican constitution guarantees its citizens rights to health, education, and housing (Gutiérrez-Rivas, 2006). These basic rights are operationalized through government programs such as the Mexican Institute for Social Security (IMSS) (health), the educational system, and the National Institute to Foment Housing for Workers (INFONAVIT). However, companies are allowed to opt out of making payments into these public programs by providing comparable benefits directly to their employees. Thus Femsa, the beverage conglomerate, has its Sociedad Famosa y Cuauhtémoc, which provides health services and educational programs for its employees. Other companies provide housing for their employees. In the United States, while employee health insurance is often provided by some firms, most social benefits are not legally required, and thus the regulatory environment for corporate social action is quite different. Consequently, in the United States greater focus is given to *explicit* CSR, defined as "corporate policies that assume and articulate responsibility for some societal interests. They normally consist of voluntary programs and strategies by corporations that combine social and business value and address issues perceived as being part of the social responsibility of the company" (Matten and Moon, 2008: 409). It is thus not surprising that the US-based scholars, as we have observed, tend to speak of CSR as "beyond compliance" behavior (McWilliams and Siegel, 2001).

Cognitive institutions include "widely shared social knowledge and cognitive categories" (Kostova and Roth, 2002: 217). This body of social knowledge is difficult to define, because it has many sources. For example, the publication of the green paper "Promoting a European Framework for Corporate Social Responsibility" by the European Commission has catalyzed discussion and action regarding firm-level social projects in the European Union. Numerous labels (Fair Trade, eco certifications, etc.), prizes, and forum discussions in Europe contribute to an environment in which there are shared expectations and knowledge regarding the social activities of companies. Firms may develop valuable reputations when their practices are consistent with citizen and customer expectations (Fombrun, 2005). Firms are also influenced by the environment to search proactively for best social practice through participation in CSR training programs and joining CSR organizations (Matten and Moon, 2008). The normative component encompasses the values and norms regarding human nature, society, and the environment held by individuals in a given country (Kostova and Roth, 2002). These values form the basis of national culture, which Hofstede (1984) calls "the software of the mind." Katz *et al.* (2001) relate Hofstede's cultural dimensions to different kinds of activism and stakeholder expectations. For example, they argue that consumer and employee activism will be high in countries such as the United States with relatively low power distance (respect for authority), low uncertainty avoidance (intolerance of ambiguity), high individualism, and moderate masculinity (less emphasis on material acquisition and greater emphasis on human relationships) compared to Latin cultures, characterized by high power distance, medium to high uncertainty avoidance, high collectivism, and generally higher masculinity.

Curiously, it appears that both explicit and implicit CSR consti-tute institutional contexts in which firms can create value through their social initiatives. In part, this result is contingent upon the kinds of background institutions in which the initiative is developed. Consistent with the explicit CSR predominant in the United States, US-based scholars expect that voluntary initiatives will lead to value creation (Burke and Logsdon, 1996) and certainly a wealth of research in the United States seems to support the idea that voluntary notions of social action are positively related to wealth creation. However, in settings where implicit CSR is significant, research in Mexico and Spain finds that involuntary CSR initiatives also create value (Husted and Allen, 2007a; 2007b; 2009). This latter result supports Porter and van der Linde (1995) who found that strict environmental regulation in Sweden was a spur to innovation and value creation for Swedish firms. These findings in countries where implicit CSR predominates seem to apply to both domestic and multinational firms. In addition, this result does not change according to the country of origin of the multinational. So that even if a multinational firm is headquartered in the United States, it is able to create value through non-voluntary initiatives when it operates in countries that are rich with implicit CSR institutions.

The lesson is that value creation is probably context dependent. Voluntary social initiatives appear to create value in countries with explicit CSR, while involuntary initiatives create value in coun-tries with implicit CSR. A company with a global, one-size-fits-all approach to social action may miss out on the differing kinds of value creation opportunities around the globe.

Conclusion

Multinational enterprises face a clear choice. They can follow the examples of BP and Caterpillar and manage local and global social issues on a case-by-case analysis of the pressures for integration and responsiveness surrounding each issue; in short all multinationals, regardless of their organizational structure, can become "trans-national" in their social strategy. Alternatively, they can ignore local subtleties and nuances in their social agenda with the attendant risks.

Although firms organized with multidomestic and transnational market strategies are generally more effective in responding to local pressures for social action, the MTV case illustrates that this is not always true. Where there is appreciable distance between the values of the firm's market segment on the one hand and the general population and powerful stakeholder groups in the host country on the other hand, management will have a more difficult job evaluating the local environment and how to respond. This, as we saw in the case of Endemol and MTV, is a particular concern in the entertainment industry.

Organizational inertia and institutional duality make managing social action in many different countries an especially difficult challenge. Fortunately, we expect that as the link between social action and strategic management becomes more clearly understood, multinationals will follow more effective approaches that evaluate the importance of local and global social issues on their own merits.

12 | *Measurement and evaluation*

Introduction

The measurement of corporate social performance (CSP) remains surprisingly primitive. Consider, for a moment, the 2007 Corporate Responsibility Report of Chevron summarized in Table 12.1. The socioeconomic indicators include workforce fatalities, days lost, incident rates, motor vehicle incident rates, diversity measures, and corporate spending on community investment. Most of the indicators deal with safety and diversity. Certainly these are important areas of concern for any major corporation, but they do not begin to capture the social impact of a firm. The only measure that looks at the firm's relationship to the community is "corporatewide spending in community investment." Yet, this indicator is an input measure – that is, it is a resource that is used in a process that can have an impact on society. It really says nothing about the impacts of that spending. Table 12.1 also includes environmental emissions and these indicators do begin to get to the issue of actual impacts. Generally speaking, environmental performance has been more amenable to measurement than social performance. It is much easier to measure the amount of greenhouse gases being emitted into the atmosphere than to measure the impact of the firm on indicators of social wellbeing like life expectancy or happiness.

Let's take one more example – the Spanish bank BBVA. Table 12.2 summarizes its social indicators for 2005–7. There is again a high focus on diversity. Workplace safety does not come into play. However, there are concerns about stakeholder (customer, employee, supplier) satisfaction, training, and time to resolve complaints. Once again, the only measure of anything not related to value chain stakeholders, deals with resources contributed to support the community.

Neither Chevron nor BBVA are unusual. As one goes from company to company, the kinds of measures of social performance are

Table 12.1: *Key corporate responsibility performance indicators at Chevron*

Key corporate responsibility performance indicators	2006	2007*
Socioeconomic		
Fatalities (workforce)	12	17 [0]
Days Away From Work Rate (workforce incidents per 200,000 hours worked)	0.09	0.07 [0.08]
Total Recordable Incident Rate (workforce incidents per 200,000 hours worked)	0.42	0.35
Company motor vehicle incidents (per million miles driven)[a]	0.82	0.82
Percent of females and non-Caucasian males at the senior executive level worldwide	21.4	24.5
Percent of females at mid-level positions and above worldwide	10.3	10.6
Total corporatewide spending in community investment (US$ millions)	90.8	119
Environmental		
Number of petroleum spills	803	826
Volume of petroleum spills (barrels)	6,099	9,245
Global VOC emissions (thousands of metric tons)	384	261
Global SOx emissions (thousands of metric tons)	118	92
Global NOx emissions (thousands of metric tons)	138	145
Number of environmental, health, and safety fines and settlements	699	684
Total GHG emissions (millions of metric tons of CO_2 equivalent)	61.5	60.7 [63.5]
GHG emissions from flaring and venting (millions of metric tons of CO_2 equivalent)	16.4	14.5
Energy efficiency performance (percentage improvement since 1992 baseline)	27	27 [27]

Notes: VOCs (volatile organic compounds), SOx (sulfer oxides), NOx (nitrogen oxides), GHGs (greenhouse gases).

[a] 2006 and 2007 data are based on a revised classification system adopted by the International Association of Oil and Gas Producers.

* Goals are shown in brackets.

Source: www.chevron.com/globalissues/corporateresponsibility/2007/performanceoverview/#b1. Accessed on January 23, 2009.

Table 12.2: *Key social performance indicators for BBVA*

	2005	2006	2007
Number of days in resolving a complaint	15	18	20
Women in management positions (Management Committee/Total Directors, and Corporate Directors/Total Directors (%)	4.73/15.82	8.48/16.61	8.76/17.33
Men and women (%)	55/45	53/47	51/49
Hours of training per employee	43	39	39
Resources for community support over operating profit (%)	1.22	1.19	1.13
Index of satisfaction of suppliers (scale: 1 to 100)	–	83	–
Index of satisfaction of customers (%)	76.3	78.5	78.6
Index of satisfaction of employees (%)	61.1	–	–

Source: www.bbva.com/TLBB/fbin/21%20indclave_tcm12–161452.pdf#tcm:
12–161780–64. Accessed on January 23, 2009.

remarkably similar. Socially oriented NGO and shareholder activists have a longstanding complaint regarding the failure to develop better measures; the usual defense is that measurement is difficult. In fact, however, there are plenty of measures and methods that already exist. The problem may be that firms rarely are interested in the effectiveness of their social projects. In a conversation with the VP of CSR at a large Indian multinational, one of the authors asked why the company did not measure the actual impacts of its social projects. His response was quite revealing. He stated that with so much need in the world, "Anything we do is helpful."

Unfortunately, such a response fails to grasp the importance of measurement as a tool to improve the effectiveness of projects or of assisting decisions about where best to invest in social projects. Not all projects provide the same social benefit for dollar invested. George

Eastman of Eastman Kodak explained why he contributed to the support of dental clinics, in these terms:

> I get more results for my money than in any other philanthropic scheme. It is a medical fact that children can have a better chance in life with better looks, better health and more vigor if the teeth, nose, throat and mouth are taken proper care of at the crucial time of childhood.[1]

Although it is unlikely that Eastman engaged in a careful analysis of the costs and benefits of dental clinics, his decision was based upon an implicit comparison of the social return from dental clinics to other social projects. Given an almost countless array of possible social projects, companies need to invest their scarce resources wisely. It only makes sense to dedicate those resources to the issues where they can have the greatest impact. By measuring impacts, managers can decide which projects within a firm's social portfolio should be developed further, simply maintained, or even discontinued so that new initiatives can be developed.

There are, of course, cases of firms concerned with the effectiveness of their social action projects and investments. In its goals for 2007 and beyond, JPMorgan Chase includes "Focus on increasing the social return, reach and impact of each dollar we invest in the community."[2] Moreover, some firms have applied the methods of cost-benefit analysis to the evaluation of their social projects. The Brazilian Banco Itaú not only engages in such evaluation, but also provides courses for NGOs, private foundations, and governmental agencies that want to learn about the economic evaluation of social projects.[3]

Moving from an altruistic focus on CSR to the realm of social strategy demands a more hard-nosed approach to evaluating the effectiveness of social action projects – not just in terms of economic value creation, but especially in terms of actual social impacts. Firms are confronted with an extraordinary array of possible projects, and they

---

[1] Accessed at www.kodak.com/global/en/corp/historyOfKodak/ eastmanTheMan.jhtml?pq-path=2/8/2217/2687/2689 on January 23, 2009.

[2] JP Morgan Chase website accessed by internet at www.jpmorganchase.com/ cm/cs?pagename=Chase/Href&urlname=jpmc/community on January 23, 2009.

[3] Fundação Itaú website accessed by internet at www.fundacaoitausocial.org. br/ on January 23, 2009.

must ensure that the projects they choose to invest in are the most effective ones.

Despite the need for improvement in the evaluation of social project impact, the continued fascination in the academic community with the relationship of social performance to financial performance remains a stumbling block to evaluation (Brammer and Millington, 2008) just as it has been to moving ahead on the research agenda (March and Sutton, 1997), as we set out in Chapter 1. In fact, the central question of the CSP literature has been its relationship to the economic impact of social action for the firm. The issue of designing social projects with the goal of increasing their social impact has largely been off the radar screen. Only recently have several management scholars turned their attention to issues of effectiveness (London, 2009).

Unfortunately, the search for firm-level measures of social performance is an important distraction from what should be the focus of our attention: evaluating the effectiveness of social initiatives. To do so requires the development of project-level measures of performance and evaluation procedure. Fortunately, once our attention is redirected to where it should be, we see immediately that a panoply of methods for evaluating social projects is available. Many of these methods are currently used by governments or intergovernmental organizations like the UN or the World Bank to examine the social impacts of poverty alleviation mega-projects. These same methods can be transported to the realm of the firm. Consequently, our purpose in this chapter is twofold. First, we will review traditional and emerging efforts to measure social performance at the corporate level. Then we will turn our attention to the real challenge: measuring the economic and social return of social action projects.

Measuring firm-level CSP

Traditional approaches

Ivan Montiel (2008) summarizes the large range of variables used by academics as measures of corporate social performance (CSP) including ethics policy communications, charitable contributions, relationships with different stakeholders, urban development, participation in minority support programs, health and safety programs, pollution control, and environmental conservation. In fact, the review of the

Chevron and BBVA cases in the introduction provides anecdotal evidence that some companies do report this kind of data. Much of this information is readily available. For example, the budget for charitable contributions is sure to be computerized and easily downloaded. Information such as the diversity of employees and suppliers does require some collaboration between HR and information systems, but this is already common at many firms. Though these measures are useful, they do not examine social impact, even at the firm level.

Even more "objective" evaluations like *Fortune's* Corporate Reputation Survey and independent ratings (the Kinder, Lydenberg, Domini social ratings or Dow Jones Sustainability Index) do not reflect actual firm social impact (Chatterji and Levine, 2006; Montiel, 2008). As mentioned earlier, environmental performance has been more amenable to measurement, at least at the plant level, because of access to data on environmental emissions provided by such public registries as the Toxic Release Inventory of the USA, the Registry of Emissions and Transfer of Contaminants in Mexico, or the National Pollutants Release Inventory of Canada.

New possibilities

Donna Wood's widely cited paper on corporate social performance opened new ground by arguing that CSP needs to take into account the "social impacts (i.e., observable outcomes) of the firm's actions, programs, and policies" (1991: 693). Max Clarkson (1995) goes a step further, asking that we set aside the ethical concerns of social action when evaluating performance – an emphasis we share. Wood and Clarkson move the discussion forward by creating a separate space in which research can focus on impacts. Wood includes within outcomes social impacts, programs, and policies. Thus, she advocates a broader research agenda that includes both direct outcomes and the externalities, positive and negative, of corporate social programs and policies.

Is there any way of measuring this overall social performance? To start, it is necessary to define accurately the firm's social objectives, which are often vague at best. To do this, we need to take a step back and ask what is a clear social objective? In 1988, economist Ben Ward wrote a prescient article offering "an alternative criterion for socioeconomic valuation" that suggests how we could proceed.

Ward's "Lexicographic Economic Performance" or LEP criterion was developed to compare public policy alternatives. Below, we explain briefly how it works and how we might apply its principles to evaluating firm social action.

LEP is divided into two parts. LEP-1 refers to the number of people whose lives are at risk or whose health is so seriously impaired as to prevent them from engaging in a normal life. LEP-2 is the number of people "who do not have adequate material resources for the practice of acceptable identities" (Ward, 1988: 764). Using these two measures, governments can compare the effectiveness of two programs: a) prohibition of the use of cell phones while driving; and b) a hot breakfast program for underprivileged children. For LEP-1, the criterion is how many lives would be saved or how would health improve. For LEP-2, the criterion is focused on the practice of healthy identities and lifestyles. In principle, a similar approach could be applied to measure the social impact of corporate policies and projects. In other words, companies could frame their social objectives in terms of lives saved, human health goals, or impacts on acceptable human identities.

Extrapolating from the LEP criterion, we urge movement in two directions. First, we agree with the idea of developing comparable measures of social impact that can be used by firms and independent raters. Second, we urge a shift in the level of analysis to the specific social project. The rest of this chapter focuses on the project-level of analysis – first in terms of economic impacts and then in terms of social impacts.

Measuring the economic impacts of social projects

Probably the most important economic impact of adding a social or environmental attribute to a product is the willingness of consumers to pay a price premium for that attribute. Certainly there are other economic benefits that may accrue to companies that engage in social projects. Much research has confirmed the ability to attract and retain employees if the company has a positive CSR reputation. Similarly, some financial investors are willing to reward companies that engage in socially responsible business practices. These are all very important economic benefits. However, to the extent that social strategy is concerned with market-based solutions to social problems and markets are driven by consumers, willingness to pay for social attributes is key. Unfortunately, at the level of a specific social project, the actual revenue generated by adding social attributes to products has been largely neglected by CSR scholars. That is why we focus on the consumer's willingness to pay (WTP). Analysts have generally measured WTP in one of at least three ways: the contingent valuation method, hedonic pricing, and conjoint analysis.

Contingent valuation method

Willingness to pay for nonmarket goods has typically been measured using the contingent valuation method (CVM). Quite simply, the researcher uses a survey instrument to ask the respondent how much he or she would pay to obtain a specific public good, like clean air or public safety. It is especially useful to examine hypothetical programs and projects, rather than actual ones. Unfortunately, CVM has a number of weaknesses. First, research indicates that CVM does not measure economic value as much as it measures the "moral satisfaction" of purchasing such goods (Kahneman and Knetsch, 1992). Another weakness of CVM is that it is subject to social desirability bias.

Despite these limitations, CVM has frequently been used in the environmental economics literature and recently, as well, in social issues research. Cohen *et al.*, (2004) evaluate the willingness to pay for crime control programs with CVM. Working from a representative sample of the US population, they found that the average household would be willing to pay between US$100 and US$150 per year for programs that reduced burglary, assault, rape, armed robbery, and murder by 10 percent. CVM has rarely been used either by CSR researchers or by business firms to measure the economic benefit of social projects.

Hedonic pricing

An alternative to CVM is hedonic pricing, which deals not with hypothetical goods, but with real ones (McWilliams *et al.*, 2006). Researchers gather price data on similar products that vary, nonetheless, on quality, size, and social or environmental attributes. By gathering data on the prices of these products and controlling for all other attributes, the researcher can determine, for example, how much consumers are willing to pay for a positive social attribute. Unfortunately, the main drawback is that hedonic pricing is not available in the case of hypothetical products or social attributes.

The hedonic price method has been used quite extensively in the valuation of public goods. Medina and Morales (2007) looked at a specific policy to increase social equity in Colombia by increasing access to public utility services. They evaluate the attribute of public utility services with the hedonic price method to estimate housing prices in Bogotá. Flippen (2004) used the hedonic price method to evaluate the attribute of neighborhood racial composition in relation to housing prices. As is the case with CVM, CSR researchers rarely use hedonic pricing to measure social attributes.

Conjoint analysis

Conjoint analysis (Wittink and Cattin, 1989; Green and Srinivasan, 1990) is used to calculate the value of specific features of products or services. It evaluates the marginal contribution of a specific attribute to a purchase. This incremental contribution is referred to as the "part-worth," which estimates the "utilities associated with each attribute ... used to define a product" (Hair *et al.*, 1998: 382). Conjoint analysis is founded on the idea that people determine the value of a product or service by aggregating the discrete chunks of value contributed by each feature. Utility, which is the theoretical foundation for determining value in conjoint analysis, is a subjective assessment of preference for each person. It includes all product or service attributes, both tangible and tacit, and as such is a metric for the individual's global preference. One can thus add the part-worths of each attribute of a product or service, to measure the total utility. Consumers are more likely to purchase products or services with higher utility values (Hair *et al.*, 1998).

Within multivariate statistics, conjoint analysis occupies a singular place in that the analyst begins by compiling an array of actual or imagined products or services by putting together specific amounts of each attribute, often displayed on a card or a computer screen. This method exposes consumers to an assortment of different options (or stimuli). Each stimulus includes discrete levels of different attributes. The consumer places the stimuli in order according to his or her likes and dislikes. Conjoint analysis presupposes that the subject's ordering of each stimulus can be decomposed into the utility derived from each of the various attributes. The utility is calculated by multiplying the part-worth by the amount of the attribute. Consequently, the subjects are engaged in a practical exercise – selecting a preferred option from a number of alternatives. Thus this method circumvents the problem of social desirability bias that plagues other methods such as CVM, because it presents the subject with an opportunity to make exchanges among the product attributes, similar to what occurs in actual decisions.

The analyst can best appreciate the unique contribution of conjoint analysis by contrasting it with CVM. CVM assesses willingness to pay by asking the buyer questions such as "what would you be willing to pay for organic milk?" In addition to the problem of whether such an inquiry measures real purchasing decisions (a weakness also common to conjoint analysis), it is subject to the difficulty of disentangling the features of the product or service from each another. For instance, organic milk may also have nutritional attributes (omega plus), be lactose-free (or not), or have a specific level of fat content (skim, 1%, 2%, whole). Conjoint analysis provides a means for taking into account an entire array of features for specific goods and services and thus getting measures of the part-worth of each attribute.

One study, which is directly relevant to companies, examined the willingness of Belgian consumers to pay for fair-trade coffee. The fair-trade certification assures, among other things, that coffee is harvested by workers who receive a fair wage for their work (de Pelsmacker *et al.*, 2005). This study found that consumers were willing to pay a price premium of 10 percent for fair-trade coffee compared to non-fair-trade coffee. WTP for most social attributes of goods and services can be estimated in a similar way.

Comparing a portfolio of social projects: real options[4]

Typically, the financial feasibility of a project is analyzed by calculating the net present value (NPV) using discounted cash flows. Often, social projects are not able to generate the short-term profits needed

---

[4] This section was drawn from Bryan W. Husted, 2005. Risk management, real options, and corporate social responsibility. *Journal of Business Ethics*, 60(2): 175–183, with permission from Springer.

to pass scrutiny (McWilliams and Siegel, 2001), as NPV excludes non-financial measures such as the value of strategic flexibility that social investments create for companies. Given that social investment can create significant flexibility for the firm, evaluation by means of the real option approach is highly recommended (Hart and Milstein, 2003). An option refers to those investments, resources, and capabilities, which provide the decision-maker with "the ability to select an outcome only if it is favorable" (McGrath, 1997: 975). Many options are based on financial instruments and stock options that have been actively traded in organized exchanges since 1973. The theory of options pricing has literally wrought a revolution in financial markets by making clear when options are mispriced, thus helping to identify profit opportunities (Black and Scholes, 1973; Merton, 1973).

In contrast to financial options, real options are based on investment projects, rather than financial assets (Kogut, 1991). Strategic management theorists soon began to see the relevance of real options logic to all decisions involving resource allocation within the firm (Bowman and Hurry, 1993). Some investments provide the firm with the opportunity to continue or discontinue further investment and thus contribute to strategic flexibility.[5]

Options confer "preferential access to future opportunities" (Bowman and Hurry, 1993: 762). Real options include both the option to undertake activities or to acquire resources (Sanchez, 1993). They allow a person or a firm to defer a decision to commit resources until after the nature of an uncertain environment has revealed itself. If future conditions turn out to be poor, then decision-makers can stop investment; if conditions turn out positively, investment may continue.

Social projects constitute a kind of investment (McWilliams and Siegel, 2001) and, as an investment, create "opportunities to expand and grow in the future" (Kogut, 1991: 21). Real social options may be divided into at least two kinds: those that generate direct versus indirect benefits (Burke and Logsdon, 1996). Direct benefits are derived

---

[5] Theorists have applied the real options logic to joint ventures (Kogut, 1991; Chi, 2000), technology investment (McGrath, 1997), research and development (Paxson, 2001), entrepreneurial failure (McGrath, 1999) and global manufacturing (Kogut and Kulatilaka, 1994). Others have even argued that strategy itself may be conceived of as a portfolio of real options (Bowman and Hurry, 1993; Sanchez, 1993; Luehrman, 1998).

from the creation of new products and services, which generate rents that are captured by the firm. Indirect benefits include the development of firm-specific assets that are of value to the firm, but require further steps in order to capture the rent potential of these assets.

In the case of social options with direct benefits, social action may act as a vehicle for innovation, providing a test of a product or service before a full-scale launch (Kanter, 1999). An example from previous chapters is *Patrimonio Hoy*, a Cemex program to provide construction credit to marginal populations. *Patrimonio Hoy* borrows from the concept of microfinance to organize customers into groups, which can borrow to purchase cement and other construction materials in quantities and with appropriate price discounts to which they would ordinarily never have access as individuals.

By solving a problem relevant to a marginalized group, social investment enables the firm to develop goods and services on a small scale. In the case of Cemex, this social option developed in Mexico provided it with the flexibility to decide whether to continue investment on a larger scale in other countries or to withhold further investment. In this case, the real option is similar to that created by R&D and technology investments generally (McGrath, 1997; Paxson, 2001). Similar analysis could be made with Wal-Mart's initial foray into eliminating plastic packaging or the decision by the Spanish transport company MRW to test-run its social strategy concept with the hiring of handicapped workers in one distribution center. McGrath (1997) takes the example of the decision to invest in pollution control technology to illustrate how a social option can be valued. These and other examples lend support to research showing that social action has been found to have a close relationship to R&D (McWilliams and Siegel, 2000).

Many real social options cannot be easily valued, however, because their benefits are less tangible. Social projects provide strategic flexibility in the form of real options by the indirect benefits they generate from goodwill fostered by social investments within the community and among consumers. Social investment creates the option, but not the obligation, for the firm to call upon stakeholders for resources it needs, for example, in the formation of a new venture (Fombrun and Shanley, 1990; Starr and MacMillan, 1990).

The value of the social option, like other real options, depends on five variables: the value of the underlying project; the exercise price; time to maturity; the risk-free interest rate; and the uncertainty or volatility of the returns making up the underlying project (Luehrman, 1998; Copeland, 2001). From a strategic point of view, if the value of the real option is greater than its price, the firm should acquire the option; otherwise, it should not.

The first variable to determine the value of a real social option is the expected value of revenues from the project's operations and the value of the underlying project (Sanchez, 1993; McGrath, 1997). The expected value of revenues from social action depends upon the demand for it. Demand is determined by the price of the good with social attributes, the cost of advertising to increase the visibility of social attributes, the level of consumers' disposable income, and the price of substitute goods (McWilliams and Siegel, 2001). Consumer tastes and demographics also affect demand for products with social attributes. As already discussed, the methods of CVM, hedonic pricing, and conjoint analysis may be used to estimate willingness to pay a price premium for these social attributes.

The value of the underlying project may arise from the access it provides to resources such as financial, human, or social capital, necessary to fundamental firm activities including launching new ventures (Starr and MacMillan, 1990) and attracting qualified employees (Turban and Greening, 1996). At the same time, the value of the underlying project may encompass, as well, costs avoided through the social option.

Methods for measuring the value of the underlying project have been well tested. Many of these methods, some already mentioned, such as avoidable costs, hedonic pricing, travel costs, contingent valuation, and social discount rates, are commonly used in the field of cost-benefit analysis (Mishan, 1988). Given the state-of-the-art in the field, the choice of which method(s) to use would depend on the specific project.

The exercise price of a social option refers to the further investments made by the firm to extract the value created by the option. The timing of the exercise of a real social option is also a critical variable that affects its value. Generally speaking, the longer one can defer the exercise of a real option, the more valuable that option will be; unless of course the asset value decays rapidly with time or there exists the threat of competitive preemption, in which case the option is more valuable if it can be exercised earlier (Bowman and Hurry, 1993; Sanchez, 1993).

The risk-free interest rate is not discussed greatly in the real options literature, although it is mentioned as a necessary element in the valuation of real options (Luehrman, 1998; Copeland, 2001). In the United States, the risk-free rate is usually measured as the return on short-maturity US treasury securities (Weston and Brigham, 1981). The higher the risk-free interest rate, the greater the value of an option (Bookstaber, 1981; Copeland, 2001). This relationship holds because the exercise price is paid in the future. As the risk-free interest rate increases, the present value of the exercise price decreases, thus increasing the value of the option itself.

Finally, the value of the social option increases as perceived environmental uncertainty increases (Bowman and Hurry, 1993; Sanchez, 1993). Increased uncertainty includes both the possibility of higher than expected, and lower than expected, returns on a project. Uncertainty refers to the variance of the expected value of the net revenues minus the costs of extracting benefits from the project (the exercise price). All factors that could increase either the variance in the expected value of net revenues or the variance in the exercise price will increase uncertainty and thus increase the value of the social option. As possible returns increase, the social option allows the decision-maker to capture positive returns, while limiting the downside outcomes that may occur if those returns do not turn out as expected. Since the option limits the possible negative returns, the decision-maker is able to capture only the benefits of the increased variance in returns and thus the value of the option increases as the variance of returns increases.

Uncertainty is also dependent upon certain boundary conditions, which affect the size and sustainability of rent streams from claims to underlying assets. Boundary conditions also influence the costs of extracting the benefits from social investments. McGrath (1997) discusses extensively the nature of these boundary conditions for technology options, many of which apply to social options. For example, stakeholders may either try to block the firm from access to valuable resources or to expropriate a portion of the firm's rent streams created by social options. Competitors may also try to match or imitate the benefits provided by social action, thus reducing rents available to the firm. In each of these cases, the boundary conditions limit the rent streams and thus the variability of the underlying asset. As the variability decreases, the value of the real social option also decreases.

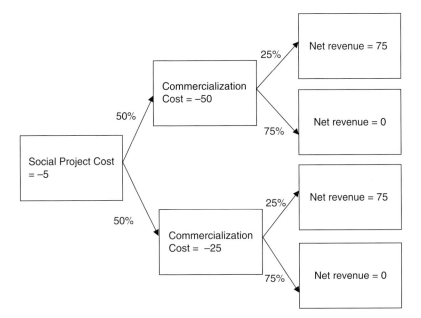

Figure 12.1: Responsible fashion option decision tree

Let's provide a brief example of how a real social option might influence a decision to invest.[6] Assume a company wants to enter the area of responsible fashion. It is thinking of launching a product line that consists of locally produced, sweatshop free clothing made of organic cotton.[7] The development of the clothing line will cost $5 million. The net present value of the commercialization costs could either be $25 or 50 million with equal probability. The net present value of revenues with government subsidies for organic cotton would probably be $75 million. If subsidies are not enacted, the net present value of revenues will be $0. There is a 25% probability that subsidies will be passed. The decision tree is depicted in Figure 1. The expected value of the social project is:

$$0.5(-50+0.25\times75+0.75\times0)+0.5(-25+0.25\times75+0.75\times0)-5=-23.75 \text{ million}$$

[6] The inspiration and logic for this example comes from McGrath (1997) who developed a similar example applied to pollution technology.

[7] This particular combination of attributes was inspired by the line of responsible clothing made by the Canadian company Me to We Style. However, the example is entirely fictitious.

With an expected loss of 23.75 million under net present value estimates, the company should not invest in the project.

However, a real option approach allows the firm to make an investment only when the outcome is favorable. Let's say that within one
year, it will become apparent whether the government will approve
subsidies or not. If the discount rate is 10% and the company can wait
and see what the government response is, then the expected value is:

$$0.9(.25[0.50\{75-50\}+0.50\{75-25\}-5]+0.75\times-5)=3.9375 \text{ million}$$

The value of the real option is positive. It still may not make sense to
proceed with the project, but the real option approach allows the strategist to place value on the strategic flexibility provided by the project.

By simply taking into account only the conditions of supply (the
cost of the option) and demand (the expected value of revenues) for
proactive social action, firms will undoubtedly under-invest in social
projects. By incorporating the value of the underlying project in terms
of the access to resources it provides, the exercise price, the timing of
the exercise of the option, the risk-free interest rate, and the uncertainty of revenues and costs associated with the underlying project into
the valuation of the real social option, the firm will be able to determine more accurately the appropriate, strategic social investment.

Measuring the social impact of social projects[8]

We have argued that the measurement and evaluation of social performance must occur at the project level. Firm-level measures of social
impact, referred to as *corporate social performance*, should reflect
the performance of a portfolio of social projects. Thus, it is necessary
to measure the results and impacts of each project or program; otherwise, firm-level measures of CSP tend to focus on inputs, rather than
outcomes. The current focus on inputs is somewhat akin to evaluating a firm's marketing success by reporting the size of its advertising
budget instead of measuring the impact of specific advertising campaigns on sales of particular products or services.

---

[8] This section draws heavily from José Salazar Cantú, and Bryan W. Husted,
2008. Measuring corporate social performance. *Proceedings of the
Nineteenth Annual Meeting of the International Association for Business
and Society*, edited by Kathleen Rehbein and Ron Roman, 149–161.

Evaluation is a word that is usually related to concepts of measurement and estimation. According to Aguilar and Ander-Egg (1992: 3), "[E]valuation is a process oriented to making a value judgment. It deals with a judgment in which one values or estimates 'some thing' (object, situation, or process), according to particular criteria of value with which one makes the judgment." They distinguish measurement and evaluation by explaining that measurement involves the quantification of something, while evaluation determines the value of this same thing. For the World Bank (2004: 248), the purpose of evaluating a project is "to determine the importance and fulfillment of the objectives, the efficiency, efficacy, impact, and/or sustainability of its development."

In social research, evaluation examines the process of developing programs and their effects. It permits the regulation of actions and social policies by reducing the probability of error in the allocation of resources and in defining the scope of target groups, and thus facilitates decision-making.

Social product or objective

The first step to consider in evaluating the effects of a social initiative is the identification of its objective, which is not always clear. Defining the objective is essential. For example, in cost-benefit analysis, the social objective is a key element in understanding impacts – tangible and intangible, direct and indirect, individual and collective – and in assessing the distributive effects upon winners and losers. Even in social action programs there are almost always some for whom the project has negative consequences.

The search for the social objective has also led to the need to define and measure concepts like the quality of life, life expectancy, and human development. The first, as noted by Becker *et al.* (2005), has been widely operationalized as GNP per capita; the second is generally measured on the basis of the expected years of life from birth, and permits comparisons around the world. Finally, human development is best measured by indicators such as income, health, and education because, as developmental economist and Nobel laureate Amartya Sen (1999) explains, an individual's capacities determine his or her prospects for escaping poverty.[9]

[9] This perspective is similar to the human capital theory of Becker (1964), since it also postulates that it is the increase in individual capacities which

Quality of life, life expectancy, and human development capture the level of human welfare by using key variables that significantly influence individual and collective welfare. However, the evaluation of corporate social projects rarely incorporates these criteria. It is customary to include general information on the amount invested and the number of beneficiaries, but more telling measures such as the increase in individual or collective liberty, health, individual capacities, and/ or in the income and savings of the target groups are unavailable. The use of basic indicators suggested by the management literature are a necessary starting point for measurement and evaluation, but must be accompanied by more meaningful indicators that transcend pure description and permit one to see the final effects upon individual and collective welfare. This approach would permit, for example, direct comparison of social programs, not only those of private firms, but also those implemented by governments and NGOs, and thus facilitate a more efficient allocation of resources.

Approaches to evaluation

Once the objectives of a social project are defined, evaluation is now possible. Although the evaluation should include each of its parts – design, implementation, and results – the last stage is of greatest interest. Social strategy programs create effects and/or impacts on diverse agents such as stockholders, employees, suppliers, customers, a battery of nonmarket stakeholders and, most prominently, the communities in which the projects are implemented. Evaluation should take into account all these diverse actors (Mosse *et al.*, 1998: 4). We will briefly review several approaches to the evaluation of social action projects: engineering economics, cost-benefit analysis, social program evaluation, social impact assessment, and impact evaluation.

Engineering economics
Engineering economics is dedicated largely to choice among alternative business investment projects. It is often targeted to the perspective of employees, stockholders, suppliers, and customers – value chain or

allows economic growth. However, Sen differs from Becker because Sen's idea of development is based on health and education as ends, not as means to achieve other ends, which is Becker's approach (Guillen, 2004).

primary stakeholders. It mostly employs quantitative approaches and focuses primarily on economic analysis that compares costs and benefits. The financial return on a project is the main concern of engineering economics as it is the chief priority for the investor; logically, donors, direct beneficiaries, and the community have less interest. Tangible and intangible externalities, such as cultural, political, or attitudinal changes, both fall outside the domain of engineering economics. For this method, economic sustainability refers to the ability of a project to pay for itself. In engineering economics, profitability usually is assumed to guarantee economic sustainability.

Engineering economics relies on the net present value and the internal rate of return of projects to determine their financial feasibility. Its weakness is the failure to incorporate qualitative and subjective assessments as well as their distributive effects and impacts on sustainability. Although much of this qualitative data can, of course, be measured statistically, this is rarely done (Jenkins, 2002).

Cost-benefit analysis

Cost-benefit analysis is also a quantitative approach that similarly uses economic analysis. Unlike engineering economics, it is especially focused on the perspective of third parties (specific individuals or groups) that may benefit from or suffer the consequences of a project. This approach enjoys a long tradition and consists of a number of tools that identify the most profitable alternatives to achieve an end.

Although profitability is relevant in cost-benefit analysis, the focus is on whether cash flow will permit the project to continue, hopefully becoming self-sufficient. Similar to engineering economics, cost-benefit analysis does not consider intangible externalities.

Redistributive effects partially returned to the literature of cost-benefit analysis when theories of economic development began to evolve from a focus on productive growth to a focus on social life, which had generally been left out. The theory of externalities and of the provision of public goods has been an important source from which part of the methodology of cost-benefit analysis has developed. However, all is not well as economists continue to assume that the impact of wealth on different groups (consumers, producers, or the government) is homogeneous. This assumption has left unresolved the puzzle of the real redistributive effects of social projects and programs.

Nevertheless, important efforts are being made to integrate this aspect into the approach (Brent, 2006).

Like engineering economics, cost-benefit analysis uses such tools as net present value analysis of social benefits and the calculation of shadow or social prices. Both approaches fail to include qualitative and subjective assessments of social projects. Non-economic determinants of individual welfare, also produced by social projects, such as changes in life prospects, familial and social relations, the quality of the natural environment, or community values, cannot be considered with cost-benefit analysis, because most of these impacts do not occur in the market or cannot be expressed in monetary terms.

Cost-benefit analysis has been used to evaluate a wide range of social projects. Nores *et al.* (2005) calculated the cost-benefit ratio of the High/Scope Perry Preschool Program for at-risk children in Ypsilanti, Michigan. At the time the program was instituted in the 1960s, children were randomly assigned to the program or a control group. Forty years later the analysts compared outcomes such as educational attainment, earnings, criminal activity, and welfare receipts. They found that participation in the program significantly increased earnings and reduced criminal activity. Assuming a 3 percent discount rate, they determined that the benefits were worth US$12.90 for every dollar spent. This kind of analysis could easily be applied to the evaluation of corporate social projects.

Despite its contribution, cost-benefit analysis has something of a dirty name among some CSR scholars. Much of its bad reputation comes from its ill-use in the case of the Ford Pinto (Gioia, 1992). In that case, Ford was confronted with evidence that the Pinto's gas tank was quite vulnerable to back-end crashes at a speed of 31 mph. A relatively low-cost solution of US$11.00 to modify the tank was rejected on the basis of cost-benefit analysis. In that analysis, the cost of US$137 million was greater than the benefit of US$49.53 million. The cost was simply the product of the US$11 repair times the 12.5 million vehicles on the road. The benefit was calculated on the basis of the savings of preventing 180 projected deaths with a value of US$200,000 per life, 180 burn injuries at a value of US$67,000 per injury, and 2,100 burned cars with a value of US$700 per car. Based on the numbers, the company did not recall the Pinto in order to repair the defect.

In addition to the absurd, insultingly low value placed on each life, it is obvious as well that the intangible externalities, both in terms of costs and benefits, were not taken into account. In cases where the life or health of a person is at stake, cost-benefit analysis can appear to be a cold, inhumane task. Those opposed to healthcare reform in the United States rallied around the idea that "government bureaucrats" would be deciding who lived and who died based on the government's willingness to pay for a particular drug or procedure. Unfortunately, these protestors did not mention that we make such decisions every day – when hospitals buy equipment, when pharmaceutical companies invest in R&D, when legislative bodies write safety standards for everything from toys to cars. In most of what we do, some calculation of costs and benefits, conscious or unconscious, thorough or superficial, is inescapable.

In the case of social strategy, cost-benefit analysis is a methodology for comparing social projects in order to determine where most effectively to invest resources. However, as the Ford Pinto case and the current healthcare reform debate demonstrate, cost-benefit analysis cannot be the only factor in the decision-making process; ethical issues must also be understood and resolved. Our concern is that frequently, not even simplest formal cost-benefit analysis is done, and social projects are either continued or terminated without a reasonable effort having been made to evaluate their effectiveness.

Social program evaluation
Social program evaluation and more recently social impact assessment (SIA) have been developed as evaluation methods that combine both quantitative and qualitative aspects. Social program evaluation, like cost-benefit analysis, is targeted to the perspective of third parties. Profitability is rarely considered as anything more than a means to permit a program's continuation. The financial sustainability of a program is seldom taken into account. Tangible externalities generally fall outside the methods of social program evaluation.

Social program evaluation does include methods which systematically incorporate qualitative information and interpret it, including intangible externalities, which are customarily excluded from more quantitative methods.

In contrast to the other methods which focus on the evaluation of impacts, social program evaluation considers the design and operation of the program, which can often be of great value, and is part of the methodological and theoretical tradition of sociology and social work, where the measurement of social variables is deeply rooted in the research tradition.[10]

One approach, explained by Riddell (1990), is to include those variables that describe the objectives of the program as determined jointly by the evaluators, developers, and beneficiaries of the program. The procedure combines cost-efficiency analysis, descriptive and correlational statistical analysis, interviews, and social network analysis.

The crippling drawback to social program evaluation is that it requires a customized format for each project, making comparisons unviable. Adoption of the method across projects is neither feasible nor desirable until researchers are able to standardize much of the procedure.

Social impact assessment

Social impact assessment (SIA) has been defined as: "The process of identifying the future consequences of a current action or proposal, which is related to individuals, organizations, and macro-social systems" (H. Becker and Vanclay, 2003: xi).[11] SIA also combines both qualitative and quantitative methods. The perspective of evaluation here is that of local and global communities. Its tools are less formal and more *ad hoc* than in the prior approaches. The objective is to achieve a strong, comprehensive understanding of the design, implementation, and results of social programs, eschewing the precision of economic-financial approaches.

Again, profitability is important only as a resource for project sustainability. However, the concern with economic sustainability is not substantiated by a preferred methodology for analyzing cash flows. In SIA, a concern with externalities is clear at least in theory, but little is done for lack of a proper methodology.

The inclusion of the social and environmental changes within SIA generally requires the participation of interdisciplinary teams. The field is still incipient and lacks its own methodology and theoretical foundations. Consequently, the tendency has been to undertake case studies in multiple stages, considering a group of indicators which may differ in each program. It appears that there is no specific guide,

---

[10] The scales and indices usually employed in sociological studies can be consulted in part 7 of Miller and Salkind (2002).

[11] Other definitions of the field can be found in Barrow (2000: 4).

but rather considerations based on specific cases. Other tools include futures studies, social network analysis, the Delphi method, interviews, statistical analysis, and interdisciplinary teams.

A fascinating example of SIA was carried out in preparation for the development of the Baku-Tbilisi-Ceyhan pipeline, by a consortium of companies led by BP. The pipeline was intended to carry oil from the Caspian Sea to the Mediterranean. The environmental and social impact assessments (ESIA) sought to determine all possible social, economic, and ecological disruptions along different proposed routes for the pipeline as well as possibilities for enhancing positive impacts. The SIAs embraced an enormous range of concerns, including the preservation of archaeological sites, safety, security, and geological hazards, as well as economic and social impacts (Blatchford, 2005). Through the ESIA process, BP and the BTC consortium were able to make commitments to reduce harm and increase benefits. Now, the conduct of the consortium can be evaluated in light of those commitments. So far, most of the commitments made by BTC, at least in the construction phase, have been fulfilled (Blatchford, 2005).

Impact evaluation

Predominantly quantitative, the field of impact evaluation (IE) has a relatively recent history.[12] Like SIA, it targets the perspective of local and global communities. Again, profitability is not important except as a resource that may permit the project's continuation, and economic sustainability is not considered in any depth. Tangible externalities generally fall outside the methods of impact evaluation, though recent methodological advances have been made that make it possible to incorporate externalities.

The amount of resources employed in a social project, the number of beneficiaries, or quantity of packages delivered, may give an idea of the social action that a firm is doing, but says nothing about the effects produced. If the purpose of a program is to improve the health of a group, it is not sufficient to count the number of packages of medicines that were distributed or the amount of money that was invested in the health program. In order to isolate effects, impact evaluation introduces experimental and quasi-experimental design. One cannot simply compare the state of health of the beneficiaries before and after

---

[12] Parker (2003) provides a worthwhile example of impact evaluation.

the program intervention since other factors could have influenced the level of health during the period in which the program took place. An adequate evaluation would compare the values of the target variables after program implementation versus the values which would have occurred in its absence. Thus the use of a control group is essential. Under this procedure, one compares a base period with a later one. The changes in a series of variables that describe the situation of two groups are tracked – those that receive the social intervention (experimental group) and those with similar characteristics that do not (the control group).

There has been a recent movement to evaluate the programs of development NGOs, which are often suited to this kind of impact evaluation. Duflo and Kremer (2005) report the evaluation of a remedial education program conducted by Pratham, an Indian NGO. This project identified children in grades 2, 3, and 4, who were lagging and still needed to learn the basic skills of the first grade. These children were withdrawn from regular classes for two hours a day to receive remedial instruction. Since Pratham wanted to expand the program to a new city, they were able to undertake a randomized experiment with half of the schools receiving a remedial teacher in the third grade and half in the fourth grade, thus permitting a comparison of third grade students who participated in the program with those who had not yet participated. In a second city, a similar experiment was run with half of the schools providing a remedial teacher for second grade and the other half for third grade. The researchers found that the program was effective, providing confidence that it made sense to scale it up.

If NGO projects are well suited to the use of randomized experiments, so are corporate social projects. A corporate partner, ICICI bank, helped pay for the evaluation of the Pratham project. One can easily imagine all sorts of creative partnerships among companies, government, NGOs, and universities to carry out this kind of evaluation. By engaging in impact evaluation, companies can make decisions about whether to roll out a specific project on a grand scale, maintain it as is, or discontinue it.

Conclusion

We have only sketched some of the available methodologies for the evaluation of social impact. The operative word is "available."

Nothing prevents companies from using these methods today. One disadvantage of the project-based focus from the perspective of the analyst is that without a common unit of account, such as LEP-1 or LEP-2, it is difficult to compare companies in terms of their social impacts. Nevertheless, the project focus is essential for corporate managers as they decide which social projects to include within the firm's social portfolio. Managers need to decide what the appropriate criteria should be for evaluating the effectiveness of social projects and how they should be compared with the firm. Project evaluations can then be tied to compensation schemes. Performance-based incentives for social-project management moves the company from a symbolic commitment to social action toward a substantive commitment. The methodology need not be complex. For example, matrices patterned on the well-known Boston Consulting Group's Growth-Share Matrix could be developed that permit comparisons among the projects and decisions with respect to continued investment or divestment; one possibility would be a 2x2 matrix with economic impact on one dimension and social impact on the other.

Our preference for project evaluation is to develop a methodology that combines quantitative and qualitative variables in straightforward constructs, tested for internal and external validity (Campbell and Stanley, 1966), which firms and researchers can use with confidence. Additionally, experimental and quasi-experimental design structures should be used wherever possible.

In order to achieve this, we first need to win the support of CSR professionals, CSR and sustainability NGOs, as well as academic organizations such as the International Association of Business and Society, the European Academy for Business in Society, and so on. Yet, this alone will be insufficient. To convince firms to make the investment in social action project evaluation, managers at some firms must first believe that social strategy is a serious option to be considered and that investment in it can pay off.

Three "stakeholders" that could help us to persuade managers to make the investment are firm strategists, business unit managers, and strategic management professors. All three are target readers for this book. All three want to know if social strategy works.

We believe the answer is yes, under the right circumstances. However, without reliable measurement and evaluation, we can't say precisely when social strategy does and does not work. Until we can, the decision to pursue social action projects will depend on the commitment (or whim) of management, and corporate social strategy will remain an interesting idea that has worked for some and not for others. That is not good enough for us.

13 | *The future of social strategy*

February 1, 2015. CNN Breaking News! Grameen Telemedicine IPO breaks all records.

The Grameen Group has just announced that it has raised a record US$100 billion in the initial public offering of its Grameen Telemedicine subsidiary. Grameen Telemedicine combines internet-based health services with recently developed revolutionary diagnostics, which permit the diagnosis of most common diseases in a matter of minutes through a simple analysis of urine, blood, and saliva. Medical doctors located in centers throughout South Asia analyze the results and provide diagnoses through internet to locations, remote and not-so-remote. Grameen Telemedicine has become the Wal-Mart of medicine, with whom it is expected to partner in order to provide healthcare services in most of the retail giant's superstores.

April 17, 2030. Bloomberg Breaking News! Certified Happiness Units trading above US$100.

Publicly traded Certified Happiness Units (CHUs) have just broken the psychological barrier of US$100. The news from the Chicago Social Exchange is that CHUs surpassed the US$100 mark at 12:32 pm today. This is a remarkable development in the short history of these financial instruments, which only began trading three years ago. Viewers will recall that CHUs were the outcome of the recent legislation requiring a minimum level of happiness throughout the nation. This legislation was made possible by breakthroughs in the measurement of national happiness and the contribution of individual organizations to happiness as a result of an alliance of psychologists, sociologists, and economists. Legislation followed, establishing specific minimums for happiness in firms with 500 or more employees. Companies may generate happiness both internally through their employees as well as externally through their products and social projects. Those companies that exceed the minimums are allowed to sell their certified excess capacity as happiness units to other companies that do not meet these targets.

These two fanciful sci-fi news stories depict possible ways that the opportunities for social strategy may evolve in the short term and twenty years from now. In this chapter, we speculate on possible futures. In order to tell our story, we will have to set a couple of ground rules. First, we assume the continuity of academics as an institution; second, multinationals will continue to be powerful economic agents. In accordance with the former, the future of social strategy as a management concept will remain tied up with CSR and stakeholder theory and the field of business and society. Strategic management will give social strategy increasing attention, though it will not be considered "mainstream" for at least several more years. Multinationals will continue to create wealth and controversy and there will be more strident demands for CSR. There will be new social legislation, demands for accountability, and markets for social capital will emerge, though corruption in international business threatens social strategy.

The fortunes of CSR

Each year in connection with the World Economic Forum in Davos, the social investment advisory firm, Innovest, publishes its list of the Global 100 – the hundred most sustainable firms on the planet. Curiously, both AIG and ING were on Innovest's list for 2008 just before the onset of the mortgage crisis. AIG bet the house on default swaps linked to collateralized debt obligations, lost everything, received nearly US$170 billion in government bailouts, and top management then decided to spend US$343,000 on a "retreat" to a resort in Arizona on November 10, 2008. On March 2, 2009, AIG announced losses of US$61.5 billion and on March 15, *The New York Times* reported: "The American International Group ... plans to pay about $165 million in bonuses by Sunday to executives in the same business unit that brought the company to the brink of collapse last year" (Andrews and Baker, 2009).

While AIG set new standards for hubris and greed, the Dutch bank ING took its government bailout with polite shamefacedness. As a result of its involvement with toxic mortgages, ING Group laid off 7,000 employees to reduce costs after suffering a loss of €1 billion in 2008 and exposure to billions more.

The 2008 financial crisis will have impacts at least through 2010. In many cases, it has forced companies to rethink their social responsibilities and responses. CSR International CEO Wayne Visser (2008) expects that corporate philanthropy will suffer significantly as a result of the crisis. Indeed there are signs that this is already happening (Alliance, 2009). Yet at the same time, social strategy, which ties social action directly to a company's core business mission, should prosper.

Sustainable value creation, by definition, requires doing business today in a way that does not sacrifice economic, social, and environmental well-being tomorrow. Stuart Hart and Mark Milstein (2003) have developed a four-cell typology of the drivers of shareholder value based on two dimensions (today – tomorrow, internal – external). They argue that tomorrow's businesses will arise from new emerging clean technologies that reduce or eliminate the company's ecological footprint and by satisfying unmet needs in order to alleviate poverty and the increasingly wide gap between haves and have-nots both within countries and between countries around the world.

The Hart and Milstein approach differs significantly from the social action and environment programs of most firms that concentrate on meeting current risks. For example, firms now engage in programs to increase eco-efficiency and prevent pollution, thus reducing costs and risks. As of December 2007, 154,572 firms from 148 countries around the world had received the ISO 14001 certification for environmental management systems (ISO 2007). However, this voluntary environmental program does not prepare companies for the new markets that will be created based on clean, disruptive technologies, or untapped markets among the rural poor, slum dwellers, and new immigrants anxious to reduce their exposure to the environment hazards, and prepared to spend what they do have on education, clean water, etc.

In contrast, the development of markets among disenfranchised groups is being led by multinationals like Santander and Cobega in Spain (Rodríguez *et al.*, 2004). Santander's International Express project targets Latin American immigrants resident in Spain by providing them with a fast, secure, reliable, and less expensive service for sending remittances back to their home countries. Some firms are thinking strategically about markets and needs that have traditionally been shuffled off to the domain of CSR and the non-profit sector. A recent example is GE's "Healthymagination" program (Loh, 2009). This major initiative within its US$17 billion health equipment business broadens its portfolio by increasing access of low-income markets to healthcare products. GE Healthcare identified a market segment eager for health information technology and lower priced high-tech health equipment targeted at prevention and specific illnesses. The firm will invest US$3 billion to develop a hundred innovations by 2015. The economic objective is the same as ever at GE: meet the company-wide target for market share and hurdle rate for return on investment. The social objective is to increase access of underserved communities and support prevention.

For more than a decade now, prominent researchers in strategic management – e.g., Kanter, Prahalad, and Hart – have been cataloging cases of firms that have consistently labored to bring needed products and services to mostly ignored markets and populations. Each example is a practical model for how economic value and social value can be joined together. Firms like GE can practice social strategy in one business unit while maintaining a traditional market strategy in another. One possible outcome is that where social strategy is effective, the satisfaction of doing so may attract other business units to experiment with social strategy as well. In future research, we hope to find that positive experiences with social strategy also improve the overall ethical climate in an organization and provide a positive influence on corporate identity.

Legislation and accountability

Although interest in CSR has increased significantly over the last decade (Vogel, 2005), significant criticism has arisen due to what is seen as the greenwashing effect of CSR (Caulkin, 2009). In Europe, there has been a reaction against CSR in recent calls for greater accountability and an enhanced role for public policy and legal sanctions in case of non-compliance (Utting, 2008). Accountability shifts attention to the failure of business to tackle tough issues like tax avoidance or inequitable distribution of value in the global supply chain that directly affect the bottom line, while pushing companies to manage their social and environmental impacts more effectively.

Consequently, there has been an increasing discussion surrounding the possibility of enacting CSR laws. Legislating CSR creates a great deal of confusion due to conflicting understandings of the concept of CSR, discussed earlier in this book. In terms of reducing undesirable social and ecological impacts, "CSR laws" already exist in the form of environmental and labor legislation. However, in another sense, CSR legislation is a contradiction in terms. Some scholars define CSR as voluntary social action that goes beyond the requirements of the law (McWilliams and Siegel, 2001). Under this approach, as soon as CSR behavior is legislated, it ceases to be CSR and simply becomes legal compliance.

Rather than quibble about definitions, we should address the real issue: when should governments enact standards that regulate the social impacts of business activity? Alternatively, we need to ask when standards should be voluntary. The severity of the economic crisis enabled, in part, by lax regulation and permissive laws promoted by business lobbyists, has already pushed government to answer, "now," to the first question. The other enabling factors of the crisis – greed, corruption, and illegal business behaviour – have placed pressure on politicians to pass new legislation on corporate governance law and CEO compensation as well.

Of course, governmental responses will vary across the world. We should expect to see significant experimenting with how firms are legally constituted and the requirements placed on them. Multinationals are likely to find that their social and environmental action programs will have to be both more global and more local at the same time. It will no longer be considered reasonable to permit lower safety and environmental standards in developing countries; accordingly, firms will have to establish worldwide minimums. At the same time, firms will also be required to adapt products and HR and marketing practices to local cultures.

Beyond these general conditions, predicting the precise demands on firms is impossible. New social issues will appear on the agenda and quickly go global. We feel reasonably certain, nonetheless, that information and digital content will play a prominent role in battles between stakeholder groups and governments with internet companies caught in the middle. Global information aggregators like Google and Yahoo have to respond to government "requests" for access to their clients' internet activities and data while free speech NGOs clamor for protection of individual rights. Legal battles on information protection can be expected worldwide; the actions of the legal systems of home and host countries in such conflicts may turn out to be more important than the legislation itself.

A second area of contention will be healthcare. Managing health-care is not just on the legislative agenda in the United States. As new medicines and treatments come to market that are effective against epidemic diseases, pharmaceutical firms and multinationals operating in developing countries will be asked to assist in providing access to life saving innovations, many of which will be much too expensive for the general population and public healthcare institutions. Here, too, firms face potential legislation, though figuring out who should pay for what and how much will be extremely difficult, with host coun-tries running the risk of chasing away foreign investment. The two other areas of certain conflict and legislation (ownership and control of natural resources and censorship of global entertainment products) we have dealt with in previous chapters – the threat of expropriation and censorship is nearly always undertaken by the authorities who cite legal restrictions on firms owning or selling these products.

Despite these conflicts that may give rise to legislation, there are practical challenges to legislating firm social action. The first obstacle is that social problems also depend, in large part, on the industry. For example, issues in the construction industry of safety and health, zon-ing, and the environment, are quite different from the issues of risk, fairness, and service to the community fundamental to the financial services industry. It is difficult to develop guidelines that would apply to anything more than the most general kinds of corporate impacts – e.g., labor, safety and environmental violations, fraud, bribery, etc. – that are already subject to legislation and where the principal failing is in funding and enforcement.

In addition, each firm brings a unique bundle of resources and cap-abilities to help reduce or eliminate negative social impacts and to fos-ter positive impacts. Legislation could enable firms to take advantage of their particular competencies in order to do the most good with a strategic interaction strategy, as discussed in Chapter 6 (Reinhardt, 1999).

Firm size is another characteristic that adds uncertainty to the future of CSR legislation. Should standards be the same for small and large companies? Germany's co-determination legislation, requiring worker representation on the supervisory board of directors, only applies to firms with 500 or more workers.

Finally, the measurement of social impacts is in its infancy. Even programs such as the Global Reporting Initiative (GRI) focus more on describing company policies that are in place, rather than on specifying standards of performance. Given the current state of the measurement of social impact, a focus on disclosure and transparency, rather than accountability, may make sense (Tapscott and Ticoll, 2003). A number of countries, including Australia, Belgium, Denmark, the Netherlands, and South Africa, already require the disclosure of social impacts of different kinds (Meisling, 2004). In the United States, the Sarbanes-Oxley Act mandates the disclosure of ethics codes for US companies.

The advantage of disclosure is that it maintains the freedom of companies to undertake social actions and reduce negative social impacts in the areas where the company can be most effective. Through disclosure, relevant stakeholders like customers, suppliers, and communities, can decide what kinds of actions they will take in response. As US Supreme Court Justice Louis Brandeis once wrote: "Sunlight is the best disinfectant."

The disadvantage of simple disclosure is that companies may continue to neglect their social responsibilities with impunity. Going beyond a legal requirement for disclosure, however, at this point in time could be unwise. Penalizing corporate accountability violations would necessitate the establishment of standards of social performance and a system of appropriate fines and punishments. Unfortunately, as previously mentioned, the state-of-the-art regarding measurement has not advanced sufficiently to allow for such standards. The most we can hope for in terms of standards currently would be the documentation of corporate efforts to internalize social externalities, similar to the documentation of efforts required by the GRI.

In the meantime, more work needs to be done in order to determine the extent to which companies should be held legally accountable for non-financial performance. For example, at present, there is no consensus with respect to the liability of companies for the non-compliance of participants in their supply chains. Creating international law that requires meeting standards across borders is highly unlikely if the recent Copenhagen Climate Change talks are an indication of the level of international cooperation we can expect.

Yet, one way or another, CSR laws will come. As new issues arise that are amenable to measurement and the establishment of liability, it is inevitable that rules regulating corporate social impacts will be enacted. These laws may not constitute a comprehensive body of law regulating CSR, but the cumulative effect may turn out to be much the same.

Regardless of the approach taken to CSR legislation – requiring simple disclosure or accountability for compliance – beyond compliance performance will always exist. No law can be so comprehensive as to contemplate all possible social responsibilities. Unanticipated issues will always arise. Thus, there will be a place for voluntary social action. Probably the most interesting opportunity exists for the development of markets for social behaviors enabled by legislation that helps to create property rights in new forms of human, social, cultural, and natural capital.

New markets for virtue

In a widely cited book, *The Market for Virtue*, David Vogel (2005) argues that although there are some product, human-capital, and financial markets that reward ethical and socially responsible behavior, less socially responsible competitors also find a place in the market. He comes to the conclusion that the market for virtue is quite limited and not likely to grow sufficiently so as to be a significant motivator for socially responsible behavior. He looks skeptically at claims that strong links between social performance and financial performance are possible.

We believe that Professor Vogel's perspective unnecessarily limits the range of markets that can be created and served. Markets do not always occur spontaneously, but may need a little help from the state. Property rights are created by government intervention, as in the case of the enclosure movement (K. Polanyi, 1944) or the development of the markets for sulfur dioxide to combat acid rain in the Northeastern USA in the 1970s. The enclosure movement, which peaked between 1760 to 1820, ended the system of cultivating crops in open fields: land was fenced and deeded to owners.

Sulfur dioxide emissions can occur both naturally through volcanic eruptions or through human activity such as the generation of electricity. The emission of sulfur dioxide combines with water vapor in clouds to create sulfuric acid. A similar process from the emission of nitrogen dioxide creates nitric acid. These acids are returned to the earth with precipitation. The acid rain has very damaging consequences for forests and fresh water bodies, changing ecosystems.

In order to reduce sulfur and nitrogen dioxide emissions, an emissions trading market was set up by the US Clean Air Act Amendments of 1990. The Acid Rain Program allows coal-burning plants to buy and sell emissions permits so as to achieve the most efficient solution to the problem of reducing these emissions. The program has achieved its goals with sulfur dioxide emissions reduced by 40 percent since 1990, and nitrogen dioxide emissions reduced by almost 50 percent (Coile, 2007).

The sulfur dioxide market created through the Acid Rain program holds the key to truly creating "markets for virtue." The kernel of this idea has been translated to the arena of climate change and greenhouse gas emissions and a new field of carbon finance has emerged (Labatt and White, 2007). Certainly, there are important differences between the sulfur dioxide case and carbon dioxide or the other greenhouse gases. Principally, the number of sources is much greater in the case of CO_2. Carbon markets have been established with mixed results in the Emissions Trading Scheme (ETS) by the European Union. Although this market has gotten off to a bumpy start because of initial problems in issuing too many emissions units, the learning curve has been helpful and carbon markets appear to be maturing as the ETS moves into its third phase. In the 2008 US elections, both presidential candidates Barack Obama and John McCain favored the implementation of a legally binding cap-and-trade system for greenhouse gases to replace the patchwork of regional attempts that currently exists. So it is possible, although not certain at this date, that mandatory carbon markets may be operating in North America in the future.

These markets represent the beginnings of markets for virtue – or vice. Certainly, this latter perspective is illustrated by one elder from the Aamjiwnaang First Nation near Sarnia, Ontario, who was left aghast by the idea of the carbon market, as she realized perceptively, that it allowed some companies to emit even greater levels of carbon – a critique also leveled by philosopher Michael Sandel (1997). The key to these environmental markets is that they provide incentives for firms to voluntarily meet and exceed emissions limits. As in the case of the enclosure movement, people and firms receive incentives to care for scarce resources in more productive ways.

According to Umair Haque (2008), the key to twenty-first century capitalism is the deepening of capital by capitalizing all sorts of goods that are currently ignored by financial markets. He writes: "And so when we capitalize rainforests, endangered species, community, the foregone opportunities of the poor, our own wellbeing – then they will finally have value: they can finally be priced, and so the fatcats of the world won't be free to destroy them with impunity." Haque, whose popular blog is attached to *Harvard Business Review*, goes over the top in suggesting that we can capitalize foregone opportunities and personal wellbeing, but the point is well taken. What we can value, we can buy and sell and, perhaps, protect.

Formalizing social, natural, and cultural capital and creating markets for them is not impossible, though our experience with sulfur dioxide and greenhouse gases, far easier to measure than intangible social and cultural capital, indicates that the creation of such markets is not easy. In order for carbon markets to function, the methodology and institutionalization of auditing projects to ensure compliance with carbon emission reduction commitments is still taking place. Undoubtedly, there will be opportunities for fraud and deception. Nevertheless, these markets will provide a number of significant benefits. First, they will provide a clear standard regarding the limits of capital depletion and a means to price scarce resources such as compliance with those standards. Second, the mechanism will be voluntary. These markets do not require firms to meet these standards, but rather provides incentives for them to do so.

Baumol (1991) has argued that business ethics and CSR are a form of corporate waste in competitive markets. In such markets, it is difficult, if not impossible, for firms to dedicate resources to what is perceived as a relative luxury. Environmental markets create a mechanism for pricing environmental resources so that firms have incentives to actually develop business missions around providing environmental products and services. They do so in a way that coordinates the action of all firms, providing benefits to society and the environment as a whole.

Hernando de Soto (2000) has traced the story of how the development of real property law in the West accelerated its economic development. He makes a vital distinction between an asset, which is anything desirable, and capital, which unlocks the potential of those assets. Land is an asset, but does not become capital until it is "represented in writing" and registered in a public way so that it can be described and traded. Clean air is desirable. Its potential as a form of capital cannot be unlocked until six conditions are met.

These conditions begin to describe the challenge of converting different kinds of resources or assets into capital (de Soto, 2000).

First, the potential of economic assets is fixed by a written representation. The useful qualities of the asset must be described. Second, some sort of system is needed to integrate these written representations so that third parties are made aware of the rights of the owners of capital. In the world of carbon finance, this is occurring with the development of formal carbon markets, like the Chicago Climate Exchange, where instruments can be traded. Third, accountability must exist by creating sanctions for the violation of rights. Fourth, assets must be made fungible so that the rights to the asset can be traded without actually selling the underlying asset (e.g., the carbon project). Fifth, as de Soto (2000: 61) explains, "Properly understood and designed, a property system creates a network through which people can assemble their assets into more valuable combinations." These new combinations are the essence of innovation and value creation (Schumpeter, 1934). Finally, transactions are protected through public registries and private services, so that property can be transferred in ways that ensure confidence and reliability. Thus, the Chicago Climate Exchange trades instruments dealing with carbon emissions without trading the actual GHG-reducing projects that they represent. It is transferred publicly with specific standards of quality in the execution of such transactions.

The challenges of creating these new forms of tradable capital are very similar to the challenges of unlocking the capital of the poor who live in irregular urban settlements. Development is almost impossible until owners receive property rights, which are well defined, and thus tradable. This process occurred for land almost 200 years ago. It is just now occurring for greenhouse gases.

It is possible that this process will repeat itself for many kinds of desirable objectives based on human, social, natural, and cultural assets. These new capital markets would allow us to value and protect much of what we value most. Those firms with well-developed social strategies will be the best positioned to take advantage of these new markets for virtue.

Threats to social strategy

From virtue, we must move to vice. Just as we have had the pleasure of postulating a future in which we value and protect virtues, we must also confront the brutal bane of corruption. In the last decade, we have been stunned by the collaborative innovation between governments and private contractors, between regulators and the creators of synthetic financial instruments to appropriate wealth. Via "legal" contracts and concessions and "legal" marketing and sales of toxic financial instruments, billions of dollars transferred into the hands of men and women who did not fairly compete for this wealth.

In the United States, this *legal corruption*, matched by an ingenious self-justification detached from any known moral code, is a far greater threat to economic and social welfare than illegal bribery and theft and Bernard Madoff's pyramid scheme.

The specifics of the corruption are amply documented. In Iraq, one of the five most corrupt countries of the world according to Transparency International's Corruption Perceptions Index (CPI), tens of billions of dollars were placed in the hands of contractors who then paid out billions to politicians and warlords.

Hurricane Katrina and unregulated health and finance industries offered billions more in suspect contracting subject to mere testimonial oversight. College student loans were corrupted by permitting loan officers to receive "consulting" payments from loan companies that often were placed on lists of "preferred lenders" by the loan officers' colleges and universities. Similar schemes were permitted by the Food and Drug Administration between pharmaceutical companies and doctors.

With the recession, a salutary backlash against unethical practices has moved government and regulatory agencies to shore up enforcement of laws and regulations as well as to update legal codes and regulatory standards. Why, we will be asked, in the final chapter of this book are we discussing corruption as a threat to social strategy? Quite simply, when the global business environment is lenient toward corruption the effect on multinationals that wish to pursue social strategy is negative. Firms with a strong social responsibility orientation and that support participative decision-making are also more likely to have a corporate identity that strives to maintain ethical behavior. In markets where corruption is tolerated – or worse, institutionalized – firms that maintain ethical standards are at a competitive disadvantage.

If this is true – which must yet be demonstrated by research – then it behooves us to review our expectations for combating global corruption. Perhaps, the most important development in international business is the spectacular growth of the BRIC (Brazil, Russia, India and China) economies, all weak performers on the CPI, whose success has thrown hundreds of billions more into the corruption pot. Their extraordinary economic success for more than a decade is a serious challenge to the long-standing view that corruption and development are incompatible. Apparently, the upper limit of corruption, before it undoes an economy, is substantially greater than many of us had thought possible.

Our evaluation of corruption in the BRIC countries, with half the world's population, must be placed in context. The emergence of the BRIC countries is an undeniable triumph for humanity, even with the social disruptions that have accompanied change. Each year, millions of people are leaving what Indian novelist, Aravind Adiga, accurately termed "The Darkness" in his Man Booker prize-winning *The White Tiger* (2008), to come into the light. Poverty is a medieval master who pits each human being against every other in a zero-sum game of "it's mine." Where there is poverty, men and women are slaves to landowners and warlords, and children are slaves to desperate parents who can neither feed nor educate them. Next to poverty, Adiga tells us, even primitive capitalism is an extraordinary opportunity. Millions in Brazil, China and India have benefited.

The case of Russia is quite different. Poverty and the culture of poverty were not the principal enemy, but the State. The State denied men and women of basic human rights. With the breakup of the Soviet Union and the end of communism, capitalism restored economic freedom, and with it personal liberties and hope. Unfortunately, in Russia, today, the State is being reconstituted as an instrument of oppression and arbitrariness. Government favoritism permits selected companies to prosper while rebellious entrepreneurs have their property expropriated and are jailed. Corruption is the business of the State.

The message to multinationals that operate in these countries is that you must participate in corrupt practices if you wish to be a player in the largest and fastest growing markets in the world. The threat this behavior represents to social strategy is clear. Inevitably, participation in corruption debilitates a firm's commitment to ethics and undermines the purpose, stability, and credibility of social and environmental strategy. Even firms that refuse involvement with corruption may be dissuaded from social strategy in an environment where corruption is tolerated and bribery is a competitive weapon. Even worse, we have worked with several firms which had always spurned all solicitation of bribes, but, in order to work in India or China or Russia, hired a local representative to whom they paid a fixed fee to manage the contractual process and government relations. In effect, they pursued a "don't ask, don't tell" strategy.

We must insist on how dangerous this practice is to social strategy. Though we know that no firm is perfect and that while one business unit may engage in admirable social action projects and another may be engaging in bribery, we believe that at some point the conflict between these two identities will manifest itself within the organization and one will win out. Attempts to bracket off or isolate units that must operate in more "complex" or "challenging" environments are destined to fail the day one such business unit posts profits that other units cannot match. The case for ethical behavior will end. We hardly need more cases like Enron, Siemens, and the 2008–9 financial crisis to confirm this argument.

Having stated the bad news, we can now point to optimistic signs. IKEA's decision to go public with its refusal to pay off bureaucrats and to halt expansion plans in Russia ought to be an example to other firms (Bush, 2009). No doubt, some will claim that IKEA has it easy. The firm is already an institution in Russia, and can, as it did in 2004, get the ear of Vladimir Putin. On the other hand, IKEA's success in Russia could have been the perfect excuse to accede to "business as usual." IKEA said no, and said so publicly and loudly. Moreover, IKEA implied that multinationals should think twice about investing in Russia and that the threat of appropriation/stealing of value created is real and constant.

As we are imagining possible futures, we should also point to positive signs with the BRIC countries. The progressive development of democratic institutions in Brazil and India should moderate corruption as the middle class broadens and education extends across social groups. In China and Russia, better educated and more secure populations will make greater demands for democratic institutions and transparency, as well. Moreover, multinationals will find low-corruption host countries pressuring them to meet global standards.

A concluding thought

Independently of the macro-environment, each firm individually will choose its path and decide its strategy. Each firm is an experiment in market and social behavior; any single business may turn out to be an opportunity for creative *instruction*.

A play on Schumpeter's "creative destruction," creative instruction is the collective learning by which an organization becomes a model for how to do something. Apple may be a model for innovation and design; the European Union a model for regional cooperation; Finland's educational system for how to teach young people; Wal-Mart for how to manage costs; MRW, the Spanish package delivery company, on how to build and sustain a social strategy.

We have restricted ourselves to positive models; the negative ones don't need more publicity. You may not agree that the models we chose are necessarily good ones; similarly we know that euro-skeptics are legion. We choose the European Union precisely because there are believers and non-believers. There are believers and non-believers when it comes to social strategy as well. We are unconcerned about the non-believers. We do care that those readers who are considering social strategy for the businesses they own and/or work in are encouraged to find creative instruction in those firms that already have chosen social strategy.

Throughout this book, we have sought to provide theoretical and practical support for social strategy. We have given special attention to multinationals. Though social enterprises and startups are inspiring, the extraordinary influence of multinationals is undeniable. In our most optimistic scenario, we can envision a group of successful social strategy multinationals, newcomers and converts, providing creative instruction for others to pursue social strategy. Is there anybody who would argue against a global economy where many more multinationals have a strong social responsibility orientation, practice participative management, and maintain high ethical standards? Perhaps Jared Diamond will turn out to be right in "Will Big Business Save the Earth?" (2009).

Bibliography

Aaer News. 2007. GE Energy's wind business has entered into patent licenses with AAER Inc. related to GE's variable speed technology for wind turbines. Aaer News, May. Accessed by internet on April 14, 2008 at www.marketmillionaires.com/canadian-stocks-global-equities/8874-aaer-news.html

Abaroa, R.M. 1999. Towards 2005: Profits, people, and the future of the regulatory state in the free market model. *Law and Policy in International Business*, 30: 131–138.

Abbott, A. 1983. Professional ethics. *American Journal of Sociology*, 88(5): 855–885.

Abratt, R. 1989. A new approach to the corporate image management process. *Journal of Marketing Management*, 5(1): 63–76.

Ackerman, R. and Bauer, R. 1976. *Corporate social responsiveness: The modern dilemma*. Reston, VA: Reston Publishing Company.

Acutt, N.J., Medina-Ross, V., and O'Riordan, T. 2004. Perspectives on corporate social responsibility in the chemical sector: A comparative analysis of the Mexican and South African cases. *Natural Resources Forum*, 28: 302–316.

Adiga, A. 2008. *The White Tiger*. New York: The Free Press.

ADM. 2009. Corporate Responsibility Report. Archer Daniels Midland. Accessed by internet at www.adm.com/en-US/responsibility/materiality/Pages/default.aspx on December 27, 2009.

Agle, B.R., Mitchell, R.K., and Sonnenfeld, J.A. 1999. Who matters to CEOs: An investigation of stakeholder attributes and salience, corporate performance, and CEO values. *Academy of Management Journal*, 42(5): 507–525.

Aguilar, M. and Ander-Egg, E. 1992. *Evaluación de servicios y programas sociales*. Madrid, Spain: Siglo XXI.

Albert, S. and Whetten, D.A. 1985. Organizational identity. In L.L. Cummings and B.M. Staw (eds.), *Research in organizational behavior*, 7: 263–295. Greenwich, CT: JAI Press.

Aldrich, H.E. 1979. *Organizations and environments*. Englewood Cliffs, NJ: Prentice-Hall.

Allen, D. B. 2007. Government regulation and the competitive advantage of nations. May 10. Accessed by internet at www.davidbruceallen. com/strategyoped/2007/05/government_regu.html on December 30, 2009.

2008. GM and Chrysler: How the US chose to fail. October 13. Accessed by internet at www.davidbruceallen.com/strategyoped/2008/10/gm-and-chyrsler.html on December 30, 2009.

Allen, W. T. 1992. Our schizophrenic conception of the business corporation. *Cardozo Law Review*, 14: 261–281.

Alliance. 2009. The financial crisis around the world. *Alliance magazine*. March 1. Accessed by internet at www.alliancemagazine.org/en/ content/the-financial-crisis-around-world on October 23, 2009.

Alvesson, M. and Berg, P. O. 1992. *Corporate culture and organizational symbolism: An overview*. Berlin: Walter de Gruyter.

Amabile, T. M. 1977. Effects of extrinsic constraint on creativity. Ph.D. dissertation. Palo Alto, CA: Stanford University.

1997. Motivating creativity in organizations: On doing what you love and loving what you do. *California Management Review*, 40(1): 39–58.

American Association of Fundraising Counsel. 2008. Giving USA 2008: The annual report on philanthropy for the year 2007. Summary accessed by internet on January 8, 2009 at www.nps.gov/partnerships/ fundraising_individuals_statistics.htm

Amit, R. and Schoemaker, P. J. H. 1993. Strategic assets and organizational rent. *Strategic Management Journal*, 14(1): 33–46.

Andersson, L. M. and Bateman, T. S. 2000. Individual environmental initiative: Championing natural environmental issues in US business organizations. *Academy of Management Journal*, 43(4): 548–570.

Andrews, E. L. and Baker, P. 2009. AIG planning to pay out huge bonuses following $170 billion bailout. *The New York Times*, March 14. Accessed by internet at www.nytimes.com/2009/03/15/business/15AIG.html?_ r=1&scp=9&sq=AIG&st=Search on December 30, 2009.

Andrews, K. 1971. *The concept of corporate strategy*. Homewood, IL: Irwin.

et al. 1965. *Business strategy and policy: Text and cases*. Homewood, IL: Irwin.

Annan, K. 2004. Address to the World Economic Forum, January 23. Accessed by internet at www.weforum.org/site/homepublic.nsf/ Content/Special+Address+by+Kofi+Annan on July 5, 2008.

Ansoff, H. I. 1965. *Corporate strategy*. New York: McGraw-Hill.

1980. Strategic issues management. *Strategic Management Journal*, 1: 131–148.

Aragón-Correa, J. A. and Sharma, S. 2003. A contingent resource-based view of proactive corporate environmental strategy. *Academy of Management Review*, 28(1): 71–88.

Arend, R. J. 2003. Revisiting the logical and research considerations of competitive strategy. *Strategic Management Journal*, 24(3): 279–284.

Argyris, C. 1993. *Knowledge for action: A guide for overcoming barriers to organizational change*. San Francisco, CA: Jossey-Bass.

Arthaud-Day, M. 2005. Transnational corporate responsibility: A tri-dimensional approach to international CSR research. *Business Ethics Quarterly*, 15(1): 1–22.

Association of Certified Fraud Examiners 2008 Report to the Nation on Occupational Fraud and Abuse. Available for download at http://vcr.csrwire.com/files/2008-rttn.pdf.

Austin, J. E., Reficco, E., Berger, *et al.* 2004. *Social partnering in Latin America: Lessons drawn from collaborations of businesses and civil society organizations*. Cambridge, MA: Harvard University Press.

Axelrod, R. 1984. *The evolution of cooperation*. New York: Basic Books.

Bach, D. and Allen, D. B. 2010. Beyond the market: What every CEO needs to know about nonmarket strategy. *MIT Sloan Management Review* SI(3): 41–48.

Bagnoli, M. and Watts, S. G. 2003. Selling to socially responsible consumers: Competition and the private provision of public goods. *Journal of Economics and Management Strategy*, 12(3): 419–445.

Banham, M. 2006. MTV launches World Aids Day awareness push. *Brand Republic*, 28 November.

Bansal, P. and Roth, K. 2000. Why companies go green: A model of ecological responsiveness. *Academy of Management Journal*, 43(4): 717–736.

Barnard, C. I. 1938. *The functions of the executive*. Cambridge, MA: Harvard University Press.

Barnett, M. L. 2007. Stakeholder influence capacity and the variability of financial returns to corporate social responsibility. *Academy of Management Review*, 32(3): 794–816.

Barney, J. B. 1986a. Strategic factor markets: Expectations, luck, and business strategy. *Management Science*, 32(10): 1231–1241.

1986b. Organizational culture: Can it be a source of sustained competitive advantage? *Academy of Management Review*, 11(3): 656–665.

1991. Firm resources and sustained competitive advantage. *Journal of Management*, 17(1): 99–120.

Baron, D. P. 1995. Integrated strategy: Market and nonmarket components. *California Management Review*, 37(2): 47–65.

2001. Private politics, corporate social responsibility and integrated strategy. *Journal of Economics and Management Strategy*, 10(1): 7–45.

2005. *Business and its environment.* Upper Saddle River, NJ: Prentice-Hall.

2007. Corporate social responsibility and social entrepreneurship. *Journal of Economics and Management Strategy,* 16(3): 683–717.

Barrow, C.J. 2000. *Social impact assessment: An introduction.* London, UK: Arnold.

Bartlett, C.A. and Ghoshal, S. 1989. *Managing across borders: The transnational solution.* Boston, MA: Harvard Business School Press.

Basu, K. and Palazzo, G. 2008. Corporate social responsibility: A process model of sensemaking. *Academy of Management Review,* 33(1): 122–136.

Bauer, R.A. 1990. The corporate response process. In L.E. Preston (ed.), *Corporation and society research: Studies in theory and measurement:* 179–202. Greenwich, CT: JAI Press.

Baumol, W.J. 1991. (Almost) perfect competition (contestability) and business ethics. In W.J. Baumol and S.A.B. Blackman (eds.) pp. 1–21.

Baumol, W.J. and Blackman, S.A.B. (eds.) 1991. *Perfect markets and easy virtue: Business ethics and the invisible hand.* Cambridge, MA: Blackwell Publishers.

Baxter, A. 2007. Aid projects build better work teams. *Financial Times,* February 27, p. 12.

Beck, G. 2005. *The real America: Messages from the heart and the heartland.* New York: Pocket Books.

Becker, G. 1964. *Human capital: A theoretical and empirical analysis, with special reference to education.* University of Chicago Press.

1976. Altruism, egoism, and genetic fitness: Economics and sociobiology. *Journal of Economic Literature,* 14: 817–826.

Becker, G., Philipson, T., and Soares, R. 2005. The quantity and quality of life and the evolution of world inequality. *American Economic Review,* 95(1): 277–291.

Becker, H. and Vanclay, F. 2003. *The international handbook of social impact assessment.* Boston, MA: Edward Elgar.

Bennis, W.G. and Slater, P.E. 1964. Democracy is inevitable. *Harvard Business Review,* 42(2): 51–59.

Bercovitch, S. 1986. *The puritan origins of the American self.* New Haven, CT: Yale University Press.

Berfield, S. 2009. Starbucks: Howard Schultz vs. Howard Schultz. *Business Week,* August 6. Accessed by internet on October 9, 2009 at www.businessweek.com/magazine/content/09_33/b4143028813542.htm

Berman, S.L., Wicks, A.C., Kotha, S., and Jones, T.M. 1999. Does stakeholder orientation matter? The relationship between stakeholder management models and firm financial performance. *Academy of Management Journal,* 42(5): 488–506.

Barnard, C. 1938. *The functions of the executive.* Cambridge, MA: Harvard University Press.

Bernstein, M. H. 1955. *Regulating business by independent commission.* Westport, CT: Greenwood Press.

Berger, P. L. and Luckmann, T. 1966. *The social construction of reality.* New York: Anchor Books.

Beyer, J., Dunbar, R. L. M., and Meyer, A. D. 1988. Comment: The concept of ideology in organizational analysis. *Academy of Management Review*, 13(3): 483–489.

Bies, R. J., Bartunek, J. M., Fort, T. L., and Zald, M. N. 2007. Corporations as social change agents: Individual, interpersonal, institutional, and environmental dynamics. *Academy of Management Review*, 32(3): 788–793.

Birgir, J. 2006. Patricia Woertz: The outsider. *Fortune*, October 2. Accessed by internet at http://money.cnn.com/2006/09/29/magazines/fortune/mpw.woertz.fortune/index.htm?postversion=2006100208 on December 28, 2009.

Black, F. and Scholes, M. 1973. The pricing of options and corporate liabilities. *Journal of Political Economy*, 81: 637–659.

Blatchford, D. 2005. Environmental and social aspects of the Baku-Tbilisi-Ceyhan pipeline. In S. F. Starr and S. E. Cornell (eds.), *The Baku-Tbilisi-Ceyhan pipeline: Oil window to the west*: 119–150. Washington, DC: Central-Asia Caucasus Institute Silk Road Studies Program of Johns Hopkins University and Uppsala University. Accessed by internet at www.silkroadstudies.org/new/inside/publications/BTC.pdf on November 14, 2009.

Bollier, D. 1996. *Aiming higher: 25 stories of how companies prosper by combining sound management and social vision.* New York: American Management Association.

Bonardi, J. P., Hillman, A., and Keim, G. 2005. The attractiveness of political markets: Implications for firm strategy. *Academy of Management Review*, 30(2): 397–413.

Bookstaber, R. M. 1981. *Option pricing and strategies in investing.* Reading, MA: Addison-Wesley Publishing Company.

Borenstein, S., Bushnell, J., and Knittel, C. R. 1999. Market power in electricity markets: Beyond concentration measures. *The Energy Journal*, 20(4): 65–88.

Bovard, J. 1995. Archer Daniels Midland: A case study in corporate welfare. Cato Institute. Accessed by internet at www.mindfully.org/Industry/ADM-Corp-Welfare.htm on December 28, 2009.

Bower, J. L., Bartlett, C. A., Uyterhoeven, H., and Walton, R. 1995. *Business policy: Managing strategic processes*, 8th edn. Chicago, IL: Richard D. Irwin.

Bowie, N.E. 1991. Challenging the egoistic paradigm. *Business Ethics Quarterly*, 1(1): 1–21.

Bowman, E.H. and Hurry, D. 1993. Strategy through the option lens: An integrated view of resource investments and the incremental-choice process. *Academy of Management Review*, 18(4): 760–782.

Boyd, B.W. and Reuning-Elliott, E. 1998. A measurement model of strategic planning. *Strategic Management Review*, 19(2): 181–192.

Boyd, B.W., Dess, G.G., and Rasheed, A. 1993. Divergence between archival and perceptual measures of the environment: Causes and consequences. *Academy of Management Review*, 18: 204–226.

Brammer, S. and Millington, A. 2008. Does it pay to be different? An analysis of the relationship between corporate social and financial performance. *Strategic Management Journal*, 29: 1325–1343.

Branco, M. and Rodrigues, L. 2006. Corporate social responsibility and resource-based perspectives. *Journal of Business Ethics*, 69(2): 111–132.

Brent, R. 2006. *Applied cost-benefit analysis*. Northampton, MA: Edward Elgar.

Breyer, S. 1979. Analyzing regulatory failure: Mismatches, less restrictive alternatives, and reform. *Harvard Law Review*, 92: 547–609.

  1982. *Regulation and its reform*. Cambridge, MA: Harvard University Press.

Brown, R. 1977. *A poetic for sociology: Toward a logic of discovery for the human sciences*. University of Chicago Press.

BT Annual Report 2000. London: British Telecom.

Buchanan, J. 1968. *The demand and supply of public goods*. Chicago, IL: Rand McNally.

Buchko, A. 1994. Conceptualization and measurement of environmental uncertainty: An assessment of the Miles and Snow perceived environmental uncertainty scale. *Academy of Management Journal*, 37(2): 410–425.

Bulow, J., Geanakoplos, J., and Klemperer, P. 1985. Multimarket oligopoly: Strategic substitutes and complements. *Journal of Political Economy*, 93: 488–511.

Burke, L. and Logsdon, J. 1996. How corporate social responsibility pays off. *Long Range Planning*, 29: 495–502.

Burlingame, D. 2001. Corporate giving. *International Journal of Nonprofit and Voluntary Sector Marketing*, 6(1): 4–5.

Bush, J. 2009. Why IKEA is fed up with Russia. *Business Week*, July 2. Accessed by internet at www.businessweek.com/magazine/content/09_28/b4139033326721.htm on November 12, 2009.

Campbell, D. and Stanley, J. 1966. *Experimental and quasi-experimental designs for research*. Chicago, IL: Rand.

Cardoso, F.H. and Faletto, E. 1979. *Dependency and development in Latin America*. Berkeley, CA: University of California Press.

Carman, J.M. and Harris, R.G. 1986. Public regulation of marketing activity, Part III: A typology of regulatory failures and implications for marketing and public policy. *Journal of Macromarketing*, 6: 51–64.

Carpenter, M.A. and Golden, B.R. 1997. Perceived managerial discretion: A study of cause and effect. *Strategic Management Journal*, 18(3): 187–206.

Carree, M.A. and Thurik, A.R. 2000. The life cycle of the US tire industry. *Southern Economic Journal*, 67(2): 254–278.

Carroll, A.B. 1999. Corporate social responsibility: Evolution of a definitional construct. *Business and Society*, 38(3): 268–295.

  2006. Corporate social responsibility: A historical perspective. In M.J. Epstein and K.O. Hansen (eds.), *The accountable corporation*, vol. III. Westport, CT: Greenwood.

Castrogiovanni, G.J. 1991. Environmental munificence: A theoretical assessment. *Academy of Management Review*, 16(3): 542–565.

Caulkin, S. 2009. Social concerns are crunched off the agenda. *The Observer*, April 5. Accessed by internet at www.guardian.co.uk/business/2009/apr/05

Chandler, A. 1962. *Strategy and structure: Chapters in the history of American industrial enterprise*. Cambridge, MA: MIT Press.

Chatterji, A. and Levine, D. 2006. Breaking down the wall of codes: Evaluating non-financial performance measurement. *California Management Review*, 48(2): 29–51.

Chen, C.C., Chen, Y.-R., and Xin, K. 2004. Guanxi practices and trust in management: A procedural justice perspective. *Organization Science*, 15(2): 200–209.

ChevronTexaco 2001. *Annual report*. San Ramon, CA: ChevronTexaco.

Chi, T. 2000. Option to acquire or divest a joint venture. *Strategic Management Journal*, 21: 665–687.

Christensen, C.M. and Bower, J.L. 1996. Customer power, strategic investment, and the failure of leading firms. *Strategic Management Journal*, 17: 197–218.

Christensen, C.M., Baumann, H., Ruggles, R., and Sadtler, T.M. 2006. Disruptive innovation for social change. *Harvard Business Review*, 84(12): 94–101.

Christensen, R., and Andrews, K. 1965. *Business policy: Text and cases*. Homewood, IL: Irwin.

Christian Aid. 2004. Behind the mask: The real face of corporate social responsibility. London: Christian Aid. Unpublished report accessed by internet at www.corporate-responsibility.org/module_images/

Christian%20Aid%20Report%20-%20Behind%20the%20mask%202004.pdf

Christmann, P. 2004. Multinational companies and the natural environment: Determinants of global environmental policy standardization. *Academy of Management Journal*, 47(5): 747–760.

Clarkson, M.B.E. 1995. A stakeholder framework for analyzing and evaluating corporate social performance. *Academy of Management Review*, 20(1): 92–118.

CNW. 2007. Wal-Mart Canada announces nationwide retrofit of store lighting. Accessed by internet at www.newswire.ca/en/releases/archive/October2007/17/c4965.html on March 18, 2008.

Coase, R.H. 1960. The problem of social cost. *Journal of Law and Economics*, 3 (October): 1–44.

Cochran, P.L. and Wood, R.A. 1984. Corporate social responsibility and financial performance. *Academy of Management Journal*, 27: 42–56.

Cohen, M.A., Rust, R.T., Steen, S., and Tidd, S.T. 2004. Willingness-to-pay for crime control programs. *Criminology*, 42(1): 89–109.

Coile, Z. 2007. 'Cap-and-trade' model eyed for cutting greenhouse gases: Method has proved successful in reducing emissions that produce acid rain pollution. *San Francisco Chronicle*, December 3. Accessed by internet at www.sfgate.com/cgi-bin/article.cgi?f=/c/a/2007/12/03/MNMMTJUS1.DTL&hw=Cap+trade+Acid+Rain&sn=001&sc=1000 on June 1, 2009.

Collins, D. 1997. The ethical superiority and inevitability of participatory management as an organizational system. *Organization Science*, 8(5): 489–507.

Collins, J. 2001. *Good to great*. New York: HarperCollins.

2009. *How the mighty fall*. Jim Collins.

Collins, J. and Porras, J. 1994. *Built to last*. New York: HarperCollins.

Collis, D.J. 1994. How valuable are organisational capabilities? *Strategic Management Journal*, 15(2): 143–152.

Copeland, T. 2001. The real-options approach to capital allocation. *Strategic Finance*, 83(4)(October): 33–37.

Corley, K.G. and Gioia, D.A. 2004. Identity ambiguity and change in the wake of a corporate spin-off. *Administrative Science Quarterly*, 49(2): 173–208.

Crane, A., Matten, D., and Spence, L. 2007. *Corporate social responsibility: Readings and cases in a global context*. Abingdon, UK: Routledge.

Crane, A., McWilliams, A., Matten, D., Moon, J., and Siegel, D.S. (eds.). 2008. *The Oxford handbook of corporate social responsibility*: 303–323. Oxford University Press.

Cuervo-Cazurra, A. 2006. Who cares about corruption? *Journal of International Business Studies*, 37(6): 807–822.

Cummings, S. 1993. Brief Case: The first strategists. *Long Range Planning*, 18: 133–135.

Daft, R. L. 1995. *Organization theory and design* (5th edn.). Minneapolis/St. Paul, MN: West Publishing Co.

Daft, R. L. and Weick, K. E. 1984. Toward a model of organizations as interpretation systems. *Academy of Management Review*, 9(2): 284–295.

Davis, I. 2005. The Biggest Contract. *The Economist*, May 26, 2005.

Davis, K. 1983. An expanded view of the social responsibility of business. In T. L. Beauchamp and N. E. Bowie (eds), *Ethical theory and business*: 94–97. Englewood Cliffs, NJ: Prentice-Hall.

de George, R. T. 1993. *Competing with integrity in international business*. New York: Oxford University Press.

de Jongh, D. 2004. A stakeholder perspective on managing social risk in South Africa: Responsibility or accountability? *Journal of Corporate Citizenship*, 15: 27–31.

de la Fuente, A. M. 2006. MTV Latam votes for election skein; Latin cabler preps new pol series. *Daily Variety*, 1 May.

de Pelsmacker, P., Driesen, L., and Rayp, G. 2005. Do consumers care about ethics? Willingness to pay for fair-trade coffee. *Journal of Consumer Affairs*, 39(2): 363–385.

de Soto, H. 2000. *The mystery of capital*. New York: Basic Books.

de Wit, B. and Meyer, R. 1994. *Strategy: Process, content, context*. Minneapolis/St. Paul: West Publishing Co.

Deal, T. and Kennedy, A. 1982. *Corporate cultures: The rites and rituals of corporate life*. Harmondsworth: Penguin Books.

Dean, T. J. and Brown, R. L. 1995. Pollution regulation as a barrier to new firm entry: Initial evidence and implications for future research. *Academy of Management Journal*, 38: 288–303.

Dechant, K. and Altman, B. 1994. Environmental leadership: From compliance to competitive advantage. *Academy of Management Executive*, 8(3): 7–20.

Demsetz, H. 1970. The private production of public goods. *Journal of Law and Economics*, 13(2): 293–306.

Dennett, D. C. 1987. *The intentional stance*. Cambridge, MA: MIT Press.

Derrida, J. 1976. *Of grammatology*. Baltimore, MD: John Hopkins University Press.

Dess, G. G. and Beard, D. W. 1984. Dimensions of organizational task environments. *Administrative Science Quarterly*, 29: 52–73.

Dewey, J. 1922. *Human nature and conduct: An introduction to social psychology*. New York: Holt.

1926. The historic background of corporate legal personality. *Yale Law Journal*, 35(6): 655–673.

1927. *The public and its problems*. New York: Holt. Republished in 1940 as *The Public and Its Problems: An Essay in Political Inquiry*. Chicago, IL: Gateway.

1935. *Liberalism and social action*. New York: Putnam.

1998. *The Essential Dewey: Volumes 1 and 2*. Edited by L. Hickman and T. Alexander. Bloomington, IN: Indiana University Press.

Diamond, J. 2009. Will big business save the earth? *The New York Times*, December 6. Accessed by internet at www.nytimes.com on December 15, 2009.

Dierckx, L. and Cool, K. 1989. Asset stock accumulation and sustainability of competitive advantage. *Management Science*, 35(12): 1504–1511.

DiMaggio P. J. and Powell, W. W. 1983. The iron cage revisited: Institutional isomorphism and collective rationality in organizational fields. *American Sociological Review*, 48: 147–160.

Donaldson, T. and Preston, L. E. 1995. The stakeholder theory of the corporation: Concepts, evidence, and implications. *Academy of Management Review*, 20(1): 65–91.

Donaldson, T. and Dunfee, T. 1994. Toward a unified conception of business ethics: Integrative social contracts theory. *Academy of Management Review*, 19(2): 252–284.

1999. *Ties that bind: A social contracts approach to business ethics*. Boston, MA: Harvard Business School Press.

Donaldson, T. and Preston, L. E. 1995. A stakeholder theory of the corporation: Concepts, evidence, and implications. *Academy of Management Review*, 20(1): 65–91.

Doty, D. H. and Glick, W. H. 1994. Typologies as a unique form of theory building: Toward improved understanding and modeling. *Academy of Management Review*, 19(2): 230–251.

Douglas, S. and Mills, K. 2000. Nonprofit fraud: What are the key indicators? *Canadian Fund Raiser*, August 16.

Downey, S. M. 1986. The relationship between corporate culture and corporate identity. *Public Relations Quarterly*, 31(4): 7–12.

Doyle, M. P. and Snyder, C. M. 1999. Information sharing and competition in the motor vehicle industry. *Journal of Political Economy*, 107(6): 1–39.

Duflo, E. and Kremer, M. 2005. Use of randomization in the evaluation of development effectiveness. In G. Pitman, O. Feinstein, and G. Ingram (eds.), *Evaluating Development Effectiveness*: 205–232. New Brunswick, NJ: Transaction Publishers.

Duncan, R. B. 1972. Characteristics of organizational environments and perceived environmental uncertainties. *Administrative Science Quarterly*, 17(3): 313–327.

Dunne, S. and Dolan, P. 2004. The anti-corporate movement: A discourse analytic perspective. Unpublished paper presented at the 20th Colloquium of the European Group for Organizational Studies, Lyublyana, Slovenia.

Dutton, J. E. and Pratt, M. G. 1997. Merck and Co., Inc.: From core competence to global community involvement. In Tichy, McGill, and St. Clair (eds.), 150–167.

Dutton, J. E., Fahey, L., and Narayanan, V. K. 1983. Toward understanding strategic issue diagnosis. *Strategic Management Journal*, 4(4): 307–323.

Dutton, J. E. and Dukerich, J. M. 1991. Keeping an eye on the mirror: Image and identity in organizational adaptation. *Academy of Management Journal*, 34: 517–554.

Dyer, J. H. and Singh, H. 1998. The relational view: Cooperative strategy and sources of interorganizational competitive advantage. *Academy of Management Review*, 32(4): 660–679.

Eguía, R. and Allen, D. B. 2004. Telefónica corporate reputation project (A). Madrid, Spain: Instituto de Empresa Business School.

Eisenhardt, K. M. and Martin, J. A. 2000. Dynamic capabilities: What are they? *Strategic Management Review*, 21(10/11): 1105–1721.

Eisenhower, D. D. 1957. A speech to the National Defense Executive Reserve Conference. November 14. Washington, DC.

Epstein, E. M. 1969. *The corporation in American politics*. Englewood Cliffs, NJ: Prentice-Hall.

Esty, D. 1999. Toward optimal environmental governance. *New York University Law Review*, 74(6): 1495–1574.

Etzioni, A. 1961. *A comparative analysis of complex organizations*. New York: Free Press.

   1998. A communitarian note on stakeholder theory. *Business Ethics Quarterly*, 8(4): 679–691.

Evan, W. M. and Freeman, R. E. 1988. A stakeholder theory of the modern corporation: Kantian capitalism. In T. L. Beauchamp and N. E. Bowie (eds.), *Ethical theory and business*: 97–106. Englewood Cliffs, NJ: Prentice-Hall.

Feddersen, T. J. and Gilligan, T. W. 2001. Saints and markets: Activists and the supply of credence goods. *Journal of Economics and Management Strategy*, 10(1): 149–171.

Fernández-Kranz, D. and Santaló, J. 2007. When necessity becomes a virtue: The effect of product market competition on corporate social responsibility. *Journal of Economics and Management Strategy*. Available at SSRN: http://ssrn.com/abstract=997007.

File, K. M. and Prince, R. A. 1998. Cause related marketing and corporate philanthropy in the privately held enterprise. *Journal of Business Ethics*, 17: 1529–1539.

Fishman, C. 2006. *The Wal-Mart effect: How the world's most powerful company really works – and how it's transforming the American economy*. New York: Penguin Press.

Fisman, R., Heal, G., and Nair, V. B. 2006. A model of corporate philanthropy. Columbia Business School Working Paper.

Fligstein, N. 1991. The structural transformation of American industry: An institutional account of the causes of diversification in the largest firms, 1919–1979. In W. W. Powell and P. J. DiMaggio (eds.), *The new institutionalism in organizational analysis*: 311–336. University of Chicago Press.

Flippen, C. 2004. Unequal returns to housing investments: A study of real housing appreciation among black, white, and Hispanic households. *Social Forces*, 82(4): 1523–1552.

Fombrun, C. J. 1996. *Reputation: Realizing value from the corporate image*. Boston, MA: Harvard Business School Press.

    2005. Building corporate reputation through CSR initiatives: Evolving standards. *Corporate Reputation Review*, 8(1): 7–11.

Fombrun, C. J. and Shanley, M. 1990. What's in a name? Reputation building and corporate strategy. *Academy of Management Review*, 33(2): 233–258.

Fombrun, C. J., Gardberg, N. A., and Barnett, M. L. 2000. Opportunity platforms and safety nets: Corporate citizenship and reputational risk. *Business and Society Review*, 105(1): 85–106.

Fortune. 2009. Global 500: Telefónica. Accessed by internet at http://money.cnn.com/magazines/fortune/global500/2009/snapshots/8221.html on December 2, 2009.

Foss, N. 2000. Strategy, bargaining, and economic organization: Some thoughts on the transaction cost foundations of firm strategy. Working paper. Copenhagen Business School.

Foucault, M. 1972. The archaeology of knowledge (trans. A. M. Sheridan Smith). New York: Pantheon.

Frederick, W. C. 1986. Toward CSR3: Why ethical analysis is indispensable and unavoidable in corporate affairs. *California Management Review*, 28: 126–141.

    1991. The moral authority of transnational corporate codes. *Journal of Business Ethics*, 10(3): 165–177.

    1994. From CSR1 to CSR2: The maturing of business-and-society thought. *Business and Society*, 33: 150–164.

Freeman, R.E. 1984. *Strategic management: A stakeholder approach.* Boston, MA: Pitman.

Freeman, R.E. and Gilbert, D.R., Jr. 1988. *Corporate strategy and the search for ethics.* Englewood Cliffs, NJ: Prentice-Hall.

Friedman, M. 1962. *Capitalism and freedom.* University of Chicago Press.

Frooman, J. 1999. Stakeholder influence strategies. *Academy of Management Review*, 24(2): 191–205.

Fry, L.W., Keim, G.D., and Meiners, R.E. 1982. Corporate contributions: Altruistic or for-profit? *Academy of Management Journal*, 25(1): 94–106.

Fukuyama, F. 1995. Social capital and the global economy: A redrawn map of the world. *Foreign Affairs*, 74(5): 89–103.

Fundación Empresa y Sociedad. 1997. La estrategia social de la empresa: Un enfoque de valor. Madrid: Fundación Empresa y Sociedad.

Galaskiewicz, J. 1997. An urban grants economy revisited: Corporate charitable contributions in the Twin Cities, 1979–81, 1987–89. *Administrative Science Quarterly*, 42: 445–471.

Garriga, E. and Mele, D. 2004. Corporate social responsibility theories: Mapping the territory. *Journal of Business Ethics*, 53: 51–71.

Gates, B. 2008. Making capitalism more creative. *Time*, July 31. Accessed by internet on August 25, 2008 at www.time.com/time/business/article/0,8599,1828069,00.html

Gatewood, R.D., Gowan, M.A., and Lautenschlager, G.J. 1993. Corporate image, recruitment image, and initial job choice. *Academy of Management Journal*, 36(2): 414–427.

Geertz, C. 1973. *The interpretation of cultures: Selected essays.* New York: Basic Books.

Ghoshal, S. 2005. Bad management theories are destroying good management practices. *Academy of Management Learning and Education*, 4(1): 75–91.

Ghoshal, S. and Moran, P. 1996. Bad for practice: A critique of transaction cost theory. *Academy of Management Review*, 21(1): 13–47.

Ghoshal, S., Bartlett, C.A., and Moran, P. 1999. A new manifesto for management. *MIT Sloan Management Review*, 40(3): 9–20.

Gilbert, C. 2005. The disruption opportunity. *MIT Sloan Management Review*, 44(4): 27–32.

Ginsberg, A. 1994. Minding the competition: From mapping to mastery. *Strategic Management Journal*, 15: 153–174.

Gioia, D.A. 1992. Pinto fires and personal ethics: A script analysis of missed opportunities. *Journal of Business Ethics*, 11(5, 6): 379–389.

Giriharadis, A. 2007. In India, poverty inspires technology workers to altruism. *The New York Times*, October 30. Accessed by internet at www.nytimes.com on December 24, 2009.

Gladwell, M. 2002. The talent myth. *The New Yorker*, July 22, 28–33.

Gloor, P. 2005. *Swarm creativity: Competitive innovation through collaborative innovation networks*. Oxford University Press.

Gnyawali, D. R. 1996. Corporate social performance: An international perspective. In S. B. Prasad and B. K. Boyd (eds.) *Advances in International Comparative Management*, 11: 251–273. Greenwich, CT: JAI Press.

Gobeli, D. H., Koenig, H. F., and Mishra, C. S. 2002. Strategic value creation. In P. H. Phan (ed.), *Technological entrepreneurship*: 3–16. Charlotte, NC: Information Age Publishing.

Godfrey, P. 2005. The relationship between corporate philanthropy and shareholder wealth: A risk management perspective. *Academy of Management Review*, 30(4): 777–798.

Goldstein, D. 2002. Theoretical perspectives on strategic environmental management. *Journal of Evolutionary Economics*, 12: 495–524.

Goll, I. and Sambharya, R. B. 1990. Corporate ideology, diversification and firm performance. *Organization Studies*, 16(5): 823–846.

Goll, I. and Zeitz, G. 1991. Conceptualizing and measuring corporate ideology. *Organization Studies*, 12(2): 191–207.

Gómez, A. 2008. Personal communication with David Allen. (Adriana Gómez is Senior Communications Officer for the International Finance Corporation of the World Bank.)

Gómez, A. and Jupe, R. 2006. IFC financing will help Mexico's Banco Compartamos reach more women. International Finance Corporation. September 20. Accessed by internet on December 1, 2009 at www.ifc.org/ifcext/pressroom/ifcpressroom.nsf/PressRelease?openform&7CAD03DE7104413B852571EF0053F447.

Granovetter, M. 1985. Economic action and social structure: A theory of embeddedness, *American Journal of Sociology*, 91(3): 481–510.

1992. Economic institutions as social constructions: A framework for analysis. *Acta Sociologica*, 35(1): 3–11.

Grant, R. M. 1995. *Contemporary strategy analysis*. Malden, MA: Blackwell.

1996. Prospering in dynamically-competitive environments: Organizational capability as knowledge integration. *Organization Science*, 7(4): 375–387.

2003. Strategic planning in a turbulent environment: Evidence from the oil majors. *Strategic Management Journal*, 24: 491–517.

2009. *Contemporary strategy analysis*, 7th edn. Malden, MA: Blackwell Publishers.

Green, P. E. and Srinivasan, V. 1990. Conjoint analysis in marketing: New developments with implications for research and practice. *Journal of Marketing*, 54(4): 3–19.

Greening, D. W. and Turban, D. B. 2000. Corporate social performance as a competitive advantage in attracting a quality workforce. *Business and Society*, 39(3): 254–280.

Greenlee, J., Fischer, M., Gordon, T., and Keating, E. 2007. An investigation of fraud in nonprofit organizations: Occurrences and deterrents. *Nonprofit and Voluntary Sector Quarterly*, 36(4): 676–694.

Griffin, J. J. and Mahon, J. F. 1997. The corporate social performance and corporate financial performance debate: Twenty-five years of incomparable research. *Business and Society*, 36(1): 5–31.

Guillén, H. 2004. Regreso hacia una economía humana: El indicador de desarrollo humano [Return to a human economy: The human development indicador]. *Comercio Exterior.* 54(1): 36–46.

Gunther, M. 2008. Wal-Mart: A bully benefactor: The giant retailer is using its power to help the global poor and protect the planet. *Fortune*, December 5. Accessed by internet at http://157.166.226.108/2008/12/02/news/companies/walmart_gunther.fortune/index.htm?postversion=2008120307 on December 26, 2009.

Gutiérrez-Rivas, R. 2006. Judges and social rights in Mexico: Barely an echo for the poorest. *Mexican Law Review*, 6 (July-December). Accessed by internet at http://info8.juridicas.unam.mx/cont/mlawr/6/arc/arc8.htm on March 24, 2009.

Habermas, J. 1975. *Legitimation crisis*. Boston, MA: Beacon.

Habitat. 2008. Habitat for Humanity. Accessed by internet at www.habitat.org on November 10, 2008.

Hafner, K., Deutsch, C. H., Fabrikant, G., Reuthling, G., and Whitmire, K. 2005. Storm and crisis: The helping hands; When good will is also good business. *The New York Times*, September 15, C1, C5.

Hair, J. F., Anderson, R. E., Tatham, R. L., and Black, W. C. 1998. *Multivariate data analysis*, 3rd edn. New York: Macmillan Publishing.

Hall, R. 1993. A framework for linking intangible resources and capabilities to sustainable competitive advantage. *Strategic Management Journal*, 14(8): 607–618.

Hambrick, D. C. and Mason, P. A. 1984. Upper echelons: The organization as a reflection of its top managers. *Academy of Management Review*, 9(2): 193–206.

Hamel, G. and Prahalad, C. K. 1989. Strategic intent. *Harvard Business Review*, 67(3): 63–76.

Hammond, T.H. 1994. Structure, strategy, and the agenda of the firm. In R.P. Rumelt, D.E. Schendel, and D.J. Teece (eds.), *Fundamental issues in strategy: A research agenda*: 97–154. Boston, MA: Harvard Business School Press.

Hansen, G.S. and Wernerfelt, B. 1989. Determinants of firm performance: The relative importance of economic and organizational factors. *Strategic Management Journal*, 10(5): 399–411.

Haque, U. 2008. How to be a 21st century capitalist. Accessed by internet on June 2, 2009 at http://discussionleader.hbsp.com/haque/2008/12/how_to_be_a_21st_century_capit.html

Harrison, J.S. and St. John, C.H. 1996. Managing and partnering with external stakeholders. *Academy of Management Executive*, 10(2): 46–60.

Hargreaves, D., Bell, P., and Fernandes, J. (eds.). 2005. The global cement report, 6th edn. Dorking, UK: Tradeship Publications Ltd.

Harrison, J.S. and Freeman, R.E. 1999. Stakeholders, social responsibility, and performance: Empirical evidence and theoretical perspectives. *Academy of Management Journal*, 42(5): 479–485.

Hart, S.L. 1995. A natural-resource based view of the firm. *Academy of Management Review*, 20(4): 986–1014.

  1997. Beyond greening: Strategies for a sustainable world. *Harvard Business Review*, 75(1): 66–76.

  2007. *Capitalism at the crossroads: Aligning business, earth, and humanity*, 2nd edn. Upper Saddle River, NJ: Wharton School Publishing.

Hart, S.L. and Christensen, C.M. 2002. The great leap: Driving innovation from the base of the pyramid. *MIT Sloan Management Review*, 44(1): 51–56.

Hart, S.L. and Milstein, M.B. 1999. Global sustainability and the creative destruction of industries. *MIT Sloan Management Review*, 41(1): 23–33.

  2003. Creating sustainable value. *Academy of Management Executive*, 17(2): 56–69.

Hart, S.L. and Sharma, S. 2004. Engaging fringe stakeholders for competitive imagination. *Academy of Management Executive*, 18(1): 7–18.

Harzing, A. 2000. An empirical analysis and extension of the Bartlett and Ghoshal typology of multinational companies. *Journal of International Business Studies*, 31(1): 101–120.

Hasseldine, J., Salama, A.I., and Toms, J.S. 2005. Quantity versus quality: The impact of environmental disclosures on the reputation of UK Plcs. *British Accounting Review*, 37: 231–248.

Hatch, M.J. 1993. The dynamics of organizational culture. *Academy of Management Review*, 18(4): 657–693.

Hatch, M. J. and Schultz, M. 2008. *Taking brand initiative*. San Francisco, CA: Jossey-Bass.

Hayek, F. 1945. The use of knowledge in society. *American Economic Review*, 35(4): 519–530.

Hax, A. C. and Majluf, N. S. 1996. *The strategy concept and process: A pragmatic approach*, 2nd edn. Upper Saddle River, NJ: Prentice Hall.

Helfat, C. 1997. Know-how and asset complementarity and dynamic capability accumulation: The case of R&D. *Strategic Management Journal*, 18: 339–360.

Henriques, I. and Sadorsky, P. 1999. The relationship between environmental commitment and managerial perceptions of stakeholder importance. *Academy of Management Journal*, 42(1): 87–99.

Heugens, P. P. M. A. R., van den Bosch, F. A. J., and van Riel, C. B. M. 2002. Stakeholder integration: Building mutually enforcing relationships. *Business and Society*, 41(1): 36–60.

Hill, C. W. L. 2007. *International Business*, 6th edn. New York: McGraw-Hill/Irwin.

Hillman, A. J. and Hitt, M. A. 1999. Corporate political strategy formulation: A model of approach, participation, and strategy decisions. *Academy of Management Review*, 24(4): 825–842.

Hillman, A. J. and Keim, G. D. 2001. Shareholder value, stakeholder management, and social issues: What's the bottom line? *Strategic Management Journal*, 22(2): 125–139.

Hillman, A., Keim, G., and Schuler, D. 2004. Corporate political activity: A review and research agenda. *Journal of Management*, 30(6): 837–857.

Hofstede, G. 1984. *Culture's consequences*. Thousand Oaks, CA: Sage.

Hosmer, L. T. 1994a. Strategic planning as if ethics mattered. *Strategic Management Journal*, 15(Summer Special Issue): 17–34.

    1994b. Why be moral? A different rationale for managers. *Business Ethics Quarterly*, 4(2): 191–204.

    1987. *The ethics of management*. Homewood, IL: Irwin.

Howard, R. 1990. Values make the company: An interview with Robert Haas. *Harvard Business Review*, 68(5): 132–144.

Howell, J. M. and Avolio, B. J. 1992. The ethics of charismatic leadership: Submission or liberation? *Academy of Management Executive*, 6(2): 43–54.

Hull, C. E. and Rothenberg, S. 2008. Firm performance: The interactions of corporate social performance with innovation and industry differentiation. *Strategic Management Journal*, 29(7): 781–789.

Husted, B. W. 1994. Transaction costs, norms, and social networks: A preliminary study of cooperation in industrial buyer-seller relationships in the United States and Mexico. *Business and Society*, 33(1): 30–57.

1998. Organizational justice and the management of stakeholder relations. *Journal of Business Ethics*, 18(2): 189–197.

2003. Governance choices for corporate social responsibility: To contribute, collaborate or internalize? *Long Range Planning*, 36: 481–498.

2005. Risk management, real options, and corporate social responsibility. *Journal of Business Ethics* 60(2): 175–183.

2007. Agency, information, and the structure of moral problems in business. *Organization Studies*, 28(2): 177–195.

Husted, B. W. and Allen, D. B. 1998. Corporate social strategy: Toward a strategic approach to social issues in management. Paper presented at the Academy of Management meetings, San Diego, CA.

2000. Is it ethical to use ethics as a strategy? *Journal of Business Ethics*, 27(1): 21–31.

2003. Strategic corporate social responsibility among multinational firms in Mexico. In P. Lewellyn and S. A. Welcomer (eds.), *Proceedings of the Fourteenth Annual Meeting of the International Association for Business and Society*, 64–67.

2006. Corporate social responsibility in the multinational enterprise: Strategic and institutional approaches. *Journal of International Business Studies*, 37(6): 838–849.

2007a. Strategic corporate social responsibility and value creation among large firms in Spain. *Long Range Planning*, 40(6): 594–610.

2007b. Corporate social strategy in multinational enterprises: Antecedents and value creation. *Journal of Business Ethics*, 74(4): 345–361.

2009. Strategic corporate social responsibility and value creation: A study of multinational enterprises in Mexico. *Management International Review*, 49(6): 781–799.

Husted, B. W. and Montiel, I. 2008. Positive and negative isomorphism in the adoption of voluntary programs: The Mexican case. Paper presented at the annual meeting of the Academy of Management, Anaheim, California, August 11.

Husted, B. W. and Salazar Cantú, J. J. 2002. The impact of industry structure on strategic corporate social responsibility: A game theoretic approach. In D. Windsor and S. A. Welcomer (eds.), *Proceedings of the Thirteenth Annual Meeting of the International Association for Business and Society*: 127–130.

2006. Taking Friedman seriously: Maximizing profits and social performance. *Journal of Management Studies*, 43(1): 75–91.

Husted, B. W. and Serrano, C. 2002. Corporate governance in Mexico. *Journal of Business Ethics*, 37(3): 337–348.

Husted, B. W., Allen, D. B., and Coduras, A. 2003. The use of corporate social strategy among large Spanish Firms. Unpublished paper presented at the European Business Ethics Network Annual Conference, Budapest, Hungary, August 30.

Hutchins, E. 1995. *Cognitions in the wild*. Cambridge, MA: MIT Press.

Inkpen, A. and Choudhury, N. 1995. The seeking of strategy where it is not: Towards a theory of strategic absence. *Strategic Management Journal*, 16(4): 313–323.

ISO. 2007. *The 2007 ISO Survey*. Accessed by internet at www.iso.org/iso/survey2007.pdf on December 30, 2009.

Itami, H. 1987. *Mobilizing invisible assets*. Cambridge, MA: Harvard University Press.

Iwata, G. 1974. Measurement of conjectural variations in oligopoly. *Econometrica*, 42: 947–966.

James, W. 1890. *The principles of psychology*. New York: Henry Holt and Company.

Jaworksi, B.J. and Kohli, A.K. 1993. Market orientation: Antecedents and consequences. *Journal of Marketing*, 57 (July): 53–70.

Jenkins, G. 2002. Stakeholder impacts. In A. Harberger and G. Jenkins (eds.). *Cost-benefit analysis*: 665–674. Cheltenham, UK: Edward Elgar.

Jensen, M. 1998. *Foundations of corporate strategy*. Cambridge, MA: Harvard University Press.

  2002. Value maximization, stakeholder theory, and the corporate object-ive function. *Business Ethics Quarterly*, 12(2): 235–256.

Jensen, M. and Meckling, W. 1976. Theory of the firm: Managerial behavior, agency costs, and capital structure. *Journal of Financial Economics*, 3(4): 305–360.

Jerome, R., Birkbeck, M., and Leger, D.E. 2002. Fallen hero. *People*, 58(7): 111–112.

Joachimsthaler, E. and Aaker, D.A. 1997. Building brands without mass media. *Harvard Business Review*, 75(1): 39–41, 44–46, 48–50.

Jones, T.M. 1995. Instrumental stakeholder theory: A synthesis of ethics and economics. *Academy of Management Review*, 20: 404–437.

Jones, T.M. and Wicks, A.C. 1999. Convergent stakeholder theory. *Academy of Management Review*, 24(2): 206–221.

Jones, T.M., Felps, W., and Bigley, G.A. 2007. Ethical theory and stake-holder-related decisions: The role of stakeholder culture. *Academy of Management Review*, 32(1): 137–155.

Judge, Jr., W.Q. and Krishnan, H. 1994. An empirical investigation of the scope of a firm's enterprise strategy. *Business and Society*, 33: 167–190.

Kahneman, D. and Knetsch, J.L. 1992. Valuing public goods: The pur-chase of moral satisfaction. *Journal of Environmental Economics and Management*, 22: 57–70.

Kahneman, D. and Tversky, A. 1984. Choices, values, and frames. *American Psychologist*, 39(4): 341–350.

Kant, I. 1964. *Groundwork of the metaphysic of morals*. New York: Harper and Row.

Kanter, R. M. 1999. From spare change to real change. *Harvard Business Review*, 77(3): 122–132.

  2009. *SuperCorp: How vanguard companies create innovation, profits, growth, and social good*. New York: Crown Business.

Karnani, A. 2007. The mirage of marketing to the bottom of the pyramid. *California Management Review*, 49(4): 90–111.

Katz, J. P., Swanson, D. L., and Nelson, L. K. 2001. Culture-based expectations of corporate citizenship: A propositional framework and comparison of four cultures. *International Journal of Organizational Analysis*, 9(2): 149–171.

Kay, J. 1993. *Foundations of corporate success*. Oxford University Press.

Keats, B. W. and Hitt, M. A. 1988. A causal model of linkages among environmental dimensions. *Academy of Management Journal*, 31(3): 570–598.

Keim, G. D. 1978. Corporate social responsibility: An assessment of the enlightened self-interest model. *Academy of Management Review*, 3: 32–39.

Kilbourne, W. E., Beckmann, S. C., and Thelen, E. 2002. The role of the dominant social paradigm in environmental attitudes: A multinational examination. *Journal of Business Research*, 55: 193–204.

Klassen, R. D. and Whyback, D. C. 1999. The impact of environmental technologies on manufacturing performance. *Academy of Management Journal*, 42(6): 599–615.

Kline, C. J. and Peters, L. H. 1991. Behavioral commitment and tenure of new employees: A replication and extension. *Academy of Management Journal*, 34(1): 194–204.

Kluckhohn, C. *et al.* 1952. Values and value-orientations in the theory of action. In T. Parsons and E. A. Shils (eds.), *Toward a general theory of action*: 388–433. Cambridge, MA: Harvard University Press.

Kogut, B. 1991. Joint ventures and the option to expand and acquire. *Management Science*, 37(1): 19–33.

Kogut, B. and Kulatilaka, N. 1994. Operating flexibility, global manufacturing, and the option value of a multinational network. *Management Science*, 40(1): 123–139.

Kostova, T. and Roth, K. 2002. Adoption of an organizational practice by subsidiaries of multinational corporations: Institutional and relational effects. *Academy of Management Journal*, 45(1): 215–233.

Kotter, J. and Heskett, J. 1992. *Corporate culture and performance*. New York: The Free Press.

Kouzes, J.M. and Posner, B.Z. 1993. *Credibility*. San Francisco, CA: Jossey-Bass.

Kytle, B. and Ruggie, J.G. 2005. Corporate social responsibility as risk management: A model for multinationals. Corporate Social Responsibility Initiative Working Paper No. 10. Cambridge, MA: John F. Kennedy School of Government, Harvard University.

Labatt, S. and White, R.R. 2007. *Carbon finance: The financial implications of climate change*. Hoboken, NJ: John Wiley and Sons, Inc.

Labelle, H. 2009. CPI 2009 video release. Accessed by internet at www.transparency.org/policy_research/surveys_indices/cpi/2009 on December 29, 2009.

Laffont, J.-J. and Martimort, D. 1997. The firm as a multicontract organization. *Journal of Economics and Management Strategy*, 6(2): 201–234.

Layard, P.R.G. and Walters, A.A. 1978. *Microeconomic theory*. New York: McGraw-Hill.

Leone, R.A. 1986. *Who profits: Winners, losers, and government regulation*. New York: Basic Books.

Lepak, D.P., Smith, K.G., and Taylor, S.M. 2007. Value creation and value capture: A multilevel perspective. *Academy of Management Review*, 32(1): 180–194.

Levy, D. 1994. Chaos theory: Theory, application and management implications. *Strategic Management Journal*, 15: 167–178.

Liedtka, J.M. 2000. In defense of strategy as design. *California Management Review*, 42(3): 8–30.

Lippman, S.A. and Rumelt, R.P. 1982. Uncertain imitability: An analysis of interfirm differences in efficiency under competition. *Bell Journal of Economics*, 13(2): 418–438.

Logsdon, J.M and Wood, D.J. 2005. Global business citizenship and voluntary codes of ethical conduct. *Journal of Business Ethics*, 59: 55–67.

Loh, S. 2009. In strategy shift, GE plans lower-cost health products. *The New York Times*, May 7. Accessed online at www.nytimes.com/2009/05/08/business/08health.html?emc=eta1 on May 30, 2009.

Lohr, A. 2004. The changing role of NGOs for business: Instruments, opponents, or professional partners? Paper presented to the EGOS Colloquium on CSR and Business Ethics, July 1–3, Ljubljana, Slovenia.

London, T. 2007. A base-of-the-pyramid perspective on poverty alleviation. Working paper. Ann Arbor, MI: William Davidson Institute at the University of Michigan.

  2009. Making better investments at the base of the pyramid. *Harvard Business Review*, 87(5): 106–113.

London, T. and Hart, S. L. 2004. Reinventing strategies for emerging markets: Beyond the transnational model. *Journal of International Business Studies*, 35: 350–370.

Lozano, G., Moxon, C., and Maass, A. 2003. Let's build their dreams: Danone Mexico and the Casa de la Amistad para Niños con Cáncer, I. A.P. Case SKE 010 of the Social Enterprise Knowledge Network.

Lozano, G., Romero, C., and Serrano, L. 2003. HEB International Supermarkets and the Banco de Alimentos de Caritas de Monterrey. Social Enterprise Knowledge Network, Case SKE004.

Luehrman, T. A. 1998. Strategy as a portfolio of real options. In J. Magretta (ed.), *Managing in the new economy*: 91–111. Boston, MA: Harvard Business School Press.

Lyotard, J.-F. 1984. *The Postmodern Condition: A Report on Knowledge*. Minneapolis, MN: University of Minnesota Press.

Mackey, A., Mackey, T.B., and Barney, J.B. 2007. Corporate social responsibility and firm performance: Investor preferences and corporate strategies. *Academy of Management Review*, 32(3): 817–835.

Madhok, A. 2006. Opportunism, trust, and knowledge: The management of firm value and the value of firm management. In R. Bachmann and A. Zaheer (eds.), *The handbook of trust research*: 107–123. Cheltenham, UK: Edward Elgar.

Mahon, J. F. and McGowan, R. A. 1998. Modeling industry political dynamics. *Business and Society*, 37(4): 390–413.

Mahon, J. F. and Waddock, S. A. 1992. Strategic issues management: An integration of issue life cycle perspectives. *Business and Society*, 31(1): 19–32.

Maignan, I., Ferrell, O. C., Hult, G. T. M., and Tomas, M. 1999. Corporate citizenship: Cultural antecedents and business benefits. *Journal of the Academy of Marketing Science*, 27(4): 455–469.

March, J. G. and Simon, H. A. 1958. *Organizations*. New York: John Wiley.

March, J. G. and Sutton, R. I. 1997. Organizational performance as a dependent variable. *Organization Science*, 8(6): 698–706.

Marcus, A. and Geffen, D. 1998. The dialectics of competency acquisition: Pollution prevention in electric generation. *Strategic Management Journal*, 19: 1145–1168.

Mares-Dixon, J., McKay, J. A., and Peppet, S. R. 1999. Building consensus for change within a major corporation: The case of Levi Strauss and Co. Accessed at www.mediate.org/Levi%20Strauss.pdf on May 24, 2004. Published in L. E. Susskind, S. McKearnen, and J. Thomas-Larmer (eds.), *The consensus building handbook: A comprehensive guide to reaching agreement*. Newbury Park, CA: Sage.

Margolis, J.D. and Walsh, J.P. 2001. *People and profits: The search for a link between a company's social and financial performance.* Rahway, NJ: Erlbaum Associates.

2003. Misery loves companies: Rethinking social initiatives by business. *Administrative Science Quarterly,* 48: 268–305.

Markides, C. 2006. Disruptive innovation: In need of better theory? *Journal of Product Innovation and Management,* 23: 19–25.

Markides, C. and Williamson, P.J. 1994. Related diversification, core competences and corporate performance. *Strategic Management Journal,* 15: 149–166.

Marquis, C., Glynn, M.A., and Davis, G.F. 2007. Community isomorphism and corporate social action. *Academy of Management Review,* 32(3): 925–945.

Matlack, C., Smith, G., and Edmondson, G. 2004. Cracking down on corporate bribery. *Business Week,* December 4. Accessed by internet at www.businessweek.com/magazine/content/04_49/b3911066_mz054.htm on November 11, 2009.

Matten, D. and Crane, A. 2005. Corporate citizenship: toward an extended theoretical conceptualization. *Academy of Management Review,* 30(1): 166–179.

Matten, D. and Moon, J. 2008. "Implicit" and "explicit" CSR: A conceptual framework for a comparative understanding of corporate social responsibility. *Academy of Management Review,* 33(2): 404–424.

Martínez, J.L. and Allen, D.B. 2000. El marketing social: de la táctica a la estrategia (Social marketing: From tactics to strategy). *Harvard Deusto Business Review,* September-October: 66–74.

Mayo, E. 1933. *The human problems of an industrialized civilization.* London: Macmillan.

McCawley, T. 2000. Racing to improve its reputation: Nike has fought to shed its image as an exploiter of third-world labour. Yet it is still a target of activists. *Financial Times,* December 21, p. 14.

McDonough, W. and Braungart, M. 1998. The next industrial revolution. *Atlantic Monthly,* October, 82–92.

McGrath, R.G. 1997. A real options logic for initiating technology positioning investments. *Academy of Management Review,* 22(4): 974–996.

1999. Falling forward: Real options reasoning and entrepreneurial failure. *Academy of Management Review,* 24(1): 13–30.

McGuire, J., Sundgren, A., and Schneeweis, T. 1988. Corporate social responsibility and firm financial performance. *Academy of Management Journal,* 31: 854–872.

McPhail, T.L. 2006. *Global communication: Theories, stakeholders, and trends.* Malden, MA: Blackwell Publishing Ltd.

McWilliams, A. and Siegel, D. 2000. Corporate social responsibility and financial performance: Correlation or misspecification? *Strategic Management Journal*, 21(5): 603–609.

2001. Corporate social responsibility: A theory of the firm perspective. *Academy of Management Review*, 26(1): 117–127.

McWilliams, A., Siegel, D., and Wright, P. M. 2006. Corporate social responsibility: Strategic implications. *Journal of Management Studies*, 43(1): 1–18.

Medina, C. and Morales, L. 2007. Stratification and public utility services in Colombia: Subsidies to households or distortion of housing prices? *Economia*, 7(2): 41–99.

Meisling, A. 2004. Global corporate social responsibility disclosure legislation. Accessed at www.goodfunds.com/news.htm on September 30, 2005.

Mendelson, N. and Polonsky, M. J. 1995. Using strategic alliances to develop credible green marketing. *Journal of Consumer Marketing*, 12(2): 4–18.

Menon, A. and Menon, A. 1997. Enviropreneurial marketing strategy: The emergence of corporate environmentalism as market strategy. *Journal of Marketing*, 61: 51–67.

Menon, A., Menon, A., Chowdhury, J., and Jankovich, J. 1999. Evolving paradigm for environmental sensitivity in marketing programs: A synthesis of theory and practice. *Journal of Marketing Theory and Practice*, 7(2): 1–15.

Merton, R. C. 1973. The theory of rational option pricing. *Bell Journal of Economics*, 4: 141–183.

Metropolitan Opera Guild. 2008. The Metropolitan Opera International Radio Broadcast Information Center accessed by internet at www.operainfo.org/about/ab_broadcast.htm on December 24, 2009.

Meyer, J. W. and Rowan, B. 1977. Institutionalized organizations: Formal structure as myth and ceremony. *American Journal of Sociology*, 83: 340–363.

Meyer, K. E. 2004. Perspectives on multinational enterprises in developing countries. *Journal of International Business Studies* 35, 259–276.

Milenio. 2009. Inicia Cemex operación en parque eólico. Milenio, January 22. Accessed by internet at www.milenio.com/node/152784 on September 30, 2009.

Miles, M. P. and Covin, J. G. 2000. Environmental marketing: A source of reputational, competitive, and financial advantage. *Journal of Business Ethics*, 23(3): 299–311.

Miles, R. E. and Creed, W. E. D. 1995. Organizational forms and managerial philosophies: A descriptive and analytical review. In B. M. Staw and L.L. Cummings (eds.), *Research in Organizational Behavior*, 17: 333–372. Greenwich, CT: JAI Press.

Miles, R. E. and Snow, C. C. 1978. *Organizational strategy, structure, and process.* New York: McGraw-Hill.

Miles, R. E., Coleman, Jr., H. J., and Creed, W. E. D. 1995. Keys to success in corporate redesign. *California Management Review*, 37(3): 128–145.

Milgrom, P. and Roberts, J. 1992. *Economics, organization and management.* Englewood Cliffs, NJ: Prentice-Hall.

Miller, D. 1987. The structural and environmental correlates of business strategy. *Strategic Management Journal*, 8: 55–76.

1988. Relating Porter's business strategies to environment and structure: Analysis and performance implications. *Academy of Management Journal*, 31(2): 280–308.

1993. The architecture of simplicity. *Academy of Management Review*, 18(1): 116–138.

Miller, D. and Friesen, P. H. 1983. Strategy-making and environment: The third link. *Strategic Management Journal*, 4(3): 221–325.

Miller, D. and Salkind, N. 2002. *Handbook of research design and social measurement.* Thousand Oaks, CA: Sage.

Miller, D. and Shamsie, J. 1996. The resource-based view of the firm in two environments: The Hollywood film studios from 1936 to 1965. *Academy of Management Journal*, 29: 519–543.

Mintzberg, H. 1973. *The nature of managerial work.* New York: Harper and Row.

1979. *The structuring of organizations: A synthesis of the research.* Englewood Cliffs, NJ: Prentice-Hall.

1983. Why America needs, but cannot have, corporate democracy. *Organizational Dynamics*, 11(4): 5–20.

1987a. Crafting strategy. *Harvard Business Review*, 65(1): 66–75.

1987b. The strategy concept I: Five P's for strategy. *California Management Review*, 29: 11–24.

1990. The design school: Reconsidering the basic premises of strategic management. *Strategic Management Journal*, 11(3): 171–195.

1991. Learning 1, planning 0: Reply to Igor Ansoff. *Strategic Management Journal*, 12(9): 463–466.

1994. *The rise and fall of strategic planning.* New York: Free Press.

Mintzberg, H. and Waters, J. 1985. Of strategies, deliberate and emergent. *Strategic Management Journal*, 6(3): 257–272.

Mishan, E. J. 1988. *Cost-benefit analysis: An informal introduction.* Boston, MA: Unwin Hyman.

Mitchell, R. K., Agle, B. R., and Wood, D. J. 1997. Toward a theory of stakeholder identification and salience: Defining the principle of who and what really counts. *Academy of Management Review*, 22(4): 853–886.

Montgomery, C.A., Wernerfelt, B., and Balakrishnan, S. 1989. Strategy content and the research process: A critique and commentary. *Strategic Management Journal*, 10(2): 189–197.

Montiel, I. 2008. Corporate social responsibility and corporate sustainability: Separate pasts, common futures. *Organization and Environment*, 21(3): 245–269.

Moon, J. and Vogel, D. 2008. Responsibility, government, and civil society. In A. Crane, A. McWilliams, D. Matten, J. Moon, and D. Siegel (eds.), *The Oxford handbook of corporate social responsibility*: 303–323. Oxford University Press.

Mosse, D., Farrington, J., and Rew, A. 1998. *Development as process: Concepts and methods for working with complexity.* London: Routledge.

Mullen, J. 1997. Performance-based corporate philanthropy: How "giving smart" can further corporate goals. *Public Relations Quarterly*, 42(2): 42–48.

Muller, A. 2006. Global versus local CSR strategies. *European Management Journal*, 24(2–3): 189–198.

Murray, K.B. and Montanari, J.R. 1986. Strategic management of the socially responsible firm: Integrating management and marketing theory. *Academy of Management Review*, 11(4): 815–827.

Nahapiet, J. and Ghoshal, S. 1998. Social capital, intellectual capital, and the organizational advantage. *Academy of Management Review*, 23: 242–266.

Nasi, J., Nasi, S., Phillips, N., and Zyglidopoulos, S. 1997. The evolution of corporate social responsiveness: An exploratory study of Finnish and Canadian forestry companies. *Business and Society*, 36: 296–321.

Navarro, P. 1988. Why do corporations give to charity? *Journal of Business*, 61(1): 65–93.

Nehrt, C. 1996. Timing and intensity effects of environmental investments. *Strategic Management Journal*, 17(7): 535–548.

Nelson, R. and Winter, S. 1982. *An evolutionary theory of economic change.* Cambridge, MA: Harvard University Press.

Newell, P.J. 2002. *Globalisation and the future state.* Brighton, UK: Institute of Development Studies.

Nores, M., Belfield, C.R., Barnett, W.S., and Schweinhart, L. 2005. Updating the economic impacts of the High/Scope Perry preschool program. *Educational Evaluation and Policy Analysis*, 27(3): 245–262.

Nowak, M.A. 2006. Five rules for the evolution of cooperation. *Science*, 314(8): 1560–1563.

Nozick, R. 1974. *Anarchy, state, and utopia.* New York: Basic Books.

O'Reilly III, C. and Chatman, J. 1986. Organizational commitment and psychological attachment: The effects of compliance, identification, and internalization on prosocial behavior. *Journal of Applied Psychology*, 71(3): 492–499.

O'Reilly III, C. and Pfeffer, J. 2000. *Hidden value: How great companies achieve extraordinary results with ordinary people.* Boston, MA: Harvard Business School Press.

O'Reilly III, C., Chatman, J. and Caldwell, D. 1991. People and organizational culture: A profile comparison approach to assessing person-organization fit. *Academy of Management Journal*, 34(3):487–516.

Obama, B. 2004. *Dreams from my father: A story of race and inheritance.* New York: Three Rivers Press.

Ogden, S. and Watson, R. 1999. Corporate performance and stakeholder management: Balancing shareholder and customer interests in the UK privatized water industry. *Academy of Management Journal*, 42(5): 526–538.

Oliver, C. and Holzinger, I. 2008. The effectiveness of strategic political management: A dynamic capabilities framework. *Academy of Management Review*: 33(2): 496–520.

Olsen, E.O. 1979. The simple analytics of external effects. *Southern Economic Journal*, 45: 847–854.

Orlitzky, M.O., Schmidt, F.L., and Rynes, S.L. 2003. Corporate social and financial performance: A meta-analysis. *Organization Studies*, 24, 403–442.

Orsato, R.J. 2006. Competitive environmental strategies: When does it pay to be green? *California Management Review*, 48(2): 127–143.

Ostroy, A. 2009. Wal-Mart's hypocritical music policy. *Huffington Post*, August 30. Accessed by internet at www.huffingtonpost.com/andy-ostroy/wal-marts-hypocritical-mu_b_272181.html?view=print on December 3, 2009.

Ouchi, W. 1981. *Theory Z: How American business can meet the Japanese challenge.* Reading, MA: Addison-Wesley.

Oxfam America. 2007. Tell Starbucks to honor their commitments to coffee farmers – E-petition accessed by internet at www.thepetitionsite.com/takeaction/335760574.

Padgett, J. 2000. Organizational genesis, identity, and control: The transformation of banking in renaissance Florence. In A. Casella and J. Rauch (eds.), *Markets and networks*: 211–257. New York: Russell Sage.

Paine, L.S. 2003. *Values shift.* New York: McGraw-Hill.

Palmer, K., Oates, W.E., and Portney, P.R. 1995. Tightening environmental standards: The benefit-cost paradigm or the no-cost paradigm? *Journal of Economic Perspectives*, 9(4): 119–132.

Papadakis, V. M., Lioukas, S., and Chambers, D. 1998. Strategic decision-making processes: The role of management and context. *Strategic Management Journal*, 19(2): 115–147.

Parker, S. 2003. Evaluación del impacto de oportunidades sobre la inscripción escolar: Primaria, secundaria y media superior. *SEDESOL, Serie: Documentos de investigación*, 6. Accessed by internet at www.sedesol.gob.mx/archivos/70/File/Docu%2006.pdf on October 17, 2005.

Pascale, R. T. 1996. The Honda effect. *California Management Review*, 38(4): 80–91.

Pascale, R. T. and Athos, A. 1981. *The art of japanese management*. New York: Warner Books.

Paul, K., Zalka, L. M., Downes, M., Perry, S., and Friday, S. 1997. US consumer sensitivity to corporate social performance: Development of a scale. *Business and Society*, 36(4): 408–418.

Paxson, D. A. 2001. Introduction to real R&D options. *R&D Management*, 31(2): 109–113.

Pearce, D., Barbier, E., and Markandya, A. 1990. *Sustainable development: Economics and environment in the third world*. London: Earthscan Publications.

Peel, M. 1998. Mind your business. *Financial Times* (Supplement on Responsible Business), May 20, p. 26–27.

Penrose, E. T. 1959. *The theory of the growth of the firm*. New York: Wiley.

Peteraf, M. A. 1993. The cornerstones of competitive advantage: A resource-based view. *Strategic Management Journal*, 14: 179–191.

Peters, T. 1998. *Thriving on chaos: Handbook for a management revolution*. New York: Harper Paperbacks.

Peters, T. and Waterman, R. 1982. *In search of excellence: Lessons from America's best-run companies*. New York: Harper and Row.

Pettigrew, A. M. 1979. On studying organizational cultures. *Administrative Science Quarterly*, 24: 570–581.

Pfeffer, J. and Salancik, G. R. 1978. *The external control of organizations: A resource dependence perspective*. New York: Harper and Row.

Phillips, R. 2003. *Stakeholder theory and organizational ethics*. San Francisco, CA: Berrett-Koehler.

Polanyi, K. 1944. *The great transformation*. Boston, MA: Beacon Press.

Polanyi, M. 1967. *The tacit dimension*. Garden City, NJ: Doubleday.

Polonsky, M. J. 1997. Broadening the stakeholder strategy mix. In J. Weber and K. Rehbein (eds.), *Proceedings of the Eighth Annual Conference of the International Association for Business and Society*: 377–382.

Poniewozik, J. 2009. Polarized news? The media's moderate bias. *Time*, November 4. Accessed by internet at www.time.com/time/nation/article/0,8599,1934550,00.html on December 15, 2009.

Popp, A., Toms, S., and Wilson, J. 2006. Industrial districts as organizational environments: Resources, networks, and structures. *Management and Organizational History*, 1(4): 349–370.

Porter, M.E. 1980. *Competitive strategy*. New York: The Free Press.

  1985. *Competitive advantage*. New York: The Free Press.

  1990. *Competitive advantage of nations*. New York: The Free Press.

  1996. What is strategy? *Harvard Business Review*, 74(6): 61–80.

Porter, M.E. and Kramer, M.R. 2002. The competitive advantage of corporate philanthropy. *Harvard Business Review*, 80(12): 56–68.

  2006. Strategy and society: The link between competitive advantage and corporate social responsibility. *Harvard Business Review*, 84(12): 78–92.

Porter, M.E. and van der Linde, C. 1995. Toward a new conception of the environment-competitiveness relationship. *Journal of Economic Perspectives*, 9(4): 97–118.

Potoski, M. and Prakash, A. 2005. Green clubs and voluntary governance: ISO 14001 and firms' regulatory compliance. *American Journal of Political Science*, 49(2): 235–248.

Prahalad, C.K. 2005. *The fortune at the bottom of the pyramid*. Upper Saddle River, NJ: Wharton School Publishing.

Prahalad, C.K. and Bettis, R.A. 1986. The dominant logic: A new linkage between diversity and performance. *Strategic Management Journal*, 7: 485–501.

Prahalad, C.K. and Doz, Y.L. 1987. *The multinational mission: Balancing local demands and global vision*. New York: The Free Press.

Prahalad, C.K. and Hamel, G. 1990. The core competence of the corporation. *Harvard Business Review*, 68(May/June): 79–91.

Prahalad, C.K. and Hammond, A. 2002. Serving the world's poor profitably. *Harvard Business Review*, 80(9): 48–57.

Preston, L.E. 1988. Editor's introduction. In L.E. Preston (ed.), *Research in corporate social performance and policy*, 10: xi–xiv. Greenwich, CT: JAI Press.

  1990. Corporate social policy and performance: A synthetic framework for research and analysis. In L E. Preston (ed.), *Corporation and society research: Studies in theory and measurement*: 66–87. Greenwich, CT: JAI Press.

Preston, L.E. and O'Bannon, D.P. 1997. The corporate social-financial performance relationship: A typology and analysis. *Business and Society*, 36(4): 419–429.

Preston, L. E. and Sapienza, H. J. 1990. Stakeholder management and corporate performance. *Journal of Behavioral Economics*, 19: 361–375.

Priem, R. L. and Butler J. E. 2001. Is the resource-based "view" a useful perspective for strategic management research? *Academy of Management Review*, 26(1): 22–40.

Rao, H. 1994. The social construction of reputation: Certification tests, legitimation, and the survival of organizations in the American automobile industry: 1895–1912. *Strategic Management Journal*, 15(S1): 29–44.

Rasmussen, E. 1989. *Games and information: An introduction to game theory.* Malden, MA: Blackwell.

Ravasi, D. and Schultz, M. 2006. Responding to organizational identity threats: Exploring the role of organizational culture. *Academy of Management Journal*, 49(3): 433–458.

Reagan, M. D. 1987. *Regulation: The politics of policy.* Boston, MA: Little, Brown and Company.

Reed, D. 2002. Employing normative stakeholder theory in developing countries. A critical theory perspective. *Business and Society* 41: 166–207.

Reinganum, J. 1984. Practical implications of game theoretic models of R&D. *American Economic Review*, 74: 61–66.

Reinhardt, F. 1998. Environmental product differentiation. *California Management Review*, 40(4): 43–73.

1999. Market failure and the environmental policies of firms: Economic rationales for "beyond compliance" behavior. *Journal of Industrial Ecology*, 3(1): 9–21.

Riddell, R. 1990. *Judging success: Evaluating NGO approaches to alleviating poverty in developing countries.* Overseas Development Institute, Working Paper 37.

Riddell, R. and Robinson, M. 1995. *Non-governmental organizations and rural poverty alleviation.* Oxford University Press.

Riesman, D., Glazer, N., and Denny, R. 1950. *The lonely crowd: A study of the changing American character.* New Haven, CT: Yale University Press.

Rindova, V. and Fombrun, C. 1999. Constructing competitive advantage: The role of firm-constituent interactions. *Strategic Management Journal*, 20: 691–710.

Roberts, P. W. and Dowling, G. R. 2002. Corporate reputation and sustained superior financial performance. *Strategic Management Journal*, 23: 1077–1093.

Robinson, K. and McDougall, P. 1998. The impact of alternative operationalizations of industry structural elements on measures of performance for entrepreneurial manufacturing ventures. *Strategic Management Journal*, 19: 1079–1100.

Rodríguez, M.A., Sabria, F., and Sánchez, P. 2004. *La cadena de suministro en la base de la pirámide*. Barcelona, Spain: CIIL.

Rondinelli, D.A. and London, T. 2003. How corporations and environmental groups cooperate: Assessing cross sector alliances and collaborations. *Academy of Management Executive*, 17(1): 61–76.

Rorty, R. 1979. *Philosophy and the mirror of nature*. Princeton University Press.

Rosenberg, N. 1990. Why do firms do basic research (with their own money)? *Research Pollicy*, 19(2): 165–174.

Roth, K., Schweiger, D.M., and Morrison, A.J. 1991. Global strategy implementation at the business unit level: Operational capabilities and administrative mechanisms. *Journal of International Business Studies*, 22(3): 369–402.

Rowley, T. 1997. Moving beyond dyadic ties: A network theory of stakeholder influences. *Academy of Management Review*, 22(4): 887–910.

Rowley, T. and Berman, S. 2000. A brand new brand of corporate social performance. *Business and Society*, 39(4): 397–418.

Ruggie, J. 2008. Protect, respect and remedy: A framework for business and human rights. Human Rights Council for the Special Representative of the Secretary-General. Accessed by internet at www.business-humanrights.org/Documents/RuggieHRC2008 on December 24, 2009.

Rumelt, R.P. 1984. Towards a strategic theory of the firm. In R. Lamb (ed.), *Competitive strategic management*: 556–570. Englewood Cliffs, NJ: Prentice-Hall.

Russo, M.V. 2001. *Institutional change and theories of organizational strategy: ISO 14001 and toxic emissions in the electronics industry*. Unpublished paper, University of Oregon, Eugene, OR.

Russo, M.V. and Fouts, P.A. 1997. A resource-based perspective on corporate environmental performance and profitability. *Academy of Management Journal*, 40: 534–559.

Rutenberg, J. 2004. Disney is blocking distribution of film that criticizes Bush. *The New York Times*. May 5, p. 28.

Ryle, G. 1949. *The concept of the mind*. London: Hutchinson.

Salazar Cantú, J.J. 2006. *La responsabilidad social de la empresa: Teoría y evidencia para México*. Ph.D. dissertation. Monterrey, Mexico: Universidad Autonoma de Nuevo Leon.

Salazar Cantú, J.J. and Husted, B.W. 2008. Measuring corporate social performance. *Proceedings of the Nineteenth Annual Meeting of the International Association for Business and Society*, edited by Kathleen Rehbein and Ron Roman, 149–161.

Sampler, J. 1998. Redefining industry structure for the information age. *Strategic Management Journal*, 19: 343–355.

Sanchez, J. L. and Sotorrio, L. 2007. The creation of value through corporate reputation. *Journal of Business Ethics*, 76(3): 335–346.

Sanchez, R. 1993. Strategic flexibility, firm organization, and managerial work in dynamic markets: A strategic-options perspective. *Advances in Strategic Management*, 9: 251–291.

Sandel, M. J. 1997. It's immoral to buy the right to pollute. *The New York Times*, December 15, sec. A, p. 15.

Savage, G. T., Nix, T. W., Whitehead, C. J., and Blair, J. D. 1991. Strategies for assessing and managing organizational stakeholders. *Academy of Management Executive*, 5(2): 61–75.

Schendel, D. and Hofer, C. 1979. Introduction. In D. Schendel and C. Hofer (eds.), *Strategic management: A new view of business policy and planning*: 1–12. Boston, MA: Little Brown.

Scherer, A. and Palazzo, G. 2007. Toward a political conception of corporate social responsibility: Business and society seen from a Habermasian perspective. *Academy of Management Review*, 32(4): 1096–1120.

Schmall, E. 2009. Compartamos to expand services as Walmex enters. Accessed by internet at www.bloomberg.com/apps/news?pid=206010 86&sid=aCuvkdjPuPlQ on December 15, 2009.

Schmidheiny, S. 1992. *Changing course: A global business perspective on development and the environment*. Cambridge, MA: MIT Press.

Schuler, D. 1996. Corporate political strategy and foreign competition: The case of the steel industry. *Academy of Management Journal*, 39: 720–737.

Schuler, D. A. and Cording, M. 2006. A corporate social performance-corporate financial performance behavioral model for consumers. *Academy of Management Review*, 31(3): 540–559.

Schultz, M. and Ervolder, L. 1998. Culture, identity, and image consultancy: Crossing boundaries between management, advertising, public relations and design. *Corporate Reputation Review*, 2(1): 29–50.

Schultz, M. and Hatch, M. J. 2002. Scaling the Tower of Babel: Relational differences between identity, image, and culture in organizations. In M. Schultz, M. J. Hatch, and M. H. Larsen (eds.), *Expressive organization*: 9–35. Oxford University Press.

Schumpeter, J. A. 1934. *The theory of economic development*. New York: Oxford University Press.

Searle, J. 1996. *The Construction of Social Reality*. New York: The Free Press.
     2005. What is an institution? *Journal of Institutional Economics*. 1(1): 1–22.

Segev, E. 1997. *Business Unit Strategy.* New York: John Wiley and Sons.

Selznick, P. 1949. *TVA and the grass roots: A study in the sociology of formal organization.* Berkeley and Los Angeles, CA: University of California Press.

  1957. *Leadership in administration: A sociological interpretation.* Evanston, IL: Row, Peterson.

Sen, A. 1970. *Collective choice and social welfare.* San Francisco, CA: Holden-Day.

  1999. *Development as freedom.* Oxford University Press.

Sennett, R. 2006. *The culture of the new capitalism.* New Haven, CT: Yale University Press.

Sethi, S.P. and Sama, L.M. 1998. Ethical behavior as a strategic choice by large corporations: The interactive effect of marketplace competition, industry structure and firm resources. *Business Ethics Quarterly,* 8(1): 85–104.

Sethi, S.P. 1978. An analytical framework for making cross-cultural comparisons of business responses to social pressures. The case of the United States and Japan. In L.E. Preston (ed.), *Research in corporate social performance and policy,* vol. I. Greenwich, CT: JAI Press.

Sexton, S. 2008. Cirque du Soleil gives back globally. Article accessed at www.himalayaninstitute.org on November 24, 2008.

Shaffer, B. 1992. Regulation, competition and strategy: The case of automotive fuel economy standards. In J.E. Post (ed.), *Research in Corporate Social Performance and Policy,* 13: 191–218. Greenwich, CT: JAI Press.

  1995. Firm-level responses to government regulation: Theoretical and research approaches. *Journal of Management,* 21: 495–514.

Shaffer, B., Quasney, T.J., and Grimm, C.M. 2000. Firm level performance implications of nonmarket actions. *Business and Society,* 39(2): 6–143.

Sharfman, M.P., Pinkston, T.S., and Sigerstad, T.D. 2000. The effects of managerial values on social issues evaluation: An empirical examination. *Business and Society,* 39(2): 144–182.

Sharma, S. 2000. Managerial interpretations and organizational context as predictors of corporate choice of environmental strategy. *Academy of Management Journal* 43(4): 681–697.

Sharma, S. and Vredenburg, H. 1998. Proactive corporate environmental strategy and the development of competitively valuable environmental capabilities. *Strategic Management Journal,* 19: 729–753.

Sharma, S., Pablo, A.L., and Vredenburg, H. 1999. Corporate environmental responsiveness strategies: The importance of issue interpretation and organizational context. *Journal of Applied Behavioral Science*, 35(1): 87–108.

Shilts, R. 1995. *And the band played on: Politics, people and the AIDS epidemic*. New York: Penguin Books.

Siegel, D.S. and Vitaliano, D.F. 2007. An empirical analysis of the strategic use of corporate social responsibility. *Journal of Economics and Management Strategy*, 16(3): 773–792.

Silk, L. and Vogel, D. 1976. *Ethics and profits: The crisis of confidence in American business*. New York: Simon and Schuster.

Simon, H.A. 1947. *Administrative behavior: A study of decision-making processes in administrative organizations*. New York: Macmillan.

Simons, T. and Ingram, P. 1997. Organization and ideology: Kibbutzim and hired labor, 1951–1965. *Administrative Science Quarterly*, 42: 784–813.

Smart, J.J.C. and Williams, B. 1973. *Utilitarianism: For and against*. Cambridge University Press.

Soros, G. 1998. *The crisis of global capitalism: Open society endangered*. New York: PublicAffairs.

Spicer, A., Dunfee, T.W., and Bailey, W.J. 2004. Does national context matter in ethical decision making? An empirical test of integrative social contracts theory. *Academy of Management Journal*, 47(4): 610–620.

Starbucks. 2006. Starbucks Corporation Social Responsibility Report 2006. Unpublished document.

Starr, J.A. and MacMillan, I. 1990. Resource cooptation via social contracting: Resource acquisition strategies for new ventures. *Strategic Management Journal*, 11: 79–92.

Staw, B.W. and Szwajkowski, E. 1975. The scarcity-munificence component of organization environments and the commission of illegal acts. *Administrative Science Quarterly*, 20: 345–354.

Stewart, J.B. 2005. *DisneyWar*, 2nd edn. New York: Simon and Schuster.

Stinchcombe, A. 1965. Social structure and organizations. In J.G. March (ed.) *Handbook of organizations*: 142–193. Chicago, IL: Rand McNally.

Strike, V., Gao, J., and Bansal, P. 2006. Being good while being bad: Social responsibility and international diversification of US firms. *Journal of International Business Studies*, 37(6): 850–862.

Sundaram, A.K. and Inkpen, A.C. 2004. The corporate objective revisited. *Organization Science*, 15(3): 350–363.

Surowiecki, J. 2009. Board Stiff. *The New Yorker*. June 1. Accessed by internet at www.newyorker.com/talk/financial/2009/06/01/090601ta_talk_surowiecki on November 16, 2009.

Sutcliffe, K. and Huber, G. 1998. Firm and industry determinants of executive perceptions of the environment. *Strategic Management Journal*, 19: 793–809.

Szwajkowski, E. 2000. Simplifying the principles of stakeholder management: The three most important principles. *Business and Society*, 39(4): 379 396.

Tapscott, D. and Ticoll, D. 2003. *The naked corporation: How the age of transparency will revolutionize business*. New York: Free Press.

Taylor, F. A. 1911. *The principles of management*. New York: W.W. Norton and Co., Inc.

Teece, D. J. 1987. Profiting from technological innovation: Implications for integration, collaboration, licensing, and public policy. In D. J. Teece (ed.), *The competitive challenge*: 185–220. Cambridge, MA: Ballinger.

  1998. Capturing value from knowledge assets: The new economy, markets for know-how, and intangible assets. *California Management Review*, 40(3): 55–79.

  2007. Explicating dynamic capabilities: The nature and microfoundations of (sustainable) enterprise performance. *Strategic Management Journal*, 28(13): 1319–1350.

Teece, D. J., Pisano, G., and Shuen, A. 1997. Dynamic capabilities and strategic management. *Strategic Management Journal*, 18: 509–533.

Thompson, J. D. 1967. *Organizations in action*. New York: McGraw-Hill.

Thompson, J. D. and Tuden, A. 1959. Strategies, structures, and processes of organizational decision. In J. D. Thompson (ed.), *Comparative studies in administration*: 195–216. University of Pittsburgh Press.

Thompson, M. S. and Thompson, S. 2006. Pricing in a market without apparent horizontal differentiation: Evidence from web hosting services. *Economics of Innovation and New Technology*, 15(7): 649–663.

Thoreen, P. W. 1981. On the profitable provision of public goods and services. *American Behavioral Scientist*, 24(4): 573–598.

Tichy, N. M., McGill, A. R., and St. Clair, L. 1997. *Corporate global citizenship: Doing business in the public eye*. San Francisco, CA: The New Lexington Press.

Tirole, J. 1988. *The theory of industrial organization*. Cambridge, MA: MIT Press.

  2001. Corporate governance. *Econometrica*, 69(1): 1–35.

Toms, J. S. 2002. Firm resources, quality signals and the determinants of corporate environmental reputation: Some UK evidence. *British Accounting Review*, 34: 257–282.

Toshiaki, O., Heikki, J., Arto, R., and Tetsuhiko, Y. 2006. Strategies, functions and benefits of forest certification in wood products marketing: Perspectives of Finnish suppliers. *Forest Policy and Economics*, 9(4): 380–391.

Treviño, L.K. and Nelson, K. 1995. *Managing business ethics: Straight talk about how to do it right.* New York: John Wiley and Sons, Inc.

Turban, D.B. and Greening, D.W. 1996. Corporate social performance and organizational attractiveness to prospective employees. *Academy of Management Journal*, 40: 658–672.

Turner, S. 1981. Opera lovers benefit from 41 year liaison between Texaco, Met. *The Ledger* (Lakeland Florida). January 14: 11.

Utting, P. 2008. The struggle for corporate accountability. *Development and Change*, 39(6): 959–975.

Varadarajan, P.R. and Menon, A. 1988. Cause related marketing: A coalignment of marketing strategy and corporate philanthropy. *Journal of Marketing*, 52: 58–74.

Vasquez, B.I. and Cueva, T.E. 2002. Normas ambientales y maquiladoras de autopartes en Matamoros y Reynosa. *Comercio Exterior*, 52(2): 119–128.

Venkatraman, N. and Grant, J.H. 1986. Construct measurement in organizational strategy research: A critique and proposal. *Academy of Management Review*, 11: 71–87.

Vian, T., McCoy, K., Richards, S.C., Connelly, P.J., and Feeley, F. 2007. Corporate social responsibility in global health: The Pfizer global health fellows international volunteering program. *Human Resource Planning*, 30(1): 30–35.

Visser, W. 2008. CSR and the financial crisis: Taking stock. November 4. Accessed by internet at http://csrinternational.blogspot.com/2008/11/csr-and-financial-crisis-taking-stock.html on October 23, 2009.

Vogel, D. 2005. *The market for virtue: The potential and limits of corporate social responsibility.* Washington, DC: The Brookings Institution.

von Clausewitz, C. 1976. *On war.* Ed. and trans. Michael Howard and Peter Paret. Princeton University Press.

von Krogh, G., Roos, J., and Slocum, K. 1994. An essay on corporate epistemology. *Strategic Management Journal*, 15 (Special Issue): 53–72.

Waddock, S.A. and Graves, S.B. 1997. The corporate social performance – financial performance link. *Strategic Management Journal* 18(4): 303–319.

Walley, N. and Whitehead, B. 1994. It's not easy being green. *Harvard Business Review*, May-June, 46–52.

Walsh, J.P. and Nord, W.R. 2005. Taking stock of stakeholder management. *Academy of Management Review*, 30(2): 426–438.

Walzer, M. 1992. Moral minimalism. In W.R. Shea and G.A. Spadafora (eds.), *The twilight of probability: Ethics and politics*, Canton, MA: Science History Publications, cited in T. Donaldson and T. Dunfee (1994): 252–284.

Ward, B. 1988. LEP: An alternative criterion for socio-economic evaluation. *Journal of Economic Issues*, 22(3): 763–778.

Wartick, S.L. and Cochran, P.L. 1985. The evolution of the corporate social performance model. *Academy of Management Review*, 10: 758–769.

Wasko, J. 2005. *A companion to television*. Malden: MA: Blackwell Publishing Ltd.

Watson Wyatt 2007. Employee ratings of senior management dip, Watson Wyatt survey finds. January 4. Accessed by internet at www.watson-wyatt.com/news/press.asp?ID=16887 on December 22, 2009.

Weick, K.E. 1993. The collapse of sensemaking in organizations: The Mann Gulch disaster. *Administrative Science Quarterly*, 38(4): 628–652.
    1995. *Sensemaking in organizations*. Thousand Oaks, CA: Sage.

Weick, K. and Daft, R. 1984. Toward a model of organizations as interpretation systems. *The Academy of Management Review*, 9(2): 284–295.

Weick, K.E. and Roberts, K. 1993. Collective mind in organizations. Heedful interrelating on flight decks. *Administrative Science Quarterly*, 38(3): 357–381.

Weiss, R.M. and Miller, L.E. 1987. The concept of ideology in organizational analysis: The sociology of knowledge or the social psychology of beliefs? *Academy of Management Review*, 12(1): 104–116.

Werbel, J.D. and Carter, S.M. 2002. The CEO's influence on corporate foundation giving. *Journal of Business Ethics*, 40(1, 3): 47–60.

Wernerfelt, B. 1984. A resource-based view of the firm. *Strategic Management Journal*, 5(2): 171–180.

Weston, J.F. and Brigham, E.F. 1981. *Managerial finance*. Hinsdale, IL: Dryden Press.

Whetten, D. 2006. Albert and Whetten revisited: Strengthening the concept of organizational identity. *Journal of Management Inquiry*, 15(3): 219–234.

Wilkins, A.L. and Ouchi, W.G. 1983. Efficient cultures: Exploring the relationship between culture and organizational performance. *Administrative Science Quarterly*, 28(3): 468–481.

Williamson, O.E. 1975. *Markets and hierarchies: analysis and antitrust implications*. New York: The Free Press.
    1985. *The economic institutions of capitalism*. New York: The Free Press.
    1991. Strategizing, economizing and economic organization. *Strategic Management Journal*, 12(2): 75–94.

1996. *The mechanisms of governance.* New York: Oxford University Press.

2000. The new institutional economics: Taking stock, looking ahead. *Journal of Economic Literature,* 38(September): 595–613.

Winter, S. 1987. Knowledge and competence as strategic assets. In D. Teece (ed.), *The competitive challenge*: 159–184. Cambridge, MA: Ballinger.

Wittink, D. R. and Cattin, P. 1989. Commercial use of conjoint analysis: An update. *Journal of Marketing,* 53(3): 91–96.

Wood, D. J. 1985. The strategic uses of public policy: Business support for the 1906 Food and Drug Act. *Business History Review,* 59: 403–432.

1991. Corporate social performance revisited. *Academy of Management Review,* 16(4): 691–718.

WorldatWork. 2009. Economic downturn leading to decline in employee commitment, morale, Watson Wyatt and Worldatwork survey finds. September 21. Accessed by internet at www.worldatwork.org/waw/adimLink?id=34569 on December 22, 2009.

World Bank 2004. *Poverty in Mexico: An evaluation of the conditions, trends, and government strategy.* Mexico, DF: World Bank Mexico.

Yip, G. 1992. *Total global strategy: Managing for worldwide competitive advantage,* Englewood Cliffs, NJ: Prentice-Hall.

Zajac, E. J., Kraatz, M. S., and Bresser, R. K. F. 2000. Modeling the dynamics of strategic fit: A normative approach to strategic change. *Strategic Management Journal,* 21(4): 429–453.

Zalka, L., Downes, M., and Paul, K. 1997. Measuring consumer sensitivity to corporate social performance across cultures: Which consumers care most? *Journal of Global Marketing,* 11(1): 29–48.

Zucker, L. G. 1987. Institutional theories of organization. *Annual Review of Sociology,* 13: 443–464.

Index